WYSIWYG GUIDE

What You See Is What You Get

THE WAY MICROSOFT® EXCEL FOR THE MACINTOSH® WORKS

Brynly Clarke

Microsoft PRESS®

Conceived, edited, and designed by DK Direct Limited and Microsoft Press.

Published by Microsoft Press.

DK DIRECT

Series Editor: Robert Dinwiddie; **Series Art Editor:** Virginia Walter
Project Editors: Gary Cockburn, Nance Fyson; **Specialist Editor:** Terry Burrows
Art Editor: Sean Edwards; **Designers:** Stephen Cummiskey, Nigel Coath, Jenny Hobson, Poppy Jenkins, Jacqueline Greene
Production Manager: Ian Paton

MICROSOFT PRESS

Acquisitions Director: Dean Holmes; **Acquisitions Editor:** Lucinda Rowley
Assistant Managing Editor: Nancy Siadek; **Technical Director:** David Rygmyr

THE AUTHOR

Brynly Clarke is a freelance computer consultant and long-time Microsoft Excel user. Microsoft Excel has contributed to the success of his projects in the UK, France, Germany, and the Czech Republic.

ADDITIONAL CONTRIBUTORS

Text Contributor: Jeff Loveridge; **Illustrators:** Anthony Bellue, Nigel Coath, Andrew Green, Janos Marffy, Coral Mula
Model Making: Sean Edwards; **Photography:** Tony Buckley, Andy Crawford, Steve Gorton, Mark Hill
Airbrushing: Janos Marffy, Roy Flooks; **Computer Assistance:** Bijan Azari, Sam Segar; **Typing Assistance:** Margaret Little

Library of Congress Cataloging-in-Publication Data

Clarke, Brynly.
The way Microsoft Excel for the Macintosh works / Brynly Clarke.
p. cm.
Includes index.
ISBN 1-55615-671-5
1. Microsoft Excel (Computer file) 2. Business--Computer programs. 3. Electronic spreadsheets. 4. Macintosh (Computer)--Programming. I. Title.
HF5548.4.M523C57 1994
650'.0285'5369--dc20 94-26963
CIP

Color Reproduction by Coulourscan, Singapore, and Triffick Technology, London, UK

Printed and Bound in the USA

123456789 QEQE 987654

Flexibook

CONTENTS

INTRODUCTION

CHAPTER ONE

Getting Started with Excel

Welcome to Microsoft Excel! In this introductory chapter you'll get started with the program and discover its principal uses. Explore the main elements of the Excel application window, learn how to use Excel's menus and toolbars, and learn how to obtain help. Practice creating, naming, and saving a simple worksheet. Perform a few calculations, add some simple formatting, and print the worksheet.

CHAPTER TWO

Worksheets

The worksheet provides a base for all of Excel's features. Practice a variety of techniques for developing, manipulating, and modifying worksheets. Use formulas and Excel's built-in functions to perform calculations, and find out how to link worksheets together.

CHAPTER THREE

Formatting & Printing

Excel has the tools to make your data look good and read easily. In this chapter you'll learn how to apply different fonts, number formats, alignment, and styles to your worksheet data. Discover how to add graphics and text boxes — and how to print your worksheets with panache.

CHAPTER FOUR

Charts & Databases

Together with worksheets, charts and databases complete Excel's major features. Charts allow you to display data from a worksheet graphically, while databases are invaluable for storing and retrieving large amounts of information. Learn how to create and modify charts, and how to compile, sort, and filter a database.

CHAPTER FIVE

Getting More from Excel

Learn about outlining and how to summarize data from related worksheets. Explore Excel's problem-solving tools and learn how to navigate large worksheets.

REFERENCE

Reference Section

About This Book

Welcome to *The Way Microsoft Excel for the Macintosh Works*, an easy-to-follow beginner's guide designed to make your introduction to Excel version 5 as smooth as possible.

The emphasis in this book is on learning Excel through practical experience: you'll familiarize yourself with the program by working through a series of examples, which have been carefully devised to cover the most frequently used of Excel's multiplicity of features. You'll follow step-by-step instructions for every procedure — and you'll find many tips and shortcuts to guide you on your way. Once you've worked through the examples, you should be able to apply the skills you've learned to a wide variety of business and home applications.

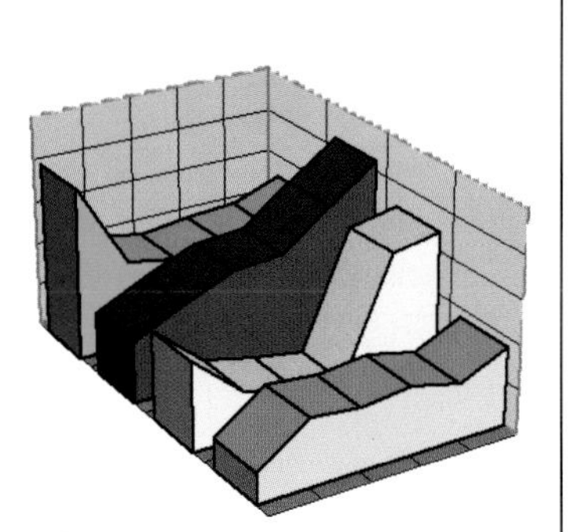

Creating Pictures
Find out how to create and modify Excel charts on pages 90 to 97.

BUILDING YOUR CONFIDENCE

We've organized this guide so that you start with some easy exercises and, building on the skills you acquire, move gradually on to more advanced topics. First you'll learn about the program itself and the elements you can see in the Excel application window. Then you'll develop a basic Excel worksheet — a simple monthly income account. You'll go on to practice some further core skills, such as the mechanics of moving and copying data, the use of formulas and functions, charting data, database creation, and how to format and print a worksheet. In the final chapter, you'll learn about some more advanced topics, such as data consolidation and Excel's problem-solving tools.

Working Smarter
Discover how to use Excel functions and the Function Wizard on pages 56 to 59.

THE WYSIWYG CONCEPT

By the way, my name's the WYSIWYG wizard. You'll find me popping up regularly in the pages that follow, handing out a few tips on getting the most from Excel.

One of the first questions you may be asking is: "Why is this book called a WYSIWYG guide?" Well, WYSIWYG stands for "What You See Is What You Get." The phrase was coined some years ago to describe computer programs with a special feature — namely that *what you see* on the screen is the same as *what you get* when you print it out. In this book, we turn the WYSIWYG concept around a little bit. The practical instructions for learning about Excel's commands and tools are accompanied by visual prompts showing exactly what is happening

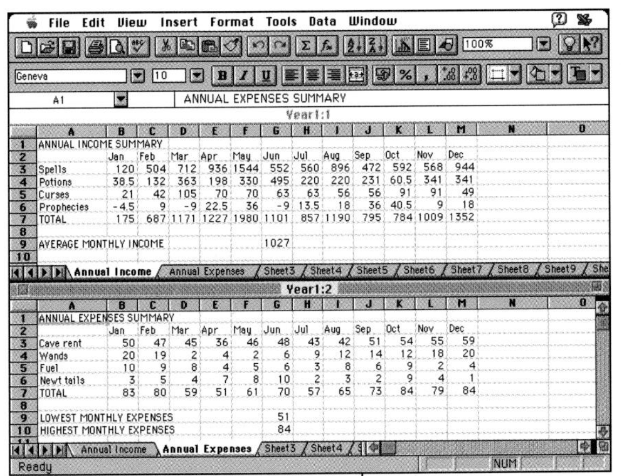

on the computer screen. In other words, *what you see* on the page is the same as *what you get* on your computer screen.

SHOTS AND FRAGMENTS

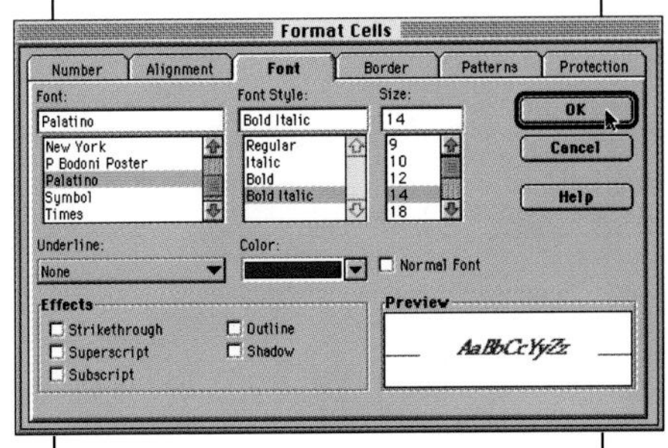

Sometimes, an instruction is accompanied by a screen "shot" (like the one at left) showing how your screen looks at a particular stage in an operation. Or you'll see a smaller box within the screen (like the one above right), called a dialog box, that allows you to specify a number of different options for the command you've chosen. At other times, you might see a series of screen "fragments" (like those shown at right), which focus on where the action is as you follow a set of instructions.

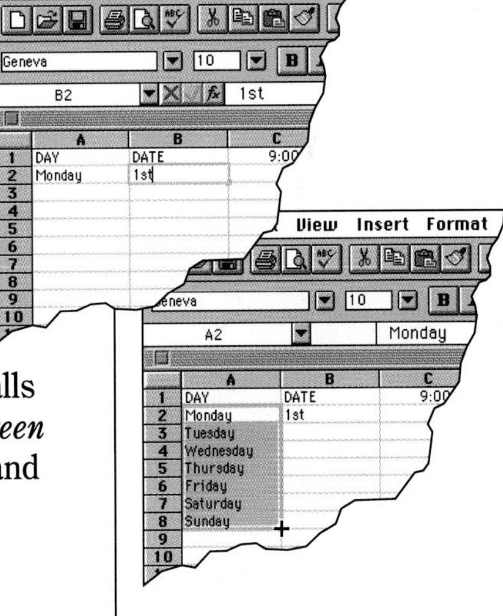

Cell Overflow!
When text that you have entered into a cell overflows into an adjacent cell, it is visible until you enter something into the adjacent cell (which will hide the overflowing text). You can solve this by widening the column or by wrapping the text (see page 71).

TIPS AND SHORTCUTS

Besides the insights that I provide, you'll see various tips scattered throughout the book in colored boxes. The *pink* boxes contain warnings about some common pitfalls you may run into when using Excel. The *green* boxes offer advice on common difficulties and suggest useful shortcuts.

REFERENCE SECTION

At the back of the book, you'll find a short Reference Section. This includes advice on organizing your workbook files and the sheets within your workbooks, a listing of useful keyboard shortcuts, some tables of mouse pointer shapes and error values, and a guide to Excel's auditing tools for tracking down the source of worksheet errors. Finally, you'll find an index to the whole volume.

Undo Formatting?
If you make a mistake when formatting, you can reverse the action if you immediately press Command and Z together or choose the *Undo* command from the *Edit* menu.

EASY READING

The only way to become comfortable with any new program is to get hands-on experience. We believe that *The Way Microsoft Excel for the Macintosh Works* will make the learning curve as easy and enjoyable for you as possible. By the end of the book, you should feel confident using the many features of Excel, and you'll be able to accomplish a wide range of tasks — from creating a basic checking account ledger to charting your company's business performance or tackling complex numerical problems. Read on!

CHAPTER ONE

Getting Started with Excel

In this introductory chapter, you'll explore some basic concepts and learn terms that will help you use Microsoft Excel effectively. You'll learn about the main elements of the Excel application window and how to enter data into the honeycomb of worksheet cells. You'll create a very simple worksheet and then make changes to your data and apply formatting so that your worksheet is easy to read and understand.

WELCOME TO EXCEL • JUMPSTART

Welcome to Excel

Ready for Action
When you start Excel 5, a workbook *opens containing a group of* sheets *that you can use as worksheets or chart sheets. The screen displays the first sheet ready for you to enter data.*

MICROSOFT EXCEL IS A POWERFUL PROGRAM that combines spreadsheet functions with sophisticated graphics and database features. The program is based on a grid of cells called a *worksheet,* into which you enter data. Using *formulas,* you can perform calculations on the data — and Excel will update the calculation results when the data changes. Excel has many uses. For example, you can set it up to monitor your bank balance and home budget or to create and manage lists — or you can create a profit and loss statement for your business and then present the information as a chart.

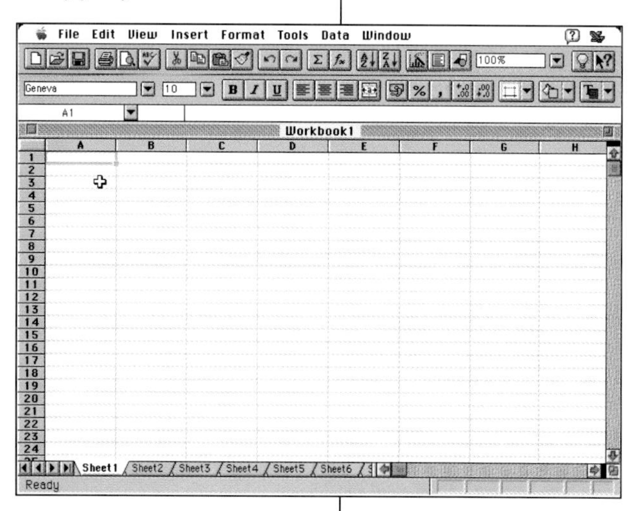

Flexible Features

You can use Microsoft Excel to:

- Organize data and present professional reports in any format you choose.
- Perform a variety of calculations, from simple arithmetic to complex financial and statistical analyses.
- Display worksheet data as graphs and charts.
- Incorporate pictures and annotations.
- Link worksheets together.
- Construct and manage databases.

System Setups!
We've assumed that you will be using a 14-inch color monitor and an Apple extended keyboard. With a larger screen, there will be differences between what you see and our screen shots. If you have a standard keyboard, you won't have access to all of the keyboard operations described.

What Equipment Do I Need?

Before you can use Microsoft Excel for the Apple Macintosh, you must have the right equipment. The minimum hardware and software requirements include:

- An Apple Macintosh with one 800-KB floppy disk drive and a hard disk drive.
- System 7 or higher and a 68020 microprocessor or higher.
- At least 16 MB free on the hard disk for the complete Microsoft Excel package. The minimum working installation of Excel requires 6.5 MB of free hard disk space.
- At least 4 MB of RAM (random access memory).
- The Microsoft Excel program disks.
- If you want to see printouts of your work, you will also need a compatible printer such as a StyleWriter II or LaserWriter.

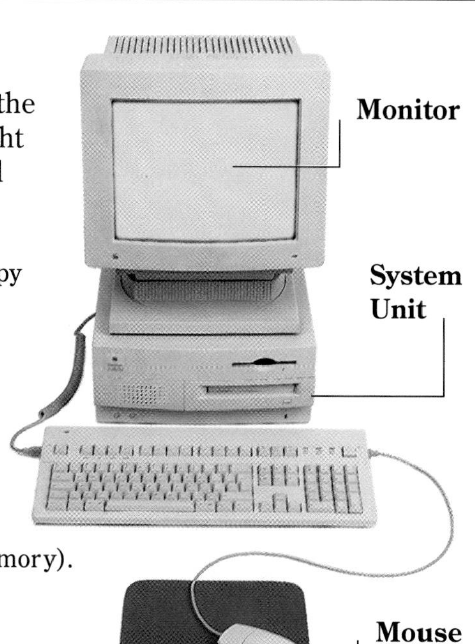

Using the Mouse

Excel is designed to be used in conjunction with a mouse, a hand-held pointing device connected to your Macintosh's keyboard. The four types of action you'll perform with the mouse are moving, clicking, double-clicking, and dragging.

- *Moving* consists of gliding your mouse over a flat surface. As you do so, a pointer moves in unison on the screen. You can position the pointer over any on-screen item.
- *Clicking* involves pressing and releasing the mouse button when the pointer has been positioned over an on-screen item.
- *Double-clicking* entails pointing to an item and then quickly pressing and releasing the mouse button twice.
- *Dragging* consists of moving the mouse while holding down the mouse button.

By using the mouse you can open and close workbooks, maneuver around worksheets and perform a variety of Excel commands, all without having to type in any keyboard instructions. For some mouse operations, however, it will be necessary to hold down the Control key at the same time as you use the mouse. Most of Excel's features can be controlled using the keyboard — for speed, this is often best — but some features, such as the toolbar buttons, can be activated only by means of the mouse.

Double Trouble?
If you are not yet accustomed to using a mouse, you may need a little practice to perfect your double-clicking technique. If the second click does not follow fast enough after the first, Excel may interpret the mouse action as two single clicks. Make sure that you don't move the mouse between clicks.

Mouse Pointer Shapes
In Excel, the mouse pointer can and does take on a variety of shapes (such as those shown below), depending on where you move it on the screen. A full table of pointer shapes can be found on page 122 in the Reference Section.

Arrow Pointer 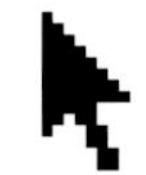

Normal Pointer in Worksheet 

I-Beam Pointer 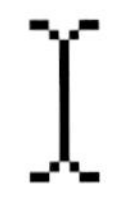

Column Width Adjuster 

Starting Excel

If Excel is not already installed on your Macintosh, follow the instructions in your manual and then within the Microsoft Excel Setup program. Once Excel has been installed, you are ready to start the program: just follow these steps.

1. Starting from the Desktop, open the folder in which you installed Microsoft Excel.

2. Position the mouse pointer over the Microsoft Excel program icon and then double-click on the mouse button. While the program loads you'll see a watch icon on screen.

Microsoft Excel

Need an Alias?
With System 7 you can make an alias of Excel and install it in the Apple menu. This means that you can launch Excel without the need to find and double-click on the program icon each time you want to start the program. If you need more information on how to do this, see your Macintosh User's Guide.

The Excel Worksheet

■ A worksheet is arranged into a series of cells, each with a unique address (for example, C3), which is determined by the column and row it occupies.

■ Columns are labeled across the top by letters. Rows are labeled down the side by numbers. Each worksheet can have a maximum of 256 columns and 16,384 rows — giving you over 4 million cells!

■ Clicking on a cell activates it. Whatever you type next appears in that cell.

■ You can manipulate data in a worksheet by selecting (highlighting) the relevant cells and performing operations on them.

■ You choose an operation by clicking on a toolbar button with the mouse, choosing a command from a menu, or pressing a combination of keys.

New to Workbooks?
A workbook consists initially of 16 blank sheets. Although *Sheet1* is displayed at first, you can access other sheets by clicking on the sheet tabs at the foot of the window. You can give the workbook and its component sheets specific names (see page 21) and you can also open new workbooks.

The Application Window

When Microsoft Excel 5 opens, you'll see a workbook window titled *Workbook1.* Associated with this there will be the the Excel menu, formula, tool, and status bars that are described below. You might need to click on the zoom box (see opposite). The first sheet (*Sheet1*) in *Workbook1* is displayed on screen.

Enter and Cancel Buttons
When you type something into the active cell, or edit its contents, these two buttons appear. You can click on the Enter button (the check mark) to confirm that your typing or editing is correct. Click on the Cancel button (the cross) if you want to start over.

Apple Icon
Clicking on this and holding down the mouse button reveals a drop-down menu that lets you get information about Excel or launch any item in the Apple Menu Items folder.

Name Box
This area tells you the address of the active cell or, if you have named the cell or range, the name of the active cell or selected range.

Close Box
Clicking here closes the workbook. If you have made any changes since you last saved the workbook you will be asked if you want to save again before the workbook closes.

Select All Button
Click here to select (highlight) the whole active worksheet.

Row Headers
Clicking on one of these selects that entire row.

Status Bar
Information about the currently-highlighted command or toolbar button is shown here, letting you know what Excel is doing or is ready to do.

Sheet Tabs
You click on these tabs to open or switch between the sheets in a workbook. The tab with a white background indicates the currently displayed sheet.

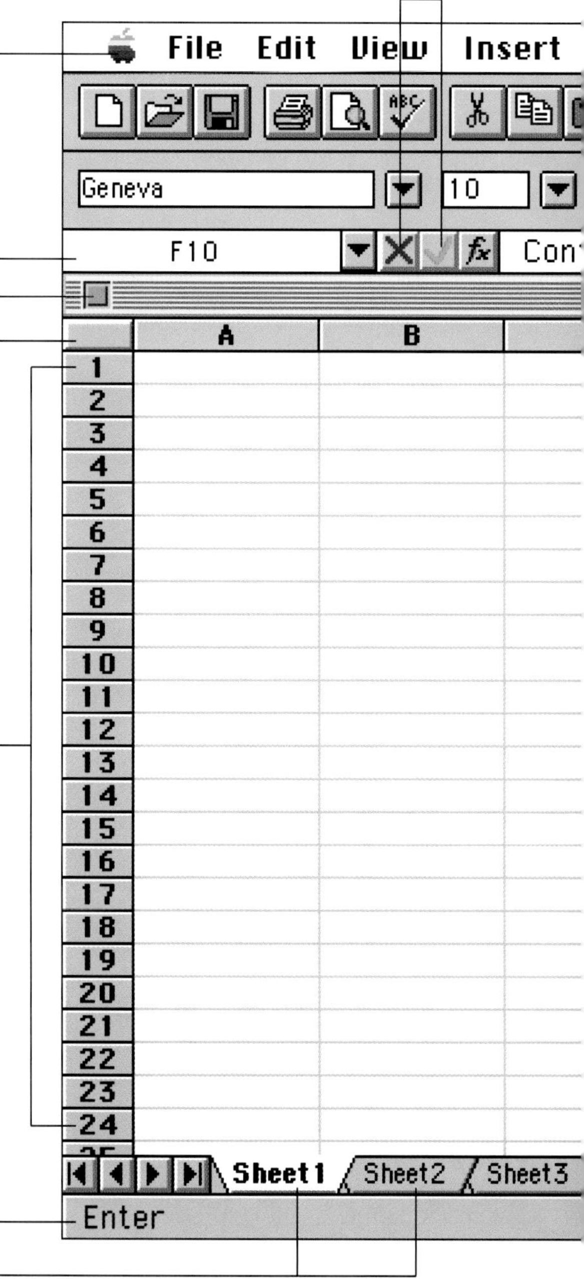

Formula Bar
Displays the contents of the active cell.

Title Bar
The name of the workbook appears here in black letters if the window is active, or in gray if it isn't. The title bar can be used to move an active window around the screen (point at the title bar and then drag it in any direction — an outline indicates the new position).

Menu Bar
When you click and hold on one of the names in this bar, a drop-down menu appears. Choosing a command from the list instructs Excel to perform a certain action.

Standard and Formatting Toolbars
You can click on the buttons in these bars to initiate some frequently used operations in Excel.

Help Icon
Clicking and holding on this opens a menu that lets you turn Balloon Help on or off or request any of the Help facilities that you installed with Excel.

Application Icon
Clicking and holding on this opens a menu that lets you move to any open program.

Zoom Box
If you have changed the size or position of a window, clicking the zoom box will resize and reposition the window to show as much as possible of the contents. If the window is already at its maximum, clicking the zoom box will return the window to its previous size and position.

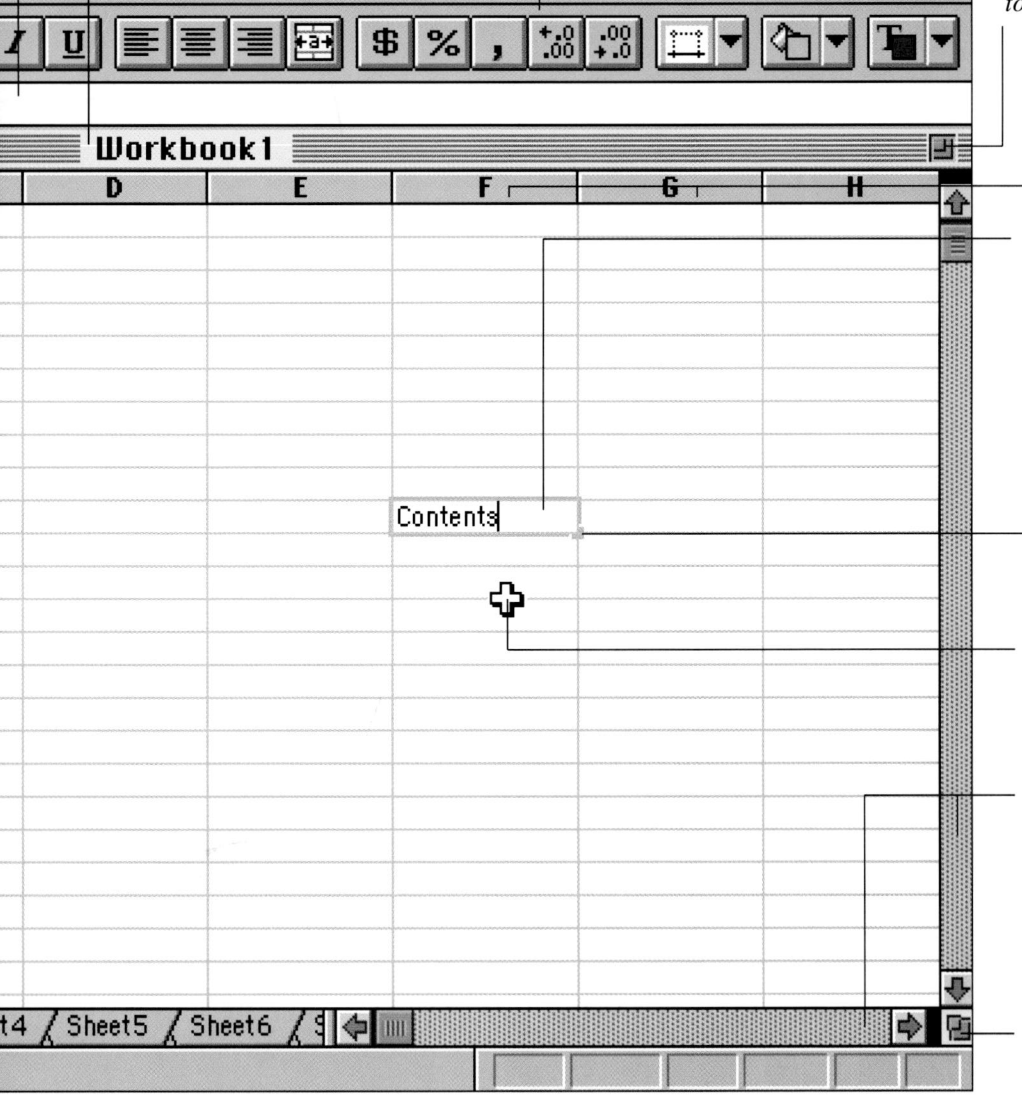

Column Headers
Clicking on one of these selects that entire column.

Active Cell
The cell to be affected by the next command is surrounded by an active-cell border. You can drag this border to move the contents of the active cell to another cell.

Fill Handle
You can drag the fill handle to create a series or to copy a cell's contents.

Mouse Pointer
The standard pointer is shown, but it can take many other shapes.

Scroll Bars
Click on the arrows at either end of these to scroll through a worksheet one row or column at a time. Drag the scroll box to scroll over longer distances.

Size Box
Dragging this lets you resize the window. An outline indicates the new size.

Wrong Command?
If you realize you have chosen the wrong command and Excel has carried it out, immediately choose *Undo* from the *Edit* menu. If the command has opened a dialog box, click on *Cancel* or *Close*.

Using the Menu Bar

Click on a name in the Excel menu bar, keeping the mouse button depressed, and you'll see a drop-down menu. Each menu displays a selection of commands. To choose a command drag the mouse pointer down to highlight it and then release the mouse button. If you choose a command followed by an ellipsis (...), a dialog box opens to let you specify further options.

Some menu commands are followed by the name of a key or combination of keys. Pressing the specified keys invokes the command.

CHOOSING A COMMAND

Now you can begin using Excel. As an example of how to choose a command from a menu, try choosing the *Open* command from the *File* menu.

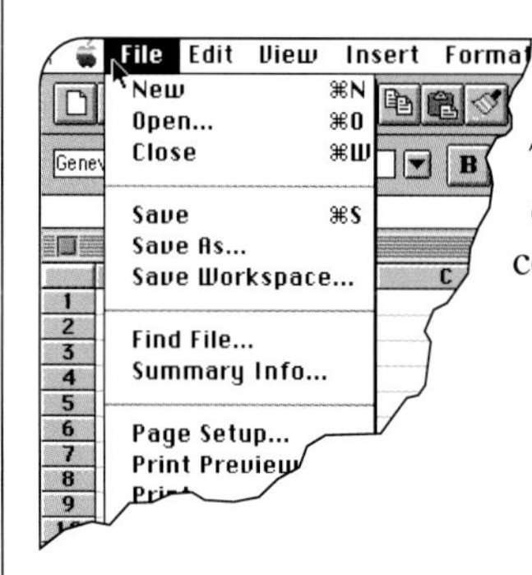

1 Click and hold on *File* in the menu bar. The *File* menu drops down, displaying a list of commands.

2 Move the pointer to *Open* and release the mouse button. A dialog box appears. Click on *Cancel* to leave it.

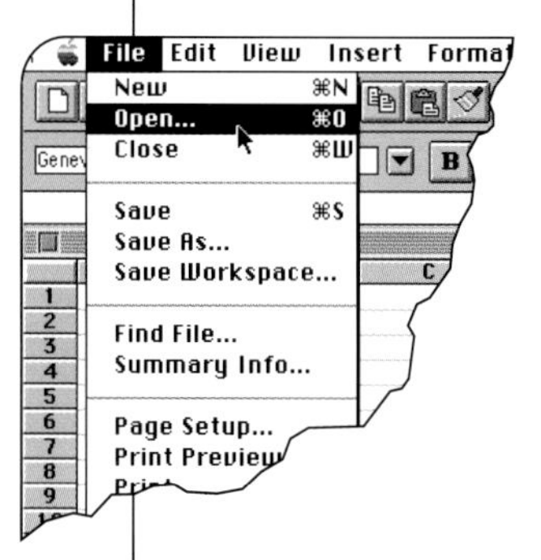

CLOSING A MENU

If you open a menu and don't find the command you want, close it by moving the pointer off the menu and letting go of the mouse button. If the pointer is in the menu bar you can move sideways to the next menu.

Menu Within a Menu?
You will find that some menu commands display a right-pointing arrowhead alongside the command. If you highlight one of these commands, a submenu appears to the right. You may then choose from the options in the submenu.

Looking Dim?
Some menu commands or dialog box labels may appear dimmed, meaning that those commands are not currently available. This may be because the command is not appropriate in the context of what has been selected on the worksheet.

The Standard Toolbar

Toolbars contain a number of commands and tools, represented as buttons. By positioning the mouse pointer over a button and clicking, you can perform actions such as creating a workbook or adding up a column of figures. Some buttons remain depressed when you click on them; clicking again reverses the action. When you open Excel 5, the Standard toolbar (shown right) and the Formatting toolbar are displayed beneath the menu bar. Other toolbars are available for your use via the *Toolbars* command in the *View* menu.

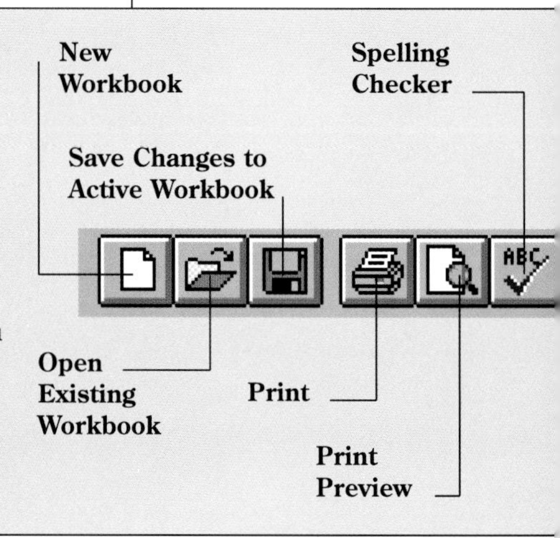

Dialog Boxes

When you choose a menu command that is followed by an ellipsis (…), a dialog box appears. A dialog box is a special window in which you give Excel more information about what you want to do next. Here are some features you will see in a typical dialog box:

Command Buttons

Clicking on a command button performs an action. Every dialog box has an OK *button for confirming the options selected. The* Cancel *button lets you withdraw without any action. The* Help *button displays information about the options. If you choose a command followed by an ellipsis (…), another dialog box appears.*

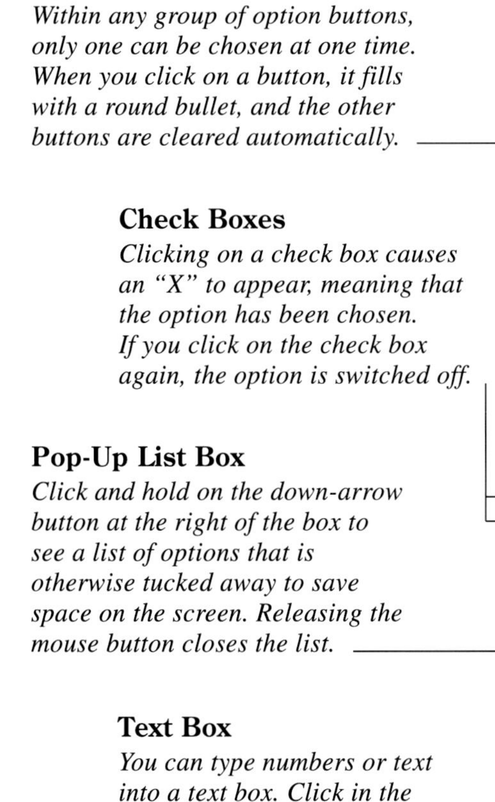

Option Buttons

Within any group of option buttons, only one can be chosen at one time. When you click on a button, it fills with a round bullet, and the other buttons are cleared automatically.

Flipcard Tabs

Some dialog boxes have several sections, or "flipcards," that can be accessed by clicking on these tabs.

Check Boxes

Clicking on a check box causes an "X" to appear, meaning that the option has been chosen. If you click on the check box again, the option is switched off.

Pop-Up List Box

Click and hold on the down-arrow button at the right of the box to see a list of options that is otherwise tucked away to save space on the screen. Releasing the mouse button closes the list.

Text Box

You can type numbers or text into a text box. Click in the box to place the insertion point, and then begin typing.

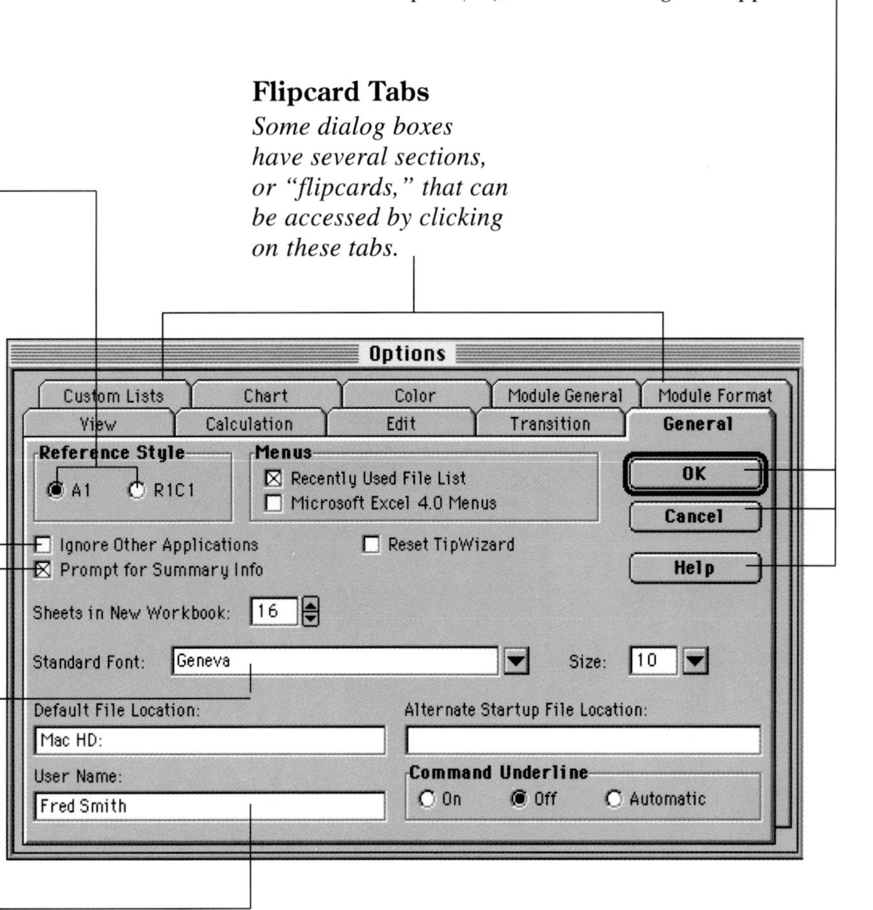

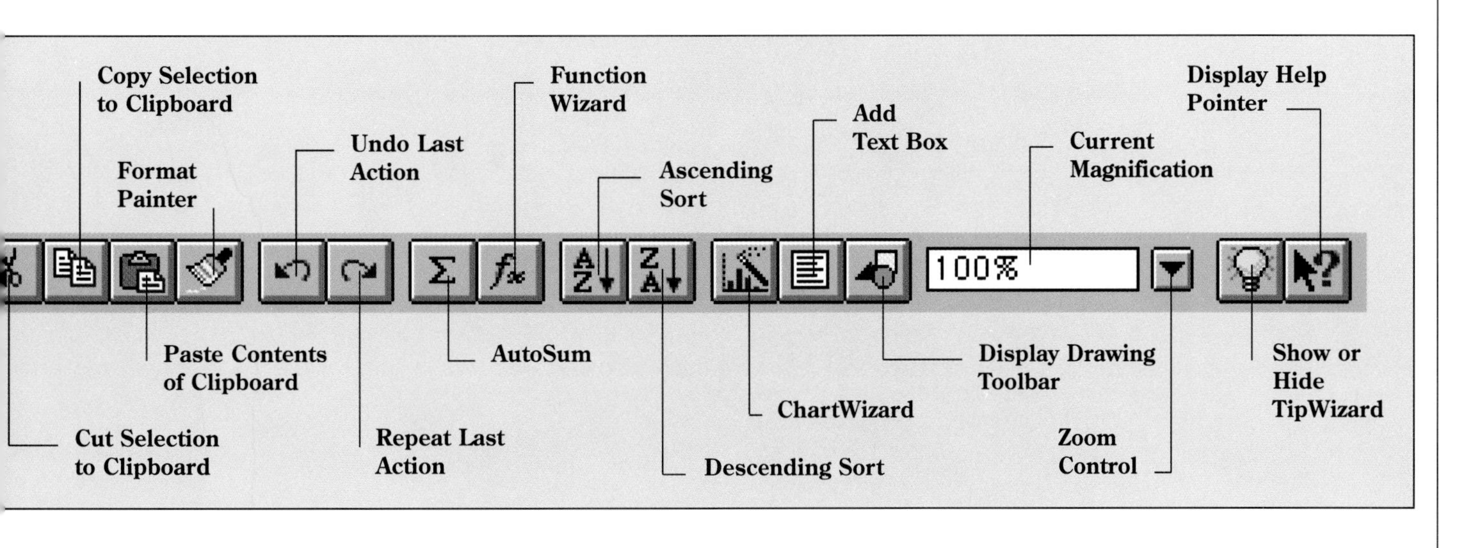

Obtaining Help

The Help Menu
Choose the Quick Preview *command for a menu of four online interactive lessons that introduce Microsoft Excel version 5. Choose* Examples And Demos *for more demonstrations and interactive tutorials.*

If you're puzzled about what to do next, you can ask for assistance from the Help menu. Click on the Help icon at the right of the menu bar, keep the mouse button depressed, and a list of options will appear. If you choose the *Microsoft Excel Help* command, a window titled *MS Excel Help* appears. Initially it displays a screen that lists the overall contents of the Help system.

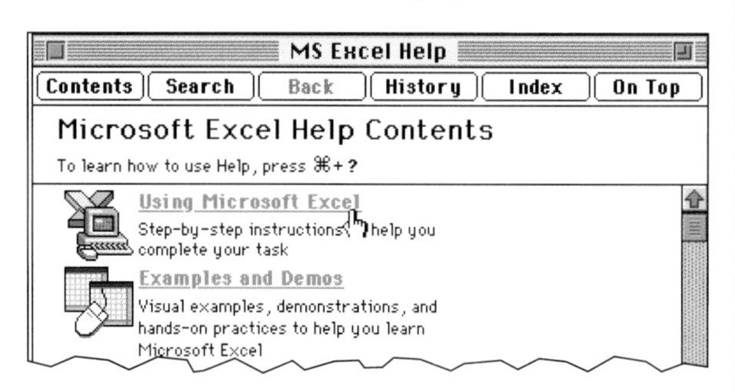

TipWizard
Click on the TipWizard button (the light bulb symbol) on the Standard toolbar, and the TipWizard will appear. The TipWizard displays a tip (in a bar above the worksheet) whenever you perform a series of actions for which there is a more efficient method.

FINDING YOUR WAY AROUND

Within the Help system, some words and phrases appear in green and are underlined. When you point to one of these "jump terms," the mouse pointer changes into a pointing hand. If you click on a jump term, Excel presents a Help screen on that topic.

Clicking on *Index* gives an alphabetical list of the Help topics available — scroll through until you find what you want. *Back* takes you to the last Help topic you looked at. You can return to any topic that you've already viewed by clicking on the *History* button and then double-clicking in the *Help History* window on the topic that you want to see again. To leave the Help system, click on the Help window's close box.

Help Button

What Is "Search"?
If you want help on a specific topic, click on the *Search* button in the *MS Excel Help* window. When the dialog box appears, type the first few letters of the topic into the box at the top. Excel displays a list of topics starting with those letters. Double-click on an entry. In the lower box a second list of topics appears. Double-click on the one most likely to help.

THE HELP POINTER

If you press Shift and Help together or click on the Help button on the Standard toolbar, the mouse pointer becomes the help pointer — a question mark next to an arrow. Click this on any menu command or toolbar button, and a screen appears explaining its function. For an explanation of the Open File button:

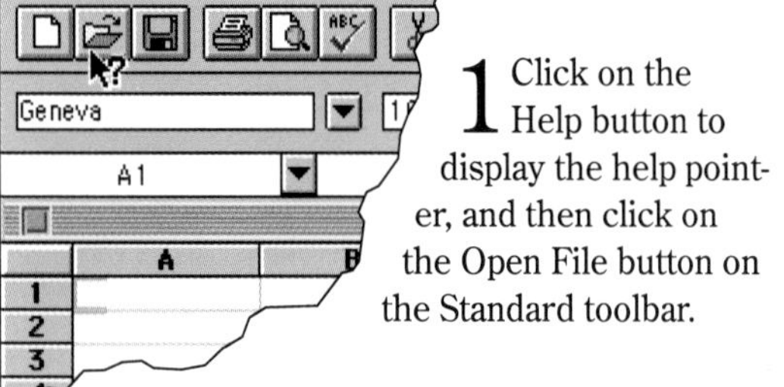

1 Click on the Help button to display the help pointer, and then click on the Open File button on the Standard toolbar.

2 A Help window appears on the screen with information about the *Open* command.

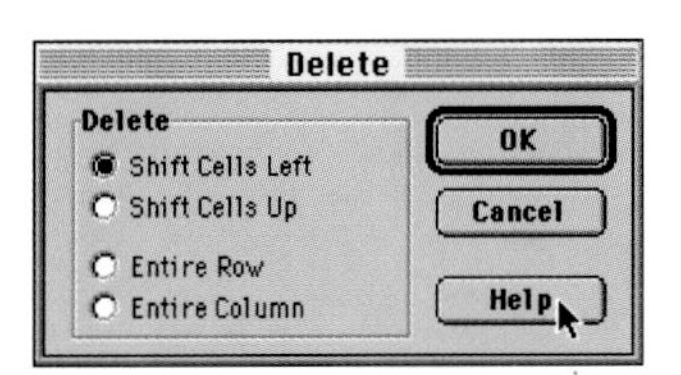

Delete Dialog Box

OTHER SOURCES OF HELP

If a dialog box is open, pressing the Help key gives context-sensitive help and is useful for obtaining information. For example, choose *Delete* from the *Edit* menu to open the *Delete* dialog box (left). Press Help, or click on the *Help* button in the dialog box, to access a Help screen about the *Delete* command.

For information about any toolbar button, point to the button. After a pause you'll see a brief description of its function (a "ToolTip") in a yellow box. For a fuller description, you can look at the status bar at the bottom left corner of the screen. With System 7 you can also use Balloon Help.

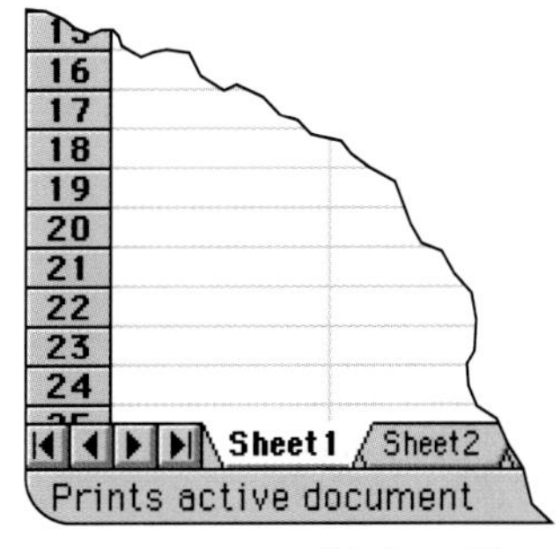

Status Bar

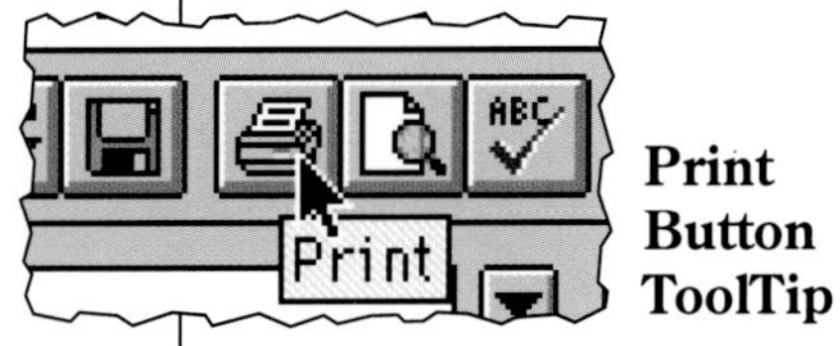

Print Button ToolTip

How to Close and Exit

When you finish what you want to do in a particular workbook, it's a good idea to close it before opening another one (otherwise it uses up part of your computer's memory unnecessarily). To close a workbook without leaving Excel, click in the close box or choose *Close* from the *File* menu. If you quit Excel (by choosing *Quit* from the *File* menu) you automatically close all open workbooks. Whenever you close or quit you are asked whether you want to save changes to the open workbooks.

Closing a Workbook

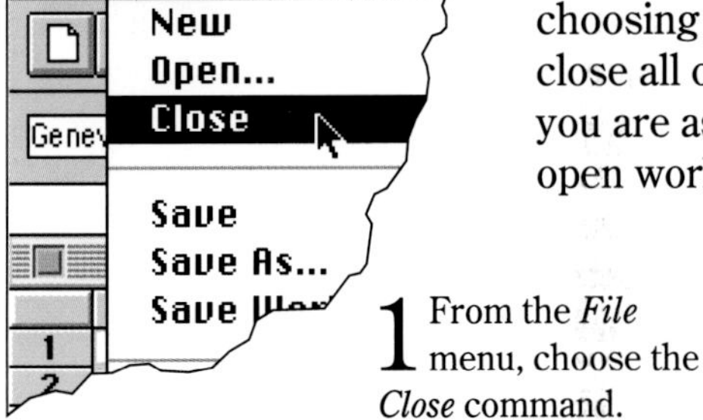

1 From the *File* menu, choose the *Close* command.

2 If you have entered anything in the workbook, a dialog box appears asking if you want to save the changes. In this instance, click on *No*. (If you want to save changes, see "Naming and Saving" on page 21.) The workbook closes, but Excel is still running.

Quitting Excel

1 To leave Excel, choose *Quit* from the *File* menu. Normally, you are asked if you want to save changes to each open workbook. In this case, you have already closed the only workbook that was open.

2 Excel shuts down and the Desktop and program icon reappear.

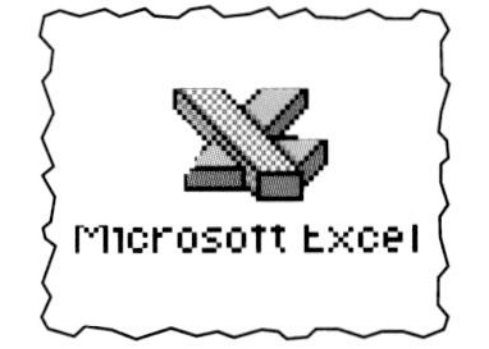

Hide and Seek!
You can hide Excel, allowing you to return to the Macintosh Desktop or go to any other program that you are also running, by clicking on the Application icon and choosing *Hide Microsoft Excel* from the Application menu. Excel is still running and is available for immediate use, but can't be seen. Going back to the Application menu and choosing *Microsoft Excel* will bring the program to the front of the screen again. The Application menu also allows you to go straight to any other program that you are using without going back to the Desktop — just choose the program name.

Jumpstart

OVER THE NEXT FEW PAGES, you'll run through the basics of creating a worksheet, entering and editing data, performing calculations, and then formatting and printing the worksheet. You'll be helping the famous wizard, Merlin, with his accounts — and also introducing yourself to some of the benefits of Excel.

Developing a Worksheet

Merlin is a wizard with an international reputation — but his business practices are still firmly rooted in the tenth century. To assist Merlin, you'll create a simple worksheet that gives details of his varied work over the last month. Don't be discouraged if you feel you are just following simple recipes at this stage. It's an excellent way to become a creative cook!

Recipe for Success
The basic ingredients of a worksheet — the items you can enter into cells — include text, numbers, dates, times, and formulas. These items can be mixed and formatted (styled) in various ways. Formulas perform calculations on values in cells, and these in turn can be the result of calculations on values in other cells — or even in other worksheets.

ENTERING DATA

On opening Excel (see page 11), you'll see a blank sheet called *Sheet1* on the screen — the first sheet in a workbook called *Workbook1*. The worksheet is ready for you to enter data. Cell A1 is the "active" cell — so the active-cell border surrounds it and A1 appears in the name box to the left of the formula bar.

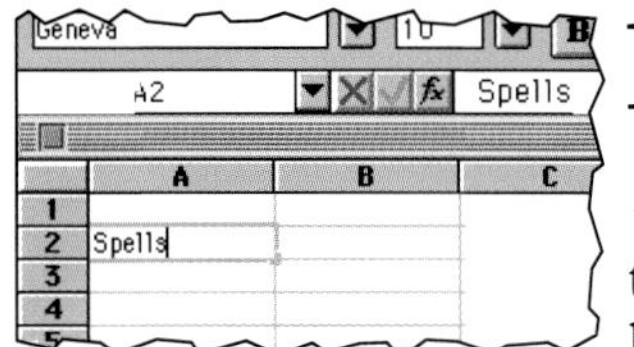

1 Click on cell A2 to make it the active cell, and then type **Spells**. As you type, the letters become visible both in the active cell and in the formula bar, and the Enter and Cancel buttons appear. In the cell, the letters are followed by a blinking vertical line (the insertion point) to indicate where the next character you type will appear.

2 If the typed entry looks correct, confirm your entry by clicking on the Enter button. If a correction is needed, press Delete to erase one character at a time and then retype correctly. Click on the Cancel button if you want to start over.

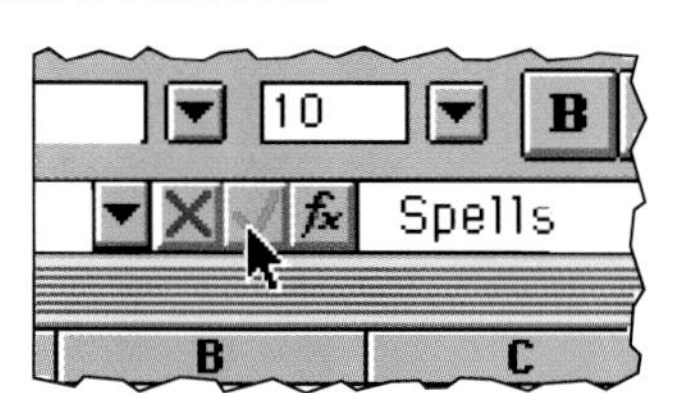

3 When you have completed your typing and clicked on the Enter button, the formula bar buttons disappear but the word **Spells** remains in cell A2 as well as in the formula bar.

Confirm Entry?
You can press the Return key instead of clicking on the Enter button to complete the entry of data into a cell. When you press Return, the next cell down becomes the new active cell. The Enter key on the numeric keypad also completes data entry but leaves the current cell active.

The Direction Keys

Other Navigation Keys

MOVING AROUND

The easiest way to make a different cell active is to move the mouse pointer over it and click. But you can also move the active cell with the keyboard:

■ *Direction keys* — each time one of these is pressed the active cell moves in the direction of the arrow.

■ *Page Up and Page Down keys* — on an extended keyboard these move the active cell up and down through the worksheet one screen at a time. If the Option (or Alt) key is held down at the same time, the active cell moves one screen left or right.

■ *Home and End keys* — on an extended keyboard these, in combination with other keys, move the active cell to a particular position. (See page 30.)

You can use the scroll bars (see page 13) to move the worksheet within the workbook window, but scrolling does not change the location of the active cell.

The Modifier Keys

The four keys shown above — Shift, Control, Option, and Command — can be used to modify the action of other keys. Pressing Command and Z together, for example, has the same effect as going to the Edit *menu and choosing* Undo. *You can learn more about keyboard shortcuts on pages 46 and 122.*

ENTERING MORE DATA

Now let's add more headings and some numbers to your worksheet. Merlin has many clients and he offers them a variety of goods and services at different rates.

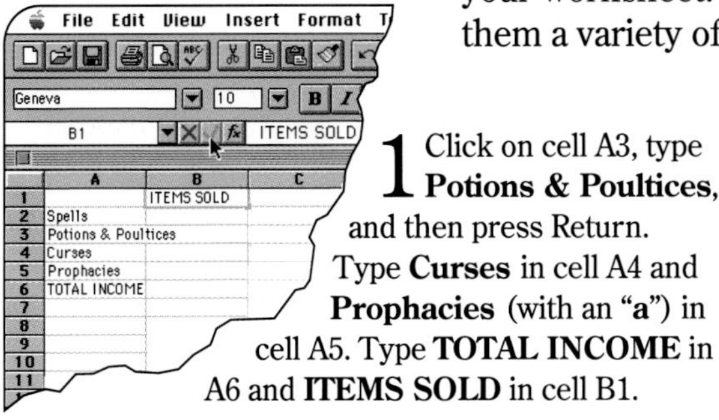

1 Click on cell A3, type **Potions & Poultices**, and then press Return. Type **Curses** in cell A4 and **Prophacies** (with an "**a**") in cell A5. Type **TOTAL INCOME** in A6 and **ITEMS SOLD** in cell B1.

2 Now type **15** in B2, **7** in B3, **3** in B4, and **-1** in B5. (Merlin gave a refund on an earlier "prophacy" that didn't come true. To get a negative number, type a hyphen before it.)

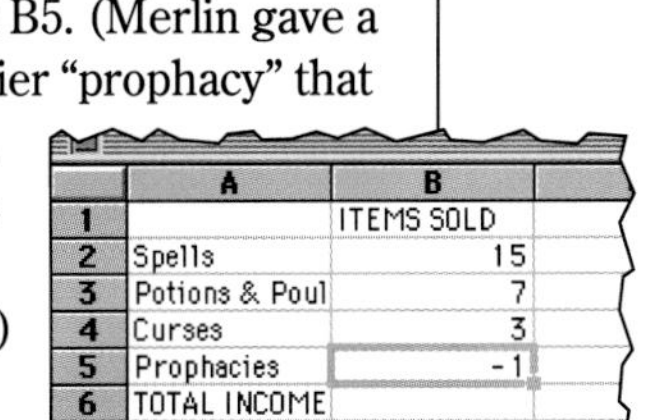

CORRECTING

You need to make a few corrections to the worksheet as it currently stands. Being almost human, Merlin miscounted the number of potions that he had sold.

	A	B
1		ITEMS SOLD
2	Spells	15
3	Potions & Poul	7
4	Curses	8
5	Prophacies	-1
6	TOTAL INCOME	

1 Click on cell B4, type **8**, and then click on the Enter button. This new data overwrites the previous cell contents.

2 You then realize that the cell address should have been B3, not B4. No problem. Simply hold down Command while you press Z. The value in cell B4 returns to **3**.

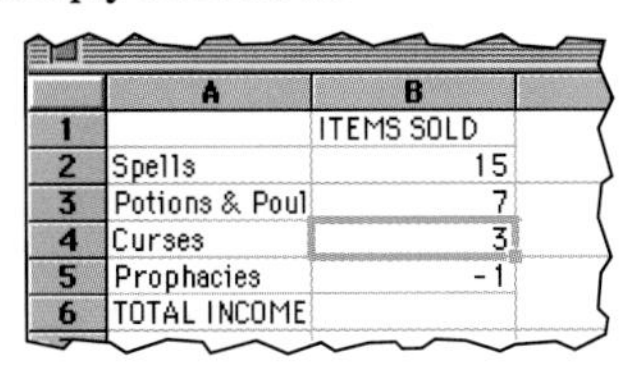

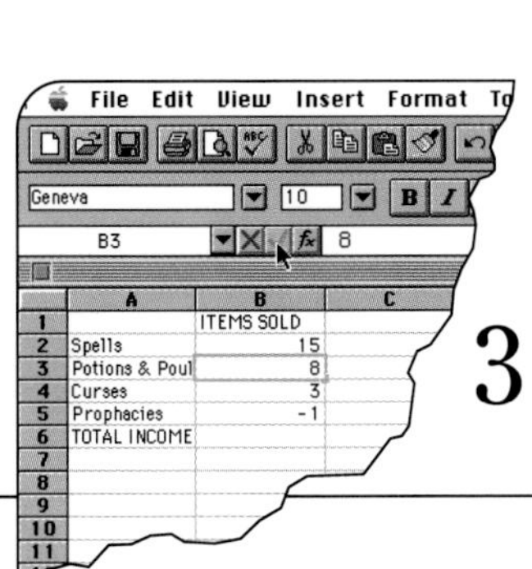

3 Now type **8** into B3, and click on the Enter button.

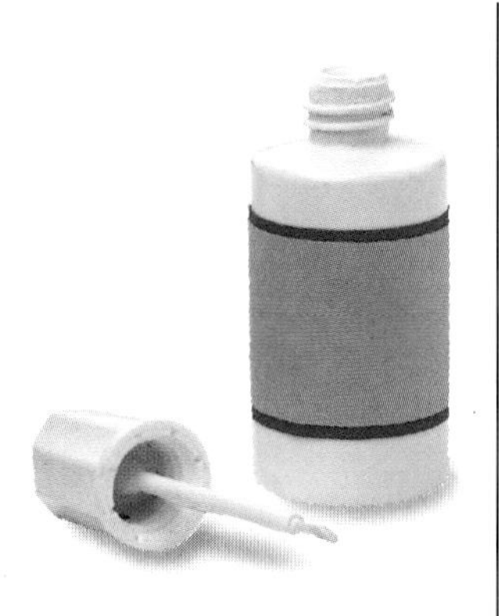

Editing

To modify the contents of a cell, you have two choices. If you activate a cell by clicking on it, the contents will appear in the formula bar, where they can be edited (see more on page 36). If you double-click on a cell, you not only activate it but can also then make changes directly within the cell.

EDITING DIRECTLY IN THE CELL

You may have realized that the word **Prophacies** in cell A5 does not look right. Merlin's spells are world-famous — but his spelling is terrible!

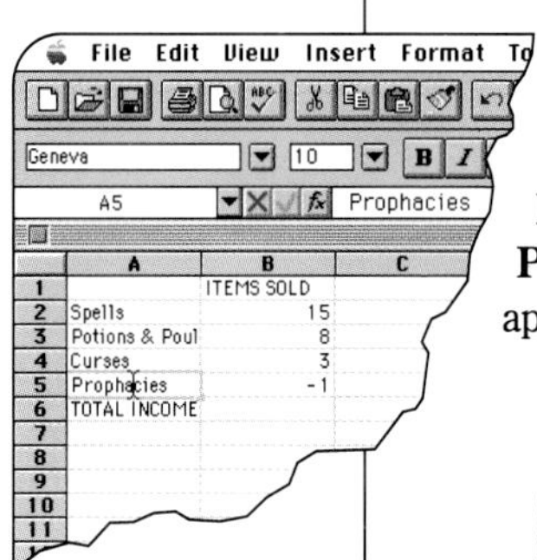

1 Double-click on cell A5 to edit directly in the cell. When moved over the cell, the mouse pointer turns into an I-beam. Position the beam between the **a** and **c** in **Prophacies**. Click and the insertion point appears between these two letters.

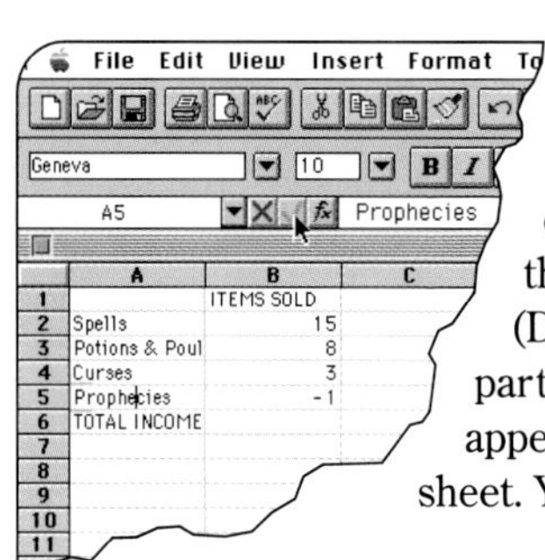

2 Press Delete and the letter **a** will disappear. Type **e**, click on the Enter button, and the correction is made. (Don't worry that the final part of the word "Poultices" appears to be lost on the worksheet. You will fix that soon.)

Spellbinding
Merlin could make good use of Excel's spell-checking facility. If you activate a single cell and then click on the Spelling Checker button on the Standard toolbar, Excel will check spelling throughout the worksheet (see more on page 55).

ENTERING MORE DATA

You now need to add some financial information to Merlin's worksheet. Merlin is paid in gold pieces — and his rates are very reasonable for someone with such special abilities!

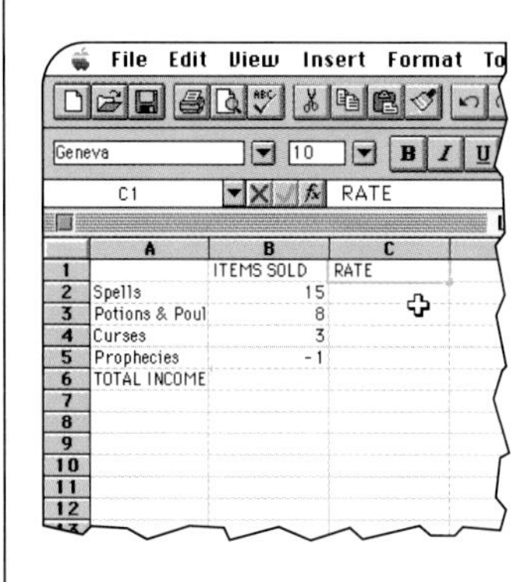

1 Click on cell C1, type the heading **RATE**, and press Enter.

2 Now type **8** into C2, **5.5** into C3, **7** into C4, and **4.5** into C5. These represent Merlin's charges for providing magic spells, potions, curses, and prophecies.

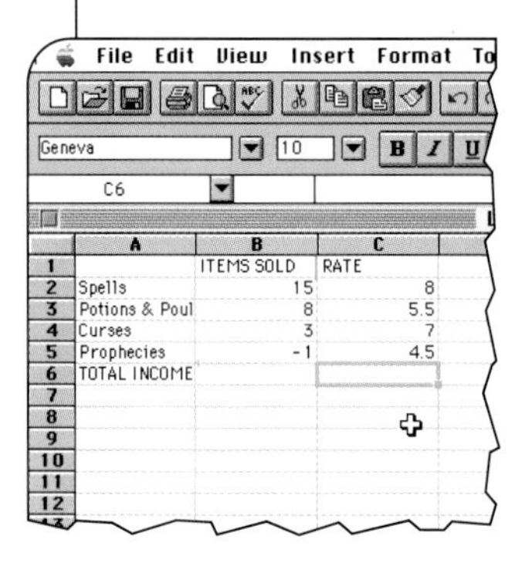

Slow Going?
You can work faster if you combine entering data and moving around the worksheet. Once you have entered something correctly in a cell, press one of the four direction keys to move to the next cell. Your data is accepted and the new cell you moved to is ready for the next typed item.

ALTERING COLUMN WIDTH

Merlin is concerned because the contents of some cells in the worksheet are not fully visible. To correct this, you need to widen column A.

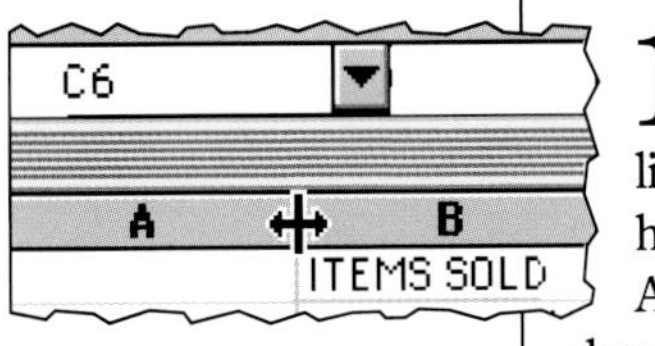

1 Move the mouse pointer over the line between the headers for columns A and B. The pointer changes to a vertical bar with two side arrows.

2 Press the mouse button and drag to the right — the gridline between columns A and B will follow the movement. Release the mouse button when the name box says "Width: 14.00." This should be wide enough for **Potions & Poultices**.

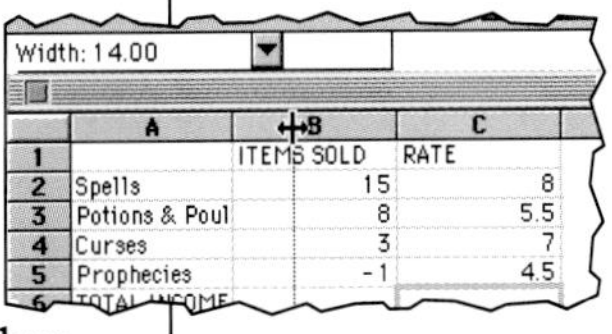

Quick Save?
You can also save by using the Save button on the Standard toolbar or the *Save* command on the *File* menu. If you have not previously saved a workbook, these actions open the *Save As* dialog box. Subsequently, they simply save changes.

Naming and Saving

Even the most reliable of computer systems cannot claim total immunity from power failures and other mishaps. When such events occur, you are likely to lose all the work done since you last saved your workbook to disk. To avoid the possibility of losing large amounts of work you should save your Microsoft Excel workbooks frequently. In this instance, as you have not saved the workbook previously, you must name it when you save it. You should also rename the worksheet into which you have been entering data.

Frozen Pointer
One symptom of software failure may be that the mouse pointer "freezes" on the screen. If this happens, press Command, Option, and Esc together, and then follow the instructions that appear on the screen.

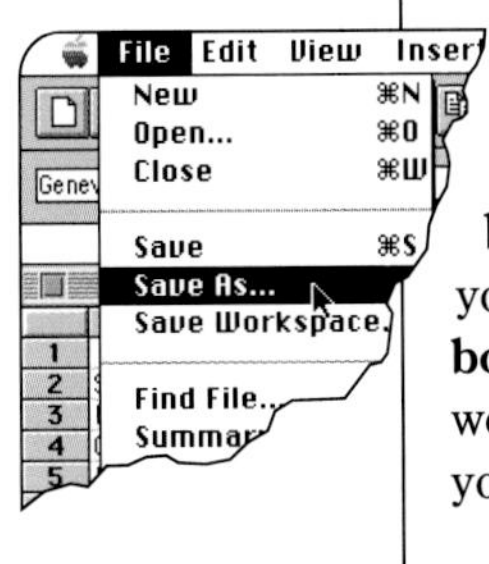

1 Choose the *Save As* command from the *File* menu. A dialog box appears. This lets you create an **Excel Workbooks** folder to keep your work in as well as rename your workbook.

2 Make sure that the new folder will be saved straight to your hard disk by opening the pop-up menu at the top and choosing your hard disk name. Click on the *New* button.

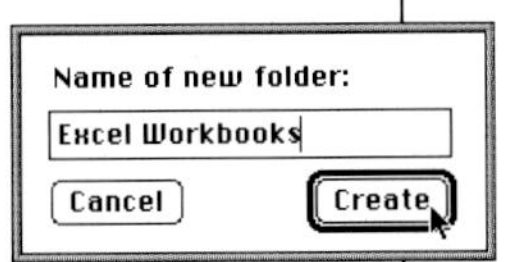

3 Type **Excel Workbooks**, then click on the *Create* button. Type **Merlin** in the *Save as* box and click on *Save*.

4 To give your worksheet a more appropriate name, double-click on the *Sheet1* tab at the foot of the window. The *Rename Sheet* dialog box appears. Type in **Jan Sales**, then click *OK*.

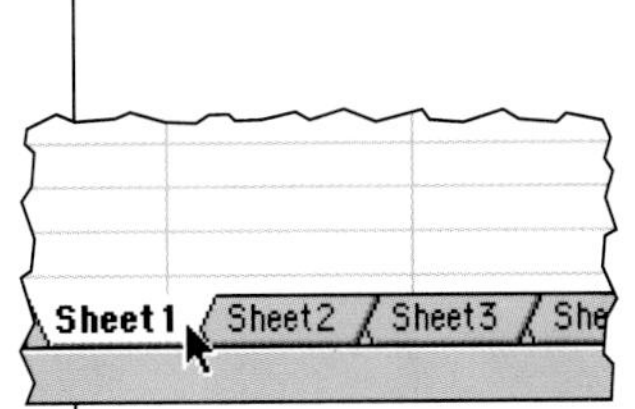

You will notice in the title bar that your workbook is now called **Merlin**. The tabs at the bottom of the screen show that the active worksheet is called **Jan Sales**.

Calculating

You can now calculate Merlin's income for the month. First you need to multiply the number of sales in each category by the appropriate rate. You'll then add up the income in each category.

To calculate using Excel, you need to employ a *formula*. You enter a formula in a cell by first typing an equal sign (=). This sign is followed by a mathematical expression, which may include numbers and references to the contents of other cells, as well as arithmetic operators (such as + and -). In Excel, you use the + sign to indicate addition, - for subtraction, * for multiplication, / for division, and ^ to raise a number exponentially (e.g., to square or cube it).

Remember School Arithmetic?
Excel follows a set order in calculations within a formula. Exponential operations are done first, then multiplication and division, with addition and subtraction last. However, you can use parentheses in your formula to override this rule. (See more on page 35.)

Using a Formula

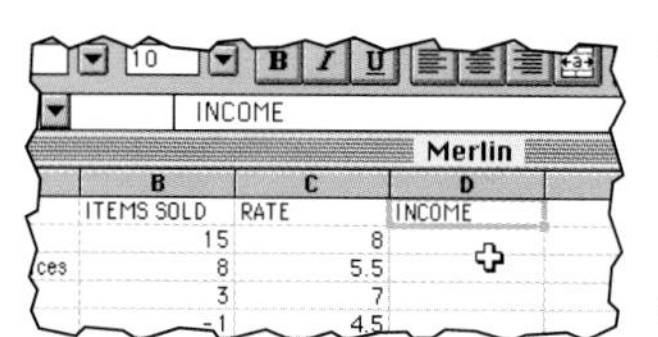

1 Type the heading **INCOME** in D1, and then press Return.

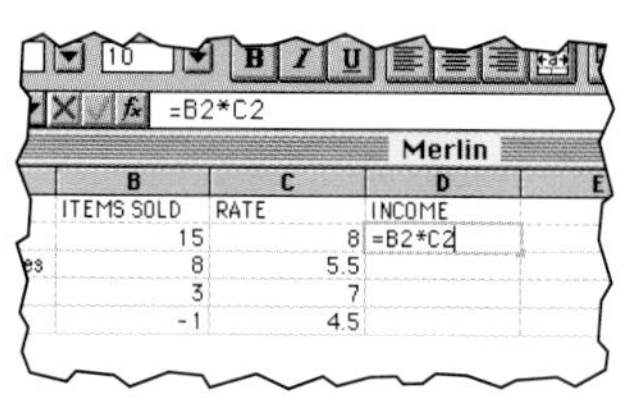

2 With cell D2 active, press the = key to start typing a formula. Because you want cell D2 to contain the contents of cell B2 (sales) multiplied by the contents of cell C2 (rate), type **B2*C2** next. Thus, the whole formula is **=B2*C2**.

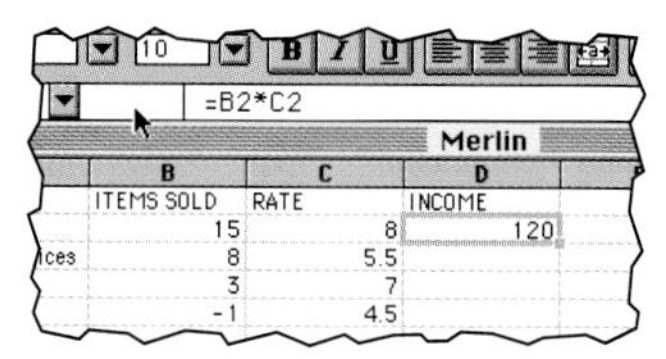

3 Click on the Enter button, and cell D2 shows the result of multiplying the values in cells B2 and C2, namely **120**. The formula itself (**=B2*C2**) is still visible in the formula bar.

COPYING A FORMULA

You could follow the same routine for each of cells D3 through D5. But a quicker way of copying cell contents (including formulas) across adjacent cells is to use the fill handle, a small square at the bottom right corner of the active cell. You can replicate the contents of the active cell by dragging its fill handle until the selection includes all the cells you want to fill.

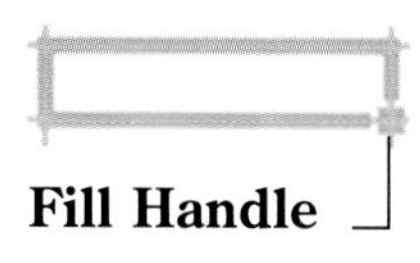

Fill Handle

1 Place the mouse pointer on the fill handle at the bottom right of the active cell border around cell D2. The pointer becomes a +.

2 Press the mouse button and drag the fill handle until the selection, which is surrounded by a gray border, extends to the foot of cell D5. Then release the button. Cells D3 to D5 fill with figures.

Why Use a Formula?
One clear benefit of a formula is that it can be used to reference cells rather than "hard data," meaning specific numbers entered into the cells. If the contents of the referenced cells change, Excel updates the whole calculation automatically.

How Big Is a Range?
A *range* is a rectangle of adjacent cells in a worksheet. For example, the range A1:C5 is the block of cells with A1 and C5 at its opposite corners. A range can be selected by clicking on a cell in one corner of the range and dragging to the cell in the opposite corner. You can erase, copy, cut, and paste ranges — and also name them for easier working (see page 60).

WHAT HAPPENED?

To understand what happened in step 2 at the bottom of the previous page, click in turn on each of the cells D3 through D5 while looking at the formula bar. You will see that each cell contains a different formula. For example, cell D4 contains the formula *=B4*C4* and cell D5 contains the formula *=B5*C5*. When you used the fill handle to copy the formula in cell D2 to the three cells below it, Excel cleverly understood that you did not want to enter the formula *=B2*C2* into each of these cells. You really wanted to fill each cell with a formula that would multiply the quantity of a category sold in column *B* with the rate in column *C* — and that is exactly what Excel has done. (See more about the effects of copying formulas on pages 50 and 51.)

ADDING UP COLUMNS

To total the numbers in a column, you can use the AutoSum button on the Standard toolbar. Excel will automatically provide the formula that sums the data.

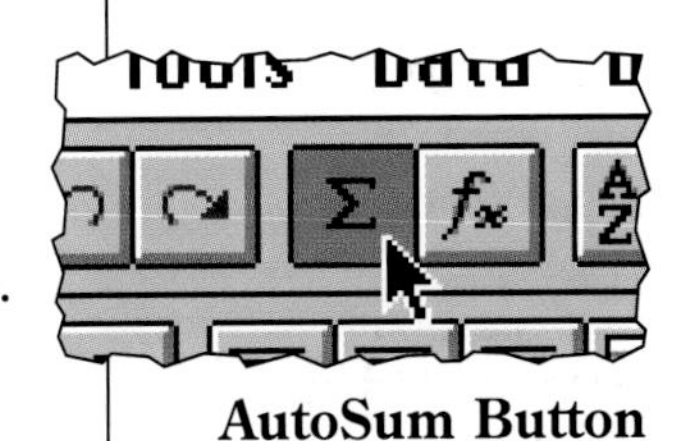

AutoSum Button

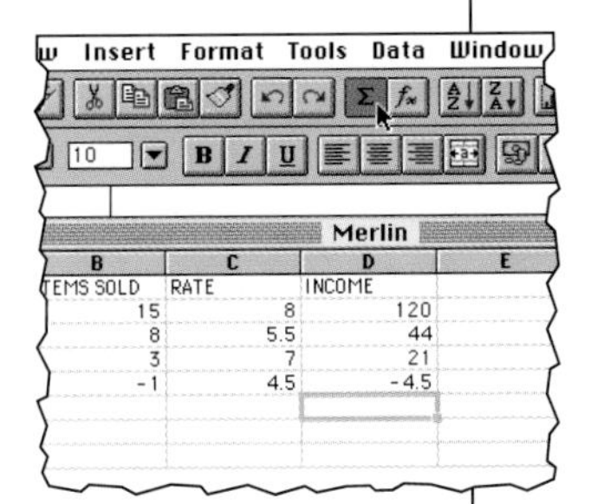

1 You have already typed **TOTAL INCOME** into cell A6. Activate cell D6 by clicking on it. Then click on the AutoSum button on the Standard toolbar.

2 The cell and formula bar both show the expression *=SUM(D2:D5)*. Using the formula SUM(D2:D5), cell D6 will display the total of cells D2, D3, D4, and D5. Click on the Enter button to enter the formula into D6.

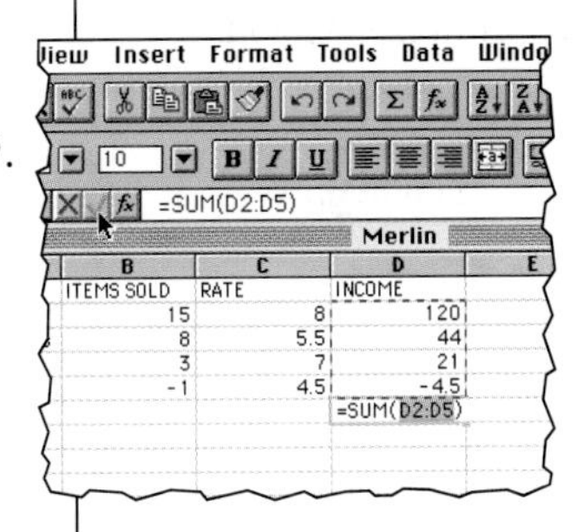

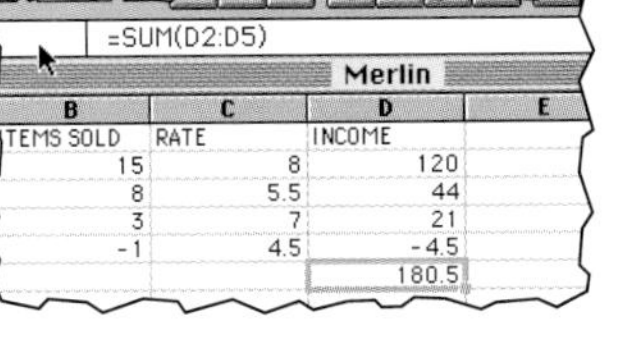

3 Cell D6 now shows Merlin's income for the month.

Merlin interrupts and says that he thinks the figure of seven potions was right after all. To make the correction, click on cell B3, type **7**, click on the Enter button — and see how the figures in D3 and D6, linked to the contents of B3, magically alter. Merlin is impressed. His eyebrows rise imperceptibly, and a barely audible "Abracadabra" escapes his lips.

Revised Worksheet

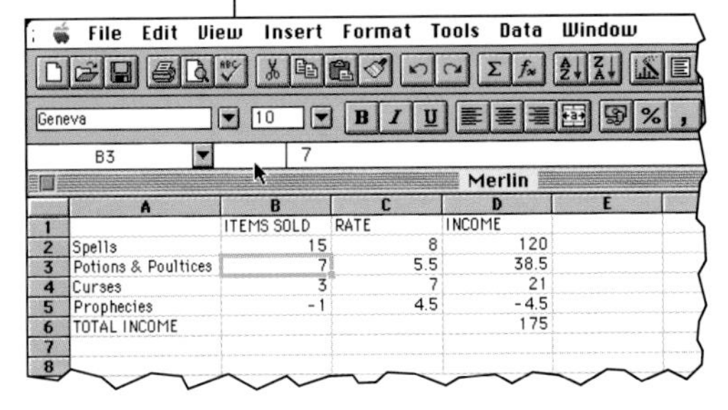

	A	B	C	D
1		ITEMS SOLD	RATE	INCOME
2	Spells	15	8	120
3	Potions & Poultices	7	5.5	38.5
4	Curses	3	7	21
5	Prophecies	-1	4.5	-4.5
6	TOTAL INCOME			175

Simple Formatting

After entering information in your worksheet, you might want to add some visual interest. Here is a brief introduction to some simple formatting techniques you can try using the Formatting toolbar. (See Chapter Three for additional detailed information on formatting options that can improve your presentation.)

ADDING BOLD AND COLOR

Changing text to bold or italic, or changing its color, are ways of adding variety and emphasis. As with all types of formatting, you must first select the cell or range of cells you wish to format.

Undo Formatting?
If you make a mistake when formatting, you can reverse the action if you immediately press Command and Z together or choose the *Undo* command on the *Edit* menu.

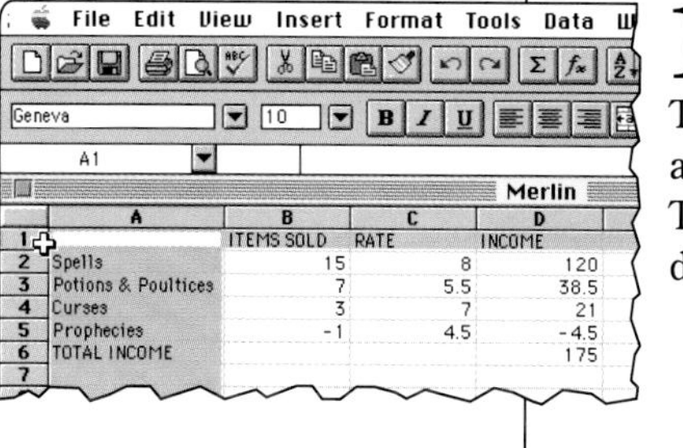

1 Click on the column A header to select the entire first column. Then hold down the Command key and click on the row 1 header. This action selects row 1, without deselecting column A.

2 Next click on the Bold button on the Formatting toolbar. The text that you selected is now displayed in bold. Increase the width of column A to 16 units (see page 21).

Bold Button

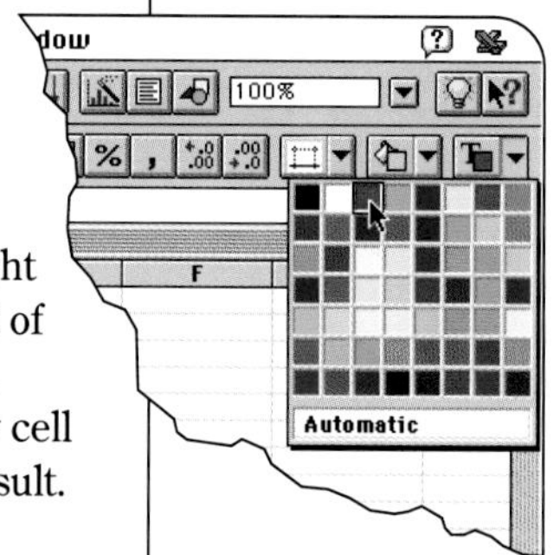

3 Now click on the down arrow to the right of the Font Color button at the far right of the Formatting toolbar. Choose a color you would like for your text labels. Click on any cell other than those highlighted to view the result.

Hiding and Displaying Toolbars

When you open Excel, the Standard and Formatting toolbars are displayed by default. Excel also has 11 other toolbars that you may want to use — you'll learn more about these later. To display or hide a toolbar, first choose the *Toolbars* command from the *View* menu. The *Toolbars* dialog box then appears. Each of the listed toolbars has a check box alongside. Using the mouse, you can check the box for any toolbar you want to display and clear the box for any toolbar you want to hide. Then click on *OK*. You can also display or hide a toolbar by using the toolbar shortcut menu. This is accessed by holding down the Control key, pointing at any part of a toolbar other than a button, and clicking on the mouse button. (See page 45 for more on shortcut menus.)

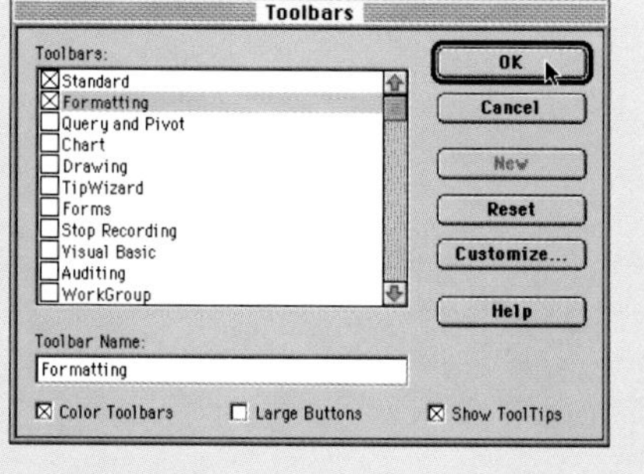

***Toolbars* Dialog Box**

CENTERING HEADINGS

Heading text usually looks best if it is centered within columns. The Center Align button on the Formatting toolbar allows you to make this change with ease.

Center Align Button

1 Select cells B1 through D1 by first selecting cell B1, and then holding down the mouse button and dragging the mouse pointer across C1 and D1.

2 Now click on the Center Align button. The column headings are centered in their cells.

NUMBER FORMATTING

Numbers as well as text can be formatted differently. Using built-in styles that Excel provides, you can express numbers in various ways, such as percentages or currencies, and put in any decimal points needed.

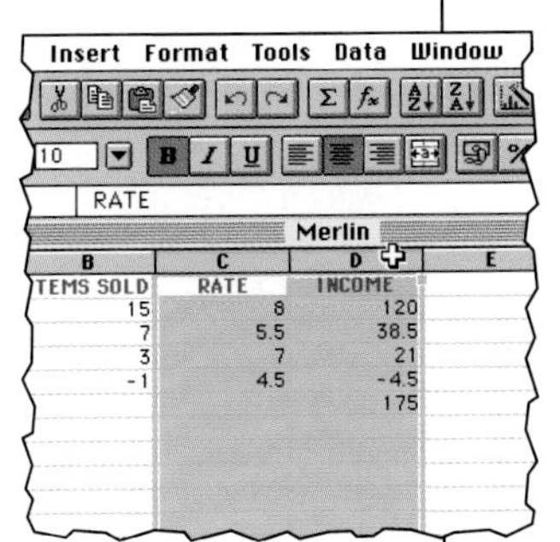

1 Select columns C and D by first clicking on the column C header and then dragging the mouse pointer into column D.

2 Click on the Comma Style button on the Formatting toolbar. This applies a decimal point and two decimal places to any selected numbers.

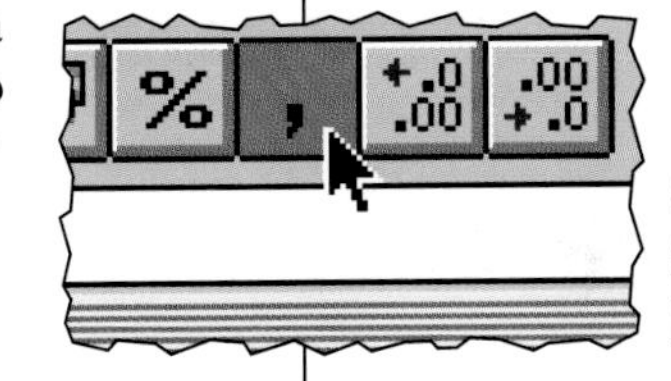

Comma Style Button

THE IMPROVED WORKSHEET

If you now click on the Save button on the Standard toolbar, Excel will save your workbook (including the **Jan Sales** worksheet you have created within the workbook) using its existing name **(Merlin)**. If you wanted to save it with a different name, you would choose *Save As* from the *File* menu. *Save As* allows you to create a new file with a new name while preserving the existing file with its existing name.

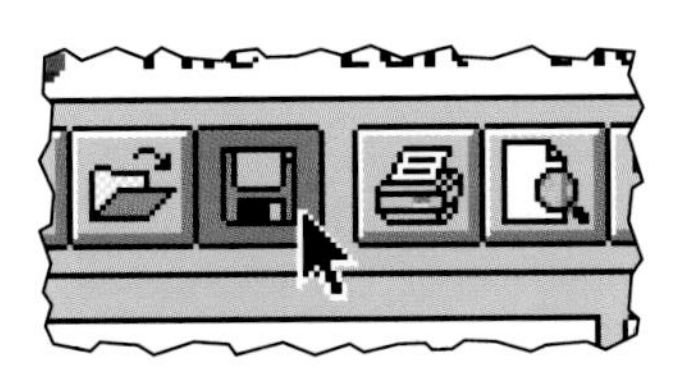

Save Button

Printing

Once your workbook is saved, you are ready to print a copy of the **Jan Sales** worksheet. The quickest way to do so is to click on the Print button on the Standard toolbar. (Unless you have a color printer, the color you have introduced on your worksheet will not show when printed.) Once you have printed, you can leave Excel by choosing the *Quit* command from the *File* menu.

Print Button

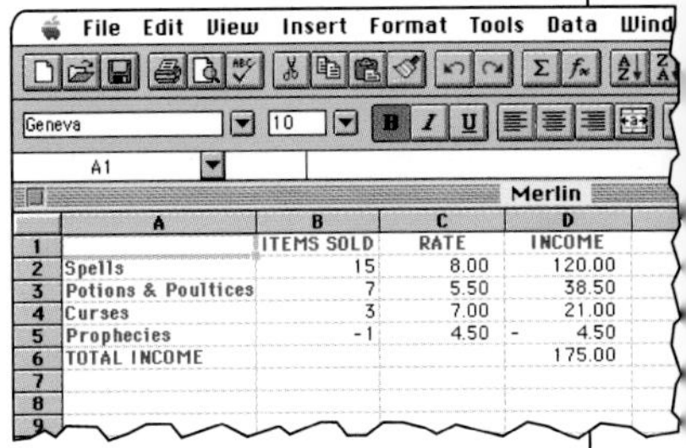

January Gains

*This is how your revised **Jan Sales** worksheet should now look.*

2

CHAPTER TWO

Worksheets

The worksheet is the real powerhouse of Excel, providing a base for all the program's features. In this chapter you'll explore the principles of worksheet construction in more detail. You'll create and modify some example worksheets, use Excel formulas to perform simple calculations, and employ some Excel functions to carry out more complex operations. You'll learn how to work with multiple worksheets and workbooks and how to link your worksheets together.

WORKSHEET BASICS • WORKSHEET MODIFICATION
WORKING SMARTER • MULTIPLE WORKSHEETS

Worksheet Basics

LET'S BEGIN OUR JOURNEY into the heart of Excel. If Excel is not running, start the program as described in Chapter One. Once again you'll see a new workbook titled *Workbook1* on the screen, ready for use. Because you are going to work on the **Jan Sales** worksheet you have already created, you need to reopen the **Merlin** workbook.

Opening a Saved Workbook

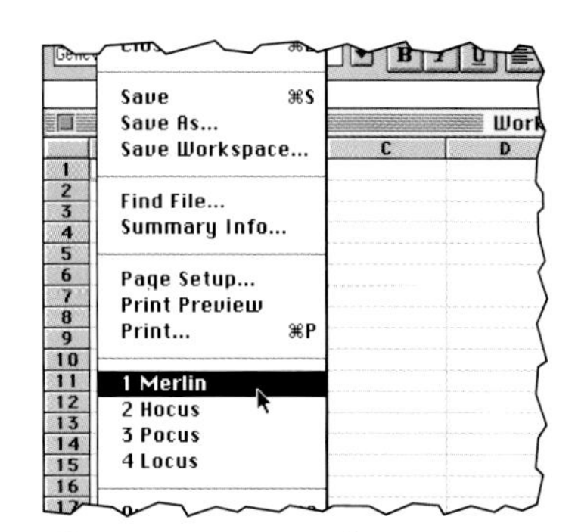

There are two methods of opening a saved workbook. If you have used the workbook recently, the simplest method is to open the *File* menu and look just above the *Quit* command. You should see a list of the last four files you have saved (see right). In this case, choose **Merlin**, which will then open. (*Workbook1* will still be open but will not be visible because it is completely hidden by the **Merlin** workbook window.)

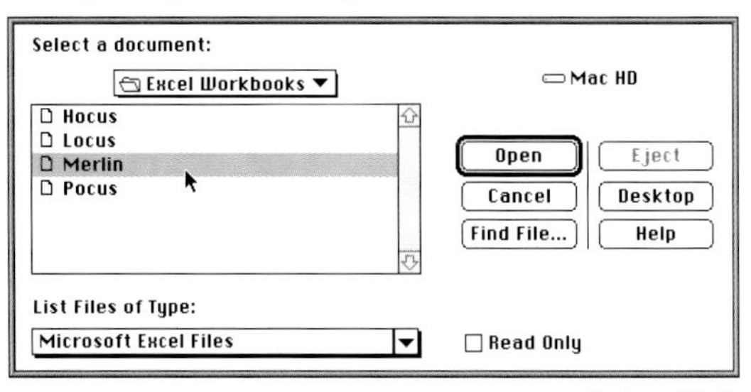

You can also open a saved workbook by choosing *Open* from the *File* menu to access the dialog box shown at left. Locate the folder or disk that contains your workbook, and then double-click on it to open it. Double-click on the workbook's name to open it. (You can use the pop-up list at the top of the dialog box to move to any folder that contains the currently active folder. Clicking on *Find File* lets you search for a file by name — see page 121.)

Shifty Dealing
You can also select cell ranges using the keyboard. Use the direction keys to move the active cell to a corner of the range you want to select. Hold down Shift while you press the direction keys, and watch how the selection expands and contracts. The Shift key can help you select a range of cells with the mouse, too. Click on one corner of the range and then hold down Shift while you click on the opposite corner.

How to Select Cell Ranges

Before carrying out operations on a worksheet, you must select the cells to be acted upon. In Chapter One you selected a single cell by clicking on it with the mouse pointer — or a range of cells by clicking and dragging. You can also select rows, columns, or the whole worksheet. When you select cell ranges instead of single cells, you can perform operations on many cells at the same time.

Remember that a range of cells is defined by the addresses of the cells at the upper left and lower right corners of the range, separated by a colon. For example, the range B2:D6 is defined as the block of cells with B2 located at the upper left corner and D6 at the lower right corner.

Selecting a Cell Range
To select any single block of cells, click on a cell in one corner, hold down the mouse button, and drag the mouse pointer to the opposite corner.

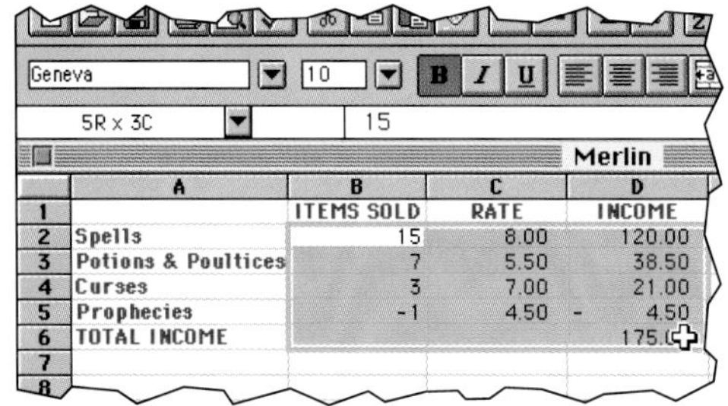

	A	B	C	D
1		ITEMS SOLD	RATE	INCOME
2	Spells	15	8.00	120.00
3	Potions & Poultices	7	5.50	38.50
4	Curses	3	7.00	21.00
5	Prophecies	-1	4.50	- 4.50
6	TOTAL INCOME			175.0

Selecting a Whole Row

To select a whole row, click on the header for that row.

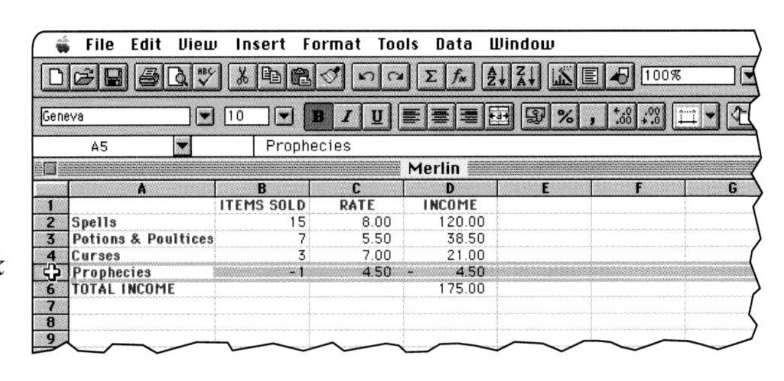

Selecting a Whole Column

To select a whole column, click on the header for that column.

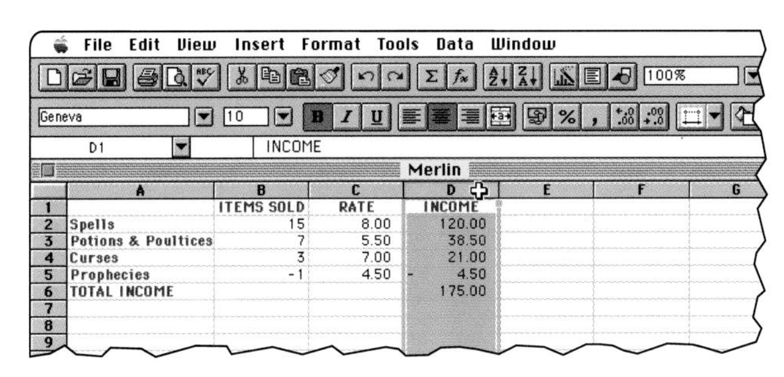

Seeing Black?
Throughout this book, we have used a light blue highlight shade to indicate selected worksheet cells. If, on your worksheets, selected cells appear black or some other color, and you want to change it, you can do so by going to the Macintosh *Color* Control Panel and changing the setting in the *Highlight color* box.

Selecting Multiple Adjacent Rows or Columns

To select two or more adjacent rows or columns, click on the header for the first row or column and then drag the mouse pointer through the headers for the adjacent rows or columns.

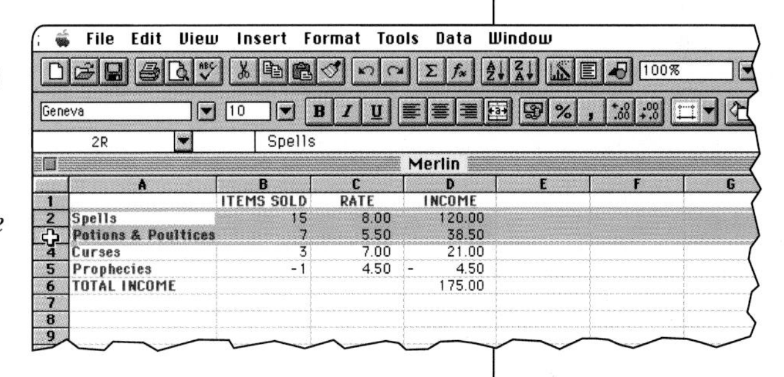

Selecting Nonadjacent Cells and Ranges

Sometimes the cells you want to select don't lie conveniently in a rectangle. To select nonadjacent cells or ranges (including whole rows and columns), hold down the Command key while you click or drag to select each cell or range.

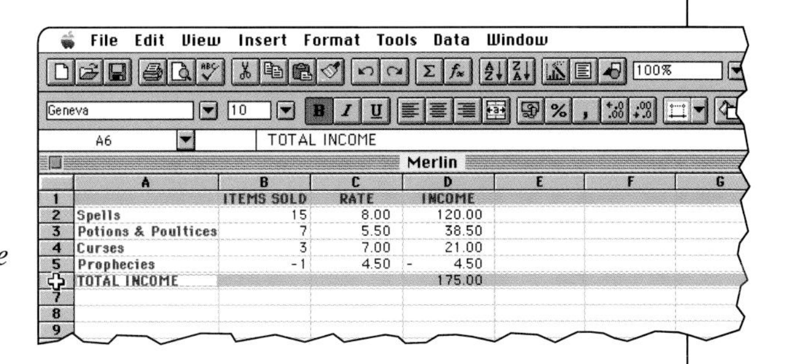

Selecting a Whole Worksheet

To select the whole worksheet, click on the Select All button at the top left of the worksheet or press Command-A.

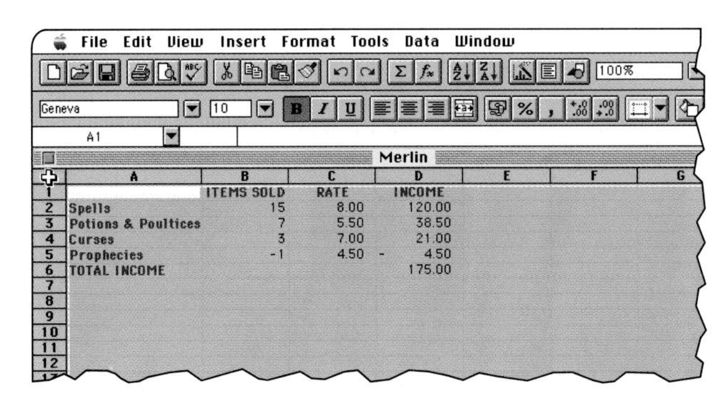

Deselecting?
To deselect any selection, click on any cell outside the highlighted cells. To deselect the entire worksheet, click on any cell.

How to Move Around the Worksheet

Few worksheets fit conveniently into the workbook window. For anything except the smallest worksheets, you'll often need to move to and work on a part of the worksheet that is not currently in view.

- *Moving* involves changing the location of the active cell.
- *Scrolling* involves moving the worksheet in the workbook window to view another part of the worksheet. You can move and scroll simultaneously when you move the active cell beyond the edge of a workbook window. Note that you can also scroll through a worksheet without moving the active cell.

Need Help Navigating?
If you lose the active cell when scrolling through a worksheet, press Command and Delete together, and the active cell will appear again. To navigate over long distances in a large worksheet, the *Go To* command on the *Edit* menu is most useful (see page 117).

Moving

You cannot click on a cell that is not visible in the workbook window. To move the active cell outside the currently visible portion of the worksheet, use the keys shown here. Try these on your **Jan Sales** worksheet.

One Cell in Direction of Arrow

To First Cell in Row

One Cell Right

One Cell Left

Right One Window

Up One Window

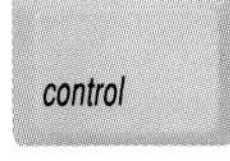
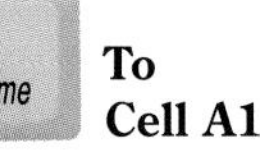

To Cell A1

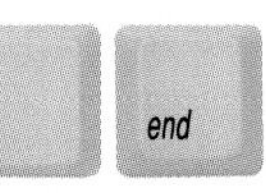

To Lower Right Corner of Worksheet

Left One Window

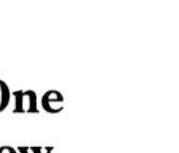

Down One Window

Scrolling

To scroll, use your mouse to click on the scroll bars at the bottom and right-hand side of the screen (see page 13). Note that these techniques do not move the active cell. Try practicing different kinds of scrolling on your **Jan Sales** worksheet.

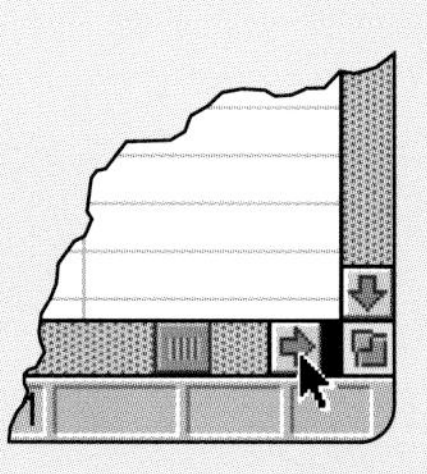

Click on a scroll bar arrow to scroll one cell at a time to the left, right, up, or down.

Keep the mouse button depressed for continuous scrolling.

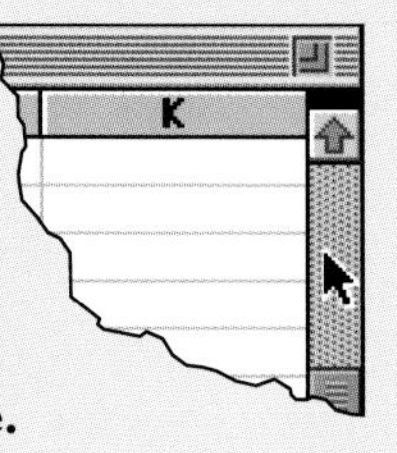

Click the scroll bar on either side of the scroll box to scroll one window at a time.

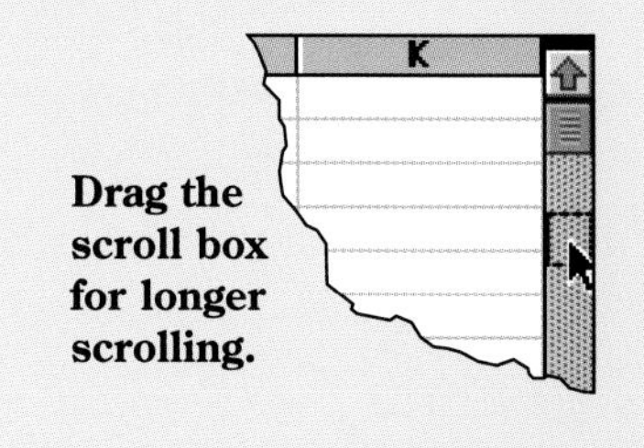

Drag the scroll box for longer scrolling.

Entering Data and Formulas

The information you can type into worksheet cells falls into two main categories — constant data (such as text, numbers, dates, and times) and formulas. When you have entered a formula into a cell, the cell displays the result calculated by the formula — which is usually (though not always) a number. A cell *value* may refer either to a piece of data you have entered directly into a cell or to the calculated result of a formula (a cell that contains a formula also has a value).

To enter data or a formula into a cell, you first make that cell active and then begin typing. What you type appears both in the formula bar and in the cell. You press Return, Enter, Tab, or a direction key, or click on the Enter button to confirm the entry. What you then see in the cell depends on Excel's interpretation of what has been entered (e.g., whether it is a number or text) and on what formatting has been applied. Some basics of how Excel interprets data are described below.

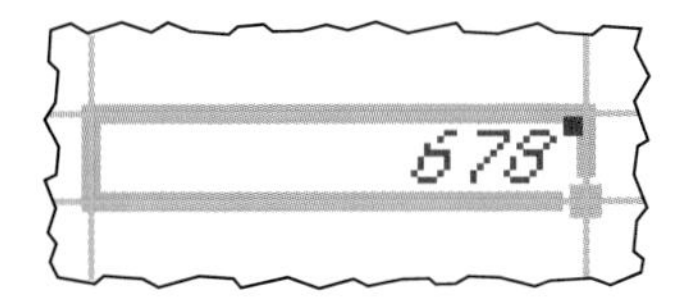

Cell Contents
Excel refers to the data or formula in a cell (which is displayed as a value*) as the cell's* contents. *A cell can also be formatted to affect the way it looks, and it can have a note attached (see page 54). The cell above has a value of 678, a special format defining its color and font, and a red flag in the top right-hand corner, which indicates that the cell has a note attached.*

Cell Overflow!
Sometimes you will find that there is too much text in a cell to fit. The excess appears to flow into the next cell to the right if that is empty; otherwise the text will appear truncated. You can solve this problem by widening the column or by wrapping the text (see page 71).

NUMBERS AND TEXT

Excel interprets any cell value that consists only of digits or certain other characters used in standard numeric expressions as a number (see "Is It a Number?" at left). The program interprets anything else (unless recognized as a date or time) as text.

1 Type a long word like **Supercalifragilisticexpialidocious** in cell H3 of your **Jan Sales** worksheet. Press the Down direction key, type **48,753,802,769** in cell H4 and press Return. A number that does not fit into a cell is displayed as a series of # marks. Overlong text flows into an adjacent cell, if that cell is empty.

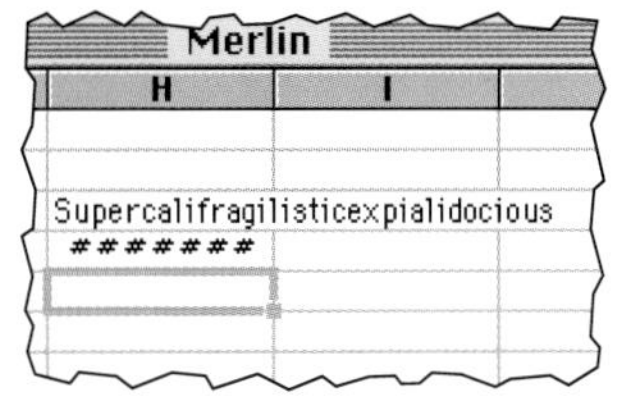

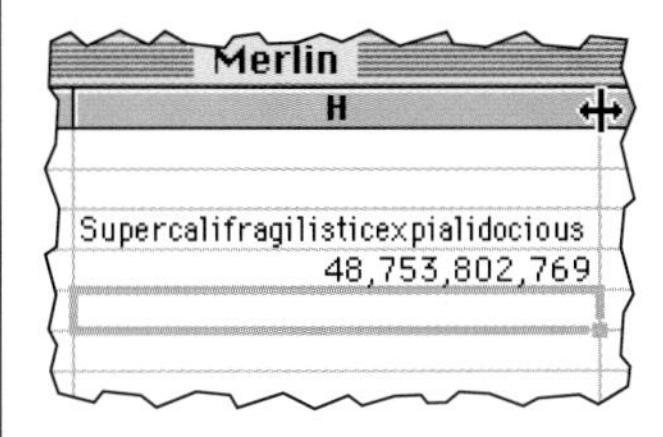

2 You can make the column fit both the text and the number by placing the mouse pointer between the H and I column headers and double-clicking.

Note that a number entered into a cell that has had no special formatting applied is automatically aligned to the right, whereas text is automatically aligned left.

Is It a Number?
Excel recognizes many standard types of numeric expression — not just series of digits — as numbers. For example, if you type **$45**, or **45%**, or **4.5**, or **-45**, these will all be interpreted as numbers, as will **4,500** and **(45)** — parentheses are often used in spreadsheets to denote negative numbers.

Numbers as Text
You can enter up to 255 text characters into any cell. If you want a number in a cell to be treated as text, as you might with a zip code, use a single quote mark before the number. You will know that Excel interprets your number as text if the entry is aligned automatically to the left instead of to the right.

Want the Time?
To enter a time in a cell, type the hour, a colon, the minutes, a space and AM or PM (if you are using the 12-hour clock), and click on the Enter button. The formula bar shows hours: minutes: seconds and AM or PM (unless your system is set up to use the 24-hour clock). Internally, Excel stores times, like dates, as serial numbers.

DATES
There are various ways to enter a date in a cell so that Excel recognizes it as a date. For example, you can type **5 Jan 94**, **5 January 94**, **1/5/94**, or **Jan 5** (assuming you are using U.S. date settings) — but not **Jan 5 94**. Pressing Control and the semicolon (;) key together will enter the current date. If Excel does not display the current date or time correctly, you need to change the system clock on your computer.

When Excel recognizes the cell contents as a date, it applies the date format most similar to what you typed — for example, if you type **1-5-94**, Excel displays **1/5/94**. It also aligns the date to the right in the cell. (If you see a date aligned left, Excel has probably not recognized it as a date.) You can change the style of the display by applying date formatting (see page 71).

In the formula bar, Excel always displays an entry that it has interpreted as a date in a form based on the setting in the *Date & Time* Control Panel, no matter how it appears in the cell. In the U.S., for example, the default setting will always display **5 January 1994** as **1/5/1994** in the formula bar. In some other countries the same date may be displayed as **5/1/1994**.

Make a Date!
Excel stores dates internally as serial numbers from 1 to 63,918, representing dates from January 1 1904 to December 31 2078. If you enter a date into a cell that has been given a format in the Number category (see page 71) it will appear as a serial number (5 July 94 is shown as 33,058). To make the date appear correctly, you must apply a date format.

A Checking Account Ledger

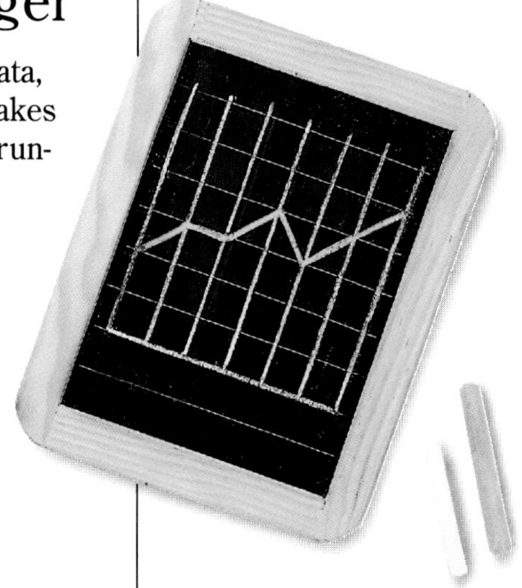

For more practice entering and manipulating data, let's set up a checking account ledger. Excel makes it easy to make changes to your ledger, keep a running balance, project future balances, and even make reconciliations on your bank statement.

As an example, you'll construct a ledger for Merlin. First close your **Merlin** workbook, without saving changes, and then reopen it again by choosing **Merlin** from the list in the *File* menu. Now open and name a new worksheet in the workbook as follows:

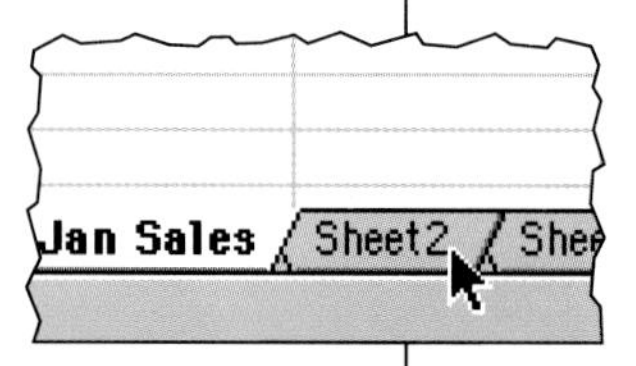

1 Double-click on the *Sheet2* tab at the bottom of the workbook window.

2 In the *Rename Sheet* dialog box, type **Checking**, and then click on *OK*.

Rename Sheet
Name
Checking
OK
Cancel
Help

When naming worksheets and workbooks you can use up to 31 characters, including spaces — the limit is set by the Macintosh operating system.

Workbooks and Worksheets

The idea of a workbook is to keep all your related worksheets (and other types of sheets that you can create in Excel, such as chart sheets) together in one file. When you open a workbook, all the sheets within it are quickly accessible by means of the sheet tabs at the foot of the workbook window. You just click on a tab to display a sheet. When you create a new workbook, you have 16 blank sheets available, but only the first six sheet tabs are visible. You can use the tab scrolling buttons or drag the tab split box to bring other sheet tabs into view.

For more on managing workbooks and worksheets, see "Multiple Worksheets" on pages 62-65 and "Managing Sheets and Workbooks" on pages 120-121.

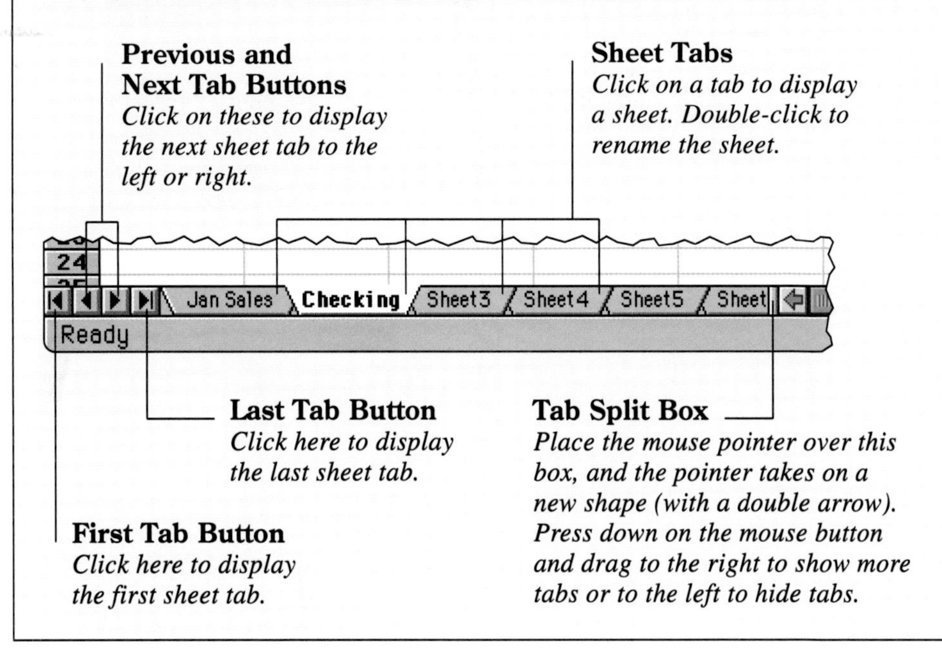

■ When you close a workbook, you can save either all or none of the changes that you have made to the workbook.

■ To add a sheet to a workbook, choose *Worksheet* from the *Insert* menu. To move a sheet within a workbook, drag its sheet tab to the new location.

■ To select several sheets, hold down Command and click on the relevant tabs. Their tabs appear white.

■ To deselect sheets, place the mouse pointer over a white tab, hold down Control and press on the mouse button, and then choose *Ungroup Sheets* from the menu that appears.

■ To delete sheets, select those sheets and then choose *Delete Sheet* from the *Edit* menu.

Entering Headings

Now you'll enter some column headings and Merlin's opening balance into the **Checking** worksheet. Selecting the range into which you are going to enter data can make data entry easier. You can use the Tab key to move the active cell through the range.

1 Click on A1, then hold down Shift and click on F2 to select the range A1:F2. You could also select the range by dragging the mouse pointer from A1 to F2.

2 Using the Tab key to move from cell to cell in the selected range, enter the column headings shown below. (Type Option-3 for the # character.) Enter the date (**31 Dec**) in cell A2, and in cell F2 type in **500** (the balance of gold pieces shown on Merlin's last bank statement).

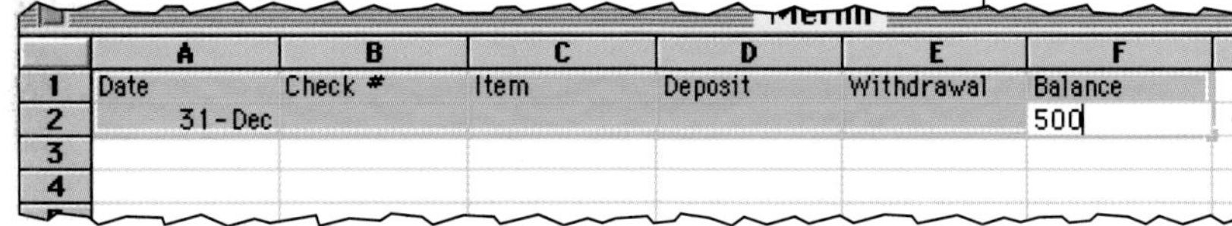

ENTERING MERLIN'S TRANSACTIONS

You can now log Merlin's transactions for January. Enter the dates, text, and numbers exactly as shown below into rows 3 through 8. Don't be concerned that the dates are not exactly in the right order. Merlin was a little haphazard in the way he recorded his transactions, but you'll sort the dates out for him in due course. Don't worry if some of the data in column C does not fit in this column, as you'll fix that shortly. And, don't worry that no amounts have been put in for the deposits shown in rows 5 and 7. You're soon going to help Merlin with formulas to calculate these.

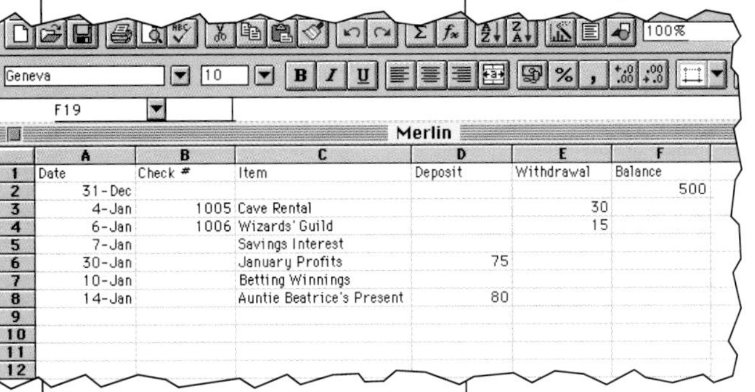

	A	B	C	D	E	F
1	Date	Check #	Item	Deposit	Withdrawal	Balance
2	31-Dec					500
3	4-Jan	1005	Cave Rental		30	
4	6-Jan	1006	Wizards' Guild		15	
5	7-Jan		Savings Interest			
6	30-Jan		January Profits	75		
7	10-Jan		Betting Winnings			
8	14-Jan		Auntie Beatrice's Present	80		
9						
10						
11						
12						

Merlin's Account

*Make sure that you type each item into the correct cell, as shown above. At this point, column C will be narrower than shown. The data in cells C6 and C8 will be partially hidden when you type **75** in cell D6 and **80** in cell D8.*

Fitting the Columns

Before going any further, you need to produce a better fit between the data in the worksheet and the columns. Some text items you have typed are partially hidden by adjacent cells. As explained previously, you can solve this by altering the widths of individual columns. You can either drag the lines between column headers to the left or right with the mouse (see page 21) or double-click on them for a "best fit" (see page 31). If you want to alter column widths to fit data over a whole range, another method is to use the *Column* command on the *Format* menu.

1 Select the range A1:F8, and then choose *Column* from the *Format* menu and *AutoFit Selection* from the submenu.

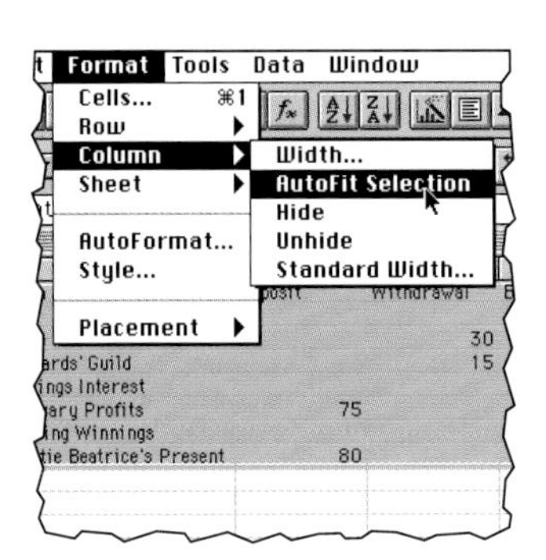

2 All the column widths are altered to fit the data.

	A	B	C	D	E	F	G
1	Date	Check #	Item	Deposit	Withdrawal	Balance	
2	31-Dec					500	
3	4-Jan	1005	Cave Rental		30		
4	6-Jan	1006	Wizards' Guild		15		
5	7-Jan		Savings Interest				
6	30-Jan		January Profits	75			
7	10-Jan		Betting Winnings				
8	14-Jan		Auntie Beatrice's Present	80			

Keeping Fit

Most methods for altering column widths also apply to row heights. If you choose the *Row* or *Column* command from the *Format* menu and then the *Height* or *Width* option from the submenu, a dialog box lets you specify widths or heights for selected rows or columns. Type the new measurement in the dialog box and then click on *OK*.

Magic Formulas

On the seventh day of each month, interest earned on the money in Merlin's savings account is paid directly into his checking account. At the moment, he has accumulated 2,500 gold pieces in his savings account and receives 6 percent annual interest on this deposit, paid in monthly instalments. Merlin is about to calculate how much interest he will earn, using paper and pencil. Relax, Merlin, and let Excel do the work!

Using the arithmetic operators * (which denotes multiplication), / (division), and % (percentage), you can create a simple formula to calculate the interest that Merlin should receive. The expression 2500*6% calculates the annual interest, and 2500*6%/12 calculates the monthly interest.

1 Click on cell D5, and then type = to start the formula. Type **2500*6%/12.** You'll see the expression appear in the cell and the formula bar as you type.

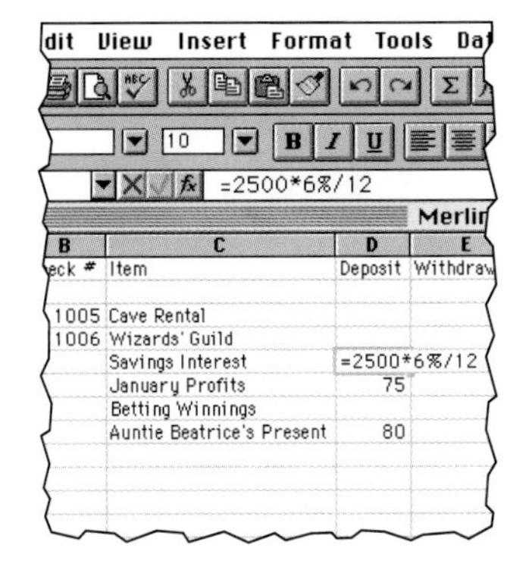

2 Click on the Enter button. The value **12.5** appears in D5, giving the calculated monthly interest on Merlin's savings.

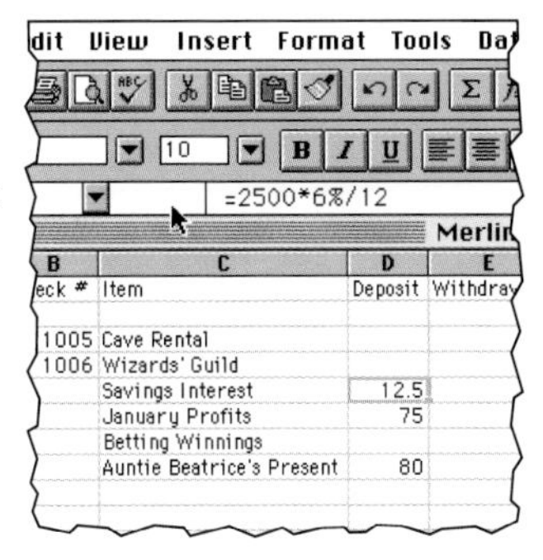

ANOTHER FORMULA

Merlin forgot to keep a record of his betting winnings, but remembers that they were 15 times his original stake, minus 2 gold pieces tax, and that his original stake was the change he received from 10 gold pieces after buying a new wand for 7 gold pieces. So, to calculate his winnings, he subtracts 7 from 10 (to compute his original stake), multiplies the result by 15, and then subtracts 2. Excel uses a strict order when carrying out calculations in formulas — exponential operations (e.g., cubing) are performed first, then division and multiplication, and finally addition and subtraction. To override this order, use parentheses.

1 Select cell D7, and then type **=(10-7)*15-2**.

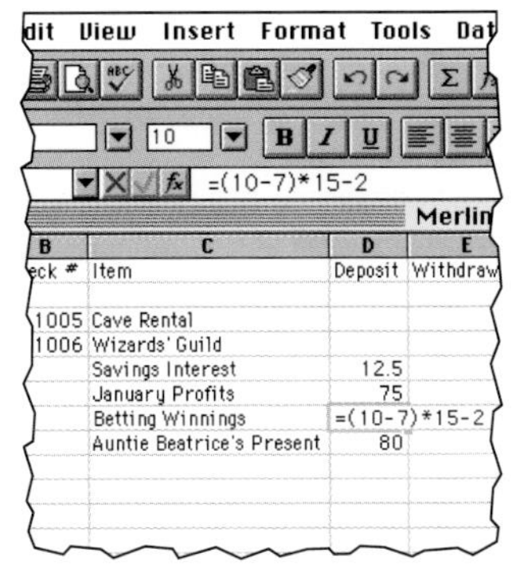

2 Click on the Enter button. The amount of the betting winnings deposit — 43 gold pieces — appears in cell D7.

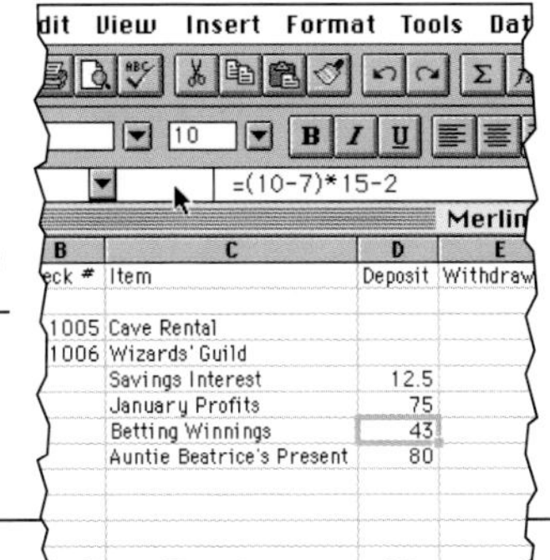

Bar Unlike Cell?
Note that after you have entered a formula in a cell, the formula bar still shows the formula — in this case, **=2500*6%/12** — but the cell itself shows the value returned by the formula, in this case, **12.5**.

Enclose It!
Be sure to put parentheses around calculations to be done first if you want to override Excel's usual order. If you had typed the Betting Winnings formula into cell D7 as **=10-7*15-2**, Excel would have multiplied 7 by 15 first, subtracted the result from 10, and then subtracted 2 from that result, giving the incorrect answer of -97.

Editing Cell Contents

The simplest way to change a cell's contents is to overwrite the contents. To do so, you select the cell, type the new data or formula, and then click on the Enter button or press Enter. To modify rather than overwrite a cell's contents, you can edit either in the formula bar or directly in the cell. To edit in the formula bar, you click on the cell to activate it and then click in the formula bar. To edit in the cell, you double-click on the cell. The mechanics of editing are similar for both methods, but editing in the cell is a little faster and lets you see straightaway how the results will look in the worksheet.

Let's try some overwriting and practice both of the editing methods on Merlin's checking ledger.

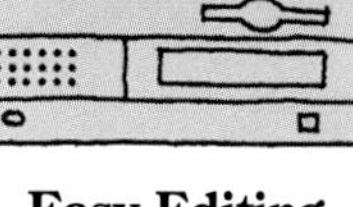

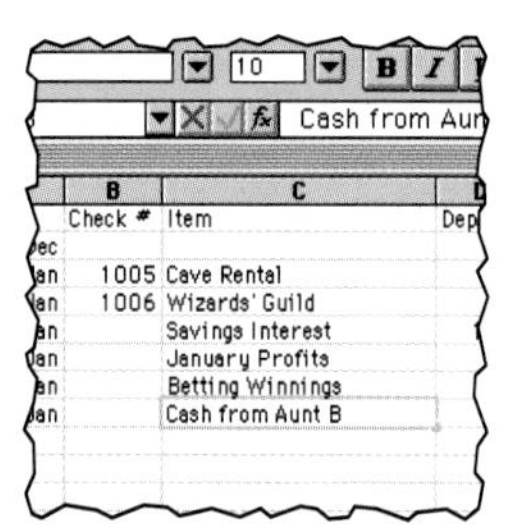

1 Select cell C8 by clicking on it. Type **Cash from Aunt B** and then press Enter. The new text will overwrite the old.

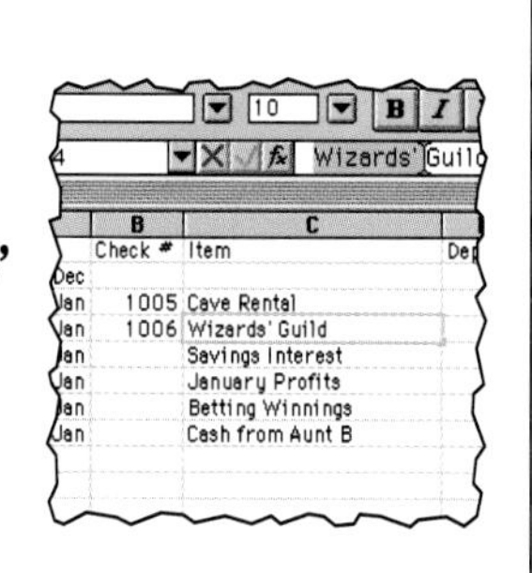

2 Select cell C4, and then position your I-beam pointer before the word **Wizards'** in the formula bar. Drag the I-beam to the right to highlight **Wizards'** and the space after it (you will see the Enter and Cancel buttons appear). Then press Delete.

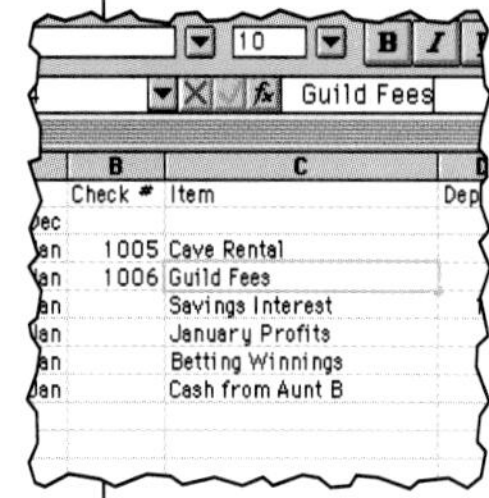

3 Click the I-beam pointer to the right of the word **Guild** in the formula bar, and then type a space and the word **Fees**. Press Enter or click on the Enter button to complete your edit.

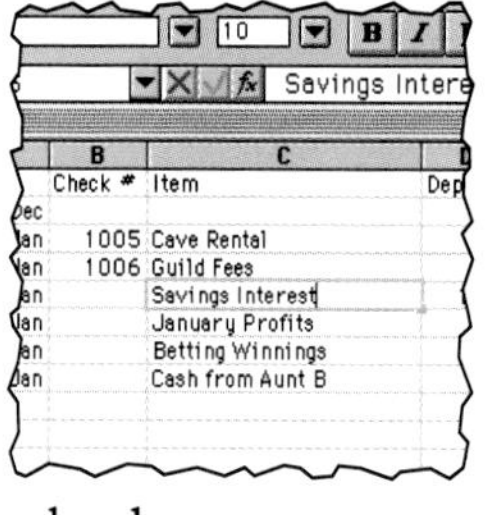

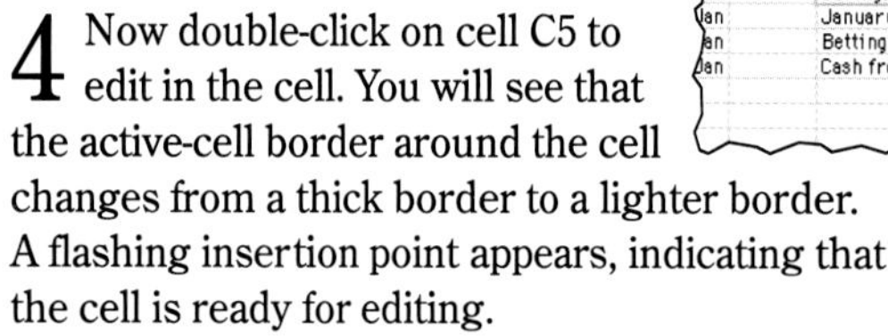

4 Now double-click on cell C5 to edit in the cell. You will see that the active-cell border around the cell changes from a thick border to a lighter border. A flashing insertion point appears, indicating that the cell is ready for editing.

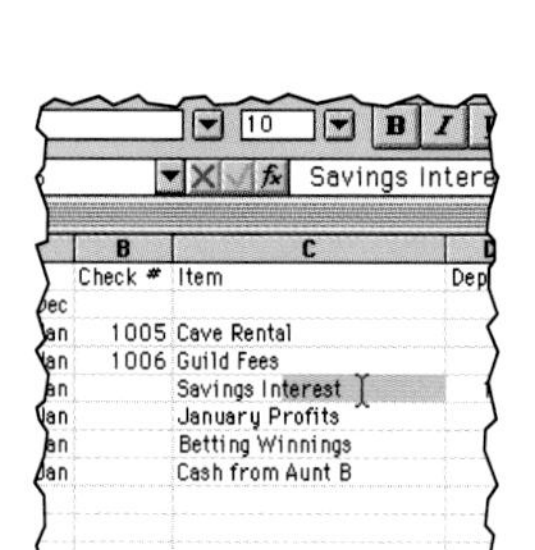

5 Click the I-beam pointer between the **n** and **t** of **Interest**, and then drag the pointer to the right to highlight the characters **terest**.

6 Now type **come** to change **Interest** to **Income**. Finally, press Enter or click on the Enter button to confirm the word change.

Easy Editing

Whether you are editing directly in the cell or editing in the formula bar, you can erase the character to the left of the insertion point by using the Delete key and erase the character to the right by using the Del key. To highlight a group of characters, drag the I-beam pointer across them. Anything you type will replace the highlighted characters. Pressing Delete (or Del) will erase the highlighted characters.

Undoing What You Did Last

The *Undo* command, which you'll find at the top of the *Edit* menu, is one of Excel's most useful timesavers. If you have made an edit that you decide to reverse, have accidentally erased a piece of text, or have entered anything you now wish to retract, you can usually use the *Undo* command to negate the last action that you performed. Remember, though, that you can only undo your last command.

Merlin decides that he would prefer not to change **Savings Interest** to **Savings Income**, so you can make immediate use of the *Undo* command.

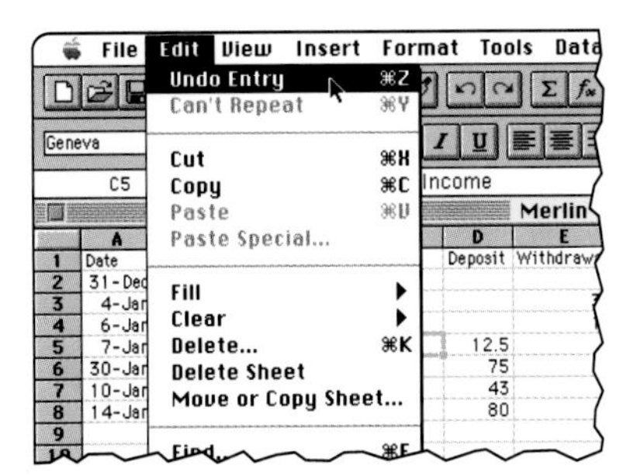

1 With cell C5 (the cell you have just edited) still selected, choose *Undo Entry* from the *Edit* menu.

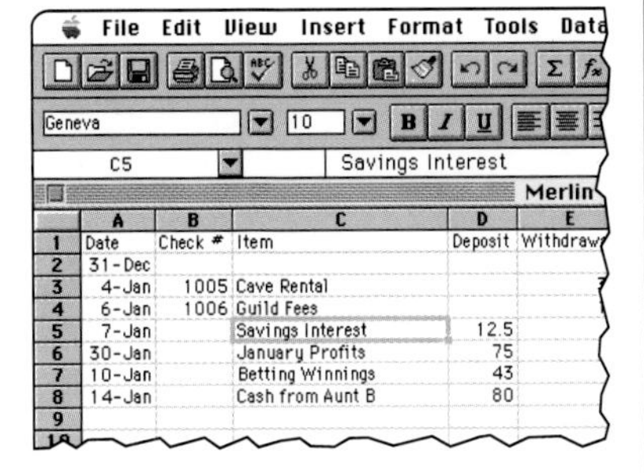

2 You will see that the contents of cell C5 revert to **Savings Interest**.

UNDOING THE UNDO
The *Undo* command can itself be undone. After you have used the *Undo* command, drop down the *Edit* menu. You will see a *Redo* command at the top of the menu. If you choose that command, you reverse the last *Undo* command that you carried out.

Change of Menu?
Some of Excel's menu commands change depending on your last action or your current selection. For example, if you have just entered text into a cell or edited a cell's contents, you will see that the command at the top of the *Edit* menu is *Undo Entry*. If you have just applied a new format to a range of cells, you will find that the top command is *Undo Format Cells*.

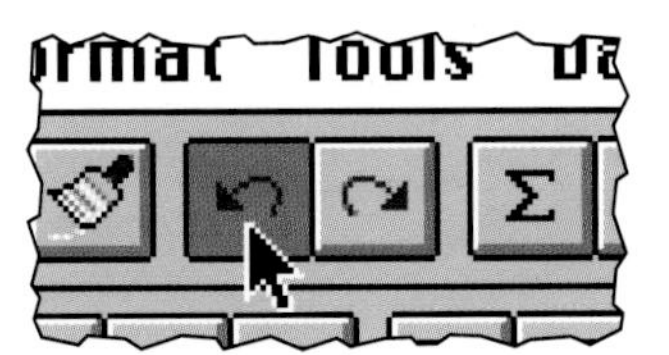

Quick Undo
Clicking on the Undo button on the Standard toolbar has exactly the same effect as choosing Undo *from the* Edit *menu. You can also undo your last action by pressing Command and Z together.*

Clearing Cell Contents

Sometimes you want to erase the contents of a cell or range. This is different from deleting, which removes the cells themselves from the worksheet (see page 48).

To clear cells, you select them and then use the *Clear* command on the *Edit* menu. This opens a submenu, where you are given a choice of clearing *All*, *Formats*, *Contents*, or *Notes*. Choosing *Contents* will remove data and formulas but will not remove notes or special formats. To clear only formatting or notes, choose the *Formats* option (see "Scrub It!" on page 76) or the *Notes* option. To clear everything, choose *All*.

Space Control!
Do not try to clear a cell by overtyping it with a space. Such a cell may look empty but it actually contains a space. This can cause problems that are difficult to trace.

CLEARING A RANGE

Merlin suddenly recalls that he spent the cash from Aunt Beatrice and never put it into his account, so it should not appear in his checking ledger.

Merlin

	A	B	C	D	E
1	Date	Check #	Item	Deposit	Withdrawal
2	31-Dec				
3	4-Jan	1005	Cave Rental		30
4	6-Jan	1006	Guild Fees		15
5	7-Jan		Savings Interest	12.5	
6	30-Jan		January Profits	75	
7	10-Jan		Betting Winnings	43	
8	14-Jan		Cash from Aunt B	80	
9					
10					

1 Select the range A8:D8, which shows **Cash from Aunt B**.

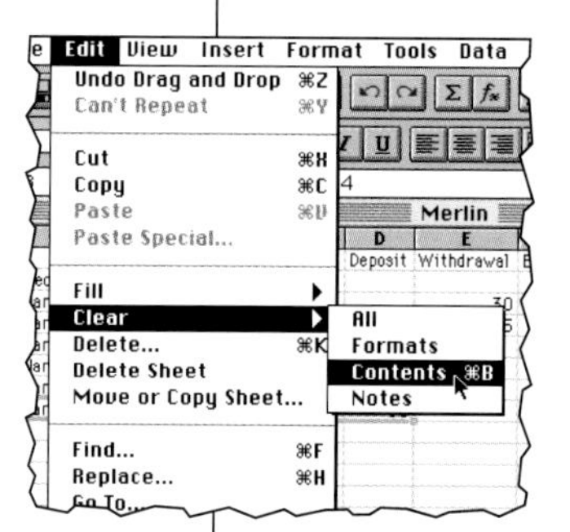

2 Choose *Clear* from the *Edit* menu, and in the submenu choose *Contents*. The entry in row 8 is cleared.

Merlin

	A	B	C	D	E	F
1	Date	Check #	Item	Deposit	Withdrawal	Balance
2	31-Dec					500
3	4-Jan	1005	Cave Rental		30	
4	6-Jan	1006	Guild Fees		15	
5	7-Jan		Savings Interest	12.5		
6	30-Jan		January Profits	75		
7	10-Jan		Betting Winnings	43		
8	14-Jan		Cash from Aunt B	80		
9						
10						
11						

Merlin now groans and says that, on reflection, he thinks it was the cash from Aunt Matilda that he spent — and that he did deposit the cash from Aunt Beatrice into the bank. You can cope with this by choosing *Undo Clear* from the *Edit* menu. Check that your worksheet is as shown at left.

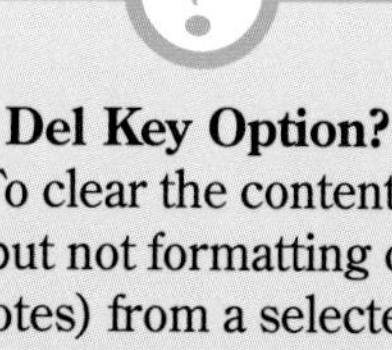

Del Key Option?
To clear the contents (but not formatting or notes) from a selected cell or range of cells, you can just select the cell or range and press the Del key.

Using Cell References in Formulas

Formulas are not restricted to operating on constant values (like the formulas you used on page 35). The values in a formula may be provided by cell references, and it is this fact that provides much of Excel's power. To use a cell reference in a formula, you can just type the cell address. When Excel calculates, it will go to the specified cell, pick up its current value, and use this value in the formula.

Fill to Clear?
Another method of clearing cell contents is to use the fill handle (see page 22). When you drag the fill handle of a selected cell or range back into the selection, the cell or range "grays out" (appears with gray shading). When you release the mouse button, the gray area is cleared of its contents.

TRACKING MERLIN'S BALANCE

Merlin wants to work out a formula that will help him to keep track of the running balance in his checking account throughout January. So for each of the cells from F3 downward (which will contain the balances on his checking account for various days in January) he needs to put in a formula that will take the previous balance, add any new deposits that have been made, and then subtract any withdrawals so as to calculate the new balance.

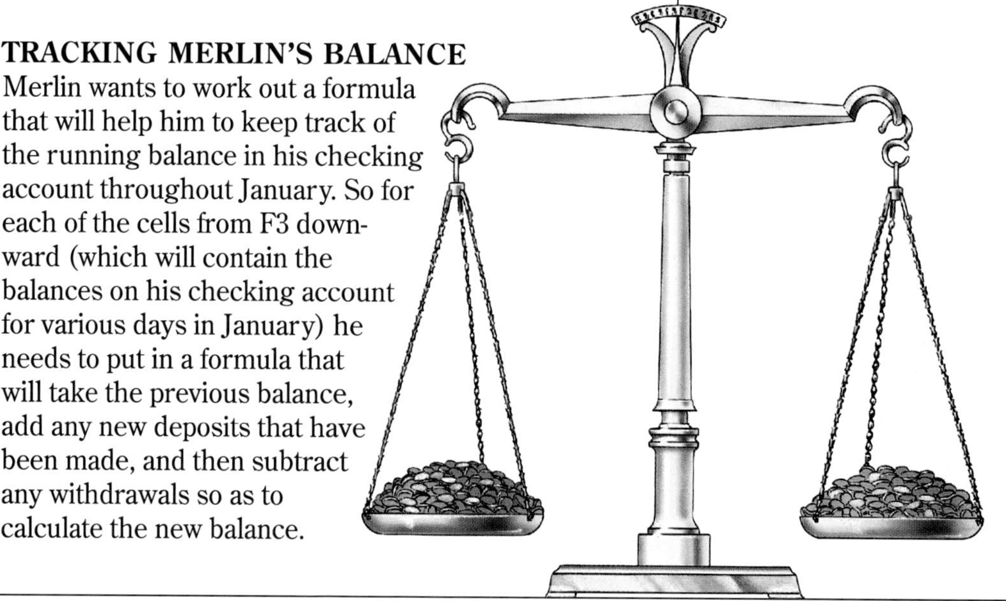

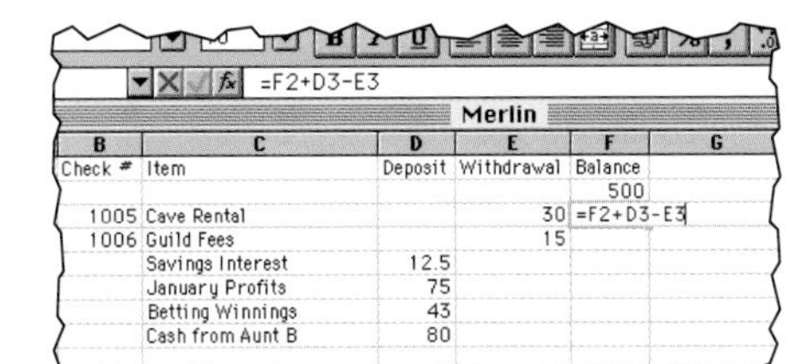

1 Select cell F3 and type the formula **=F2+D3-E3.**

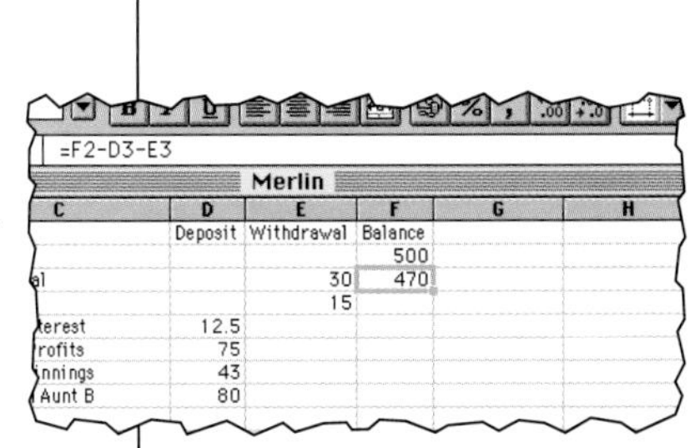

2 Click on the Enter button. Cell F3 will now reflect Merlin's new January 4th balance — 470 gold pieces.

Creating Cell References by Pointing

In cell F4, you need the formula **=F3+D4-E4**. This time, try entering cell references in the formula using a method known as "pointing." When you click on a cell while entering a formula, that cell's address is inserted into your formula.

1 Select cell F4, type =, and then click on F3. This sets the value in F3 (the previous balance) as the starting point for your formula. The cell reference appears in F4 and in the formula bar. A marquee (moving border) frames F3.

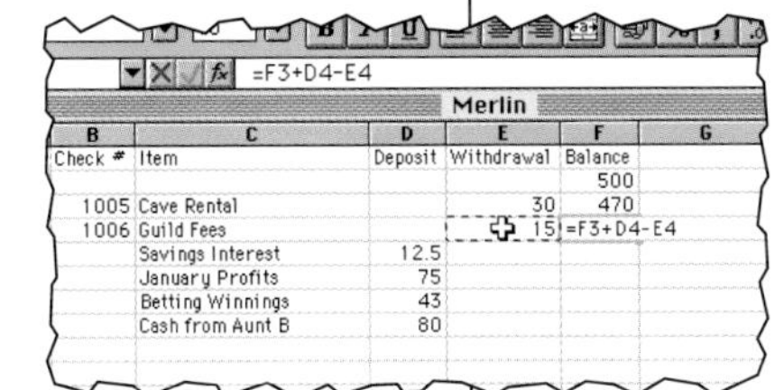

2 Type a plus sign, and then click on cell D4. Now type a minus sign and click on cell E4. Both cell F4 and the formula bar will now show the whole formula, namely **=F3+D4-E4.**

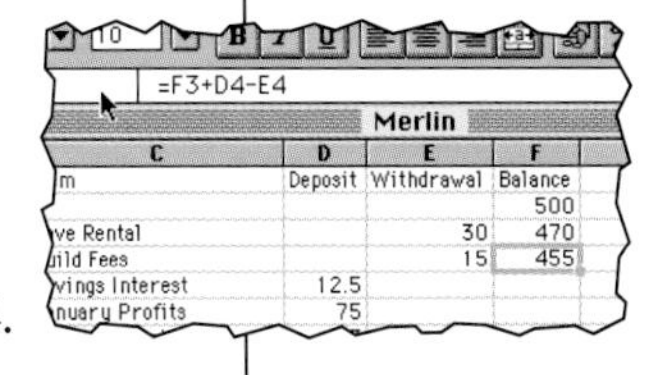

3 Click on the Enter button. The January 6th balance (455 gold pieces) appears in cell F4.

Think Before You Click!
Note that when you are entering a formula, you cannot complete your entry and move the active cell by clicking on another cell. If you click on another cell when entering a formula, Excel will include the cell's address as part of the formula.

You could enter a similar formula in every cell in column F to calculate Merlin's running balance. Or you could copy the formula in cells F3 or F4 to other cells in column F. You will see the usefulness of this when you reach page 50. First, you'll learn more about ways of building and modifying worksheets. Choose *Save* from the *File* menu, or click on the Save button, to save your changes to the **Merlin** workbook.

Worksheet Modification

EXCEL PROVIDES A VARIETY of techniques for building a worksheet and rearranging its contents. You can create series of values. You can easily move or copy cells and ranges to other parts of the worksheet. You can also insert and delete cells, rows, and columns — and do combined operations such as copying and inserting at the same time.

Initially, you'll practice creating series, copying and moving constant cell data — such as text, dates, and numbers — and inserting and deleting cells. Then you'll look at some special considerations that apply to moving or copying cells containing or referenced by formulas. First try some simple filling, copying, and moving using these techniques:

- **AutoFill** (a mouse technique for copying the contents of cells into adjacent cells or creating series) and **Fill** (a menu command for copying the contents of cells into adjacent cells)
- **Drag and Drop** (best used for moving and copying operations within the part of your worksheet that shows in the workbook window)
- **Cut, Copy, and Paste** (best used for moving or copying operations over longer distances)

Intuitive Stretch
*Excel's AutoFill can recognize the start of a series of numbers and extend it. On a blank part of a worksheet, enter **5** and **10** in adjacent cells, one above the other. Select both cells, and then drag the fill handle at the bottom right corner of the lower cell downward and release the mouse button. You'll see that a series has been created. AutoFill also recognizes single values that are frequently extended into series. Try entering **January** in a cell, and then drag its fill handle down six cells.*

Basic Moving and Copying

The principles of moving and copying worksheet data are as follows:

- You can move or copy the contents of single cells or cell ranges. Every move or copy involves at least two cells or ranges. Data is moved or copied from the source cell (or range) to one or more target cells (or ranges).
- In a copy operation, the contents of the source cell or range remain unchanged. In a move operation, the source cell or range is cleared (emptied of its contents).
- In either a move or a copy operation, the contents of the target cell or range are overwritten. (Sometimes Excel displays a message alerting you that a replacement is about to be made).

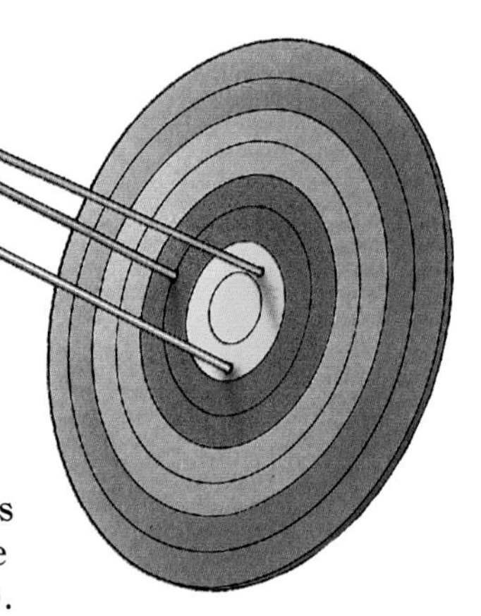

Besides simple moving or copying, you can insert the source cell (or range) instead of overwriting the contents of the target. You can also move or copy only parts of the cell using *Paste Special* (see "Paste Special?" on page 75).

Creating an Appointment Log

In your **Merlin** workbook, open a new worksheet by clicking on the *Sheet3* tab, and then rename the worksheet **Appointments** (see page 32). You'll use this worksheet to create a diary for Merlin's business meetings. You'll develop the appointment log by using AutoFill and Fill, and then rearrange his sessions using drag and drop; cut, copy, and paste; and cut, copy, and insert paste. Finally, you'll carry out still more modifications by inserting and deleting some cells and ranges.

Using AutoFill

1 Enter **DAY** into cell A1, **DATE** into cell B1, **9:00 AM** into cell C1, and **9:30 AM** into cell D1 (being careful to leave a space between the minutes and **AM**). Type **Monday** into A2 and **1st** into B2.

2 Select the range C1:D1. Position your mouse pointer on the fill handle at the lower right corner of D1, where it changes into a +.

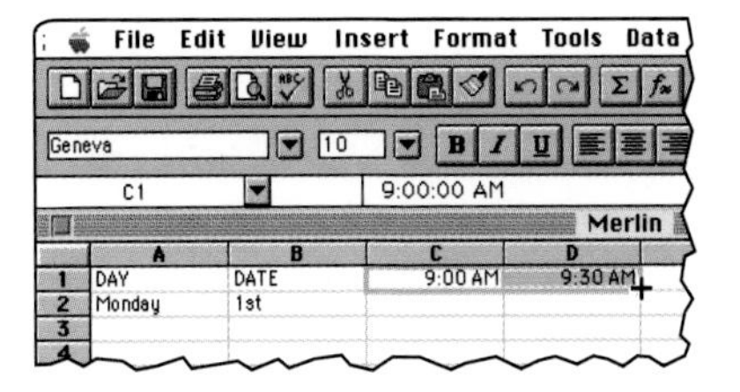

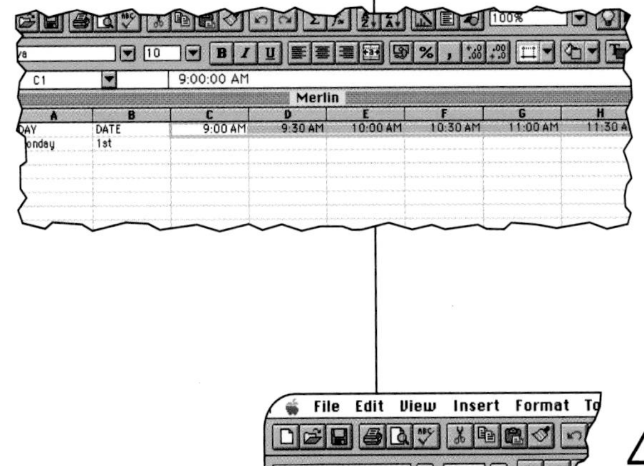

3 Press the mouse button and drag the fill handle to the right until the selection extends to the right edge of cell H1. Then release the button. AutoFill is smart; it spotted the start of a half-hour series and extended it. Note that you had to select both C1 and D1 for Excel to create the series. If you had selected only C1, Excel would have created an hourly series.

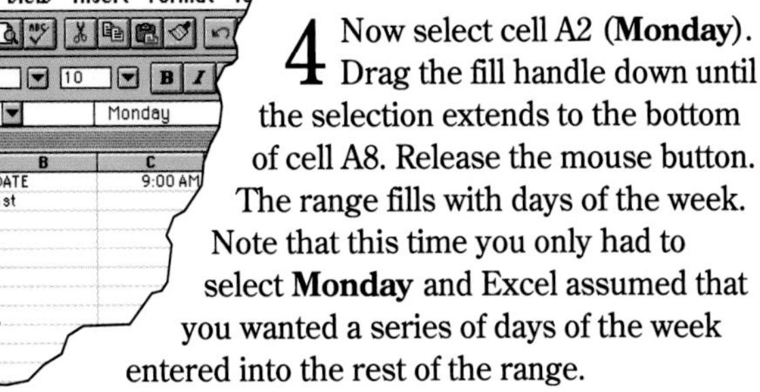

4 Now select cell A2 (**Monday**). Drag the fill handle down until the selection extends to the bottom of cell A8. Release the mouse button. The range fills with days of the week. Note that this time you only had to select **Monday** and Excel assumed that you wanted a series of days of the week entered into the rest of the range.

Fill Control!

In some cases, when you drag the fill handle of a single cell, you may find that AutoFill has created a series when all you wanted was a simple duplication of the cell's contents. To force a simple copy instead of a series, hold down the Option key while you drag the fill handle.

REPEATING AN AUTOFILL

You can use the *Repeat* command from the *Edit* menu to carry out the most recently executed action again — whether an AutoFill, a menu command, or the action of a toolbar button. Like the *Undo* command (see page 37), *Repeat* is a real timesaver.

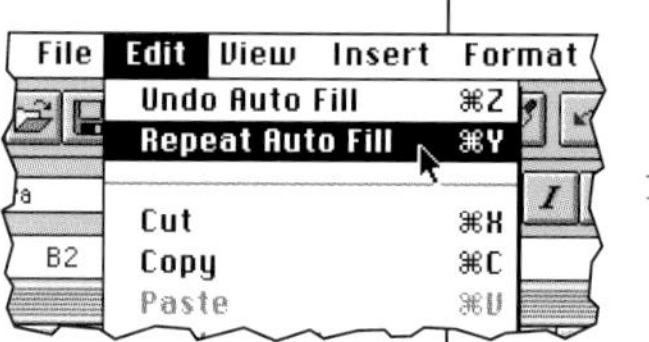

1 Select cell B2 and choose *Repeat Auto Fill* from the *Edit* menu.

	A	B	C
1	DAY	DATE	9:00 AM
2	Monday	1st	
3	Tuesday	2nd	
4	Wednesday	3rd	
5	Thursday	4th	
6	Friday	5th	
7	Saturday	6th	
8	Sunday	7th	

2 The range B3:B8 fills with a series of values from **2nd** to **7th**, repeating the AutoFill you just carried out in column A. Double-click on the line between the headers for columns A and B to narrow column A, and then on the line between column headers B and C to narrow column B.

Repeat Performance?
Don't confuse the *Repeat* command with the *Redo* command, which reverses an *Undo* (see page 37). The *Repeat* command is performed most often on a cell or range different from the original selection. It can be especially useful for repeating formatting. The *Repeat* command on the *Edit* menu varies according to what you did last. For example, after a clear operation, you would see *Repeat Clear* on the *Edit* menu.

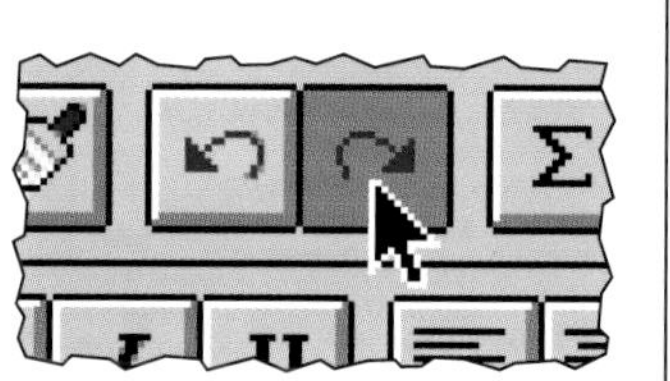

Quick Repeat
The Repeat button on the Standard toolbar has exactly the same action as the Repeat *command on the* Edit *menu.*

MORE FILLING

Let's continue developing Merlin's appointment log. Enter **Queen G** into cell C2, **Dr. Fang** into D2, **Gandalf** into E2, and **Lancelot** into F3. Next type **Arthur** into C4 and **Ms. Black** into D4, as shown.

AutoFill and Fill can be used not only to create series but also to copy cell contents into ranges. For example, two of Merlin's clients want to make several appointments throughout the week, keeping the same hours.

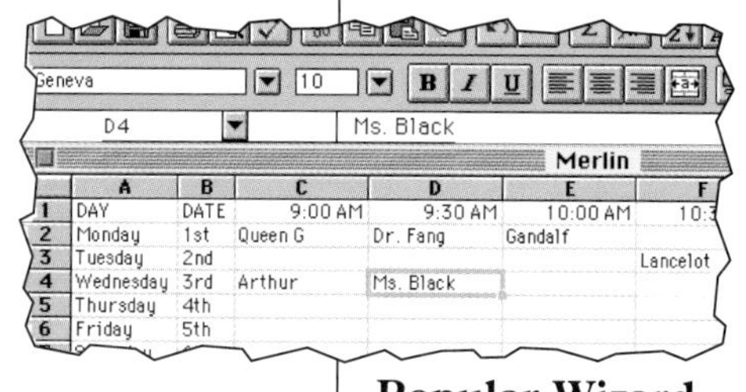

Popular Wizard
Merlin has no trouble filling his appointments log.

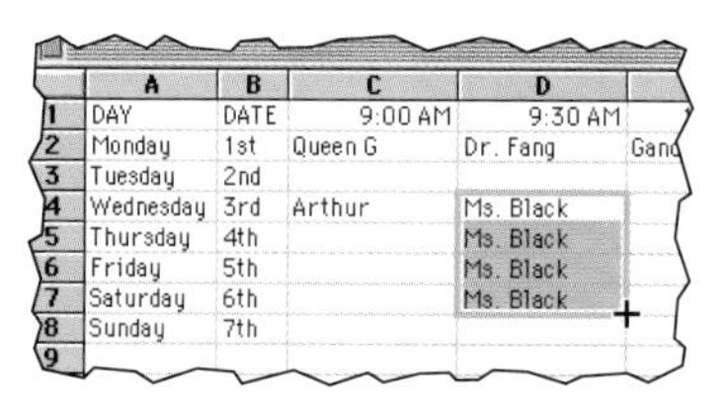

1 Select cell D4 (**Ms. Black**), and drag the fill handle to the bottom of D7. The range D5 to D7 fills with **Ms. Black.**

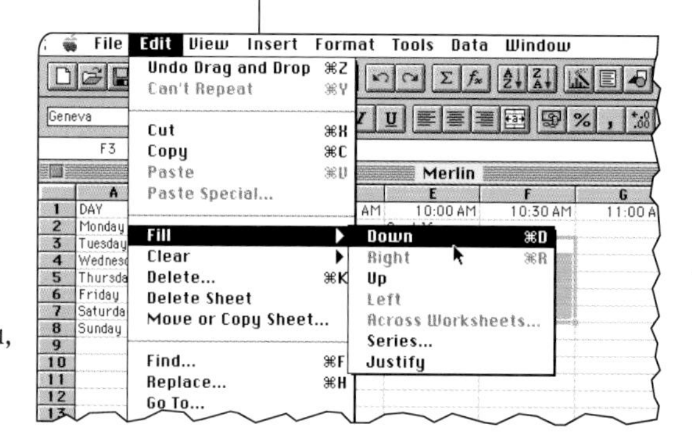

2 Select the range F3 to F7, and then choose *Fill* from the *Edit* menu. In the submenu, choose *Down*. The range F4 to F7 fills with **Lancelot**.

Quick Fill?
The *Fill* command on the *Edit* menu can be used to copy the contents of a cell or cells at the edge of a selected range into the rest of the range. The *Fill* command has a submenu from which you can choose *Down*, *Right*, *Up*, or *Left*, depending on whether the cell contents to be copied are at the top, left, bottom, or right of the selected range.

Drag and Drop

Merlin's clients are constantly asking to rearrange their appointments, but you can cope with this easily on the worksheet by using move and copy techniques.

MOVING BY DRAG AND DROP

Gandalf has cancelled his Monday 10:00 AM meeting with Merlin, but Queen G says she wants to move to that vacant slot. This provides a good opportunity to practice a move by drag and drop.

1 Select cell C2 (**Queen G**). Position the mouse pointer over its active cell border. The pointer will change to the normal Macintosh arrowhead.

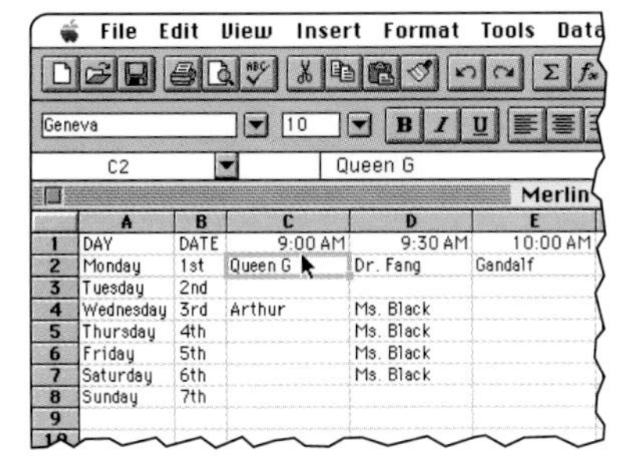

2 Press the mouse button and drag your mouse to the right. A gray border in the shape of a single cell travels with the mouse pointer. You can drag it wherever you like, but in this instance drop it (by releasing the mouse button) onto cell E2 (**Gandalf**).

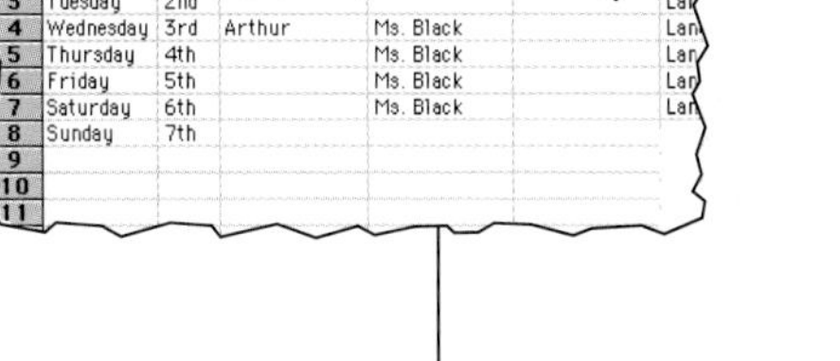

3 A message box asks you to confirm that you want to replace the existing contents of cell E2. Confirm the replacement by clicking on *OK*. You will see that cell C2 is now empty and its previous contents have overwritten cell E2.

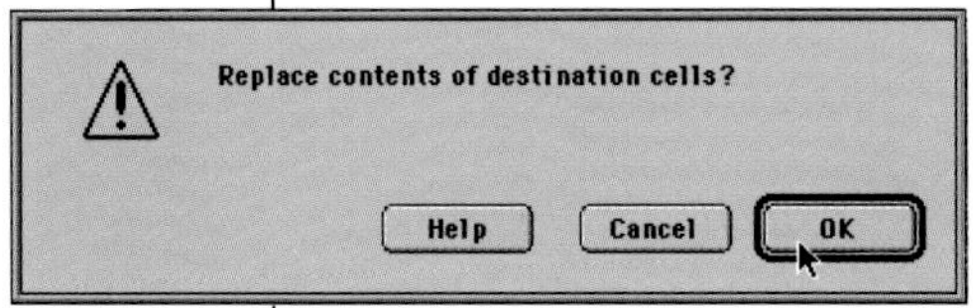

COPYING BY DRAG AND DROP

Both Dr. Fang and Queen G now want to arrange additional Wednesday morning meetings with Merlin, at the same times as their Monday appointments. Merlin agrees and thinks that he can fix this (believing he can talk Ms. Black out of her 9:30 AM visit), but it requires a copying operation. To copy cell contents using drag and drop, you hold down the Option key during the operation.

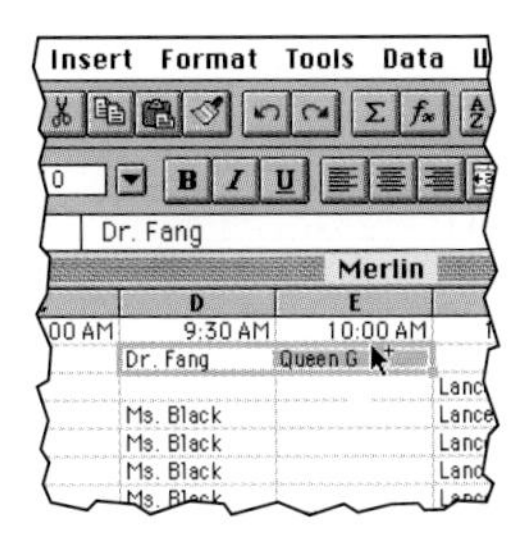

1 Select the range D2:E2 (**Dr. Fang** and **Queen G**). Hold down Option, and then position the mouse pointer over the active range border. The pointer becomes an arrowhead accompanied by a tiny plus sign.

2 Drag the border down until it is positioned over the range D4:E4. Release the mouse button and then the Option key. This time no message will appear to warn that you will overwrite D4. Note that the contents of D2:E2 have been copied to D4:E4.

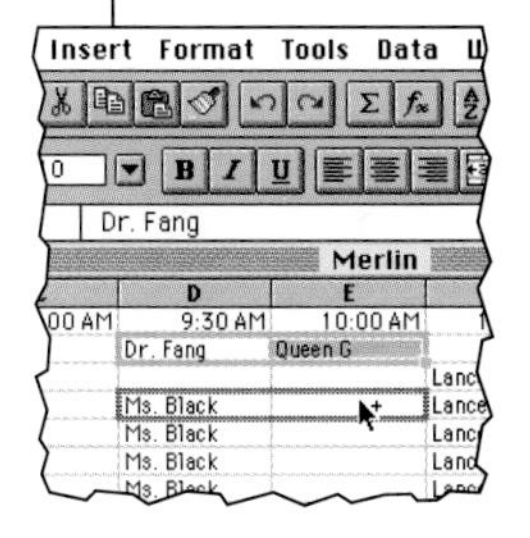

Cut, Copy, and Paste

Sometimes, you may want to copy or move data over long distances on a worksheet, or make multiple nonadjacent copies, or move data between different worksheets, between workbooks, or even between different Macintosh applications. You can perform these maneuvers by means of cut, copy, and paste operations — techniques that use a part of your computer's memory called the Clipboard as a temporary storage area.

The *Cut* and *Copy* commands put the contents of selected cells into the Clipboard. The *Paste* command puts the Clipboard data into your worksheet. After a copy and paste, the copied data stays in the Clipboard and can be pasted again if you want — until you replace it by cutting or copying another selection into the Clipboard. You can perform cut, copy, and paste operations using commands on the menu bar, shortcut menu commands (see opposite page), toolbar buttons, or the keyboard. The examples below use toolbar buttons and menu commands.

Corner It!
When pasting a range of cell contents, you don't need to select the whole target range — just the top left corner. Pasting is like hanging wallpaper. You anchor what you are pasting at the top and let the rest unfurl downward. If you do select a target range, it must be the same size and shape as your source range, or Excel will display an error message.

MOVING BY CUT AND PASTE

Dr. Fang now wants to move his Monday 9:30 AM meeting with Merlin to Friday 9:00 AM. Using a simple cut and paste operation, you can put the source data into the Clipboard and then paste it over the target cell, which simultaneously clears the source cell. Note that you can paste a selection that has been cut only once, as it is then removed from the Clipboard.

Cut Button

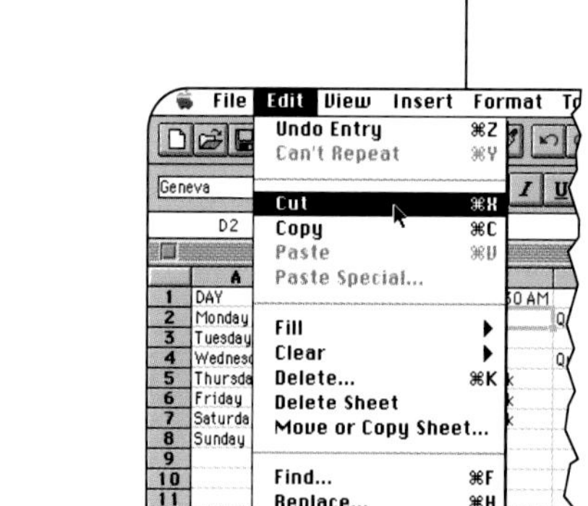

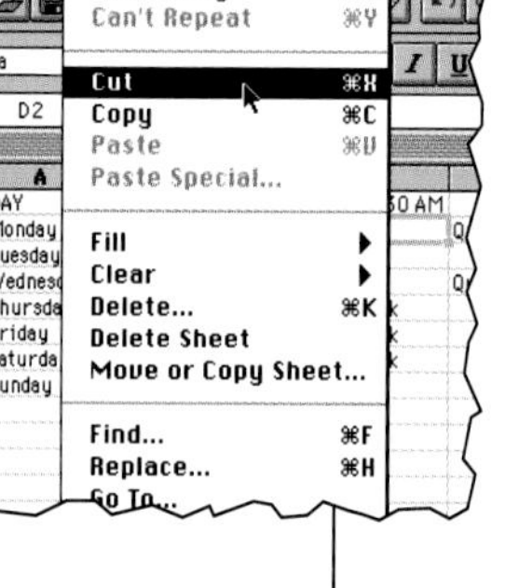

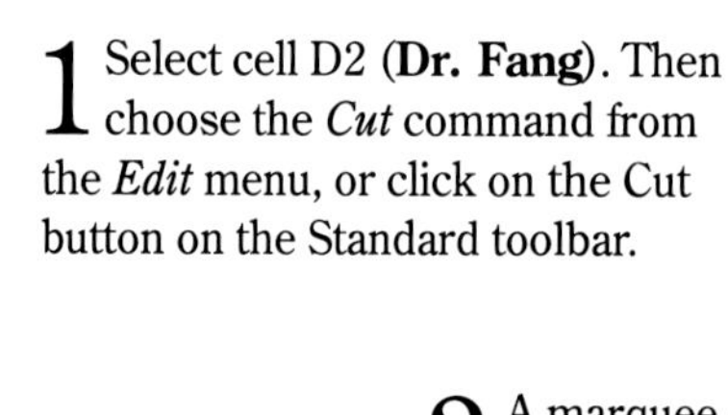

1 Select cell D2 (**Dr. Fang**). Then choose the *Cut* command from the *Edit* menu, or click on the Cut button on the Standard toolbar.

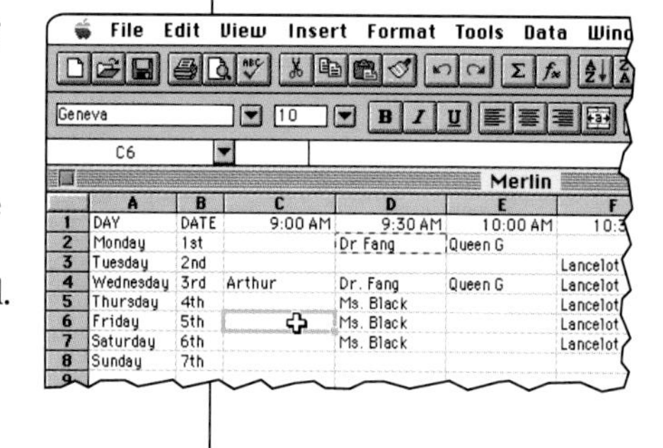

2 A marquee (moving border) frames cell D2. The status bar says "Select destination and press ENTER or choose Paste." Click on cell C6 to make it the target cell.

Paste Button

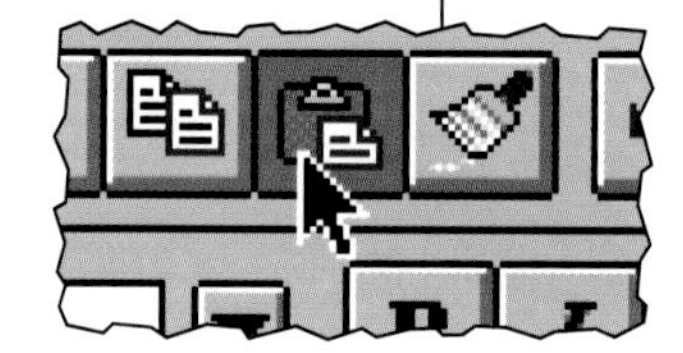

3 Choose *Paste* from the *Edit* menu, or click on the Paste button on the Standard toolbar. The contents of D2 are pasted into C6, and D2 is cleared.

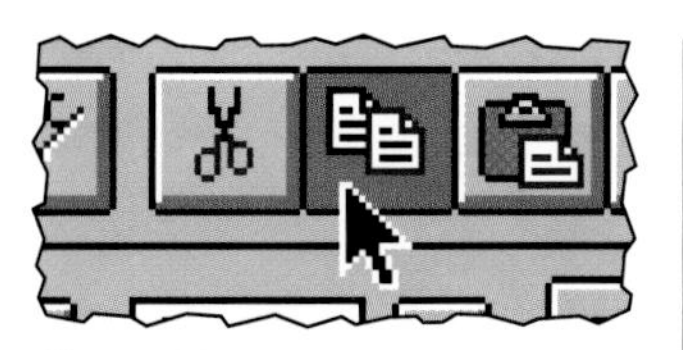

Copy Button

COPYING BY COPY AND PASTE

Arthur now contacts Merlin to arrange several more appointments. This calls for a copy and multiple paste. Copied data stays in the Clipboard after a paste, so multiple pasting of copied data is straightforward.

1 Select cell C4 (**Arthur**) and then choose *Copy* from the *Edit* menu or click on the Copy button on the Standard toolbar.

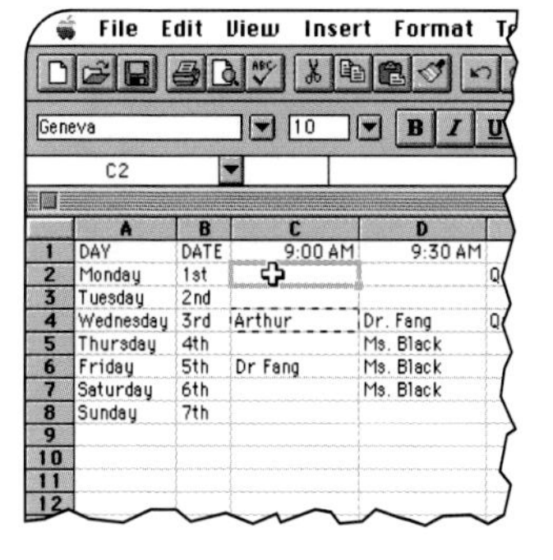

2 A marquee appears around C4. Select cell C2 to make it the target cell, and then choose *Paste* from the *Edit* menu or click on the Paste button on the Standard toolbar.

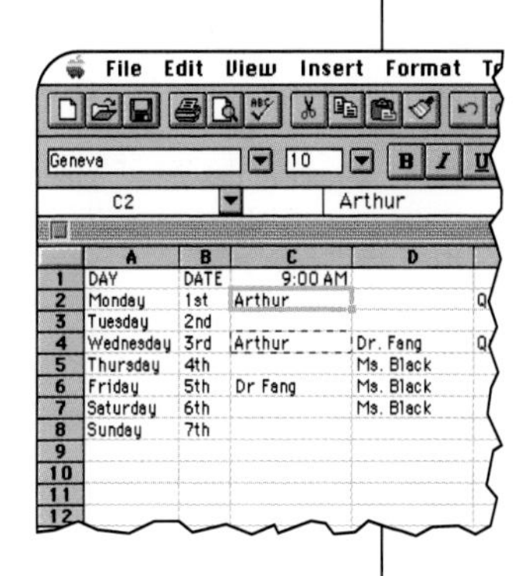

3 You will see that **Arthur** has been copied to cell C2. However, a marquee remains around cell C4. This indicates that you can paste the same data again, as many times as needed.

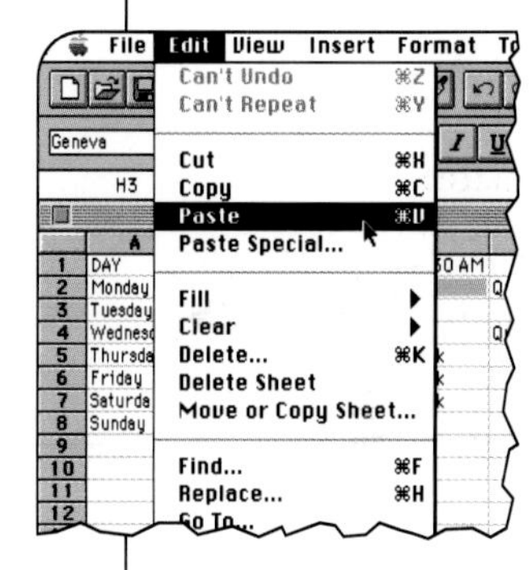

4 Select cell D2, hold down Command, select cell H3, and then choose *Paste* from the *Edit* menu. Finally, press Esc to remove the marquee.

Being Choosy?

Remember that in addition to containing a value and/or a formula, a cell may also have a special format and possibly a note attached (see page 54). When you copy or move, all of these are copied or moved. But by using the *Paste Special* command instead of *Paste*, you can choose whether to copy the value, formula, format, or note. (See "Paste Special?" on page 75.)

Cell Shortcut Menu

Shortcut Menus

When you place your mouse pointer over any cell in your worksheet and hold down Control as you press down on the mouse button, the cell underneath the pointer is selected, and at the same time you will see a shortcut menu, like the one shown at left. You can choose a command from the menu by moving down to the command name. The cell shortcut menu is specific to worksheet cells and contains commands such as *Cut*, *Copy*, *Paste*, *Delete*, and *Clear Contents* that are commonly applied to cells. Some other parts of the Excel workbook window — such as the column and row headers, toolbars, the title bar, and the worksheet tabs — also have shortcut menus with commands appropriate to those parts of the screen. Experiment with these shortcut menus by holding down Control and mouse-clicking on the relevant areas. If you make a mistake, you can undo it by pressing Command-Z.

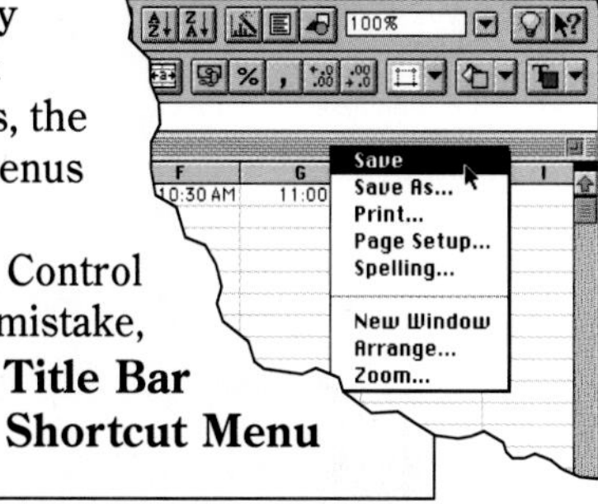

Title Bar Shortcut Menu

Worksheet Tab Shortcut Menu

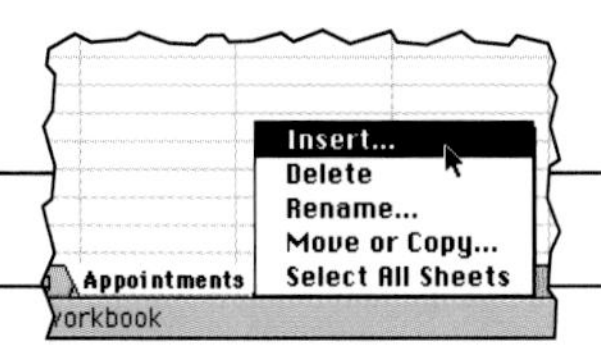

Fabulous Four
At the bottom of the keyboard lie the fabulous four cut, copy, paste and undo keys — X, C, V, and Z. Paired with Command, these keys provide shortcuts for cutting, copying, pasting and undoing in all Macintosh applications.

Cut, Copy, and Insert

So far, you have carried out only simple move and copy operations. In these operations, the contents of the target cell(s) are overwritten with the contents from the source cell(s). However, you can also insert cut or copied data so that the target cells are shifted down or to the right instead of being overwritten. This operation is known as an insert paste — and is much like putting a new building block into a wall by shifting the existing blocks to create a "hole."

The mechanics of performing a cut or copy and insert paste are similar to an ordinary cut or copy and paste. You use the *Cut* or *Copy* command to cut or copy the source data to the Clipboard, but then instead of using the *Paste* command, you use the *Cut Cells* command from the *Insert* menu to insert cut cells and the *Copied Cells* command to insert copied cells.

Mouse Maneuver?
Cells can also be moved or copied and inserted using drag and drop. For moving and inserting, hold down Shift during the operation. For copying and inserting, hold down both Shift and Option. These mouse techniques are a little tricky, so try using the menu commands first.

COPYING AND INSERTING

Ms. Black now calls Merlin and insists that she must see him on Monday morning at 10:00 AM. Merlin thinks he can arrange this by putting Queen G's Monday appointment off until 10:30 AM, but doing this calls for a copy and insert paste.

When you use menu commands to perform a copy and insert paste, a dialog box appears that gives you the choice of moving worksheet cells to the right or downward to accommodate the source data. In this instance, Merlin needs to move **Queen G** to the right.

Quick Combinations
Some more shortcuts that you can perform with Command and a second key are given below. There's a more comprehensive list on page 122.

+ F Find
+ K Delete Cells

+ I Insert Cells
+ 1 Format Cells

1 This time use the shortcut menu to choose the *Copy* command. With the mouse pointer over cell D5 (**Ms. Black**), hold down Control, click on the mouse button and then choose *Copy*. A marquee frames D5.

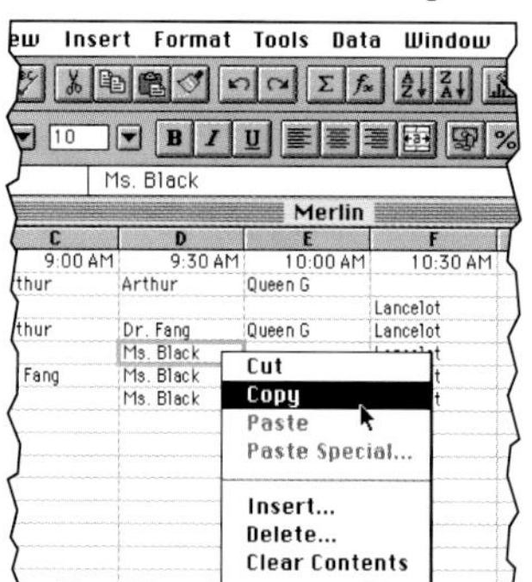

2 Select cell E2 and then choose the *Copied Cells* command from the *Insert* menu.

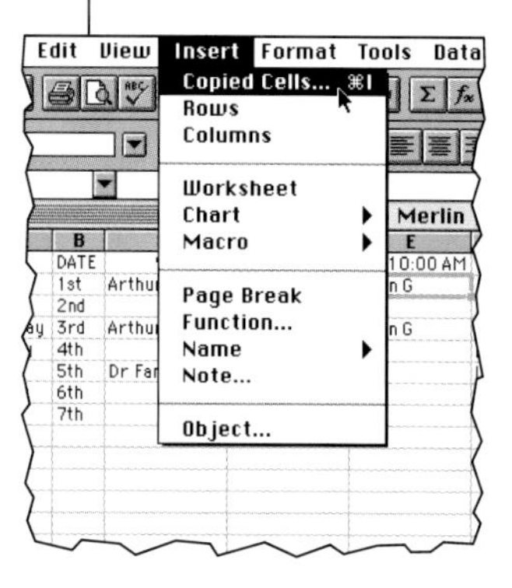

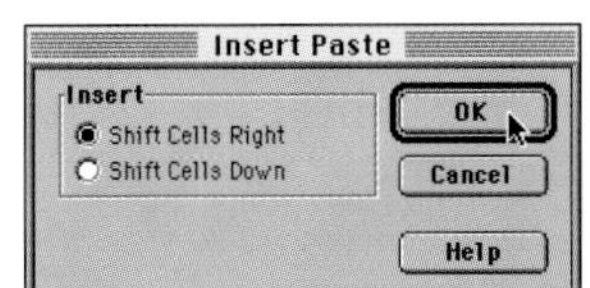

3 The *Insert Paste* dialog box appears and asks if you want to shift existing cells down or to the right to create a hole for "**Ms. Black**." Click on *Shift Cells Right*, and then click on *OK* to confirm.

4 **Ms. Black** is inserted into E2, and the existing contents of E2 (**Queen G**) shift one cell to the right. Press Esc to clear the marquee.

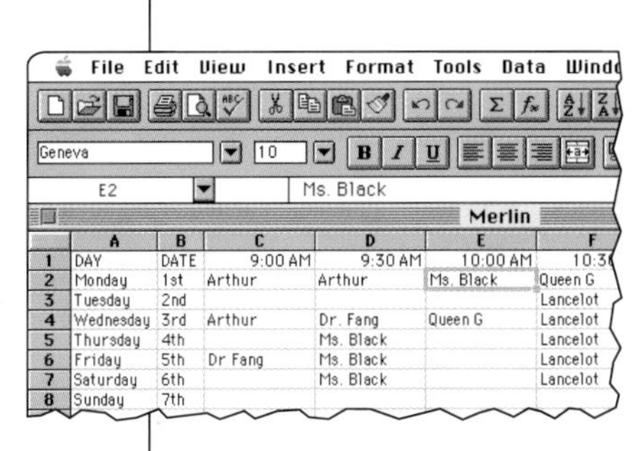

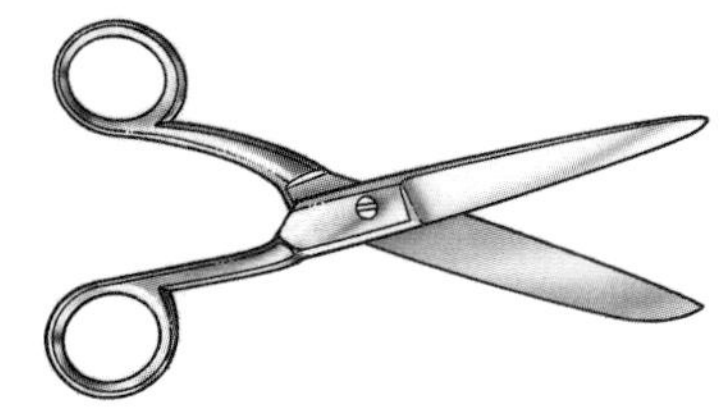

CUTTING AND INSERTING

Queen G now phones to request that her Wednesday appointment be moved to 9:00 AM. Looking at the appointment log, Merlin sees that this can be achieved by moving both Arthur's and Dr. Fang's appointments so that each is half an hour later, thus creating a vacant slot at 9:00 AM for Queen G. The whole shift can be achieved easily by means of a cut and insert operation.

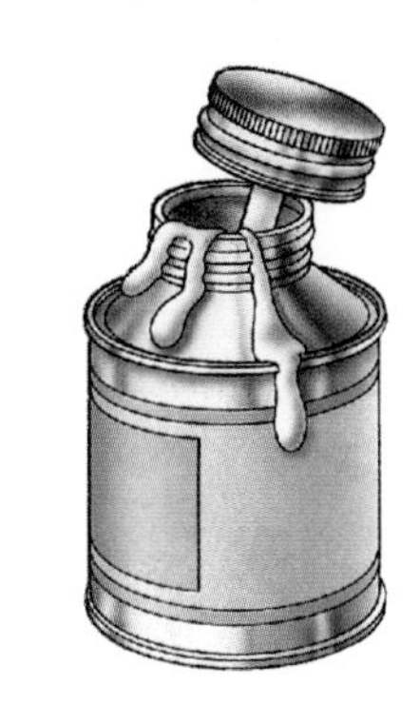

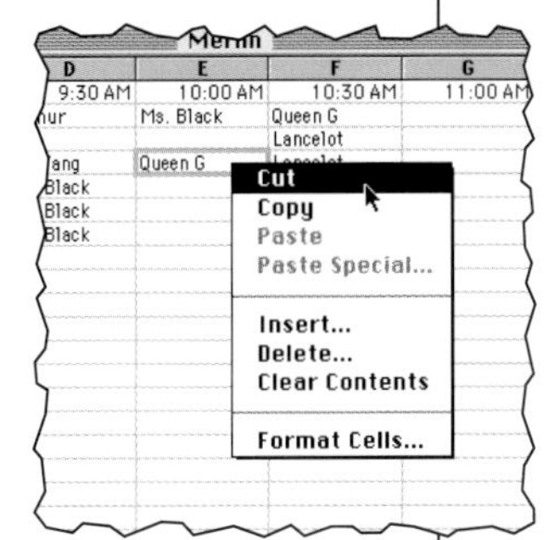

1 Select cell E4 (**Queen G**) and then choose *Cut* from the cell shortcut menu (hold down the Control key as you click on the cell). A marquee appears around E4.

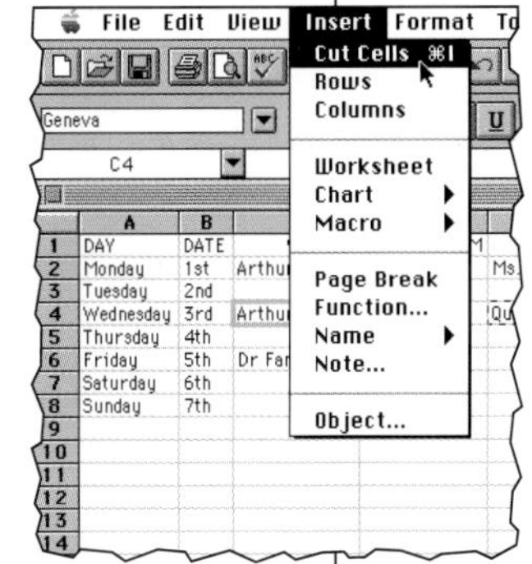

2 Select cell C4 and then choose the *Cut Cells* command from the *Insert* menu.

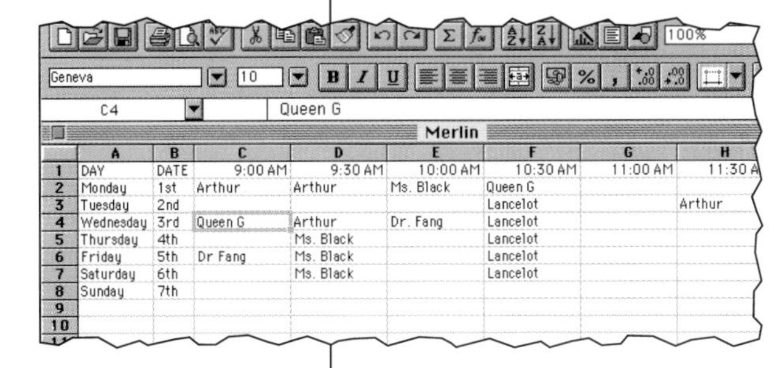

3 Inspect the worksheet and you will see that **Queen G** has been cut from E4 and inserted into C4.

In the course of this operation, the cut cell (E4) was actually deleted from the worksheet and then reinserted at C4. Because the source and target cells for the move were in the same row, no dialog box appeared to ask whether you wanted to shift cells to the right or down to accommodate the inserted cell. Excel simply closed up the hole in E4 by shifting C4 and D4 one cell to the right, creating a space in C4 to insert **Queen G.**

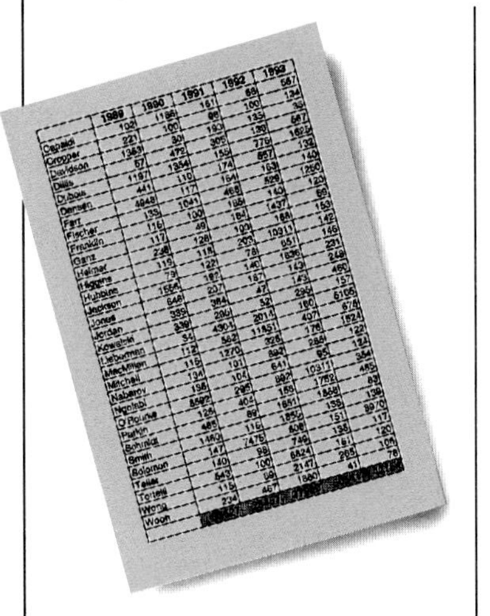

Inserting and Deleting Rows, Columns, and Cells

By using the *Rows*, *Columns*, and *Cells* commands from the *Insert* menu, and the *Delete* command from the *Edit* menu, you can insert or delete cells, rows, or columns to change your worksheet.

Not Possible!
Excel does not allow you to perform delete or insert operations when multiple nonadjacent areas of the worksheet are selected.

INSERTING ROWS AND COLUMNS

To insert new rows or columns, you must select an appropriate number of rows or columns in the position where you want the new ones to appear. You then choose the *Rows* or *Columns* command from the *Insert* menu. For example, Merlin thinks it might be helpful to insert two blank rows at the top of the appointments worksheet to improve the appearance of his diary.

A Two-Row Insert

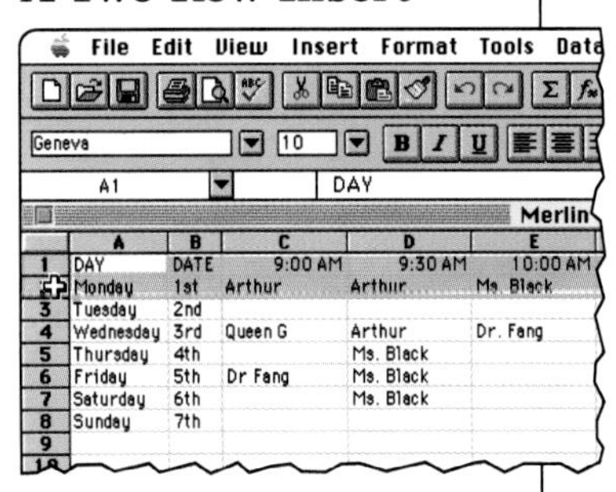

1 Click on the header for row 1 and drag the mouse pointer down to select both rows 1 and 2.

2 Choose *Rows* from the *Insert* menu. Two blank rows are inserted in rows 1 and 2, and the rows below are shifted downward.

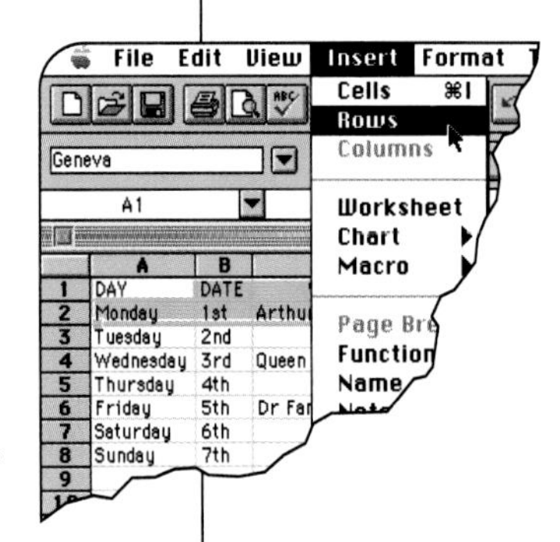

DELETING ROWS AND COLUMNS

To delete rows or columns, you select the rows or columns that you want to remove from the worksheet and then choose *Delete* from the *Edit* menu.

Merlin decides that he does not need an 11:00 AM column in his appointment log. He can use this time instead for pursuing his hobby — mystical research.

What Moves Where?
When you insert or delete rows, existing rows below are automatically shifted down (with an insert) or up (with a delete). There is no effect on the rows above the deleted or inserted rows. When you insert or delete columns, existing columns to the right are shifted right (with an insert) or left (with a delete).

A One-Column Delete

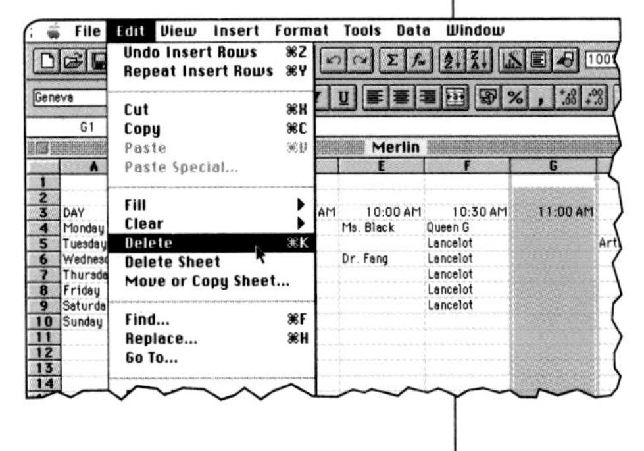

1 Select column G by clicking on its header. Then choose *Delete* from the *Edit* menu.

2 Column G is removed from the worksheet, and the columns to the right shift to the left, which closes the gap.

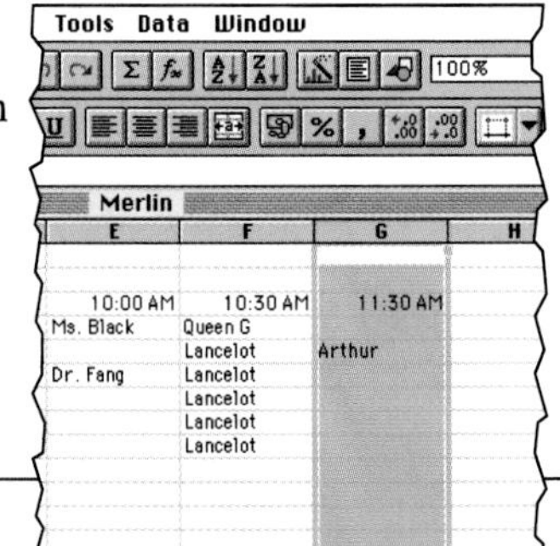

INSERTING AND DELETING CELLS

When you insert or delete a single cell or a range of cells (as compared to whole rows or columns), you need to decide in what direction it is best to shift other cells in the worksheet. For example, Merlin realizes that Monday is the third day of the month, and not the first, as he had originally thought. He suggests correcting his diary by deleting cells B4 and B5 from the worksheet.

Deleting Two Cells

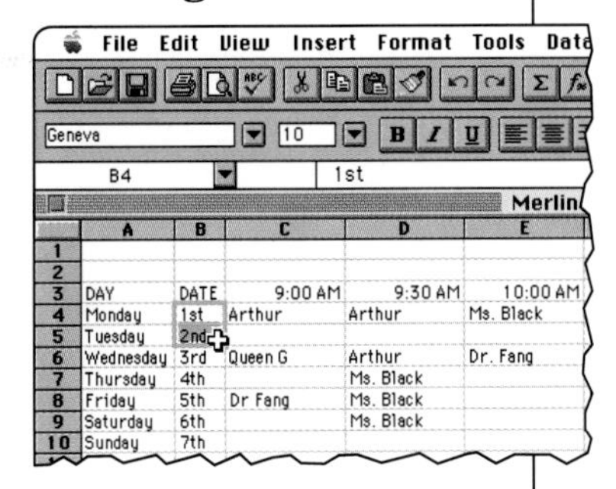

1 Select the range B4:B5, and then choose *Delete* from the *Edit* menu.

2 The *Delete* dialog box appears. Choose *Shift Cells Up*, and then click on *OK*. B4 and B5 are deleted, and the cells in column B below B5 shift up two cells.

Note that if you had chosen *Shift Cells Left* you would have confused Merlin's appointments log considerably by shifting all his Monday and Tuesday appointments with clients to half an hour earlier. You now need to enter **8th** into cell B9 and **9th** into cell B10.

Finally, Merlin decides it would be best to separate weekend appointments from those on Monday through Friday and suggests inserting blank cells in A9:F9.

Delete — or Clear?
Before using the *Delete* command, consider whether you would be better off using the *Clear Contents* command. Remember that clearing cells erases their contents but has no effect on the structure of the worksheet. Deleting cells removes the cells themselves and causes other cells in the worksheet to shift.

Inserting a Range of Cells

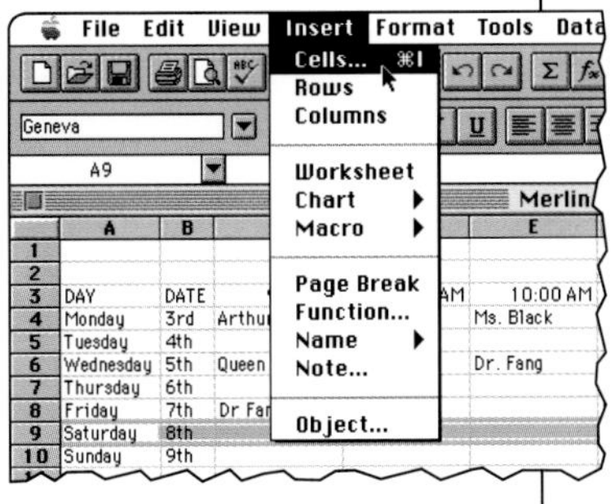

1 Select the range A9:F9, and then choose *Cells* from the *Insert* menu.

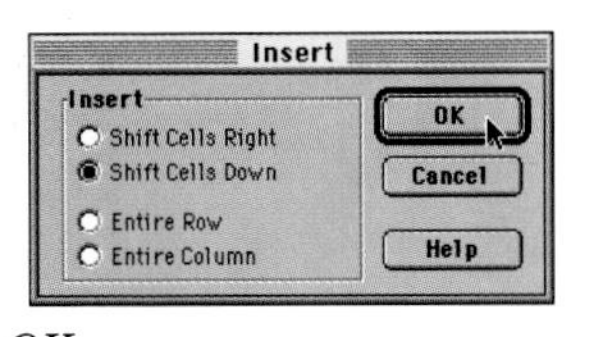

2 The *Insert* dialog box appears. Choose *Shift Cells Down,* and then click on *OK*.

The **Appointments** worksheet is now as shown at right. Because Merlin and his clients are happy with the alterations, click on the Save button on the Standard toolbar to save all the latest changes to the **Merlin** workbook.

Next you'll return to the **Checking** worksheet to look at the effects of moving or copying cells that contain formulas or cells that are referenced by formulas.

Merlin's Diary
Merlin has a busy week ahead of him.

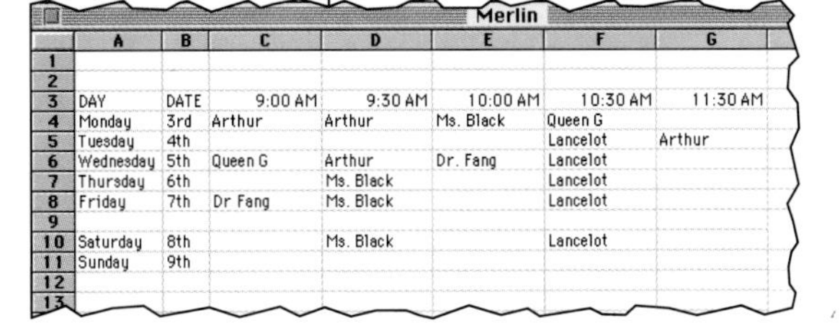

	A	B	C	D	E	F	G
1							
2							
3	DAY	DATE	9:00 AM	9:30 AM	10:00 AM	10:30 AM	11:30 AM
4	Monday	3rd	Arthur	Arthur	Ms. Black	Queen G	
5	Tuesday	4th				Lancelot	Arthur
6	Wednesday	5th	Queen G	Arthur	Dr. Fang	Lancelot	
7	Thursday	6th		Ms. Black		Lancelot	
8	Friday	7th	Dr Fang	Ms. Black		Lancelot	
9							
10	Saturday	8th		Ms. Black		Lancelot	
11	Sunday	9th					
12							
13							

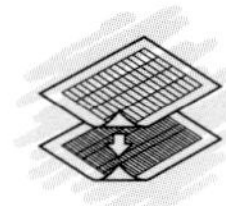

Copying and Moving Formulas

Special considerations apply when you are copying or moving cells that contain or are referenced by formulas. Cell references in formulas can be either relative or absolute. A *relative* cell reference points to a cell that has a particular address *relative* to the cell containing the formula. Therefore, if the formula is copied to another cell, relative cell references in the formula are updated accordingly. An *absolute* cell reference, in contrast, always refers to the same worksheet cell. An absolute cell reference is indicated by $ signs in front of the row and column designators — for example, $A$3.

Relative or Absolute?
An example of a formula containing a relative cell reference would be =D4 within cell F4. Excel interprets this as "equal to the cell two cells to the left." If the formula were to be copied to F6, it would therefore be updated to =D6. An example of a formula containing an absolute reference would be =$D$4 in cell F4. If copied to cell F6 (or any other cell) this formula would still refer to cell D4.

COPYING A FORMULA THAT CONTAINS RELATIVE CELL REFERENCES

To see what happens when you copy a formula that contains relative references, click on the **Checking** sheet tab in your **Merlin** workbook.

1 Click on cell F4. It contains the formula **=F3+D4-E4**, which are all relative cell references. Drag the cell's fill handle down to the bottom of cell F8. This copies the formula in F4 to cells F5 through F8.

=F3+D4-E4

Merlin

	A	B	C	D	E	F
1	Date	Check #	Item	Deposit	Withdrawal	Balance
2	31-Dec					500
3	4-Jan	1005	Cave Rental		30	470
4	6-Jan	1006	Guild Fees		15	455
5	7-Jan		Savings Interest	12.5		
6	30-Jan		January Profits	75		
7	10-Jan		Betting Winnings	43		
8	14-Jan		Cash from Aunt B	80		
9						

2 Release the mouse button and then look at the formulas in each of the cells F5 through F8.

F5 =F4+D5-E5

Merlin

	A	B	C	D	E	F
1	Date	Check #	Item	Deposit	Withdrawal	Balance
2	31-Dec					500
3	4-Jan	1005	Cave Rental		30	470
4	6-Jan	1006	Guild Fees		15	455
5	7-Jan		Savings Interest	12.5		467.5
6	30-Jan		January Profits	75		542.5
7	10-Jan		Betting Winnings	43		585.5
8	14-Jan		Cash from Aunt B	80		665.5
9						

You will see that each formula is different from the formula in cell F4. For example, the formula in F5 is **=F4+D5-E5**. That is because the cell references were updated when the formula in cell F4 was copied to the four cells directly below it. Each formula adds the deposit and subtracts the withdrawal in its *own* row to the previous balance — giving the correct running balance figures.

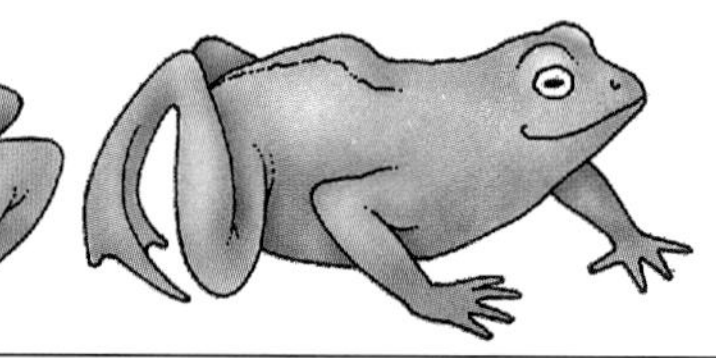

All Gone!
If you delete a cell referenced by a formula elsewhere on the worksheet, a #REF! error appears in the cell containing the formula. The error occurs because the cell contents that had been referenced no longer exist.

COPYING A FORMULA THAT CONTAINS ABSOLUTE CELL REFERENCES

Sometimes you want to copy a formula to a different location but you want the cell references in the formula to continue to point to the same cells in the worksheet. For this purpose, you use absolute cell references.

Merlin wants to project his worksheet many months ahead. You can copy recurring transactions, such as the cave rental, from January to subsequent months. However, Merlin would prefer that if, say, his cave rental changes, he can alter the rental for each month with a single edit. To provide for this, you need to create a "master" copy of the recurring transactions in a separate part of the worksheet, and then arrange that each month's recurring transactions refer to this master copy using absolute cell references.

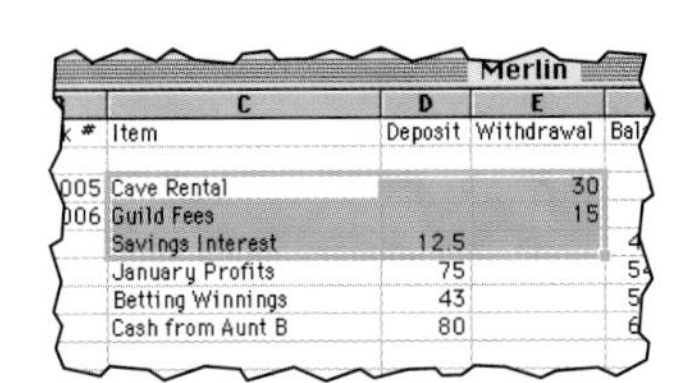

1 Select cells C3 through E5. These contain the transactions that Merlin thinks will be the same each month. Hold down the Option key and drag the range border across the worksheet, dropping the block into the cell range G1 through I3. Scroll to the right so that you can see column I.

2 Click on cell E3 and enter the formula **=$I$1**. Click on the Enter button and you will see that it returns the value in cell I1 — **30**. Now enter **=$I$2** in cell E4 and **=$H$3** in cell D5.

COPYING THE TRANSACTIONS

You can now copy the recurring transactions to the subsequent months. Because the formulas in cells E3, E4, and D5 use absolute cell references, when you copy the formulas they will always refer to the values in cells I1, I2, and H3.

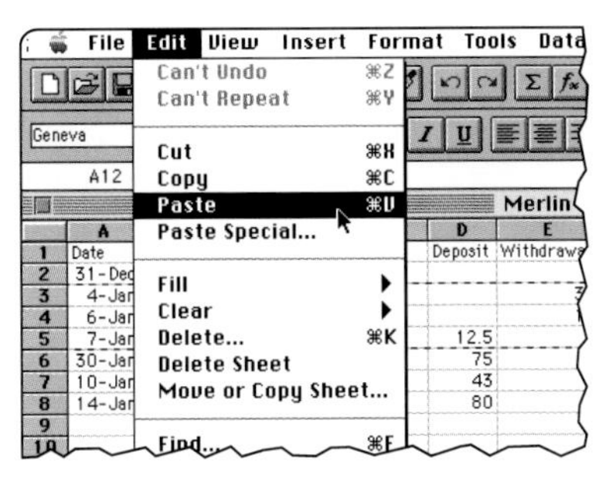

1 Select cells A3 through E5 and choose *Copy* from the *Edit* menu. Paste the range contents into A12:E14 and then into A18:E20 using the *Paste* command from the *Edit* menu. Look at one of the copied formulas, such as the one in cell E12; it still refers to cell I1.

2 Edit the dates on the worksheet. In cells A12 to A14, change the month to February. In cells A18 to A20 change it to March.

3 The check numbers for February and March are obviously now wrong. Select cells B12 through B19, choose *Clear* from the *Edit* menu, and choose *All* from the submenu. Merlin can fill these in later.

4 Now click on cell F8, and use the fill handle to fill the running balance formula all the way down to cell F20.

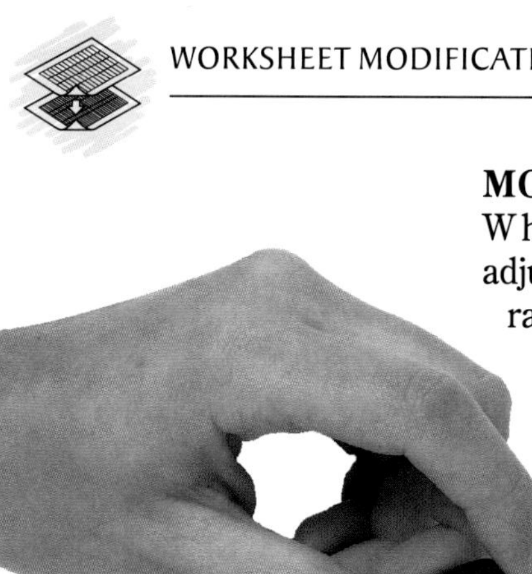

MOVING FORMULAS

When you move cells containing formulas, Excel adjusts all relative references to cells *within* the moved range. However, there is no change in references to cells *outside* the moved range. This usually produces the desired result, but always check that the outcome is as you expected.

1 Click on cell F20 and look in the formula bar. It contains the formula **=F19+D20-E20**.

2 Now select the range A20:F20, move this range down one row using drag and drop, and then click on cell F21. It contains the formula **=F19+D21-E21**. Note that the references to D20 and E20 have been updated, because these cells were *within* the moved range, while the reference to F19, which was not moved, remains the same.

3 Undo the change by choosing *Undo Drag and Drop* from the *Edit* menu.

Check Your Changes!
Because of the way Excel updates references when you move or copy data or formulas, it's easy to change the layout of a worksheet without altering the way the worksheet works. However, it's a good idea always to check affected formulas after a copy or move.

COPYING AND MOVING CELLS REFERENCED BY FORMULAS

Copying cells referenced by formulas has no effect on the formulas. However, if you *move* a cell or a range of cells that are referenced by formulas, Excel adjusts the formulas automatically to reflect the new locations of the referenced cells. This applies whether the cell references are relative or absolute.

Merlin decides that he wants to move the contents of cells G1 through I3 out of the way to improve the appearance of the worksheet.

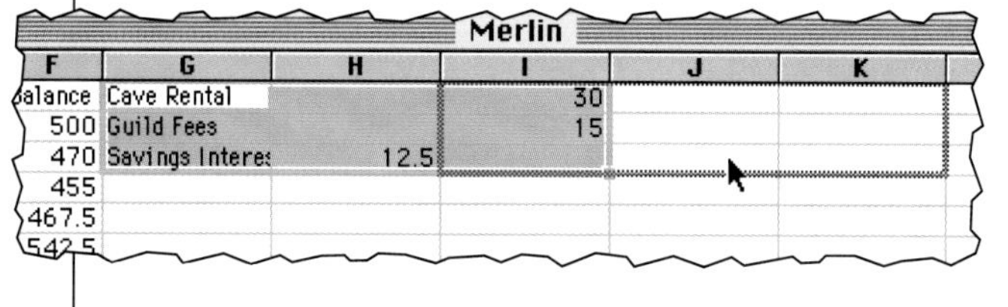

1 Select the cell range G1 through I3. Drag and drop the highlighted range into the range I1 through K3.

2 Click on cell E3 and look in the formula bar. Notice that the cell reference in the formula has changed from \$I\$1 to \$K\$1 to reflect the new location of the cave rental fee.

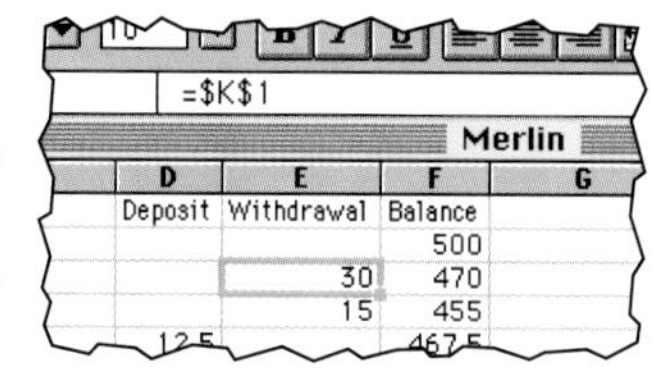

1 Click on cell E3. Choose *Copy* from the *Edit* menu. Now choose *Paste Special* from the *Edit* menu. The *Paste Special* dialog box is displayed.

Converting Formulas to Values

Merlin is concerned that if his cave rental changes later on in the year, and if he alters the amount in cell K1 to reflect this, the rental amounts for months that have already passed will also change because they are linked to cell K1 by formulas. Excel has a solution to this problem — as each month passes, Merlin can replace the formulas in that month's recurring transactions with the transaction values themselves.

2 Click on *Values* under *Paste*, and then click on *OK*. This pastes the value returned by the formula in E3 over the formula.

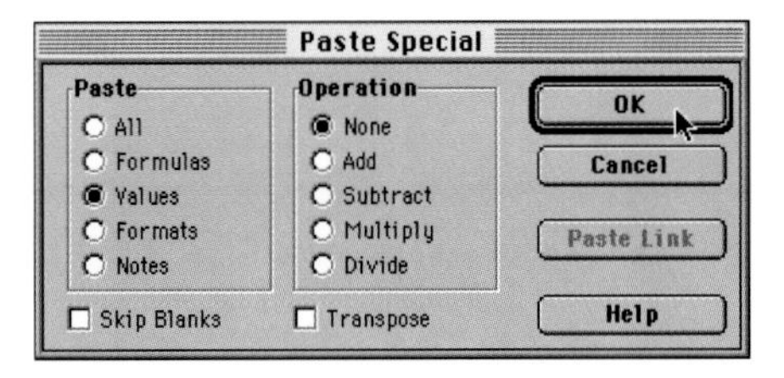

3 E3 now contains the value 30, and changes to the value of K1 will no longer affect it. Use the same method to convert the formulas in cells E4 and D5 to constant values. Now Merlin can change any of his projected fixed transactions without changing his record of the amounts already transacted.

C Item	D Deposit	E Withdrawal	F Balance
			500
Cave Rental		30	470
Guild Fees		15	455
Savings Interest	12.5		467.5
January Profits	75		542.5

Staying Constant
You can also convert a formula to a constant value by selecting the cell containing the formula, clicking in the formula bar, and then pressing Command-=. This key combination calculates the formula in the formula bar and replaces it with its value. Press Enter to confirm the change.

Sorting Worksheet Data

Merlin wants to sort the January transactions in his worksheet so that they are arranged by date. First he needs to enter one additional transaction — a check that he wrote to his tailors. You can add it by entering **12 Jan** in A9, **1007** in B9, **Taillors** in C9 (don't worry about the misspelling for now), and **30** in E9.

To sort the transactions, you use the *Sort* command. Before you sort your data, you must select the range of cells that you want to sort. You also need to decide which row or column to sort by — in this case column A, because it contains the dates — and whether to sort in ascending or descending order.

1 Select the cell range A3 through E9 and then choose *Sort* from the *Data* menu.

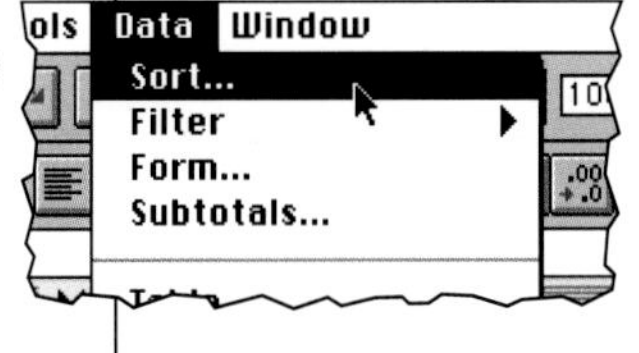

2 The *Sort* dialog box is now displayed. Column A is already displayed under *Sort By*, and the *Ascending* option is checked, so you don't need to make any changes. Click on *OK*.

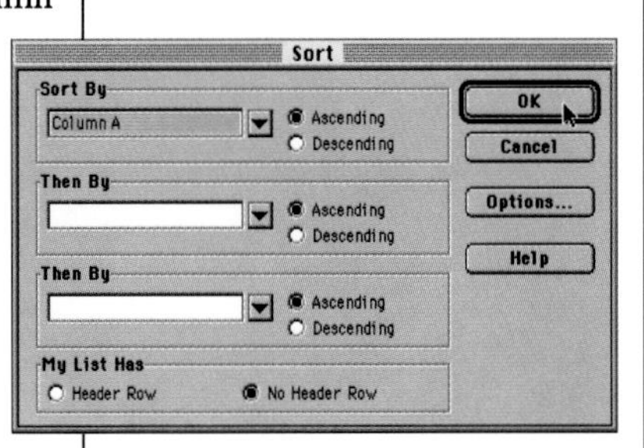

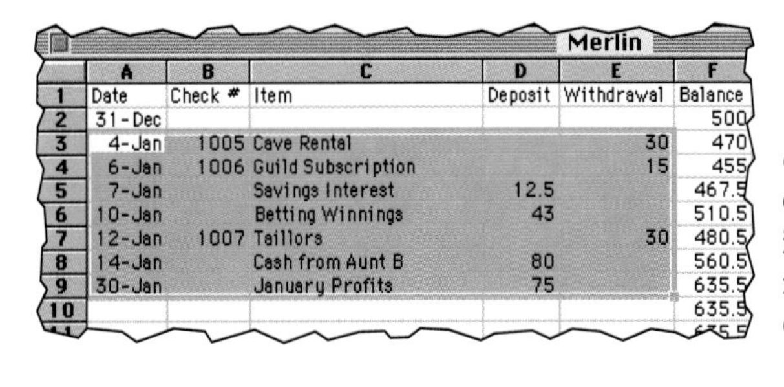

	A	B	C	D	E	F
1	Date	Check #	Item	Deposit	Withdrawal	Balance
2	31-Dec					500
3	4-Jan	1005	Cave Rental		30	470
4	6-Jan	1006	Guild Subscription		15	455
5	7-Jan		Savings Interest	12.5		467.5
6	10-Jan		Betting Winnings	43		510.5
7	12-Jan	1007	Taillors		30	480.5
8	14-Jan		Cash from Aunt B	80		560.5
9	30-Jan		January Profits	75		635.5
10						635.5

3 You can see that January's transactions are now sorted in ascending date order. For more on the *Sort* command and dialog box, see page 103.

Other Types of Worksheet Modification

Merlin is pleased with his **Checking** worksheet — he can enter the details of any transactions he intends to make over the next few months and obtain an instant assessment of how it will affect his running balance. But he wants to make a few final amendments.

Just Looking?
The *Find* command in the *Edit* menu is similar to the *Replace* command. In the *Find* dialog box, you type whatever you want to find into the *Find What* box and click on *Find Next*. When Excel finds a cell that matches the criteria you specified, that cell becomes active.

FIND AND REPLACE

Excel allows you to search for occurrences of specified cell contents and replace them with other values. You can search for and replace constant data, such as text or numbers, or formulas. You can perform your search either on a selected range of cells or on a whole worksheet. Merlin has decided that he wants to change some of the text items in his worksheet.

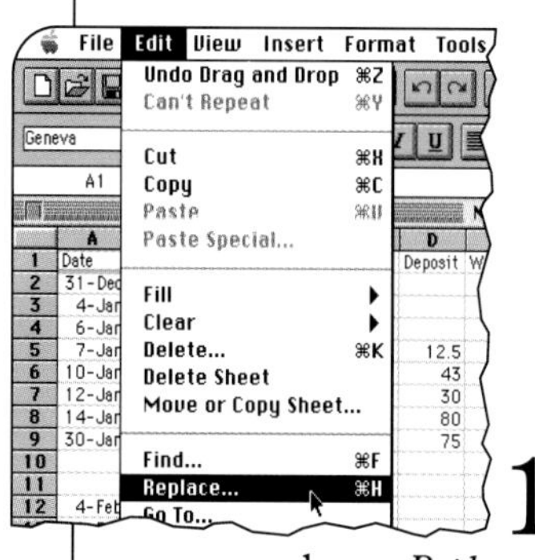

1 Click on cell A1 and then choose *Replace* from the *Edit* menu. The *Replace* dialog box is displayed.

2 In the *Find What* box, type in **Guild Fees**. Then click in the *Replace with* box, and type in **Guild Subscription**. Click on *Replace All*. Look at cells C4, C13, and C19 — you'll see that the contents have been replaced.

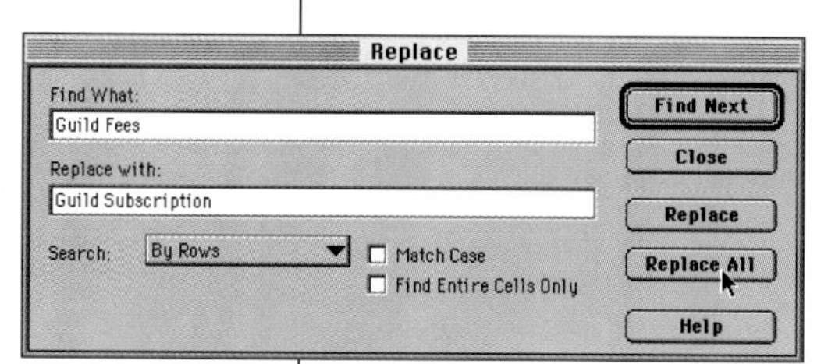

Many options are available when you are searching and replacing. For example, you can instruct Excel to match all of a cell's contents or just a part. For a description of all the options available, click on the *Help* button in the *Replace* dialog box.

CELL NOTES

Worksheets are easy to create but can be difficult to understand later if you change them. Excel lets you annotate your worksheets by attaching notes to cells. These notes are not visible in the worksheet.

1 Select cell C6 (**Betting Winnings**) and choose *Note* from the *Insert* menu. The *Cell Note* dialog box is displayed.

2 In the *Text Note* box, type **King John won at 15-1**. Click on *OK*; the dialog box will close and this note will be attached to the cell listed in the *Cell* text box (C6).

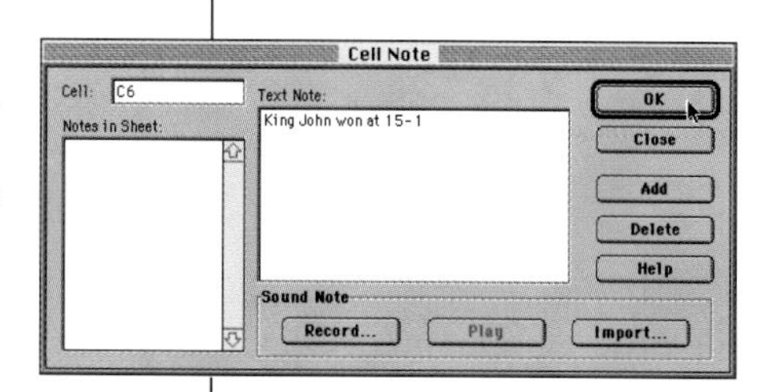

3 You will see that cell C6 now has a small red flag in the top right-hand corner, indicating that it has a note attached.

You can use the *Cell Note* dialog box to add a series of notes to different cells in the worksheet. For each note, first double-click in the *Cell* box. Type the address of the cell you want to contain the note, or click on the relevant cell in the worksheet to add its address to the *Cell* box. Then double-click in the *Text Note* box and type the text of the note. Click on *Add* and repeat the process for your next note. Click on *OK* when you have added all the notes to your worksheet.

CHECKING YOUR SPELLING

Excel's spelling checker provides a quick way to check the spelling in your worksheet. The spelling checker queries the spelling of any word it cannot find in its dictionary. You can check the entire worksheet by selecting a single cell or any part of the worksheet by selecting a range of cells.

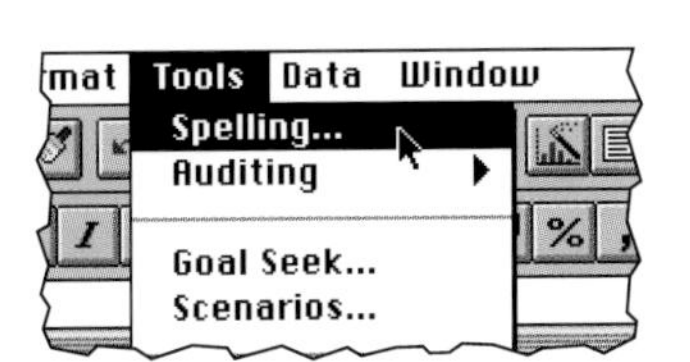

1 Select cell A1 and choose *Spelling* from the *Tools* menu or click on the Spelling Checker button on the Standard toolbar. The *Spelling* dialog box appears.

2 Excel queries the word **Taillors**. It suggests that the correct spelling is **Tailors**. Click on *Change* to accept that suggestion.

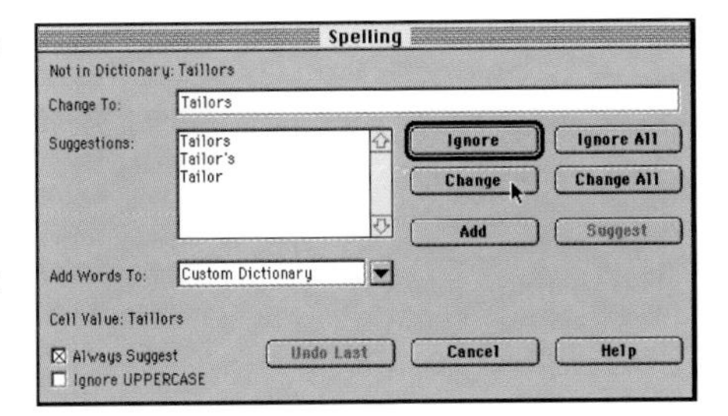

The spelling checker often provides several alternative suggestions for a misspelled word. If you don't like the suggestion in the *Change To* box, click on one of the alternatives listed under *Suggestions* and then click on *Change*. If you click on the *Change All* or *Ignore All* button, the spelling checker will change or ignore all examples of a word that is not in its dictionary.

HIDING A COLUMN OR ROW

Excel lets you hide columns or rows and then make them visible again at a later stage. Merlin would prefer that his betting winnings do not show, in case his disapproving mother sees the worksheet.

1 Select row 6, which contains the gambling winning. Choose *Row* from the *Format* menu. From the submenu, choose *Hide*.

2 Row 6 is now hidden from view. You can unhide it by selecting rows 5 and 7 and then choosing *Row* from the *Format* menu again. This time choose *Unhide* from the submenu. You can now close your **Merlin** workbook, saving all changes that you have made.

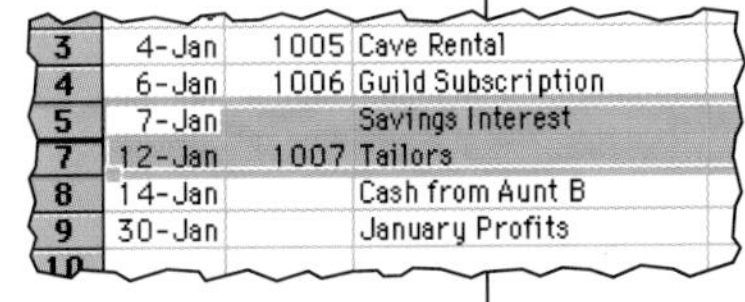

3	4-Jan	1005	Cave Rental
4	6-Jan	1006	Guild Subscription
5	7-Jan		Savings Interest
7	12-Jan	1007	Tailors
8	14-Jan		Cash from Aunt B
9	30-Jan		January Profits

Notes on Notes!
To review the notes in a worksheet, choose the *Note* command from the *Insert* menu again. Within the *Cell Note* dialog box, all notes in your worksheet are listed in the *Notes in Sheet* box. If you click on one, the full text of the note appears in the *Text Note* box, where it can be amended. You can remove the note by clicking on *Delete*.

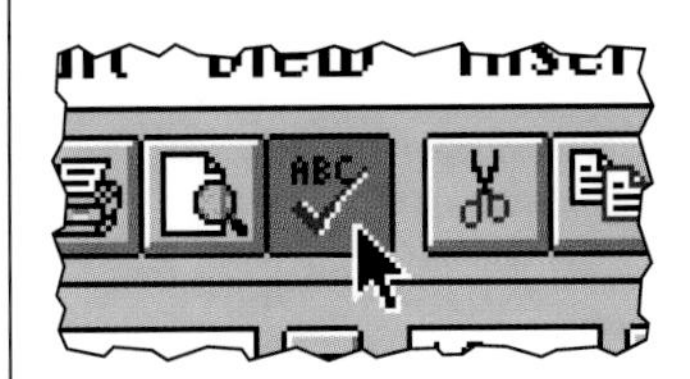

Spelling Checker Button
Clicking on this button on the Standard toolbar is a quick way of activating the spelling checker.

Working Smarter

EXCEL HAS MANY FEATURES that can make your worksheets easier to create. For example, Excel allows you to enter data into several worksheets at once using group edit. Excel functions are similar to the simple formulas that you have already used but allow you to perform more advanced mathematical operations. Your worksheets can be made more comprehensible and easier to use by naming cells and cell ranges.

Grouped Worksheets

Excel lets you add data to several worksheets at a time. This is known as a group edit. To see how to do this, let's set up annual income and expense sheets for Merlin. Open a new workbook by clicking on the New Workbook button on the Standard toolbar. Save the workbook as **Year1** in the **Excel Workbooks** folder that you created earlier. Rename *Sheet1* as **Annual Income** and *Sheet2* as **Annual Expenses**.

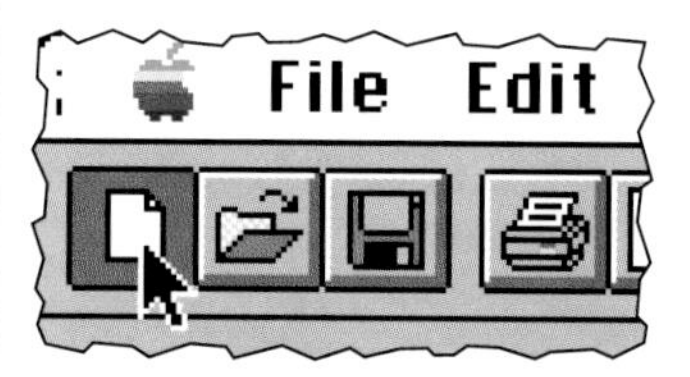

New Workbook Button

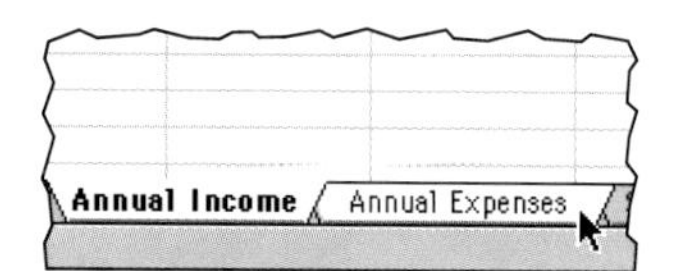

1 Click on the **Annual Income** sheet tab. Hold down Command and click on the **Annual Expenses** sheet tab. The tabs for both sheets are now highlighted. You will see *[Group]* appear after *Year1* in the title bar. Any operations you perform will now be performed on both sheets.

2 To set column widths, select columns B through M. Choose *Column* from the *Format* menu and *Width* from the submenu. In the *Column Width* dialog box, enter a value of **4** and click on *OK*.

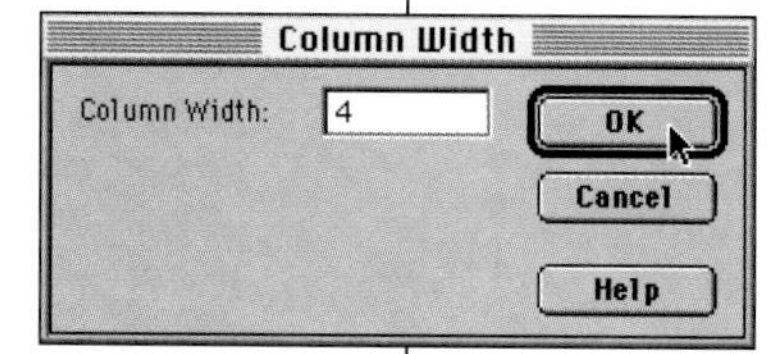

3 Enter the labels shown at right. If you now select the **Annual Expenses** worksheet, you will see that the same data appears on both sheets. Click on the **Annual Income** sheet tab again.

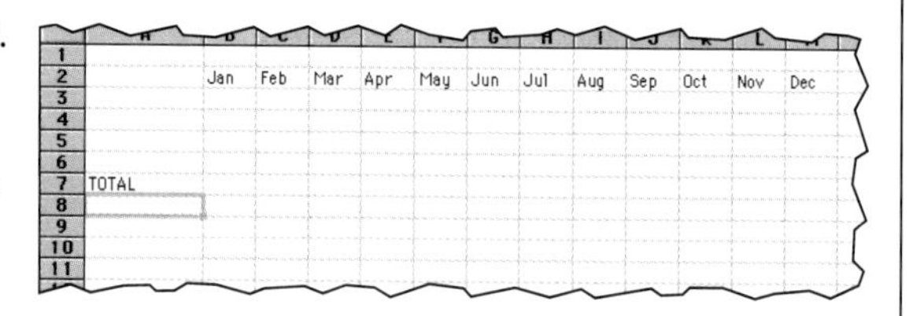

Using Worksheet Functions

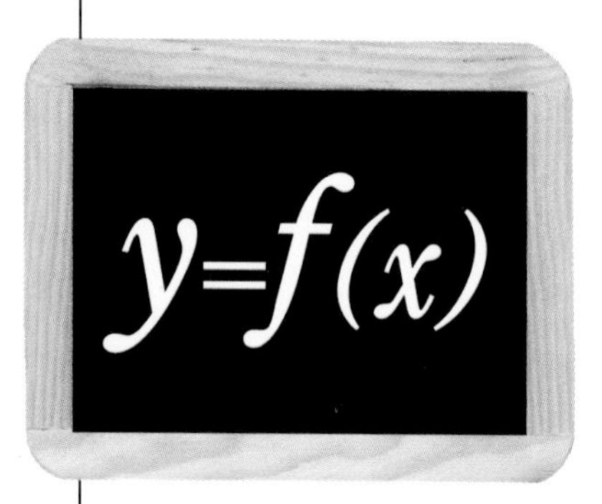

Excel functions provide a shorthand for formulas that would be long or complex to enter. Each different function performs a specific operation, using one or more *arguments*, a list of which has to be supplied in parentheses after the function name. For example, the SUM function (which you already used in the guise of the AutoSum tool in Chapter One) adds up a series of values. To use this function, you simply type =SUM into a cell, followed, in parentheses, by the range of cells whose values you wish to add. The range reference is the SUM function's argument.

No Use for Summary Info?

If you do not want to be prompted for summary information each time you save a new workbook, choose *Options* from the *Tools* menu and clear the *Prompt for Summary Info* check box on the *General* flipcard.

What Are Arguments?

A function's arguments — the information that you supply for the function to carry out its specific operation — can be values, cell references, named ranges, and other types of information. Different functions require different types of arguments.

USING THE FUNCTION WIZARD

Excel guides you through the creation of functions with a feature called the Function Wizard. The Function Wizard provides the form of the function and helps you enter the specific information you need to complete the argument. Let's use the Function Wizard to add the SUM function to your worksheets. You'll enter the numerical data on which the function can operate afterwards.

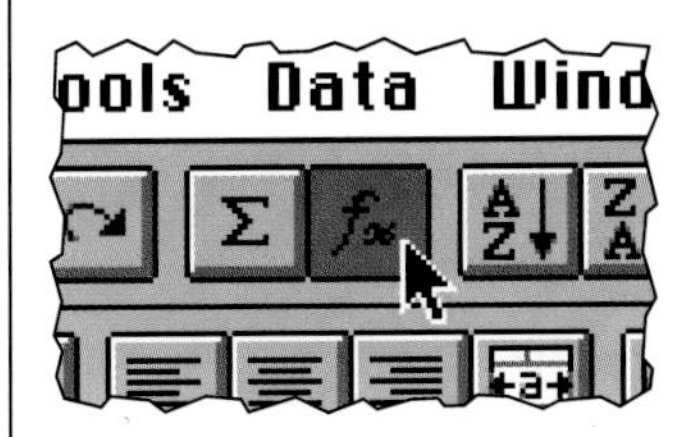

1 Click on cell B7, and then click on the Function Wizard button on the Standard toolbar.

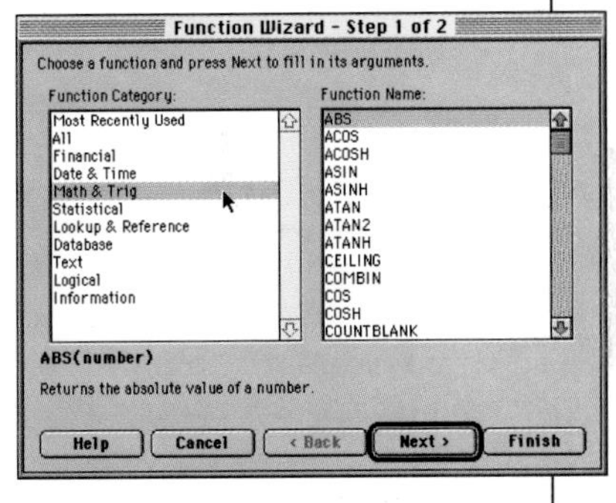

2 The first *Function Wizard* dialog box is displayed with a list of all the categories of functions on the left-hand side. The box on the right-hand side lists the functions within that category. Click on *Math & Trig* in the left-hand box.

Function Wizard - Step 1 of 2
Choose a function and press Next to fill in its arguments.
Function Category: Most Recently Used, All, Financial, Date & Time, Math & Trig, Statistical, Lookup & Reference, Database, Text, Logical, Information
Function Name: ROUNDUP, SIGN, SIN, SINH, SQRT, SUBTOTAL, SUM, SUMIF, SUMPRODUCT, SUMSQ, SUMX2MY2, SUMX2PY2, SUMXMY2
SUM(number1,number2,...)
Adds its arguments.
Help | Cancel | < Back | Next > | Finish

3 To find SUM in the right-hand box, click on the top function and press the S key. This takes you to the first function beginning with S. Scroll down, choose *SUM*, and click on the *Next* button.

4 The second *Function Wizard* dialog box appears. You will see a flashing insertion point in the *number1* box where you enter the required arguments — in this case, select the range B3:B6 by clicking on cell B3 in your worksheet and dragging down through B6. Click on *Finish* in the *Function Wizard* dialog box.

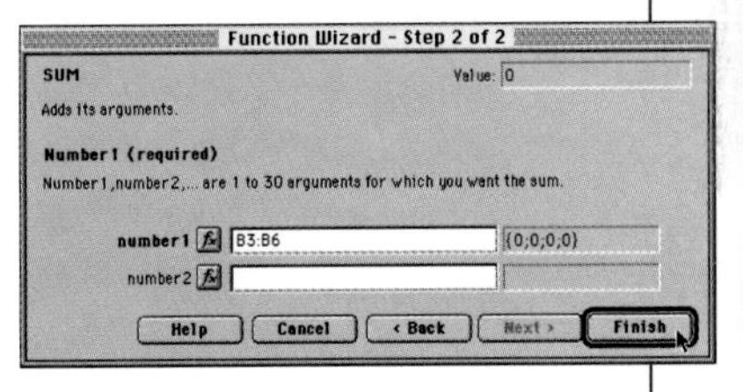

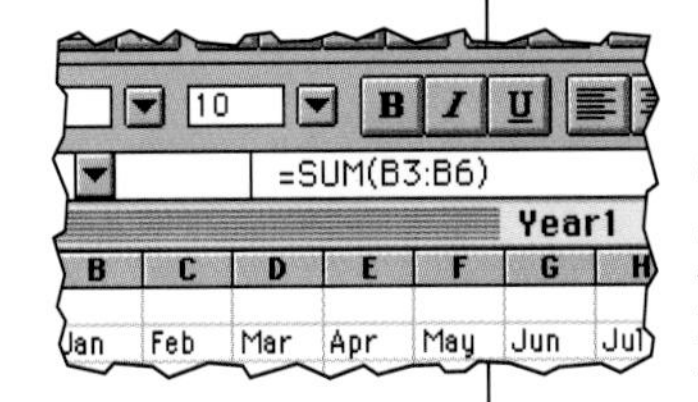

5 If you look in the formula bar with cell B7 still selected, you will see that the formula *=SUM(B3:B6)* is displayed in full. Now use the fill handle to copy this formula into the range C7:M7. For now, the whole range fills with zeroes.

Ungroup Sheets
Insert...
Delete
Rename...
Move or Copy...
Select All Sheets

Shortcut Menu

You are still working on both worksheets. You no longer want to do this, so hold down Control, point to the **Annual Income** sheet tab and hold down the mouse button. Choose *Ungroup Sheets* from the shortcut menu.

Now enter the data in row 1 and rows 3 through 6 shown at right — the monthly totals are calculated automatically.

A	B	C	D	E	F	G	H	I	J	K	L	M
ANNUAL INCOME SUMMARY												
	Jan	Feb	Mar	Apr	May	Jun	Jul	Aug	Sep	Oct	Nov	Dec
Spells	120	504	712	936	1544	552	560	896	472	592	568	944
Potions	38.5	132	363	198	330	495	220	220	231	60.5	341	341
Curses	21	42	105	70	70	63	63	56	56	91	91	49
Prophecies	-4.5	9	-9	22.5	36	-9	13.5	18	36	40.5	9	18
TOTAL	175	687	1171	1227	1980	1101	857	1190	795	784	1009	1352

Calculating Averages

Excel provides many simple but useful functions for statistical analysis of worksheet data. On his annual income summary, Merlin would like to calculate his average monthly income over the whole year. To do this, you can use the AVERAGE function on the **Annual Income** worksheet.

1 In cell A9 type **AVERAGE MONTHLY INCOME.** Now click on cell G9.

	A	B	C	D	E	F	G	H
1	ANNUAL INCOME SUMMARY							
2		Jan	Feb	Mar	Apr	May	Jun	Jul
3	Spells	120	504	712	936	1544	552	560
4	Potions	38.5	132	363	198	330	495	220
5	Curses	21	42	105	70	70	63	63
6	Prophecies	-4.5	9	-9	22.5	36	-9	13.5
7	TOTAL	175	687	1171	1227	1980	1101	857
8								
9	AVERAGE MONTHLY INCOME							
10								

2 Click on the Function Wizard button on the Standard toolbar.

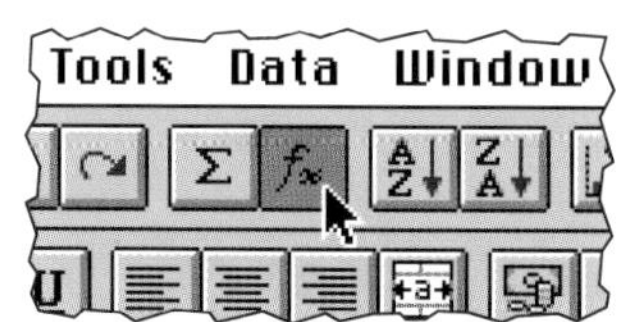

3 In the first *Function Wizard* dialog box, select *Statistical* from the *Function Category* box. Then choose *AVERAGE* from the *Function Name* list. Click on the *Next* button.

4 The second *Function Wizard* dialog box appears. To specify the values for which you want the average, click on cell B7 and drag through M7 (you may have to move the dialog box first by dragging its title bar). Click on the *Finish* button.

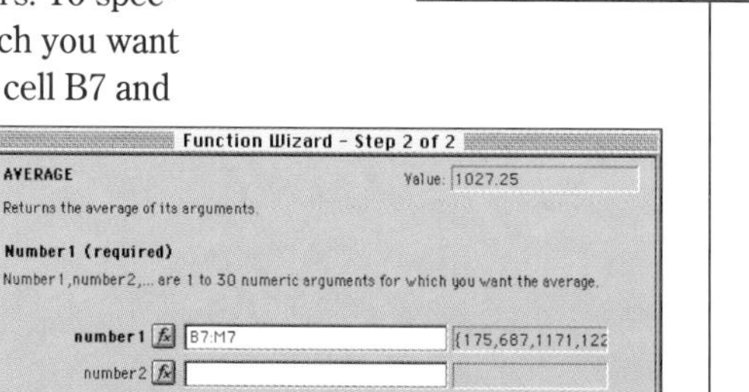

5 You can see that the monthly average income — **1027** — is now displayed in cell G9.

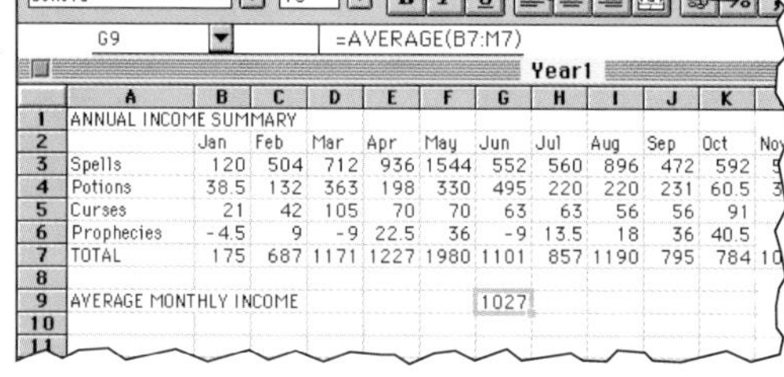

G9 =AVERAGE(B7:M7)

Year1

	A	B	C	D	E	F	G	H	I	J	K
1	ANNUAL INCOME SUMMARY										
2		Jan	Feb	Mar	Apr	May	Jun	Jul	Aug	Sep	Oct
3	Spells	120	504	712	936	1544	552	560	896	472	592
4	Potions	38.5	132	363	198	330	495	220	220	231	60.5
5	Curses	21	42	105	70	70	63	63	56	56	91
6	Prophecies	-4.5	9	-9	22.5	36	-9	13.5	18	36	40.5
7	TOTAL	175	687	1171	1227	1980	1101	857	1190	795	784
8											
9	AVERAGE MONTHLY INCOME						1027				
10											

Funky Functions

Don't be put off by some of the complex-looking functions that Excel offers. There are some familiar functions as well, such as SQRT (calculates the square root of a number) and ROUND (rounds a number to a specified number of digits). For descriptions of specific functions, click on *Reference Information* in the *MS Excel Help* Contents screen, then choose *Worksheet Functions* and browse through the lists of functions.

Minimum and Maximum

The MIN and MAX functions allow you to select the lowest and highest values from a range of cells. Before trying them out, set up Merlin's annual expenses summary. Click on the **Annual Expenses** sheet tab. Enter the data shown at left into cell A1 and the range A3 through M6. Excel will automatically calculate the totals in row 7 because you already entered the SUM function.

	A	B	C	D	E	F	G	H	I	J	K	L	M
1	ANNUAL EXPENSES SUMMARY												
2		Jan	Feb	Mar	Apr	May	Jun	Jul	Aug	Sep	Oct	Nov	Dec
3	Cave rent	50	47	45	36	46	48	43	42	51	54	55	59
4	Wands	20	19	2	4	2	6	9	12	14	12	18	20
5	Fuel	10	9	8	4	5	6	3	8	6	9	2	4
6	Newt tails	3	5	4	7	8	10	2	3	2	9	4	1
7	TOTAL	83	80	59	51	61	70	57	65	73	84	79	84

Now you can use the MIN and MAX functions to display Merlin's lowest and highest monthly expenses.

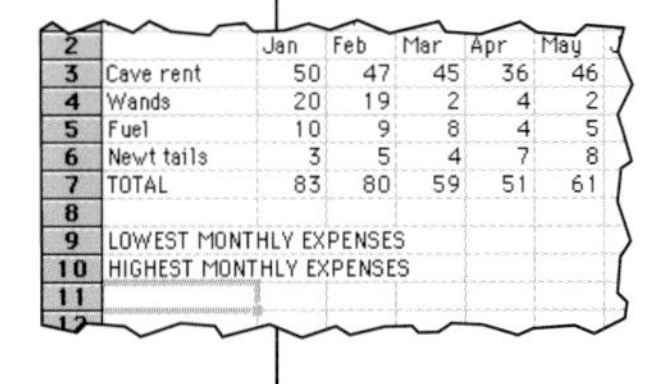

1 Click on cell A9 and enter **LOWEST MONTHLY EXPENSES**. Click on cell A10 and enter **HIGHEST MONTHLY EXPENSES**.

2 Click on cell G9 and then on the Function Wizard button.

3 From the *Function Wizard* dialog box, choose *Statistical* under *Function Category*. Scroll down to *MIN* under *Function Name*. Click on *MIN*, and then click on *Next*.

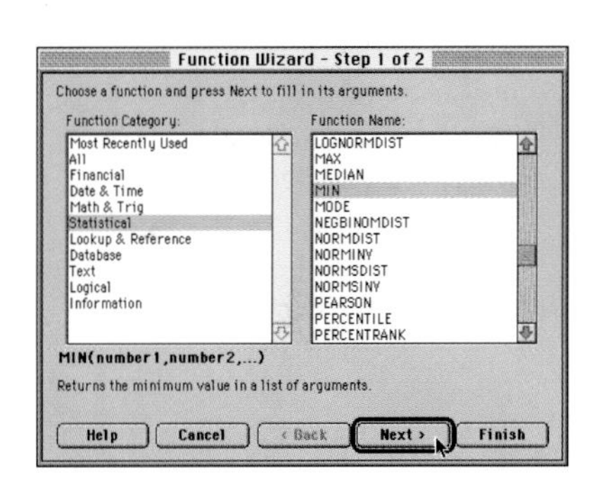

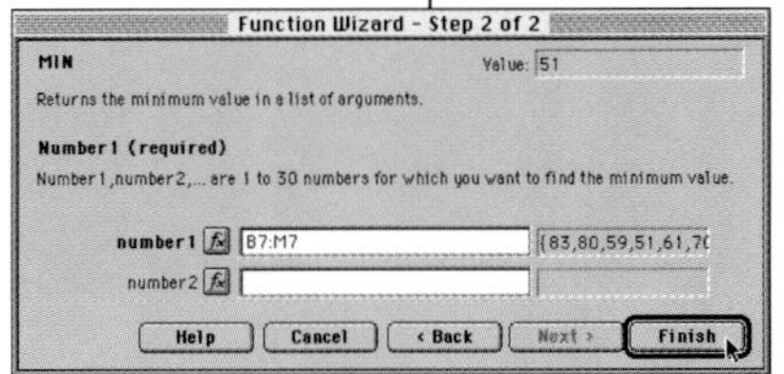

4 Click on cell B7 and drag across through cell M7 to specify the range of values from which you want Excel to find the lowest value. Your cell range is displayed in the *number1* box. Click on *Finish*.

Error Alert!
Sometimes when you are using formulas and functions, Excel alerts you to a problem in calculating a formula and displays an error value, such as #DIV/0!, #NAME?, #N/A!, or #VALUE!, in one or more cells. For an explanation of error values, see page 123 in the Reference Section.

5 The MAX function works in a similar way. Click on cell G10, and then click on the Function Wizard button. In the first dialog box, choose *Statistical* under *Function Category*, and *MAX* under *Function Name*. Click on *Next*.

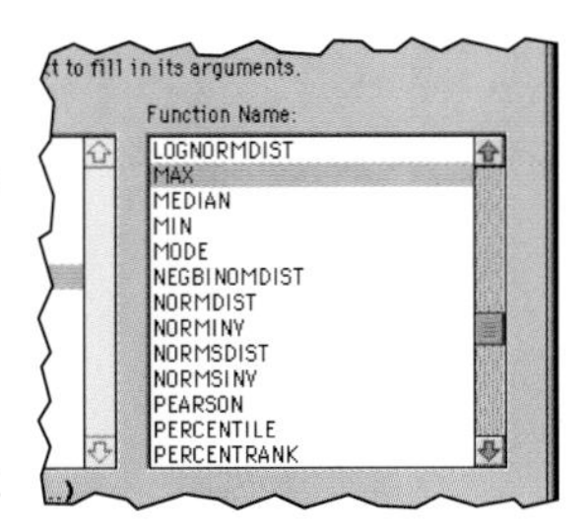

6 Click on cell B7 and drag across through cell M7. Then click on *Finish*.

7 Merlin's lowest and highest monthly expenses are displayed in cells G9 and G10. Before you go any further, save the workbook.

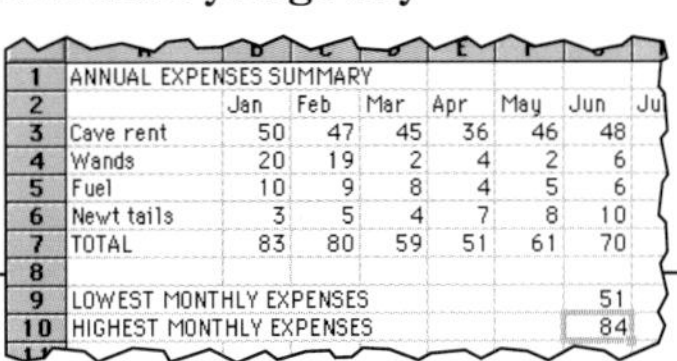

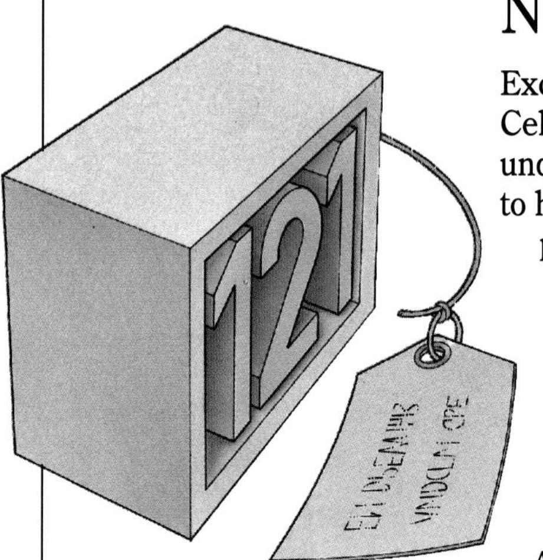

Naming Cells and Ranges

Excel allows you to give names to cells or cell ranges. Cell and range naming can make worksheets easier to understand and use. For example, you can use names to help you navigate through large worksheets (see page 117), and you can use names instead of cell or range references when linking one worksheet to another (see page 64). Using names can also help you avoid errors when writing formulas. For example, if you mistype a name in a formula, you'll get an error message; if you mistype a cell address, you won't get a warning, just an incorrect result.

Before you start naming cells, click on the **Annual Income** sheet tab.

Name with Care!
Cell or range names can contain any type of character except spaces or hyphens. However, names must always start with a letter (A-Z), and they must not look like cell references. It is always a good idea to make names as meaningful as possible, especially if you are likely to keep and use your worksheet for more than a few days.

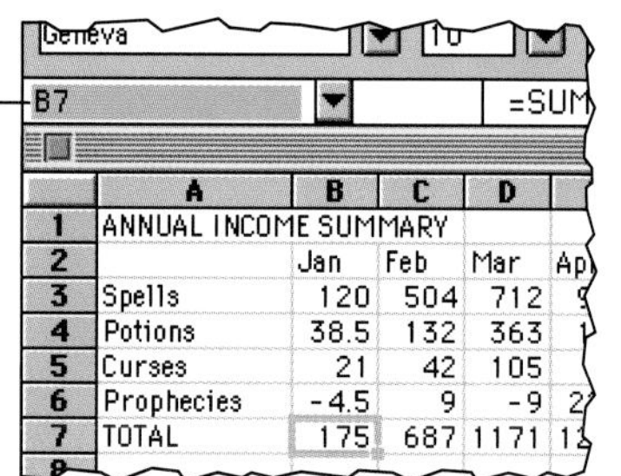

Name Box

1 Click on cell B7, and then click in the name box at the left of the formula bar. The cell reference B7 is highlighted.

2 Type the name **TotalJan** to overwrite B7 and press Enter. B7 can now be referred to as either B7 or **TotalJan**.

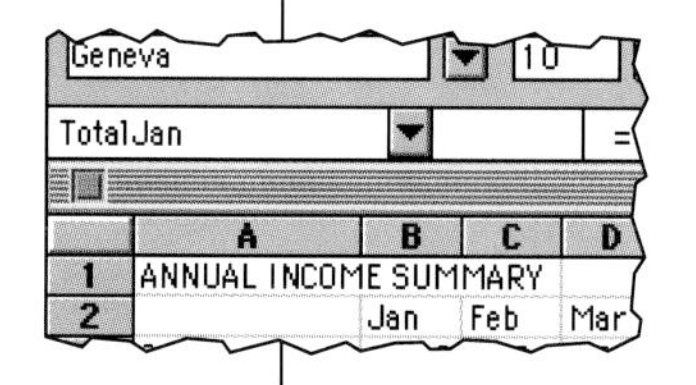

Repeat this procedure for the remaining eleven months in cells C7 through M7, naming them **TotalFeb** through **TotalDec**.

NAMING CELL RANGES

You can name cell ranges as well as individual cells. You can select a block of cells and name individual ranges of cells within the block using existing column and row headings.

Case Sensitive?
When you are naming cells or ranges, Excel does not mind if they are typed in upper case or lower case. For example, **Total**, **total**, and **TOTAL** are all treated as exactly the same name.

View Insert Format Tools Data
Cells... ⌘I
Rows
Columns
Worksheet
Chart
Macro
Page Break
Function...
Name
Note...
Object...
Define... ⌘L
Paste...
Create...
Apply...

1 Select the cell range A2 through M7, and then choose *Name* from the *Insert* menu. From the submenu, choose *Create*.

2 The *Create Names* dialog box appears. Excel suggests naming ranges within the block of cells using the labels in the top row and left-hand column. Click on *OK*.

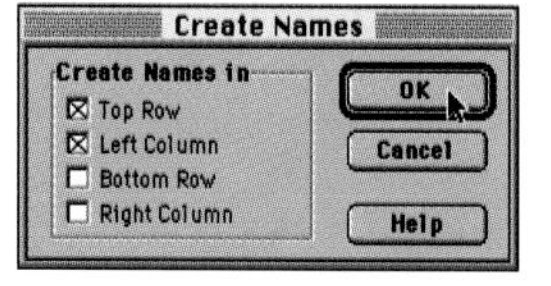

3 You can view the names by clicking on the down arrow next to the name box in the formula bar. Scroll through the pop-up list of names that appears.

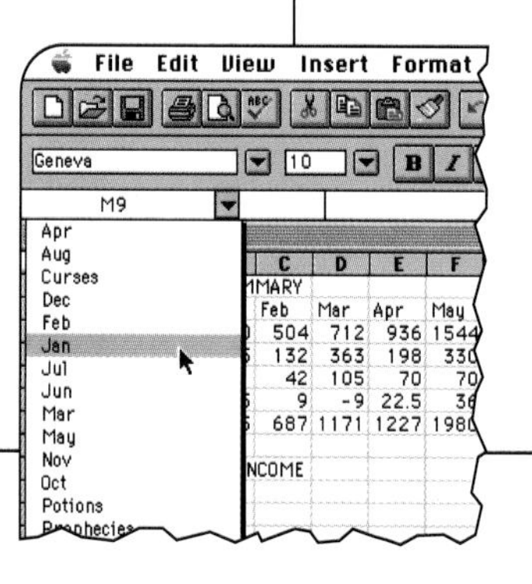

The list of names includes named individual cells, such as **TotalApr** (the name for cell E7), and named ranges, such as **Jul** (which refers to the range H3:H7) and **Curses** (which refers to the range B5:M5). Choose **Spells** from the pop-up list of names and you will see the range B3:M3 selected in the worksheet. Look in the name box and you will see the name of the range — **Spells**. This range can now be referred to as either B3:M3 or **Spells**.

Unique Names!
You can use a particular name only once in any workbook. For example, you cannot give the same name to identical cells or ranges within two different worksheets in the same workbook or to two ranges within the same worksheet.

NAMES IN FORMULAS

At the moment all your worksheet formulas are still using cell or range references. For example, the formula in cell G9, which calculates the average monthly income, is **=AVERAGE(B7:M7)**. However, formulas can easily be converted so that they use names instead of cell or range references. For example double-click on cell G9 and edit the formula in this cell to **=AVERAGE(TOTAL)**. When you press Enter, you will see that because **TOTAL** is the name for the range B7:M7, the new formula returns the same result as it did previously.

G9 =AVERAGE(TOTAL)

Year1

	A	B	C	D	E	F	G	H	I	J	K	L
1	ANNUAL INCOME SUMMARY											
2		Jan	Feb	Mar	Apr	May	Jun	Jul	Aug	Sep	Oct	Nov
3	Spells	120	504	712	936	1544	552	560	896	472	592	568
4	Potions	38.5	132	363	198	330	495	220	220	231	60.5	341
5	Curses	21	42	105	70	70	63	63	56	56	91	91
6	Prophecies	-4.5	9	-9	22.5	36	-9	13.5	18	36	40.5	9
7	TOTAL	175	687	1171	1227	1980	1101	857	1190	795	784	1009
8												
9	AVERAGE MONTHLY INCOME						=AVERAGE(TOTAL)					
10												
11												

It isn't necessary to use manual methods to incorporate names into your formulas; Excel has a facility that lets you convert your formulas automatically. Start by selecting the cell range A2 through M7.

Intersecting Names
You can specify the area of a worksheet where two ranges intersect by typing the two range names separated by a space. After creating names for ranges in your worksheet, try entering **=Aug Spells** into a blank cell in your worksheet. The value in cell I3 (the point where the two ranges **Aug** and **Spells** intersect) is displayed.

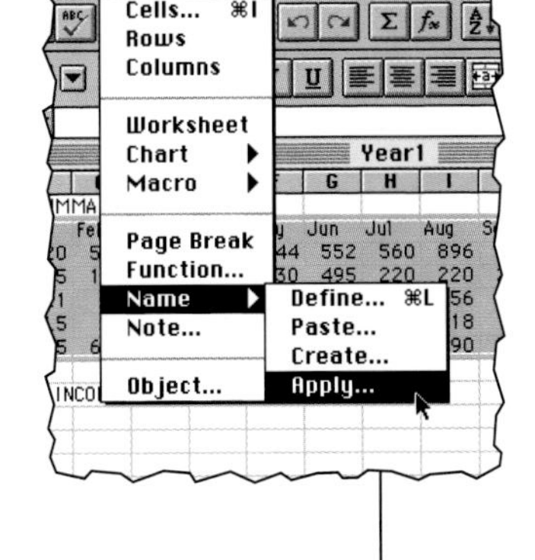

1 Choose *Name* from the *Insert* menu and *Apply* from the submenu. The *Apply Name* command searches for formulas in selected cells and replaces cell or range references with names defined for them.

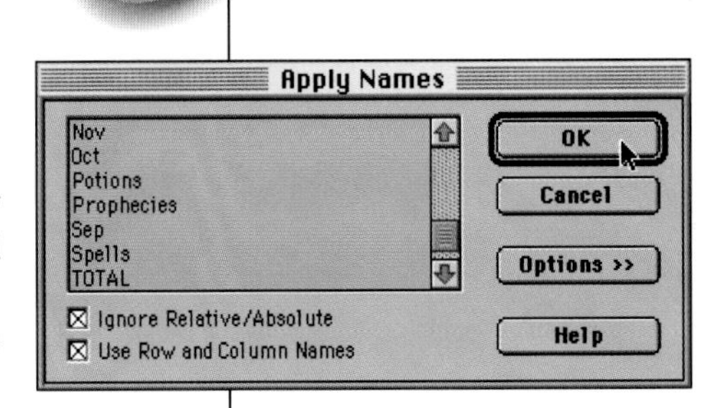

2 The *Apply Names* dialog box appears. Check that all your row and column names (such as **Jan** and **Spells**) are highlighted under *Apply Names* (if they are not, click on each in turn). Then click on *OK*.

All the formulas in your selected cell range have now been converted. You can check this by clicking on cell B7. The formula has changed from **=SUM(B3:B6)** to **=SUM((Spells Jan):(Prophecies Jan))**. Now save your **Year1** workbook.

Multiple Worksheets

EXCEL LETS YOU VIEW and manipulate more than one workbook or worksheet at the same time. This makes it easier to copy and paste data from one worksheet or workbook to another. You can also create Excel links so that changes to the data in one worksheet are automatically reflected in another worksheet, even in a different workbook. In this section, you'll link Merlin's annual income and expense worksheets to a new annual profit worksheet.

Arranging Workbook Windows

Each Excel workbook appears in its own window and can display only one worksheet at a time. If you want to view more than one worksheet, from the same or from a different workbook, you will need to manage the windows to make the best use of the limited screen space. Besides using the mouse to activate, reposition, and resize windows, you can manage windows by choosing commands from the *Window* menu.

Vanishing Window? Sometimes you might find that a workbook window "disappears" behind another, so that it is totally obscured. You can still find it, though, either by choosing from the list of open windows on the *Window* menu, or by using the keyboard shortcut Command-F6 to cycle around the open windows.

THE WINDOW MENU

The *Arrange* command in the *Window* menu opens a dialog box that gives you options for arranging all the windows you have open. For example, windows can be arranged horizontally or tiled. The *Hide* and *Unhide* commands can be used to make specified windows disappear or reappear. All open windows are listed at the bottom of the menu, with a check marking the currently active window. You can activate any window in this list by clicking on it.

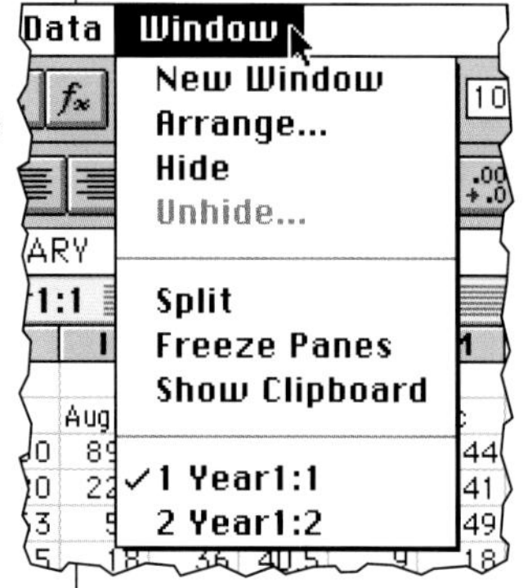

To see how multiple viewing works, let's look at two worksheets from the same workbook at the same time. With the workbook **Year1** open, activate the **Annual Income** worksheet.

1 Choose *New Window* from the *Window* menu. This produces a duplicate version of the **Year1** workbook. This is not a new workbook, simply a second window containing the same workbook.

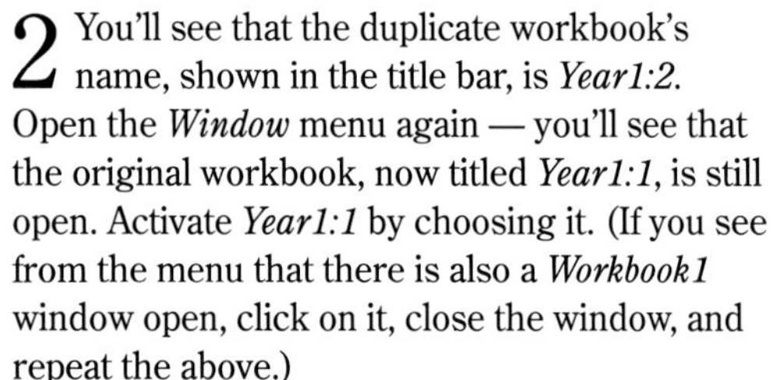

2 You'll see that the duplicate workbook's name, shown in the title bar, is *Year1:2*. Open the *Window* menu again — you'll see that the original workbook, now titled *Year1:1*, is still open. Activate *Year1:1* by choosing it. (If you see from the menu that there is also a *Workbook1* window open, click on it, close the window, and repeat the above.)

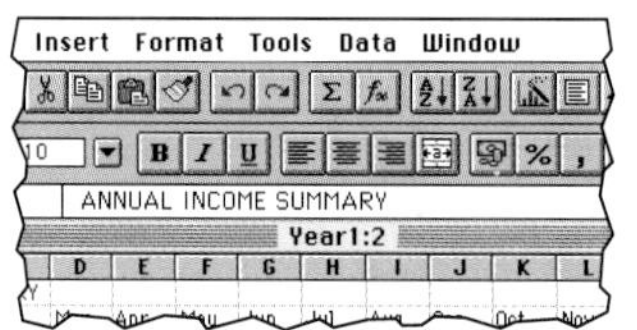

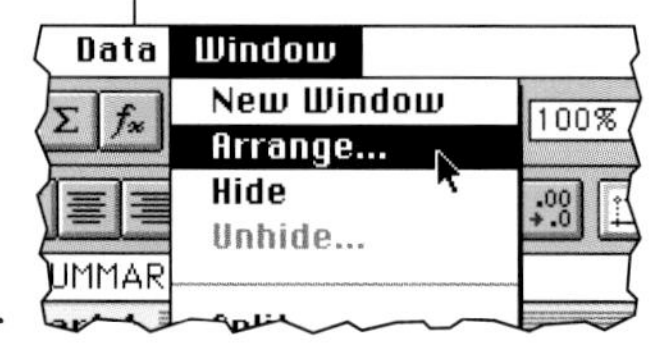

3 Choose *Arrange* from the *Window* menu. The *Arrange Windows* dialog box is displayed.

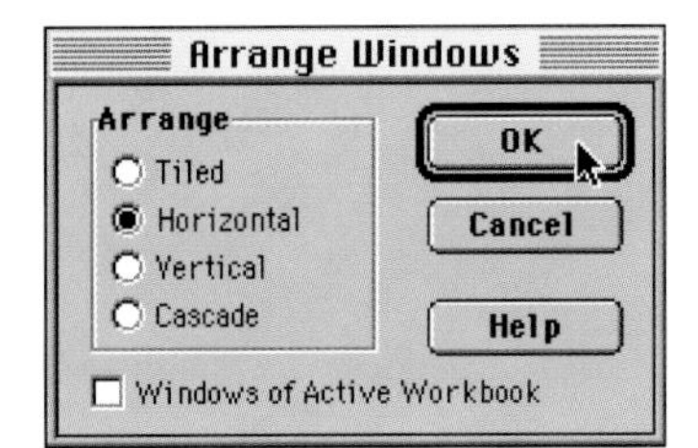

4 Choose *Horizontal* under *Arrange*, and then click on *OK*.

5 You can now see both copies of **Year1**. Activate the lower window by clicking on it, and then click on the **Annual Expenses** sheet tab. You can now view both the **Annual Income** and **Annual Expenses** worksheets at the same time.

Copying Data Between Worksheets

To see how to copy and link data between worksheets, let's create a new worksheet, view it with the two worksheets in **Year1** that are currently open, and then copy some data into it. Activate the upper window (**Year1:1**), double-click on *Sheet3* and rename it **Annual Profit**.

1 Make the widths of columns B through M consistent with the other worksheets. Select the columns, choose *Column* from the *Format* menu, *Width* from the submenu, enter **4** into the dialog box, and click on *OK*. Enter the labels shown above in columns A and N. Choose *New Window* and then *Arrange* from the *Window* menu.

2 In the *Arrange Windows* dialog box, click on *Horizontal* and then on *OK*. If you click on the **Annual Income** tab in the **Year1:1** window, you will now see all three worksheets — **Annual Profit**, **Annual Income**, and **Annual Expenses**.

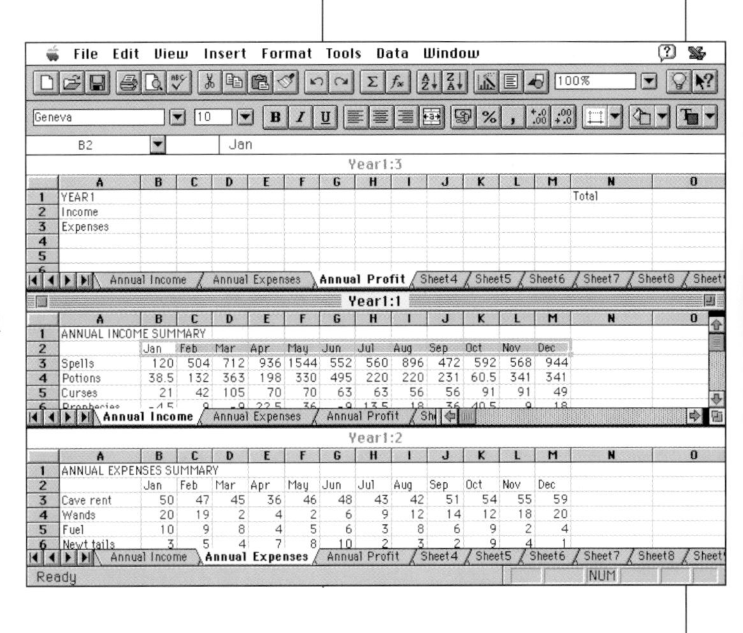

3 To see how simple it is to copy data between windows, you can copy the month labels from **Annual Income** into **Annual Profit**. Click on **Annual Income** and select the cell range B2 through M2. Choose *Copy* from the *Edit* menu.

4 Finally, click on **Annual Profit** and select cell B1. Choose *Paste* from the *Edit* menu.

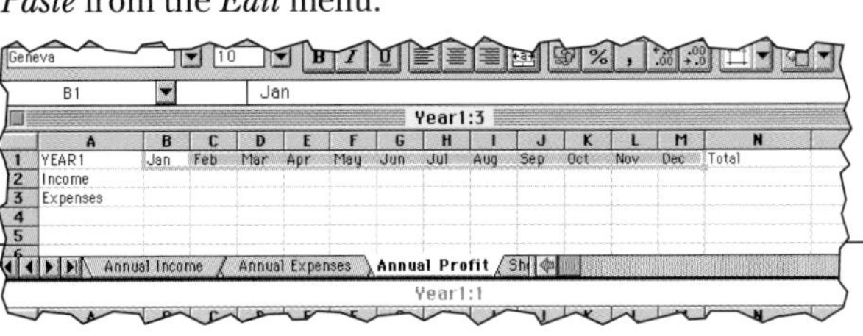

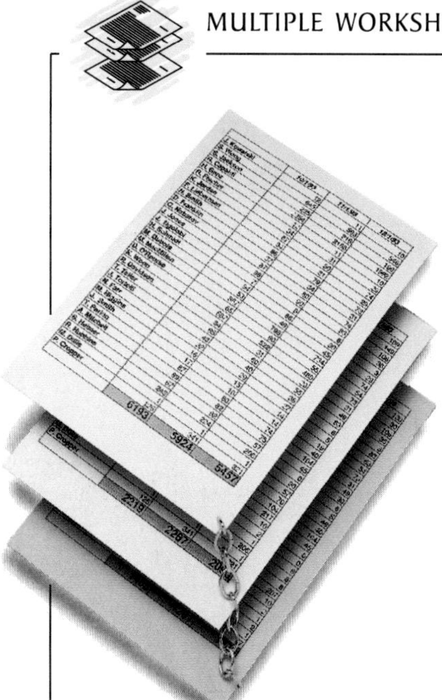

Linking Your Worksheets

The ability to link worksheets and workbooks is one of Excel's most powerful features. For example, you can link data from a number of worksheets into a summary worksheet in the same or a different workbook knowing that any changes in the source data will be reflected in the summary, or dependent, worksheet.

EXCEL LINKS

An Excel link consists of an external reference indicator (represented by an exclamation mark), used to "point" to the cell or cell range in the worksheet from which the data is coming. Any changes made to this source data are transmitted to the dependent worksheet. You can create links by using the *Paste Special* command, by typing in external references directly, or by pointing.

PASTING A LINK

In our example, **Annual Income** and **Annual Expenses** are the source worksheets, and **Annual Profit** is the dependent worksheet. Let's use the *Paste Special* command to link the total expenses for each month into the profit summary sheet.

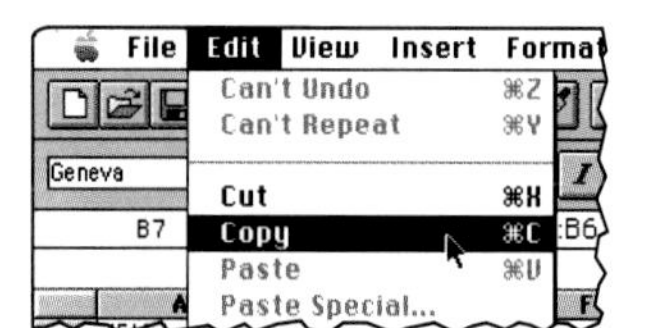

1 Click on the **Annual Expenses** worksheet. Scroll down to and click on cell B7. Choose *Copy* from the *Edit* menu.

2 Click on **Annual Profit** and then on cell B3. Choose *Paste Special* from the *Edit* menu. The *Paste Special* dialog box is displayed.

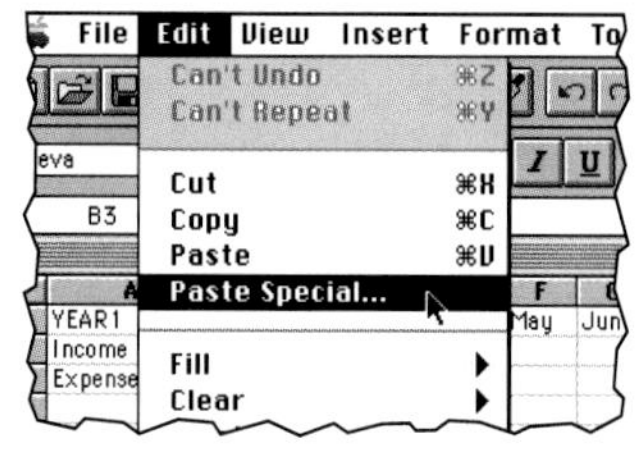

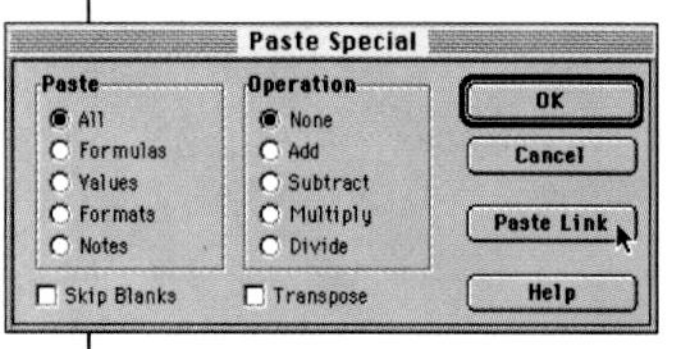

3 In the dialog box, click on the *Paste Link* button.

4 Look at the formula bar. You'll see that you have created a link to a cell in **Annual Expenses**. The formula refers to cell $B$7, preceded by the external reference indicator (!) and the worksheet name.

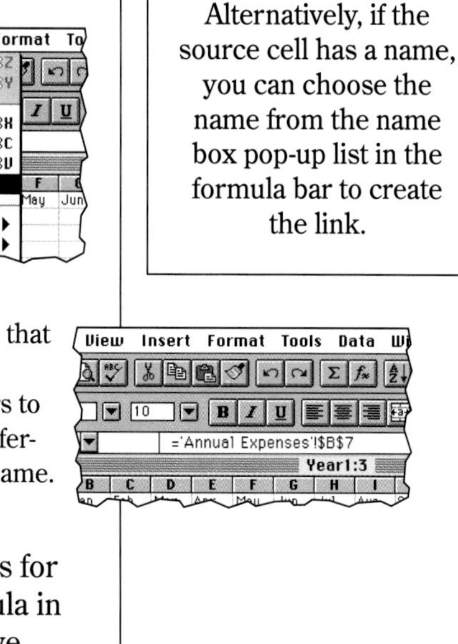

You can use a shortcut to copy the total expenses for the other eleven months. By changing the formula in cell B3 from an absolute reference to a relative reference you will be able to copy the formula across using the drag and fill method.

Double-click on cell B3, and edit the formula so that it reads **='Annual Expenses'!B7**. Now drag the fill handle across to cell M3. Click on cell C3 — you can see that it now contains the formula **='Annual Expenses'!C7**.

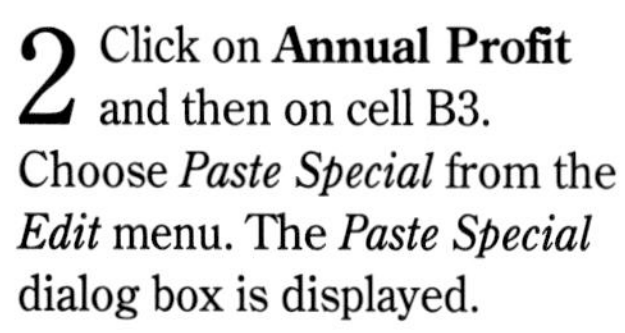

Pointing and Linking
You can also create an Excel link by "pointing" with the mouse. Select the cell in the dependent worksheet to contain the link, type **=**, activate the source worksheet, and then point to and click on the cell that contains the source data. Finally, press Enter. Alternatively, if the source cell has a name, you can choose the name from the name box pop-up list in the formula bar to create the link.

TYPING A LINK

If your worksheets contain named cells, and you know the names you want to use, it may be quicker to type in the links manually. Use this method to link the income data in **Annual Income** to **Annual Profit**.

1 In cell B2 of **Annual Profit**, enter the formula **=TotalJan**. Click on the Enter button, and you'll see the value from cell B7 of the **Annual Income** sheet displayed. Because the name **TotalJan** can be used only once in the **Year1** workbook, the formula need not contain the worksheet name.

2 To link the other monthly income totals, select cell B2 and drag the fill handle across to cell M2. Edit each cell individually, replacing **Jan** with the correct month.

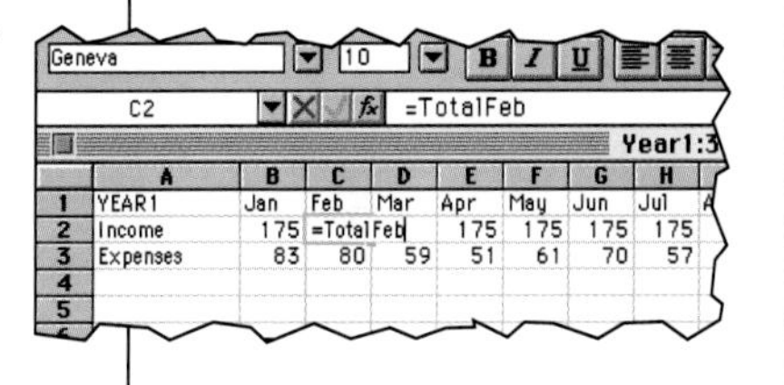

3 Complete the **Annual Profit** worksheet by selecting N2:N3 and clicking on the AutoSum button on the Standard toolbar. Then select cell N4 and type **=N2-N3**.

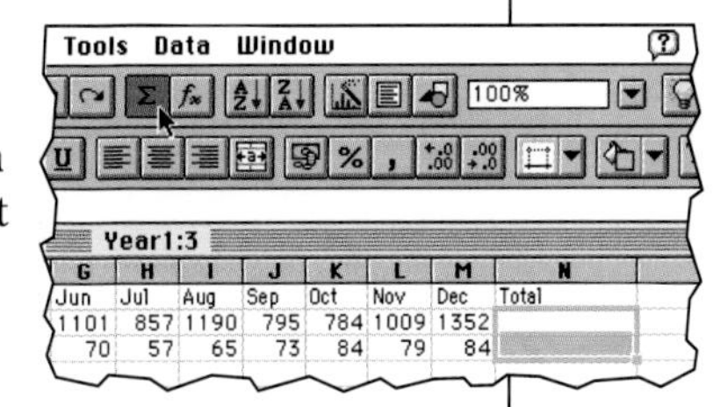

TESTING THE LINKS

You can test whether the links are working by altering data in a source worksheet and checking that the changes are reflected in the dependent worksheet. A customer who received some faulty spells in December asked for his money back. As a result, Merlin's December income has fallen. Select cell M3 in the **Annual Income** worksheet and replace **944** with **920**. When you press Enter, the value in cell M2 of the **Annual Profit** falls to 1328.

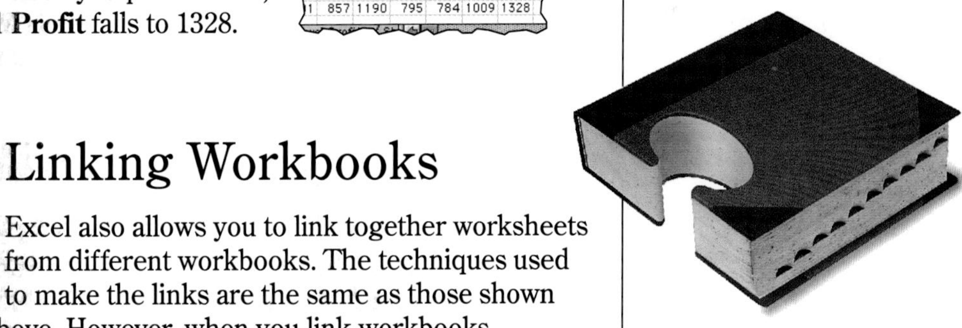

Linking Workbooks

Excel also allows you to link together worksheets from different workbooks. The techniques used to make the links are the same as those shown above. However, when you link workbooks together, the linking formulas must also include the workbook name. In the example above, if the **Annual Income** and **Annual Expenses** worksheets were in a workbook called **Inc & Exp**, you would have to type the formula **=Inc & Exp!TotalJan** into cell B2 of the **Annual Profit** worksheet. The source workbook does not even have to be open — the linking formula expands to include the workbook's location, allowing the workbook to be found.

Now close the **Year1:2** and **Year1:3** windows by clicking on their close boxes (top left-hand corner of each window). Maximize the remaining window, and then close the **Year1** workbook, saving all changes.

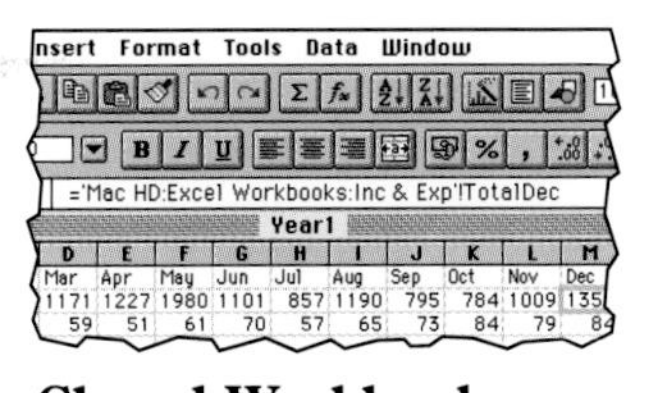

Closed Workbooks

If the source worksheet is not open, the formula is automatically expanded to include the file location.

Which Folder?

When linking worksheets from different workbooks, it is always advisable to save the source and dependent workbooks within the same folder.

3

CHAPTER THREE

Formatting & Printing

Excel not only takes all your data-calculation and manipulation in stride, it also has the tools to make data look good and read easily — on screen, in presentations, and on the printed page. In this chapter you'll learn about the use of fonts, number formatting, alignment, and styles. You'll discover how you can add graphics and text boxes to your worksheets, and you'll learn how to print out worksheets that are attractive and convey professional accuracy.

ON LINE
Reset
MENU
Print Fonts
ENTER
Test
FORM FEED
Continue
Alt
+
–

Formatting Worksheets

EXCEL GIVES YOU CONSIDERABLE control over how data appears, both on screen and on paper. You can choose font and type size as well as typographical effects such as bold, italic, and underlining. You can control how text and numbers are aligned across cells or ranges, and how numbers and dates are displayed. By using colors, borders, and shading patterns, you can emphasize different parts of your worksheet. Once you have formatted your data, you can protect cells from accidental or unauthorized changes.

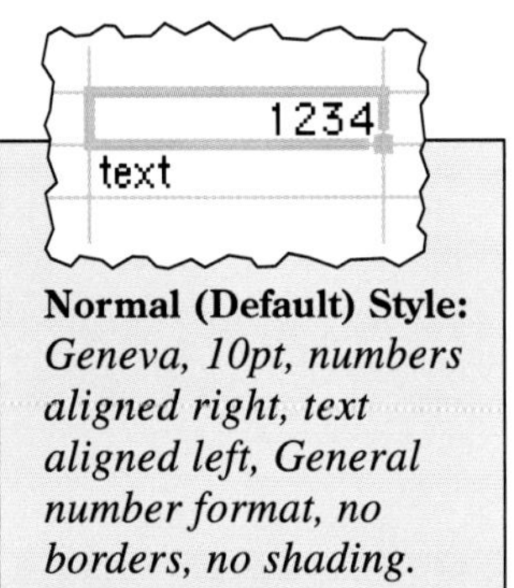

Normal (Default) Style: *Geneva, 10pt, numbers aligned right, text aligned left, General number format, no borders, no shading.*

Formatted Example: *Times, 12pt, red, bold, center-aligned horizontally, Currency number format, outline borders, and light blue shading.*

Formats and Styles

In Excel, a cell's *format* includes attributes such as font, alignment, number format, borders, and shading. A cell's protection attributes (see page 76) are also part of its format. You can quickly apply many types of formatting to selected cells or ranges using buttons on the Formatting toolbar. For more detailed formatting, use the *Format Cells* dialog box. This can be accessed via the *Cells* command on the *Format* menu or the *Format Cells* command on the cell shortcut menu.

A *style* is a defined and named set of formatting attributes. An "unformatted" cell is actually formatted with the Normal (default) style. At the left, you will see two unformatted cells showing the Normal style and the same cells with different formatting attributes applied.

Easy Formatting
Excel provides some special features for formatting worksheets and for copying and applying formats. For tabular data, try using AutoFormat (see page 74). The format painter (also page 74) allows quick copying of formats from one cell to others. You can save any format you create as a style (see page 75), which you can apply later to any worksheet in the same workbook.

The Formatting Toolbar

The Formatting toolbar allows you to choose some common formatting options without using menu commands. It includes buttons for altering font and type size, aligning cell contents, or applying some special effects such as bold or italic, cell borders, cell color, and font color.

The style buttons (Currency, Comma, and Percent) let you apply three built-in styles that affect the way numbers look in cells. The decimal place buttons allow you to increase or decrease the number of decimal places displayed with numbers.

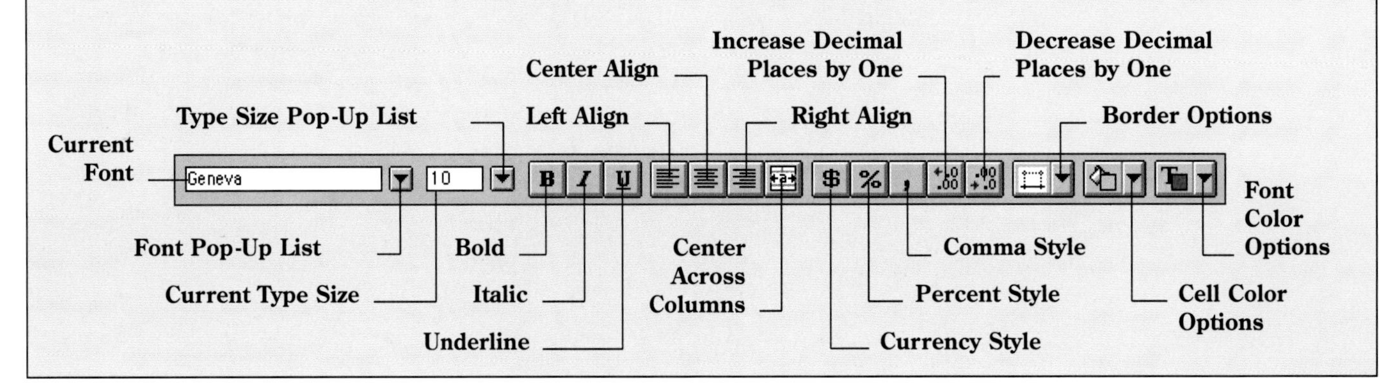

Fonts

Strictly, a font is a specific combination of a typeface (such as Geneva or Helvetica), a type size, and a type style (such as italic or bold). In Excel, the term font is used to mean simply typeface. Choosing the right fonts can be vital for creating attractive and easy-to-read worksheets. But be careful not to use too many fonts on a page or the overall appearance may suffer.

The fonts available to you in Excel depend both on the fonts installed on your Macintosh and on the type of printer you use. Apart from TrueType fonts (see box at right), there may be fonts that are available on screen but not on your printer, and vice-versa.

Times

Zapf Chancery

R

Geneva

TrueType or PostScript?
Excel and other System 7 applications have access to the TrueType family of fonts. These appear the same on screen as they do when printed, and type size can be changed, or scaled, to any point size. For the very best results, though, you may want to consider using PostScript fonts and Adobe Type Manager, a combination that lets you use publication-quality printers.

CHANGING FONTS

To see how formatting in Excel works, you'll practice applying various types of formatting attributes to a copy of one of the worksheets you have created so far. First, you'll change a font. Open the **Year1** workbook, copy it by saving it as **Year1A**, and then display the **Annual Income** worksheet.

1 Select row 2, which contains the months.

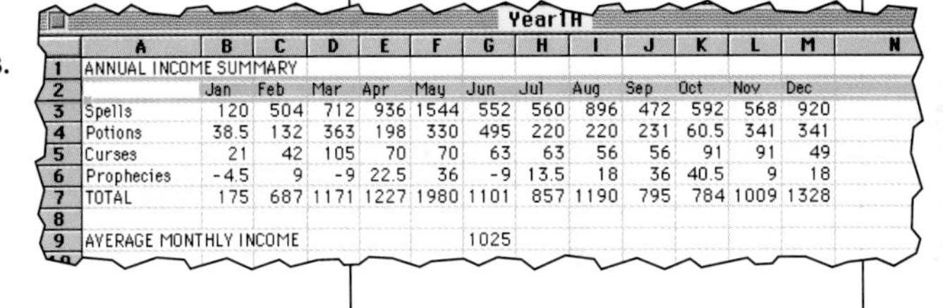

Year1A

	A	B	C	D	E	F	G	H	I	J	K	L	M
1	ANNUAL INCOME SUMMARY												
2		Jan	Feb	Mar	Apr	May	Jun	Jul	Aug	Sep	Oct	Nov	Dec
3	Spells	120	504	712	936	1544	552	560	896	472	592	568	920
4	Potions	38.5	132	363	198	330	495	220	220	231	60.5	341	341
5	Curses	21	42	105	70	70	63	63	56	56	91	91	49
6	Prophecies	-4.5	9	-9	22.5	36	-9	13.5	18	36	40.5	9	18
7	TOTAL	175	687	1171	1227	1980	1101	857	1190	795	784	1009	1328
8													
9	AVERAGE MONTHLY INCOME						1025						

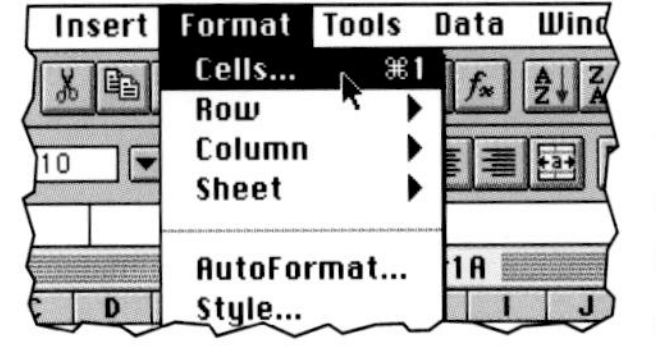

2 Choose *Cells* from the *Format* menu or the *Format Cells* command from the cell shortcut menu. The *Format Cells* dialog box appears. Click on the *Font* tab.

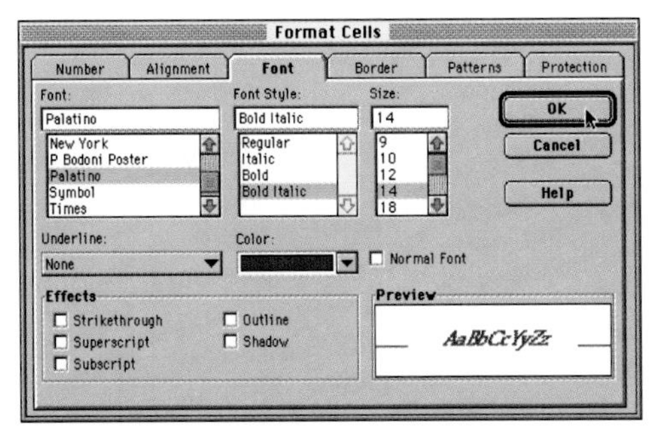

3 In the *Font* flipcard, choose *Palatino* from the *Font* list. You can also select a font style, type size, and other effects such as *Underline* or *Strikethrough* from the *Font* flipcard. Choose *Bold Italic* from the *Font Style* list, *14* pt from the *Size* list, and a dark color from the *Color* pop-up list. Excel displays how the text will look in the *Preview* box. Click on *OK*.

Format Characters?
With Excel version 5, you can apply font formatting to individual characters in cells. Simply double-click on the cell, select the characters you wish to format, and then apply whatever font, type size, font style, and color you wish to those characters.

4 Select the range A3:A7 and choose *Repeat Format Cells* from the *Edit* menu.

5 Because you increased the type size, you need to adjust column widths. Select the range A2:M7, choose *Column* from the *Format* menu and then *AutoFit Selection* from the submenu.

MORE FONT FORMATTING

Now try using the pop-up lists on the Formatting toolbar to apply some more font formatting to the **Annual Income** worksheet.

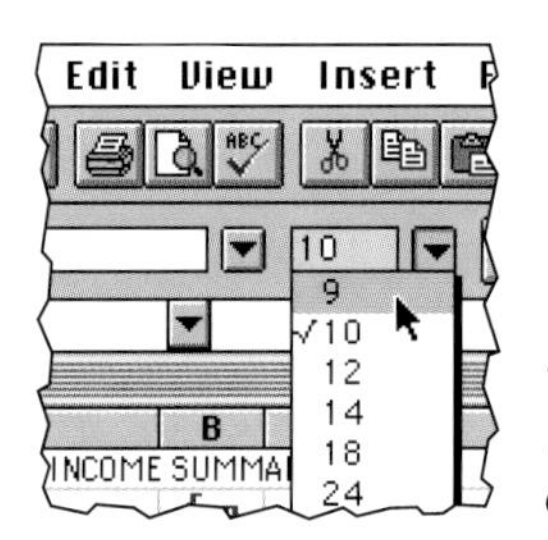

1 Select the range B3:M7 and choose *9* pt from the type size pop-up list on the Formatting toolbar.

2 Select cell A1 (ANNUAL INCOME SUMMARY), hold down Command, and select the range A9:G9, containing the average monthly income data.

3 Choose *Times* from the font pop-up list on the Formatting toolbar. Choose *18* pt from the pop-up type size list.

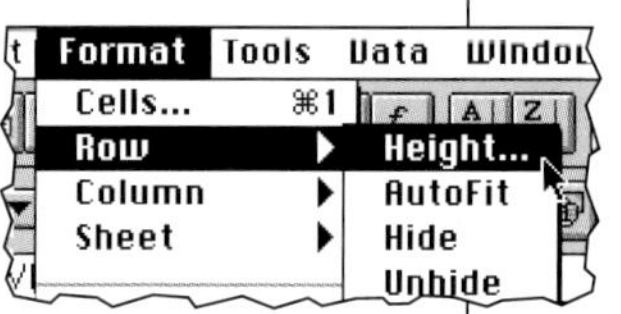

4 The row heights adjust automatically, but you can also control this yourself. With A1 and the range A9:G9 still selected, choose *Row* from the *Format* menu, *Height* from the submenu, enter **25** in the *Row Height* dialog box, and click *OK*.

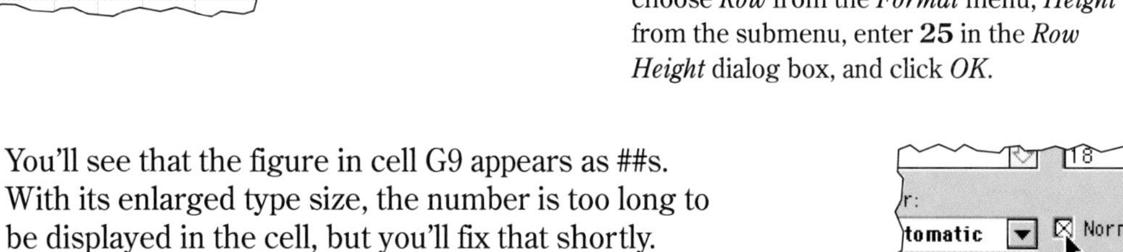

You'll see that the figure in cell G9 appears as ##s. With its enlarged type size, the number is too long to be displayed in the cell, but you'll fix that shortly.

Back to Normal

If you ever want to change cells back to the default font (Geneva 10 pt), select the cells, access the Format Cells *dialog box, and in the* Font *flipcard, check the* Normal Font *box, and click on* OK.

Altering Alignment

Using buttons on the Formatting toolbar, you can align data in various ways — left-aligned, right-aligned, centered, or centered across several cells. The *Alignment* flipcard in the *Format Cells* dialog box provides some extra options: you can align data at the top, center, or bottom within cells, wrap text onto several lines, or even rotate it sideways. Try centering data within a range of cells and also vertically centering some data.

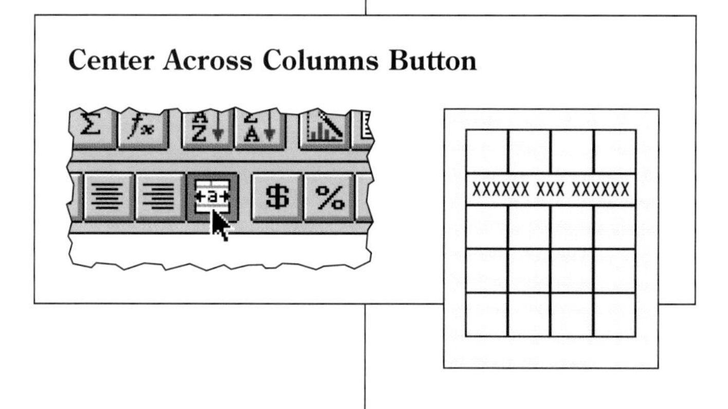

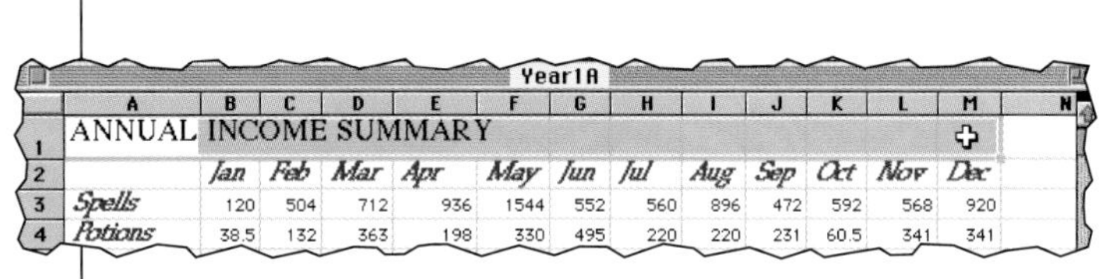

1 Select the range A1:M1, and then click on the Center Across Columns button on the Formatting toolbar.

2 The heading in cell A1 is centered horizontally in the selected range. Now select the range G9:I9 and click on the Center Across Columns button again. You will now be able to see the figure 1025.25.

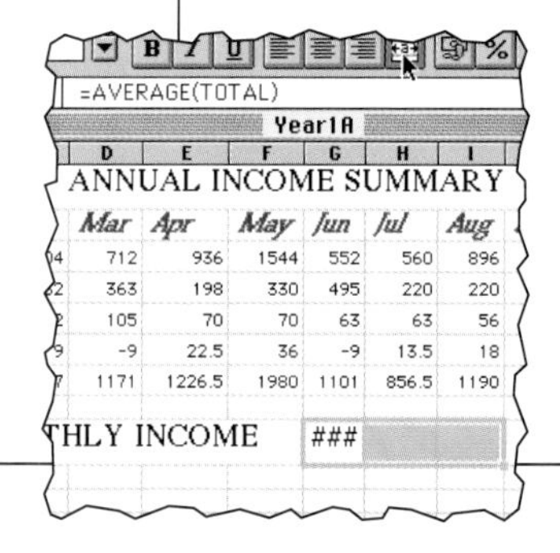

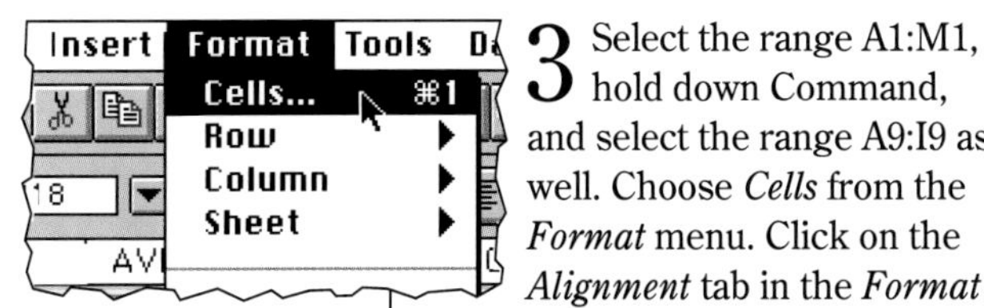

3 Select the range A1:M1, hold down Command, and select the range A9:I9 as well. Choose *Cells* from the *Format* menu. Click on the *Alignment* tab in the *Format Cells* dialog box.

4 Within the *Alignment* flipcard, choose *Center* under *Vertical* and click on *OK*.

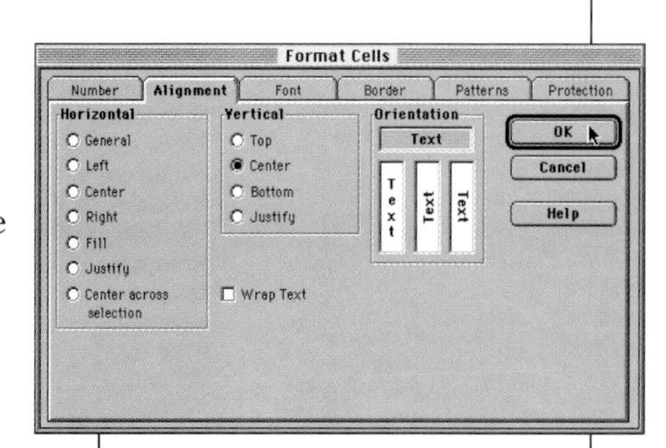

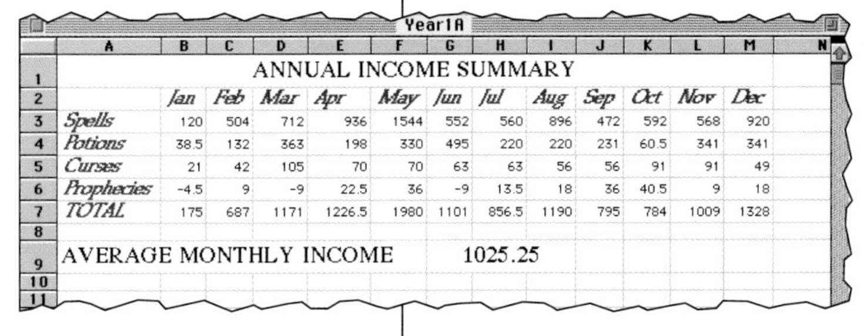

5 The selected data is center-aligned vertically, and the worksheet should now appear as shown at left.

General Who?
All unformatted cells have the General numeric format which is part of the Normal style. Numbers, dates, and times are shown much as they are entered into cells, with a few exceptions. For example, numbers typed surrounded by parentheses are displayed as negative. Very small numbers will appear in scientific notation.

Wrap It?
If you have problems displaying a long text label in a cell, try wrapping it onto several lines. Select the cell containing the label, access the *Format Cells* dialog box, check *Wrap Text* in the *Alignment* flipcard, and click on *OK*.

Formatting Numbers, Dates, and Times

Excel offers a selection of built-in numeric formats, and it is easy for you to define new ones. The built-in formats fall into different categories such as number, currency, date, time, percentage, and fraction.

Numeric formats have codes defining the decimal places to display, the order for displaying days and months in dates, and so on. To apply a numeric format, select the cells and then access the *Number* flipcard in the *Format Cells* dialog box. When you choose from the *Category* list, a list appears in the *Format Codes* box. The code you choose shows in the *Code* edit box.

Number Format Codes

Each number format code can contain up to four fields, separated by semicolons. The first field defines the format that will be given to positive numbers, the second for negative numbers, the third for zero values, and the fourth for text. This table shows how Excel displays 1500, -1500, and 0.5 using some built-in numeric formats.

Category	Format Code	Positive	Negative	Decimal
Default	General	1500	-1500	0.5
Number	0	1500	-1500	1
Number	0.00	1500.00	-1500.00	0.50
Number	#,##0	1,500	-1,500	1
Currency	$#,##0;-$#,##0	$1,500	-$1,500	$1
Currency	$#,##0;[RED]-$#,##0	$1,500	-$1,500*	$1
Currency	$#,##0.00;-$#,##0.00	$1,500.00	-$1,500.00*	$0.50
Percentage	0%	150000%	-150000%	50%
Scientific	0.00E+00	1.50E+03	-1.50E+03	5.00E-01
Fraction	# ?/?	1500	-1500	1/2

*Displayed in red

CHANGING NUMBER FORMAT

Now try altering the numeric format of some data in your **Annual Income** worksheet. At present, all the data has a General numeric format.

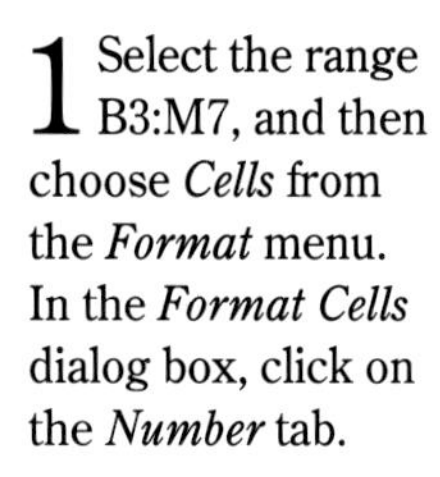

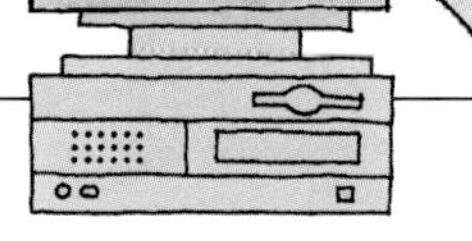

1 Select the range B3:M7, and then choose *Cells* from the *Format* menu. In the *Format Cells* dialog box, click on the *Number* tab.

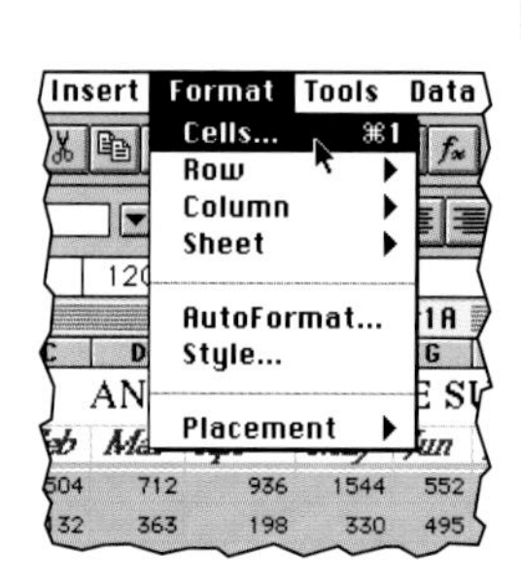

2 In the *Number* flipcard, click on *Number* under *Category*, and choose #,##0; [RED] -#,##0 from the *Format Codes* list box. This format will include a comma with all numbers over 1000, rounds all decimal numbers to the nearest whole number, and will display any negative numbers in red and with a minus sign. Click on *OK*.

3 The negative numbers in the cells in row 6 are now shown with minus signs and in red, and all numbers above 1000 (except the figure in cell G9) have commas.

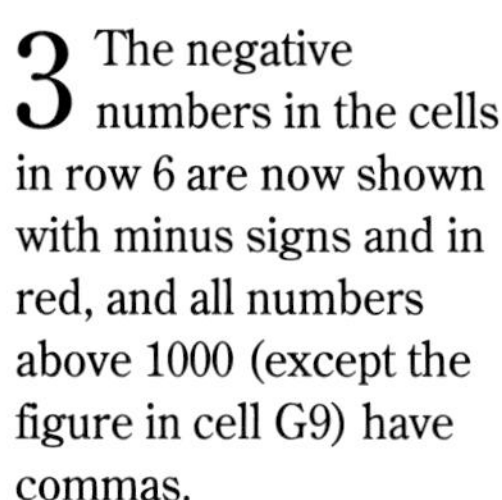

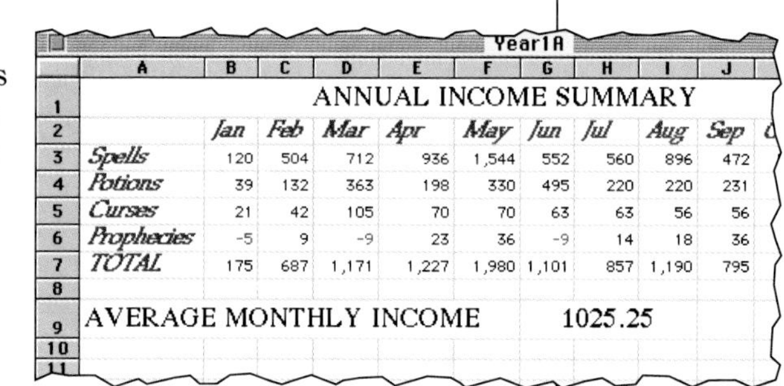

Year1A

	A	B	C	D	E	F	G	H	I	J
1				ANNUAL INCOME SUMMARY						
2		Jan	Feb	Mar	Apr	May	Jun	Jul	Aug	Sep
3	Spells	120	504	712	936	1,544	552	560	896	472
4	Potions	39	132	363	198	330	495	220	220	231
5	Curses	21	42	105	70	70	63	63	56	56
6	Prophecies	-5	9	-9	23	36	-9	14	18	36
7	TOTAL	175	687	1,171	1,227	1,980	1,101	857	1,190	795
8										
9	AVERAGE MONTHLY INCOME						1025.25			
10										

Cut the Clutter

Carefully consider the purpose of your worksheet before applying numeric formats. In financial statements, accuracy is important, but save the $ or other currency symbol for totals and other important values you want to emphasize. For presentations, appearance is the key. Restrict the number of decimal places you display, to suppress needless zeroes.

Comma, Currency, and Percent Style Buttons

Three buttons on the Formatting toolbar — the Comma, Currency, and Percent Style buttons — provide a quick way to apply three types of number format to your selected cells. More precisely, each applies a simple style consisting solely of a number format (see page 75).

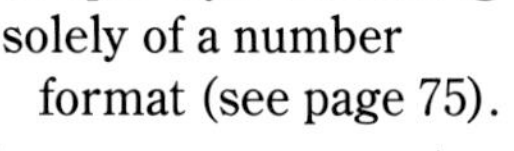

Comma Style Button
The Comma Style button adds a comma to numbers over 1000, displays numbers with a decimal point and two decimal places, and displays negative numbers in parentheses.

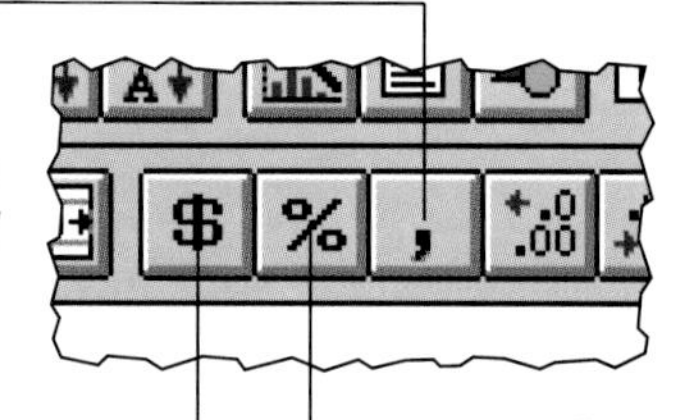

Currency Style Button
The Currency Style button applies the same format as the Comma Style button but adds a $ symbol before the number.

Percent Style Button
The Percent Style button converts numbers into percentages. For example, it converts 0.5 to 50%.

Button Picking!
Note that clicking on the down arrow next to the Borders button on the Formatting toolbar opens up a palette from which you can choose an option. Clicking on the button itself applies the option you last selected, which is displayed on the button. The same rule applies to the Color and Font Color buttons.

Borders and Shading

One important objective of formatting is to visually group data that belong together. Every cell has four borders and any or all can be emphasized. You can apply borders to a cell or range by means of the Borders button on the Formatting toolbar. Alternatively, the *Border* flipcard in the *Format Cells* dialog box allows you to choose a combination of border options, styles, and colors. Choose *Outline* if you want a border all around the selected cell or range.

Another way to add emphasis and separate data is through block patterns and color. You can choose from a range of color and pattern options by using the Color button on the Formatting toolbar, or you can use the *Patterns* flipcard in the *Format Cells* dialog box.

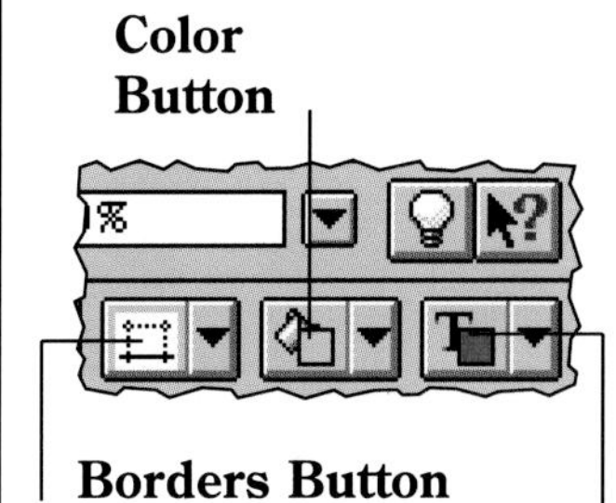

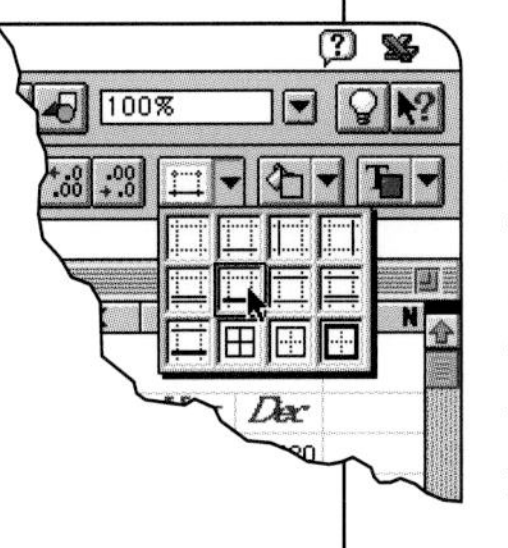

1 Select cells B6 through M6, click on the arrow next to the Borders button on the Formatting toolbar, and choose a thick bottom border from the palette.

2 Now select the range G9:I9. Access the *Format Cells* dialog box, and choose the *Border* tab.

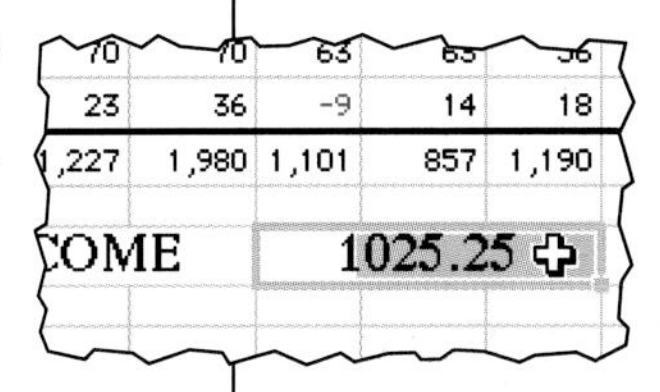

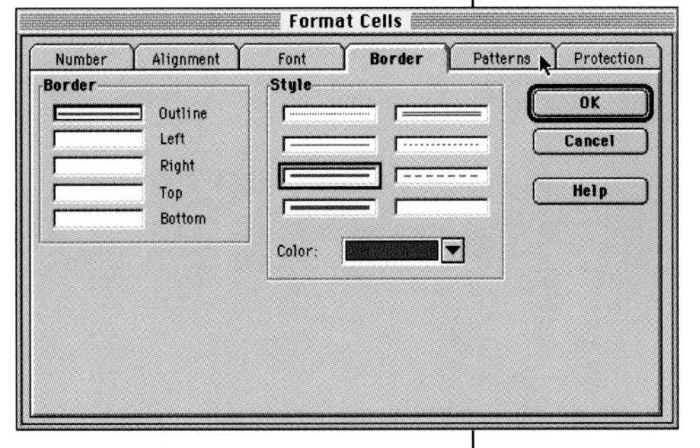

3 In the *Border* flipcard, choose *Outline* under *Border*, a moderately thick line under *Style*, and a dark color from the *Color* box. Then click on the *Patterns* tab.

4 In the *Patterns* flipcard, choose a light shade (such as cream) and click on *OK*.

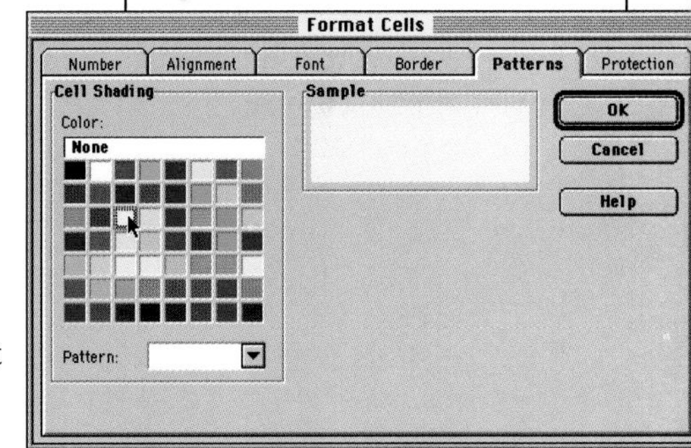

The formatted **Annual Income** worksheet should now look as shown below, with all the changes in number format, center aligning, and font changes, as well as the addition of borders and shading. If you wish, change any of the formatting elements until you achieve a result that you find satisfying. Then save the **Year1A** workbook by choosing *Save* from the *File* menu.

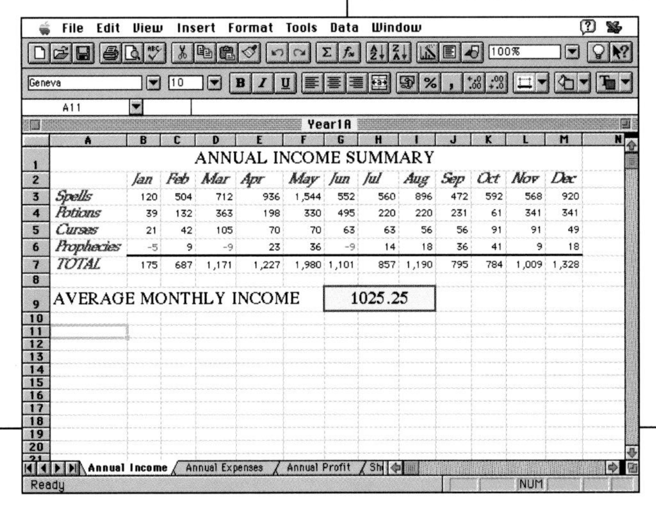

	Jan	Feb	Mar	Apr	May	Jun	Jul	Aug	Sep	Oct	Nov	Dec
Spells	120	504	712	936	1,544	552	560	896	472	592	568	920
Potions	39	132	363	198	330	495	220	220	231	61	341	341
Curses	21	42	105	70	70	63	63	56	56	91	91	49
Prophecies	-5	9	-9	23	36	-9	14	18	36	41	9	18
TOTAL	175	687	1,171	1,227	1,980	1,101	857	1,190	795	784	1,009	1,328

ANNUAL INCOME SUMMARY

AVERAGE MONTHLY INCOME 1025.25

Reverse Shading?
If you apply dark shading to a cell, its contents may be more readable if they are reversed into white. Select the cell, click on the arrow next to the Font Color button on the Formatting toolbar and choose white.

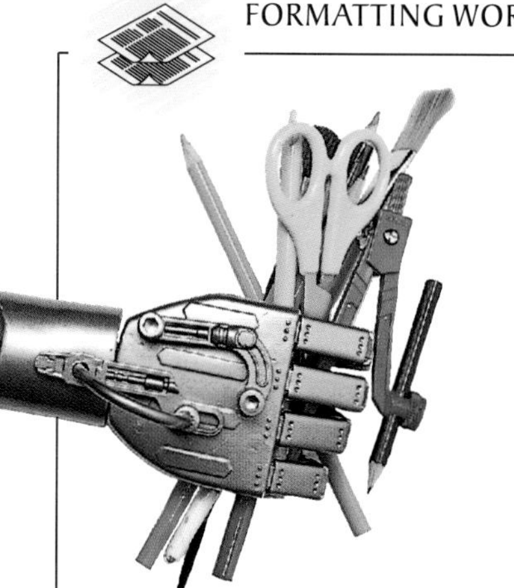

AutoFormat

To format a worksheet that contains data in tabular form, you can make Excel do most of the work by using the AutoFormat feature. To see how it works, open the **Annual Expenses** worksheet in the **Year1A** workbook. You'll format the table contained in the range A1:M7. Select any cell in this range, and then choose *AutoFormat* from the *Format* menu.

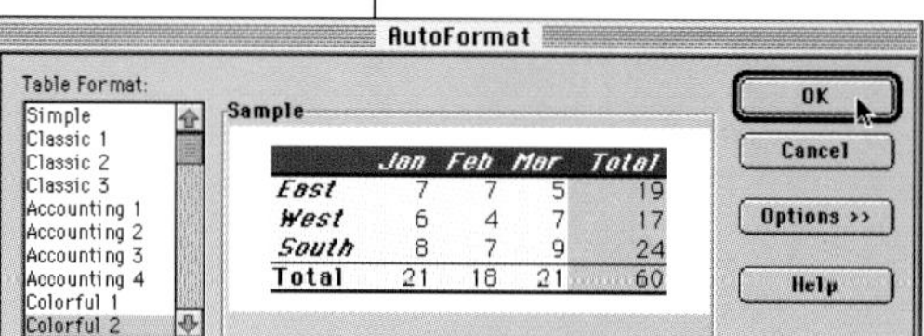

1 The *AutoFormat* dialog box appears with a list of the table formats available and a *Sample* box to show you what the highlighted format looks like. Choose *Colorful 2* from the *Table Format* list, and then click on *OK*.

Auto Impact!
Using AutoFormat may cause row heights and column widths to change for your entire worksheet. To prevent this happening, click on *Options* in the *AutoFormat* dialog box, and under *Formats to Apply*, clear the *Width/Height* check box before clicking on *OK*.

2 The automatic formatting is applied. If you wish, experiment with some of the other table formats.

	A	B	C	D	E	F	G	H	I	J	K	L
1	ANNUAL EXPENSES SUMMARY											
2		Jan	Feb	Mar	Apr	May	Jun	Jul	Aug	Sep	Oct	Nov
3	Cave rent	50	47	45	36	46	48	43	42	51	54	55
4	Wands	20	19	2	4	2	6	9	12	14	12	18
5	Fuel	10	9	8	4	5	6	3	8	6	9	2
6	Newt tails	3	5	4	7	8	10	2	3	2	9	4
7	TOTAL	83	80	59	51	61	70	57	65	73	84	79
8												
9	LOWEST MONTHLY EXPENSES						51					
10	HIGHEST MONTHLY EXPENSES						84					
11												
12												

Copying Formats

Excel provides a very useful tool for copying formats — the format painter. To copy a format from one cell to a single cell or range, you first select the cell with the format you want to copy, click on the Format Painter button on the Standard toolbar, and then select the range where you want the format "painted." Try this on your **Annual Expenses** worksheet.

Multiple Paint?
If you want to copy a format from a selected cell to several nonadjacent cells or ranges, double-click on the Format Painter button, "paint" the cells you wish to take on the format, and press Command-Period or Esc when you have finished.

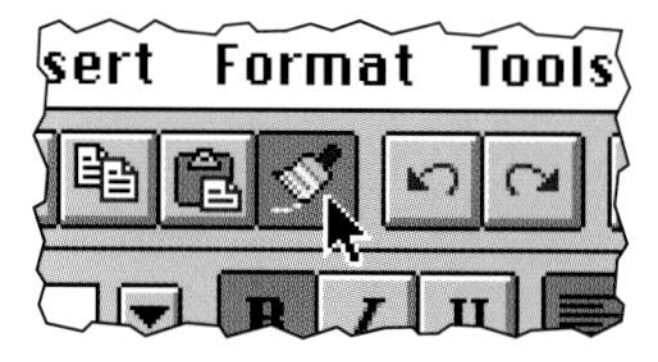

1 Select cell A7 and then click on the Format Painter button. You'll see the normal mouse pointer is accompanied by a paintbrush symbol.

2 Drag the mouse pointer to select or "paint" A9:G10.

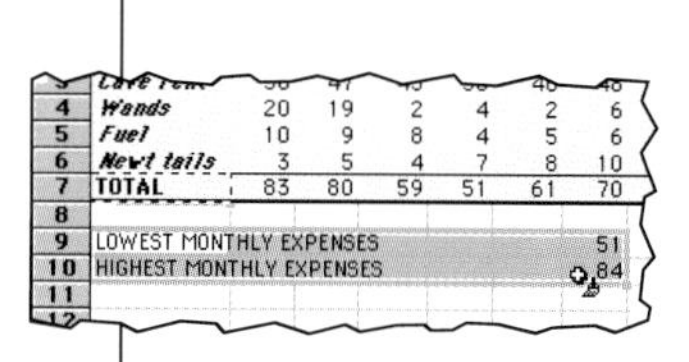

3 When you release the mouse button, the selected range takes on the same format as cell A7.

Styles

A style is a defined and named list of formatting attributes. In addition to the Normal style, Excel comes with five other built-in styles. Each of these has only one formatting attribute — a number format. The built-in styles include the Currency, Comma, and Percent styles that you met on page 72. Two others, Comma (0) and Currency (0), are similar to the Comma and Currency styles — but omit the use of a decimal point and decimal places.

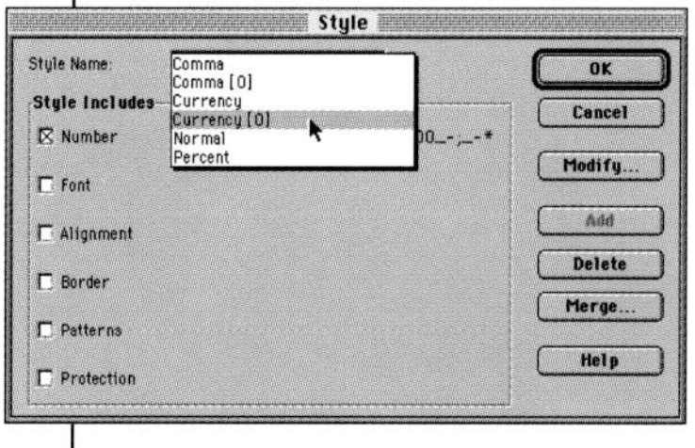

Style Dialog Box
Any of the built-in styles can be applied to a selected cell or range by choosing Style *from the* Format *menu. Within the* Style *dialog box (shown above), you can choose from the drop-down* Style Name *list. Note that you can also apply the Comma, Currency, and Percent styles by means of buttons on the Formatting toolbar.*

DEFINING A NEW STYLE

Using the *Style* dialog box, you can create and name new styles. A style can be created using any combination of formats — font, alignment, number format, border, pattern, and cell protection. When you apply the style to a cell, the style's formatting attributes replace the existing, equivalent attributes in that cell. Any attributes not defined in the style stay unchanged. To see how this works, open the **Annual Income** worksheet in the **Year1A** workbook again. You'll define a style, which you can then apply to some cells in this worksheet.

Paste Special?
Excel provides an alternative to the format painter for copying cell formats only. You select the source cell(s), use the *Copy* command in the *Edit* menu, select the target cell(s), and then choose *Paste Special* from the *Edit* menu. In the *Paste Special* dialog box, choose *Formats* under *Paste*, and then click on *OK*.

1 Select cell B3 and then choose *Style* from the *Format* menu. In the *Style* dialog box, you will see *Normal* listed in the *Style Name* box, and under *Style Includes*, you'll see a list of the formatting attributes that define the *Normal* style.

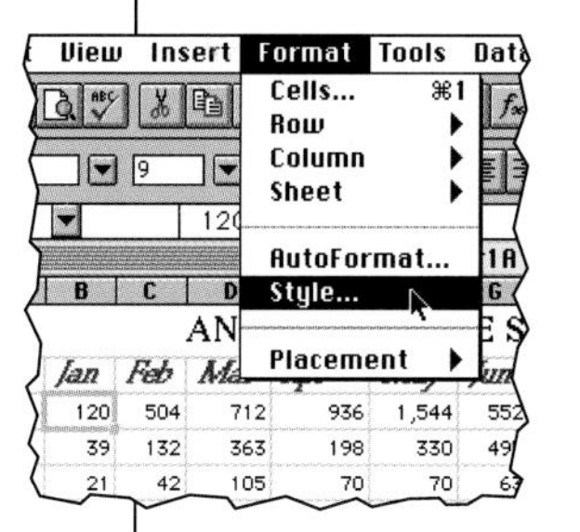

2 Type **BlueTimes** into the *Style Name* box. Clear the *Number*, *Alignment*, *Border*, and *Protection* check boxes. The attributes that are not checked will not be defined for this style. Click on the *Modify* button. The *Format Cells* dialog box appears. Click on the *Font* tab.

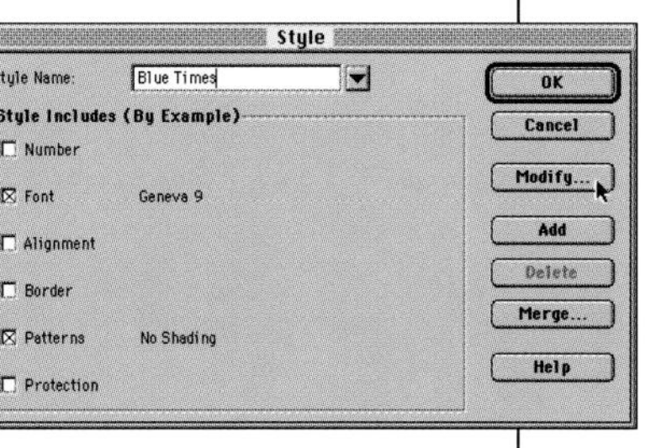

3 In the *Font* flipcard, choose *Times* under *Font*, *Bold* under *Font Style*, *9* pt under *Size*, and choose a dark blue from the *Color* pop-up list. Click on the *Patterns* tab, and in the *Patterns* flipcard choose a light gray under *Color*. Click on *OK*. You have now defined the **BlueTimes** style. Click on *OK* in the *Style* dialog box.

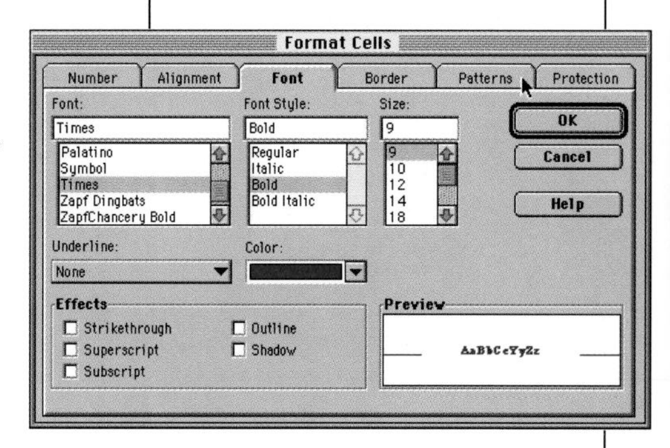

APPLYING THE NEW STYLE

Now that you have created a new style, you can apply it to a range in the **Annual Income** worksheet. Select the range B3:M7, choose *Style* from the *Format* menu, and then do the following:

1 In the *Style* dialog box, click on the down-arrow button next to the *Style Name* box, and choose *BlueTimes*. Click on *OK*.

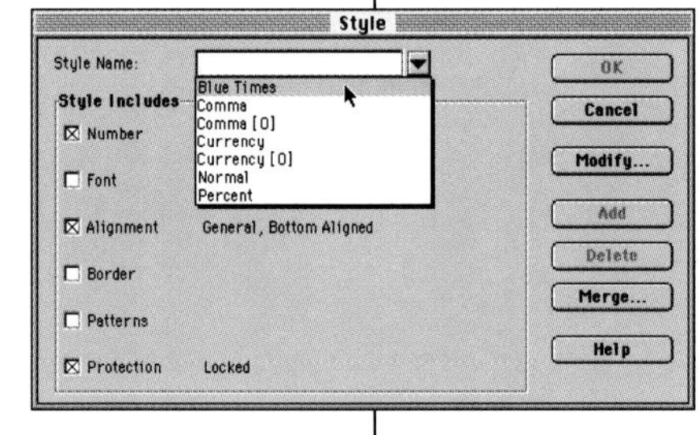

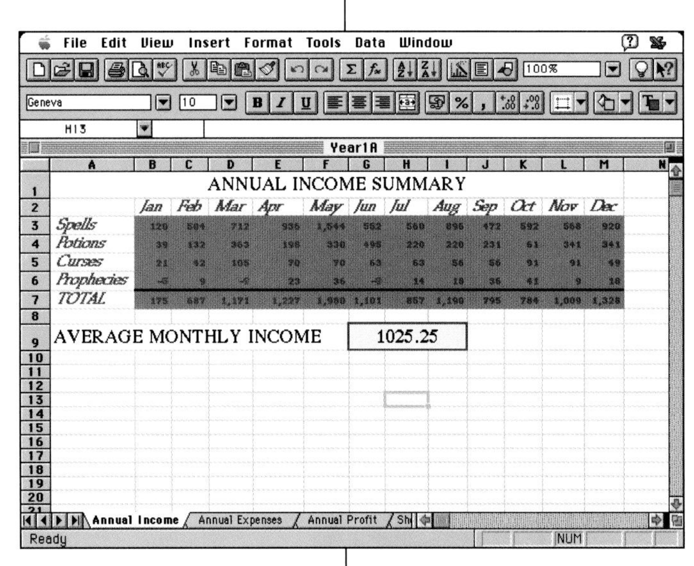

2 The BlueTimes style is applied to the selected range, giving the result shown at left.

Note that formatting attributes not defined in the style — such as numeric formats — have not changed in the worksheet. Thus, the negative values in B6 and D6 are still displayed in red because that is part of the numeric formatting of those cells, not their font color.

Scrub It!
When experimenting with formatting a worksheet, sometimes you'll decide the styling you've applied doesn't work and you'd prefer to start again. You can return the formatting of any selected cell or range to the Normal style by choosing the *Clear* command on the *Edit* menu and the *Formats* option from the submenu.

Cell Protection

Having developed a worksheet, you may want to instruct Excel to protect all or part of it from accidental or unauthorized changes. You may also want to hide some cell formulas. You can override the protection that Excel provides when you want to make changes but you can stop others from doing the same by using a password.

Protection operates at two levels. Every cell has protection attributes that are a part of its format. However, these individual attributes take effect only after you have turned on overall worksheet protection by choosing the *Protection* command from the *Tools* menu.

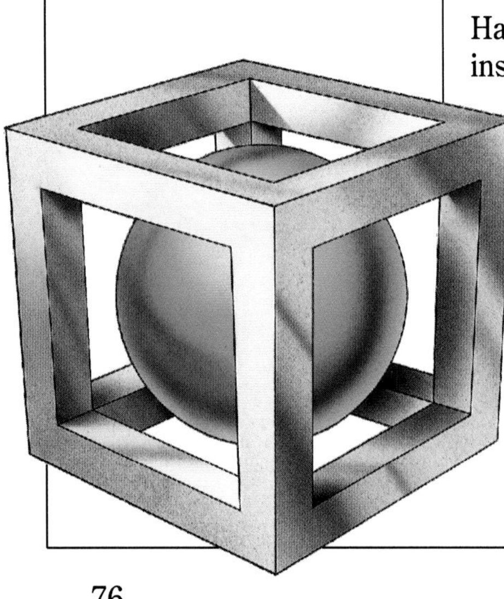

More Security?
In addition to the options for protecting worksheets described on this page, you can prevent anyone from opening a workbook or saving changes to it except by means of a password. For more information on these forms of protection, see "Workbook Security" on page 123 of the Reference Section.

LOCKED AND HIDDEN CELLS

A cell can have either or both of two protection attributes: it can be *locked* or *hidden*. When worksheet (or workbook) protection is turned on, the contents of a locked cell cannot be changed, and any formula in a hidden cell will not be displayed. By default, all the cells in a worksheet are locked but not hidden. You can alter the protection attributes of a cell by accessing the *Protection* flipcard in the *Format Cells* dialog box.

To see how cell protection operates, open the **Annual Expenses** worksheet.

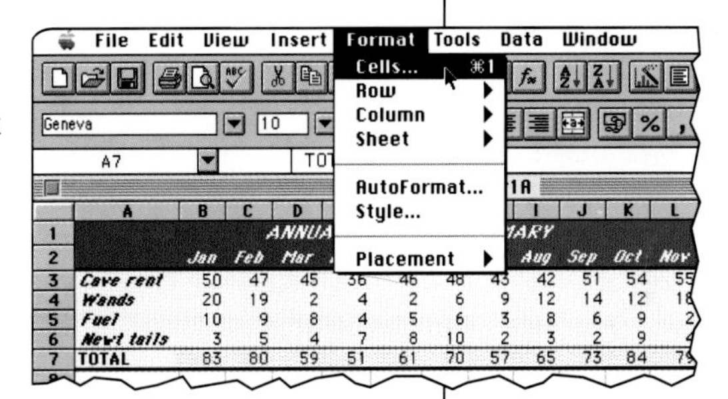

1 Select the range A7:M7. Choose *Cells* from the *Format* menu, and then click on the *Protection* tab in the *Format Cells* dialog box.

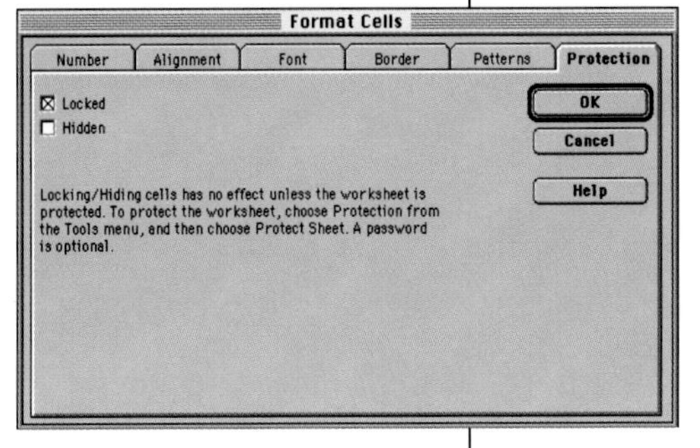

2 The *Protection* flipcard shows the default cell protection attributes. *Locked* is checked and *Hidden* is clear. Check the *Hidden* box so that the cells you have selected have this attribute as well. Then click on *OK*.

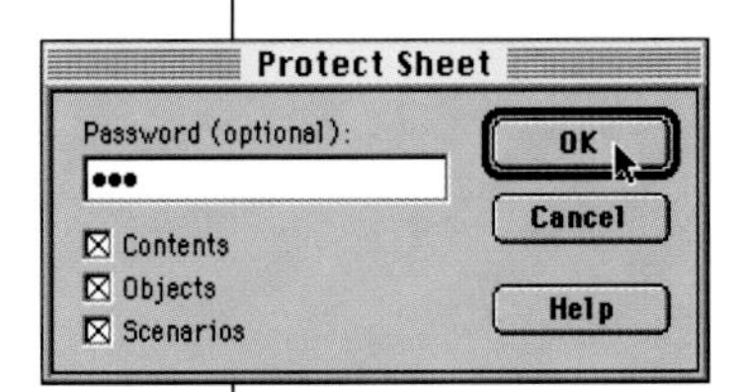

3 Choose *Protection* from the *Tools* menu and *Protect Sheet* from the submenu. The *Protect Sheet* dialog box allows you to specify a protection password. Type **WIZ** in the *Password* box. You will see a dot instead of each letter. Click on *OK*. You then confirm the password by typing it again.

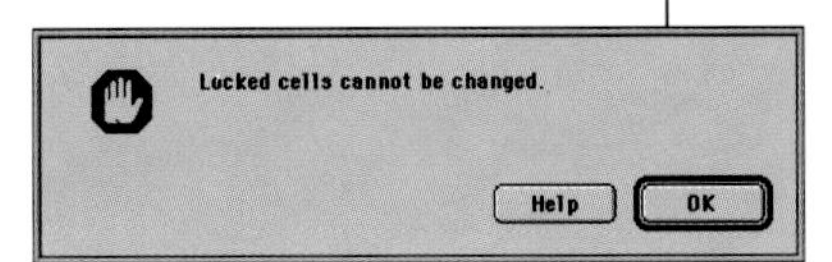

4 The worksheet is now protected. Try to change a cell and you will see an error message because all cells are locked. Click on a cell in the range A7:M7. Nothing shows in the formula bar because these cells are hidden as well as locked.

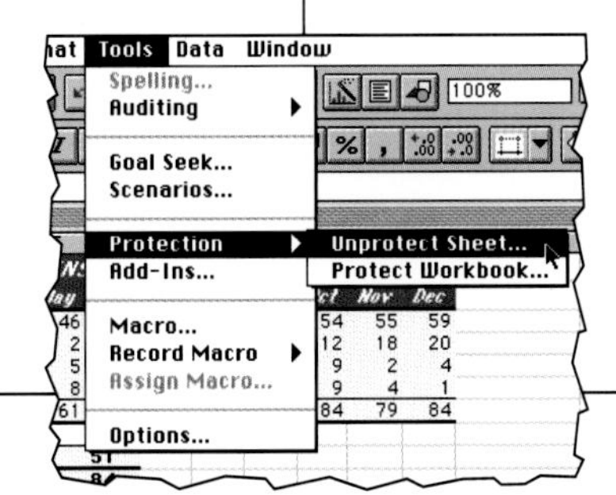

5 To disable hiding and locking of cells, choose *Protection* from the *Tools* menu again and *Unprotect Sheet* from the submenu. Type **WIZ** again in the password box and press Enter. The worksheet is no longer protected. Now close the **Year1A** workbook.

Foiled!
When a worksheet is protected, you cannot perform formatting, even on cells that are not locked. Many commands on the *Edit*, *Format*, and *Insert* menus are dimmed. You'll find that you cannot perform operations such as filling, copying, clearing, inserting, or deleting, and you cannot alter column widths or row heights.

Adding Graphics

YOU CAN ENHANCE THE APPEARANCE of your worksheets with "graphic objects." A graphic can be a single shape or a picture created from a group of shapes drawn with Excel's Drawing toolbar, a text box, or an embedded chart (see page 90).

Floating Toolbar ?
When a toolbar appears in the middle of your worksheet, it is "floating." You can move it anywhere on the screen by dragging its title bar, or alter its shape by dragging its size box. Double-click anywhere on the toolbar, except on a button, and it becomes a long horizontal bar at the top of the window. Double-click on it again, and it reverts to a floating toolbar.

Artistic License
The toolbar contains twenty-one buttons that allow you to draw shapes, manipulate them, and add various special effects.

The Drawing Toolbar

You can display the Drawing toolbar by clicking on the Drawing Toolbar button on the Standard toolbar (see page 15) or by holding down Control, clicking on any toolbar and then choosing *Drawing* from the shortcut menu. To draw a shape, first click on a drawing button. The mouse pointer changes to a +. Click the pointer on the worksheet, drag it to form the shape, and release the mouse button. You can then click on another drawing button to draw another shape. If you want to draw a series of same-type shapes, double-click on a button. Click on the button again or press Esc to finish and return to the normal mouse pointer.

Tools on the Drawing Toolbar

The functions of the buttons on the Drawing toolbar are described below. Holding down Shift when drawing has the effects described. If you hold down Command when drawing, Excel fits the shape to the cell grid of the worksheet.

Straight Line Tool
Draws straight lines; hold down Shift to constrain the line to horizontal, vertical, or a 45° angle.

Arrow Tool
Draws an arrow; hold down Shift to constrain the arrow shaft to horizontal, vertical, or a 45° angle.

Freehand Line Tool
Draws freehand lines.

Outline and Filled Rectangle Tools
Draw outline and filled rectangles; hold down Shift to make perfect squares.

Outline and Filled Ellipse Tools
Draw outline and filled ellipses (ovals); hold down Shift to produce perfect circles.

Outline and Filled Arc Tools
Draw outline and filled arcs; hold down Shift for quarter-circles.

Outline and Filled Freeform Tools
Draw any kinds of freehand and polygon shapes. Double-click, or click on the starting point, in order to finish the shape.

Text Box
Draws a box in which you can enter text.

Selection
Used to trace a rectangular frame that selects all shapes within its borders.

Reshape
Lets you change the shape of polygons.

Group
Connects two or more selected objects.

Ungroup
Disconnects a selected object into its parts.

Bring to Front
Brings selected object in front of other objects.

Send to Back
Sends selected object behind other objects.

Create Button
Lets you draw a button for assigning a macro.

Pattern
Applies pattern and pattern color to an object.

Drop Shadow
Adds a shadow to a selected object.

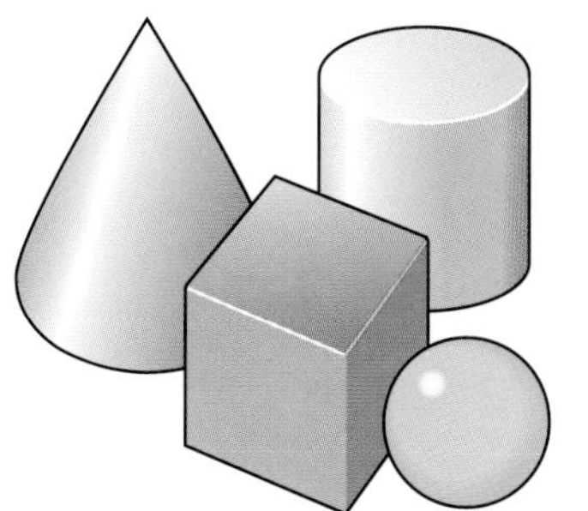

Drawing and Manipulating Objects

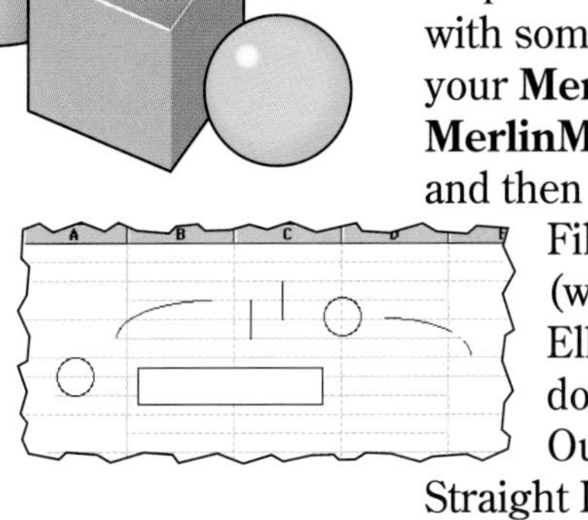

To practice using the Drawing toolbar and working with some shapes, open a new sheet (*Sheet4*) in your **Merlin** workbook and rename the sheet **MerlinMobile**. Display the Drawing toolbar, and then draw the shapes shown at left. Use the Filled Rectangle tool to draw the rectangle (which is filled in white), the Outline Ellipse tool to draw the two circles (hold down Shift when dragging the mouse), the Outline Arc tool to form the two arcs, and the Straight Line tool to draw the two vertical lines.

SELECTING OBJECTS

Having created an object, you may want to resize, move, copy, format, or delete it. But first you must select it. When an object is selected, it displays a frame with small black squares called handles. These handles are visible, but the frame itself is not.

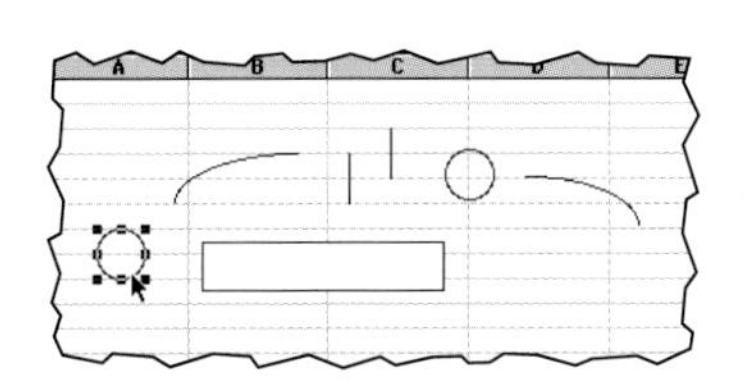

Single Selection
To select a filled shape, place the mouse pointer on the shape so that the pointer changes to an arrow, and click. To select an outline object, click on its edge.

Multiple Selection
To select multiple objects, hold down Shift and click on each object in turn. Alternatively, you can click on the Selection button on the Drawing toolbar, and then drag a frame around all the objects you want to select.

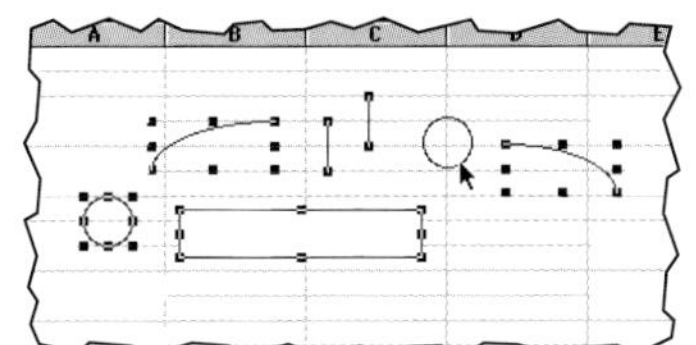

RESIZING AND MOVING OBJECTS

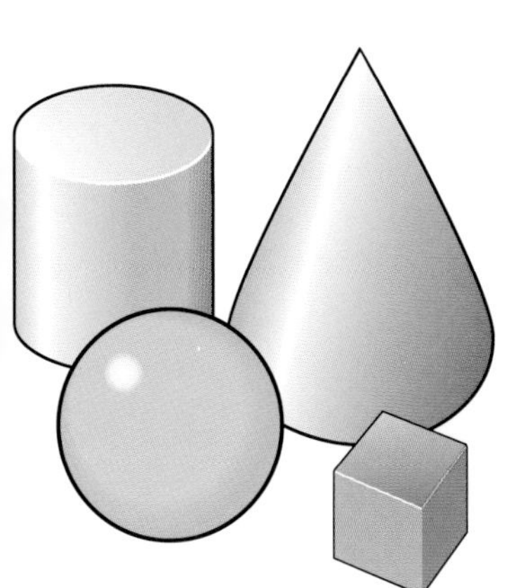

To resize an object, select it and then drag one of the selection handles. To resize horizontally and vertically at the same time, drag a corner handle. To move an object, drag its edge. Holding down Shift while you drag constrains the movement to horizontal or vertical.

1 Lengthen the filled rectangle you drew by selecting it and dragging the selection handle to the right.

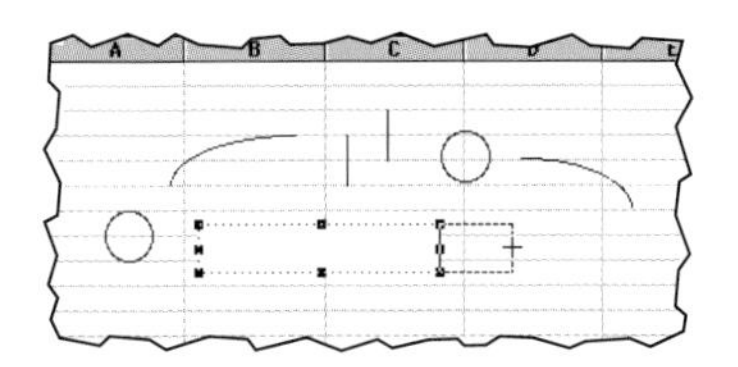

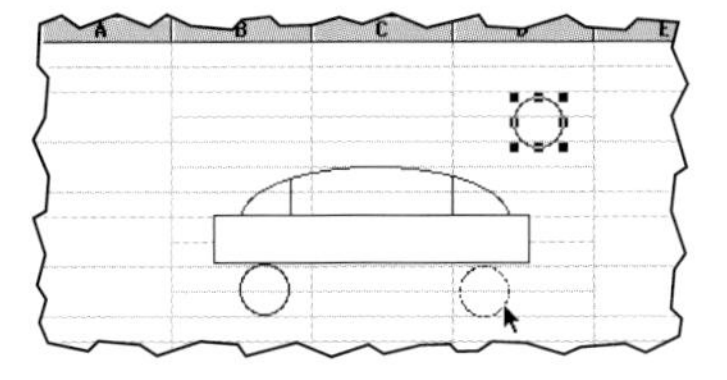

2 Now select each of the other shapes in turn and drag them into position around the rectangle to assemble the "MerlinMobile."

Get Together!
You may want to draw separate shapes and then group them to form a single object. To do so, select the shapes you want to combine and then click on the Group button on the Drawing toolbar. A grouped object can be manipulated without displacing its parts. However, you can't alter the individual parts of a grouped object. If you want to disconnect a grouped object into its parts, select it and then click on the Ungroup button.

More — or Less?
Holding down Option when you move an object duplicates it. You can also use cut, copy, and paste to move and copy objects. Pressing the Delete key will delete any currently selected objects.

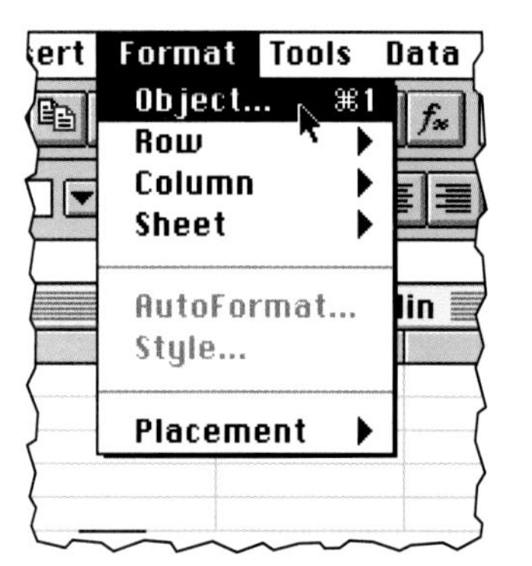

FORMATTING OBJECTS

To format an object, you select it and then choose the *Object* command from the *Format* menu. The *Patterns* flipcard within the *Format Object* box (which varies according to the object selected) allows you to control the style, color, and weight of lines, arrows, or object borders. You can fill shapes with patterns and colors, create rounded corners for rectangles, and more. The *Patterns* flipcard includes a sample to show what your object will look like with the options you have chosen.

Quick Format?
Double-clicking on the edge of any object, including a text box, both selects the object and brings up the *Format Object* dialog box.

1 Select one of the shapes comprising the MerlinMobile and choose *Object* from the *Format* menu.

2 In the *Patterns* flipcard of the *Format Object* dialog box, choose any style, color, and weight you like for the shape's border from the pop-up lists under *Border*, and any fill color you like from the colors under *Fill*. If you wish, click on the down-arrow button next to *Pattern*. Choose a pattern and a pattern color from the options that appear. Click on *OK*.

3 Your chosen border, color, and pattern options will be applied to the object.

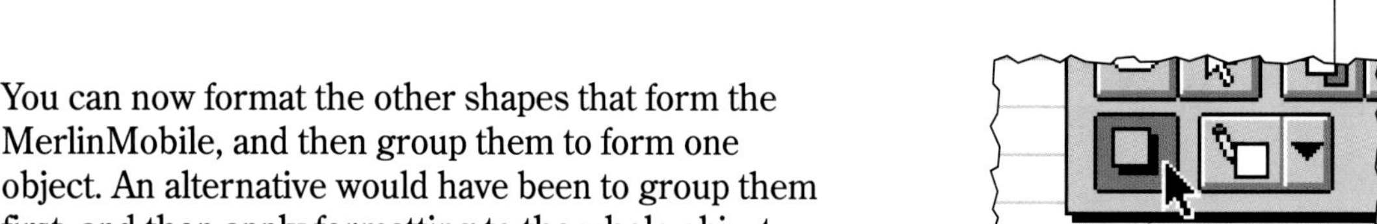

You can now format the other shapes that form the MerlinMobile, and then group them to form one object. An alternative would have been to group them first, and then apply formatting to the whole object.

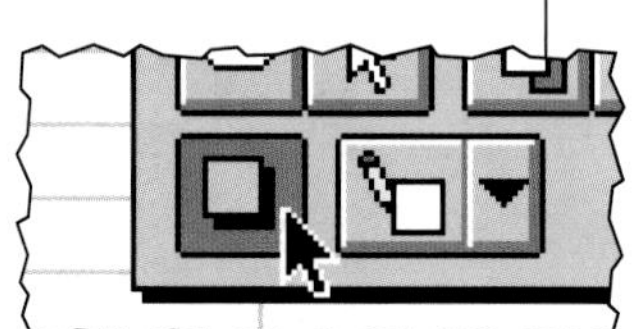

Drop Shadow Button
Clicking on the Drop Shadow button on the Drawing toolbar allows you to add an attractive shadow effect to selected shapes.

Text Boxes

One of the most useful objects is the text box. To create a text box, click on the Text Box button on the Standard or Drawing toolbar and then click and drag on the worksheet. When you start typing, text fills the box. You can apply font formatting to individual text characters using the Formatting toolbar or the *Format Object* command. If you select the whole box, you can apply the same types of formatting as you can to cells and their contents. You can also resize a text box.

Text Box Button

1 Open the **Jan Sales** worksheet in the **Merlin** workbook. Call up the Drawing toolbar and move it below the data by dragging its title bar. Click on the Text Box button, and then click and drag roughly from E4 to G8 to form a text box as shown.

2 Type **January**, press Return to force a new line, and then type **Special Offer**. Select the text box, and then choose *Object* from the *Format* menu.

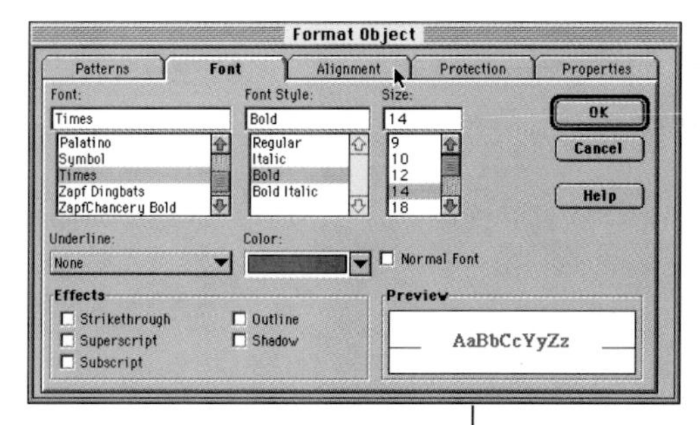

3 In the *Format Object* dialog box, click on the *Font* tab. In the *Font* flipcard, choose a font, color, font style, and size. Then click on the *Alignment* tab, and in the *Alignment* flipcard set *Text Alignment* to *Center* both horizontally and vertically. Click on *OK*.

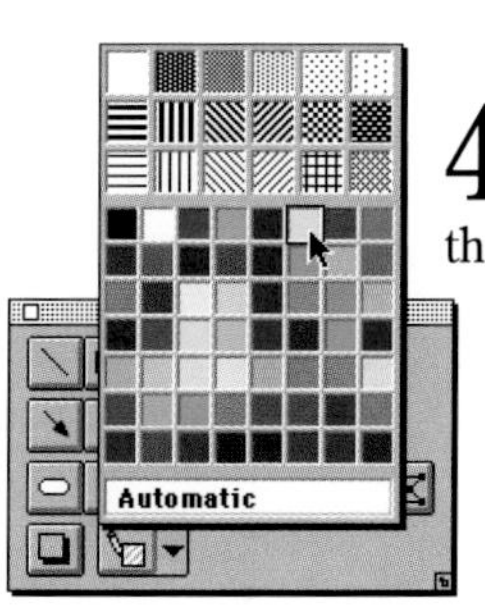

4 With the text box still selected, click on the down arrow next to the Pattern button on the Drawing toolbar. Choose a pattern and then a pattern color for the text box.

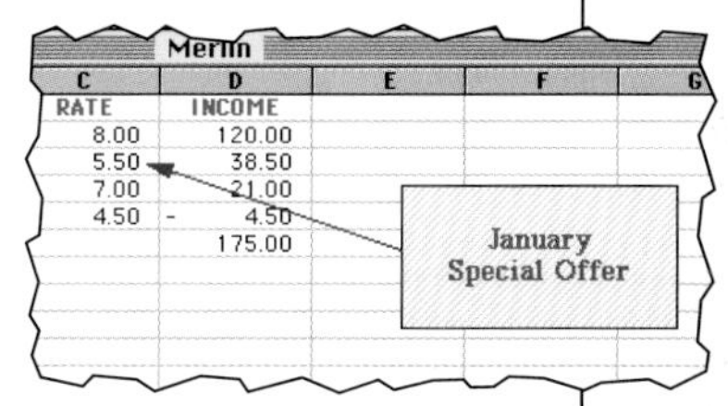

5 Click on the Arrow tool and drag from the edge of the text box to the edge of cell C3. With the arrow still selected, choose *Object* from the *Format* menu, and in the *Patterns* flipcard, choose the style, color, and weight of the line, and the style, width, and length of the arrowhead. Click on *OK*.

Hot Properties?
The *Properties* flipcard within the *Format Object* dialog box lets you control what happens to a graphic object if you change underlying cells. You can specify that the object can move and resize with changes, move with cells but stay the same size, or be unaffected by changes to the cells underneath. A check box lets you define whether or not the object will print.

LAYERING OBJECTS

Graphic objects can be imagined as floating in layers on the worksheet. The Bring to Front and Send to Back buttons on the Drawing toolbar allow you to superimpose objects in the order that you want. Overlapping objects can be used to create special effects.

Tricky Clicking!
Every object has a shortcut menu with commands (such as *Cut*, *Copy*, *Format Object*, and *Send to Back*) that can be accessed by pointing to the object and clicking the mouse button while holding down Control. But take care when performing this on non-filled objects. If you miss the edge, you will select the cell underneath.

1 Click on the Outline Rectangle button and drag on the worksheet roughly from E10 to G15 to draw a separate rectangle about the same size as your text box. Fill the rectangle with a dark shade of gray by choosing *Object* from the *Format* menu and choosing gray from the *Patterns* flipcard.

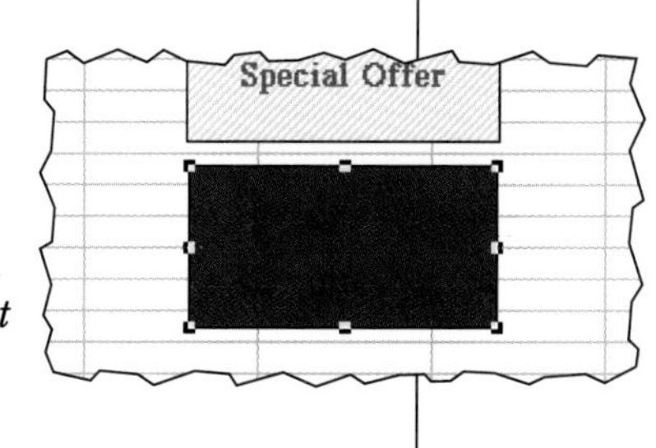

2 Drag the gray rectangle to cover most of your text box.

3 Click on the Send to Back button, then deselect the gray rectangle by selecting a worksheet cell. The gray rectangle now appears partially hidden behind the text box, creating a deep shadow effect. Now close the **Merlin** workbook, saving all changes.

Printing

PRINTING A WORKSHEET can be as simple as clicking on a toolbar button — but to print the worksheet exactly as you want may require a little more planning. Do you want to print the whole worksheet or only a part? Would you prefer to fit what you want to print onto one page or several pages? Do you want to include column titles on every page? You can also choose options such as the number of copies to print — and you can use Print Preview to fine-tune your worksheet's appearance before you print.

Print Preview

Print Preview Button

To practice printing with Excel, open the **Checking** worksheet in your **Merlin** workbook. You'll start off by looking at some ways in which you can control printing of the whole worksheet. Begin by clicking on the Print Preview button on the Standard toolbar. The Print Preview window displays your worksheet exactly as it will appear when it is printed and allows you to change aspects of your page layout before you print. Click on the *Margins* button. The main features of the Print Preview window are shown below:

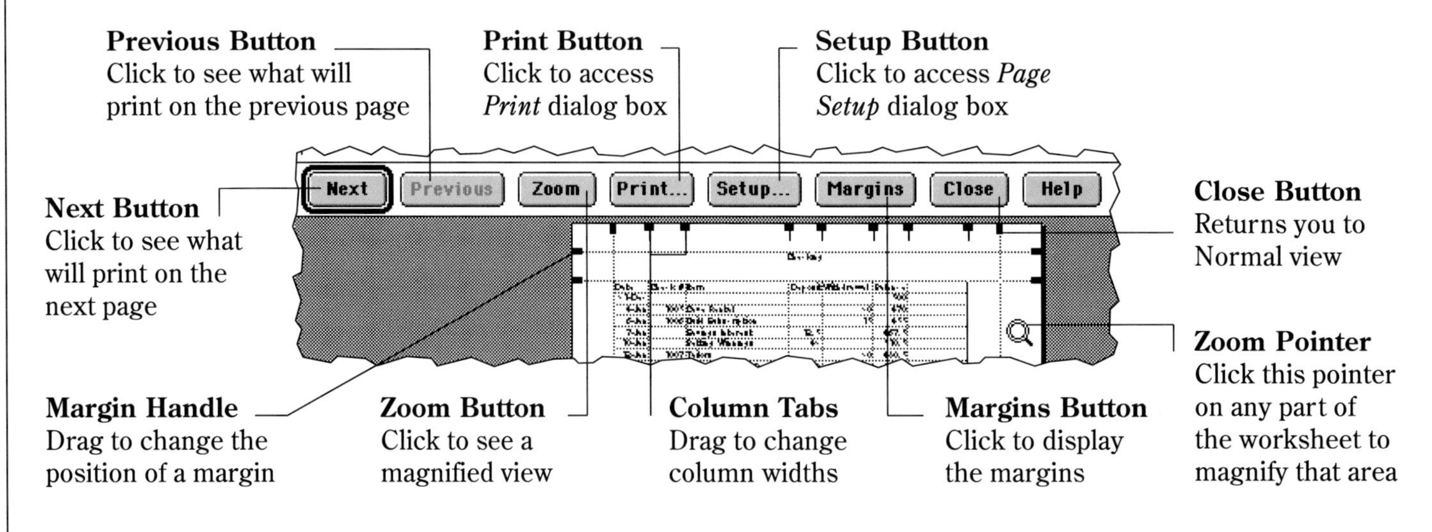

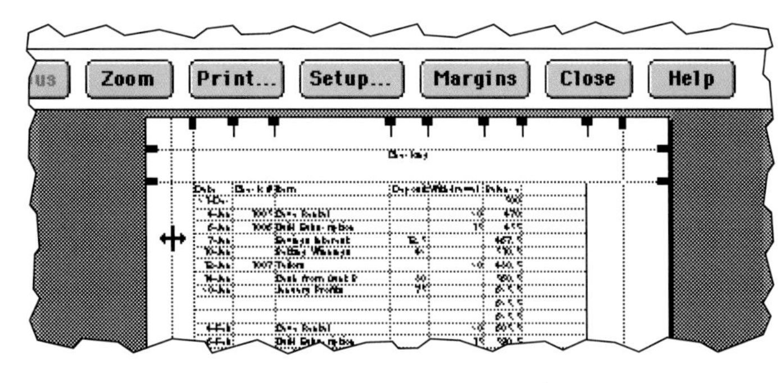

CHANGING MARGINS

Try altering the margin settings. First put the mouse pointer on the left margin and drag the margin to the left. While you are dragging, the current margin setting is displayed on the status bar at the bottom left-hand corner of the screen. Drag the margin until it is set to *0.50* inches. If you set the right margin to the same value, you'll see that a little more of your worksheet now appears on the page.

Fitting onto a Page

Fitting an oversized worksheet (like your **Checking** worksheet) onto one printed page is a common printing problem. Altering the margins will help sometimes, but margins that are too narrow can make a document look cramped. Fortunately, Excel provides a number of solutions to this problem.

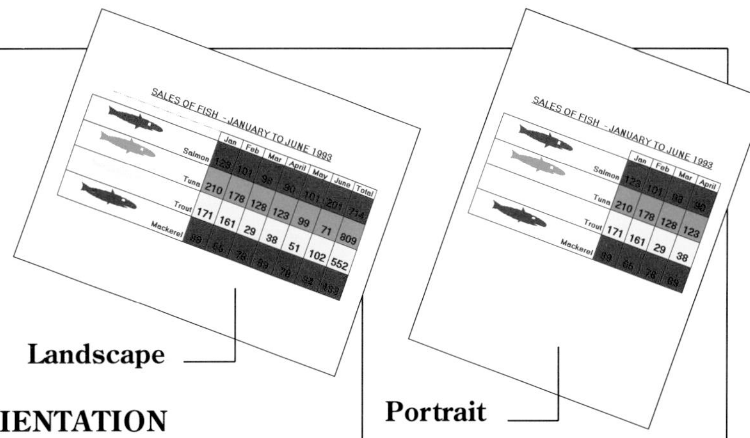

Landscape

Portrait

CHANGING PAGE ORIENTATION

Changing to landscape orientation is often useful for printing worksheets that are wider than they are long. Before changing the orientation of your **Checking** worksheet, drag the worksheet's left and right margins back to their original settings of *0.75* on each side.

1 Click on the *Setup* button in the Print Preview window. The *Page Setup* dialog box appears. Click on the *Page* tab to display the *Page* flipcard.

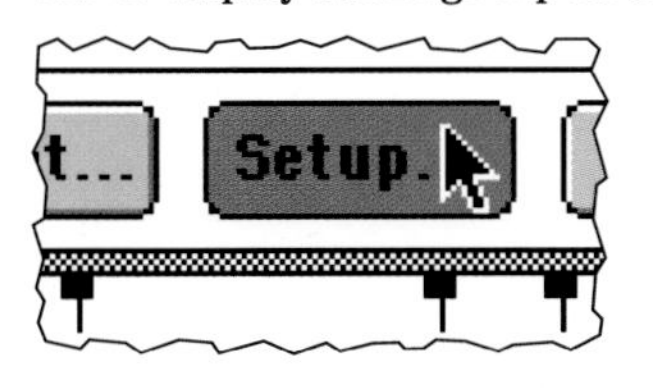

2 Click on *Landscape* under *Orientation*, and then click on *OK*. In Print Preview you will see that the worksheet is now set up to be printed horizontally across the page (*Landscape*) instead of vertically.

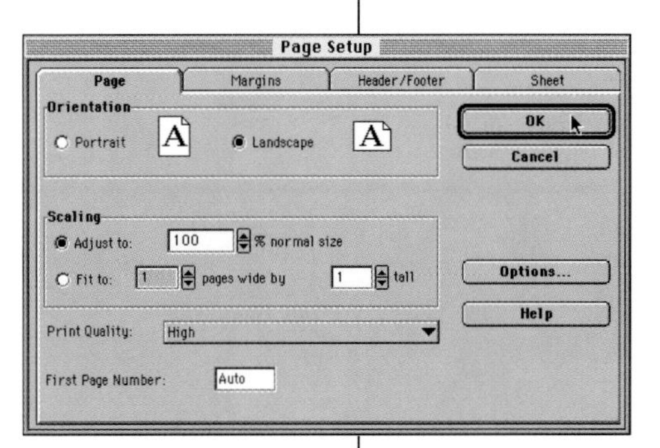

SCALING TO FIT

Now try another technique. You can instruct Excel to scale your worksheet so it fits exactly on the printed page. Click on the *Setup* button again to access the *Page Setup* dialog box.

1 In the *Page* flipcard, choose *Portrait* under *Orientation*, and under *Scaling*, click on the *Fit to* option. Return to Print Preview by clicking on *OK*.

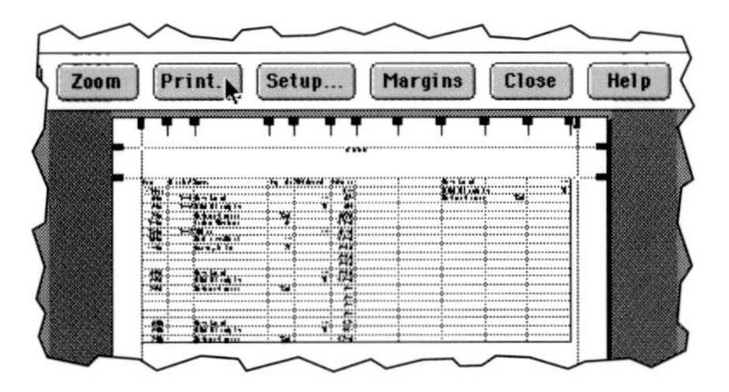

2 In the Print Preview window, you will see that the worksheet has been scaled down to fit the page in *Portrait* orientation. Click on the *Print* button.

3 The dialog box at right appears allowing you to choose options such as the range of pages and numbers of copies to print. Make sure that *Selected Sheets* is chosen in the bottom left hand corner, and choose as many copies as you want to print in the *Copies* box. Click on *Print*. Each copy of the worksheet should print on a single page.

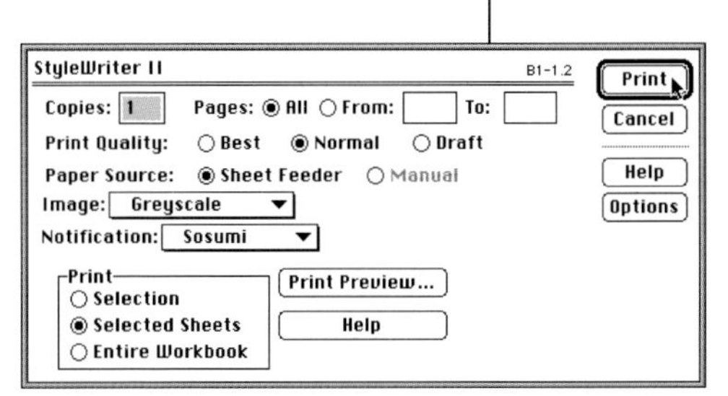

Printing Part of a Worksheet

Sometimes you may decide to print only part of your worksheet. To do this, you must define a print area within the *Page Setup* dialog box. This time, access the *Page Setup* dialog box by choosing *Page Setup* from the *File* menu. In the *Page* flipcard, click on the *Adjust to* option under *Scaling* and increase the percentage in the *Adjust to* box to *100%* to return your **Checking** worksheet to normal scale. Then click on the *Sheet* tab.

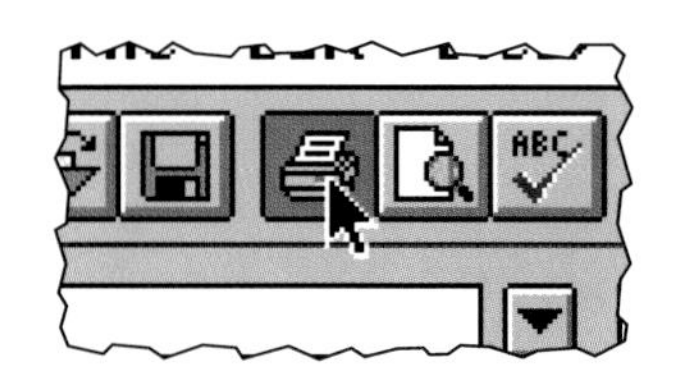

Button Bypass
The Print button on the Standard toolbar bypasses all dialog boxes and uses the print settings that you last defined.

1 In the *Sheet* flipcard, click in the *Print Area* box. To set the range A1:F14 as the print area, click on cell A1 in the worksheet and drag the mouse pointer to cell F14. Release the mouse button when you see *$A$1:$F$14* in the *Print Area* box. Click on *OK*.

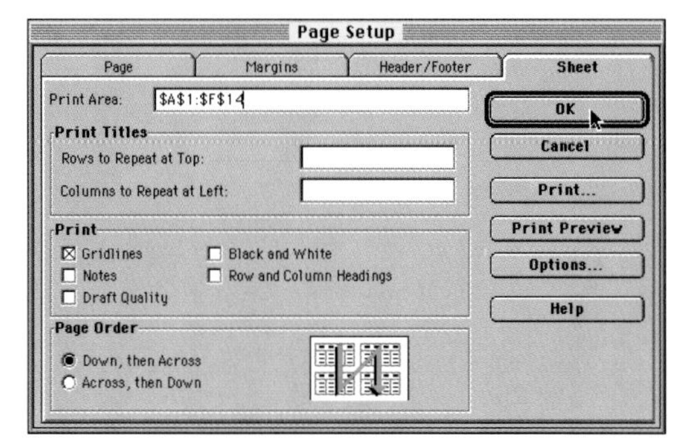

Merlin

	A	B	C	D	E	F
1	Date	Check #	Item	Deposit	Withdrawal	Balance
2	31-Dec					500
3	4-Jan	1005	Cave Rental		30	470
4	6-Jan	1006	Guild Subscription		15	455
5	7-Jan		Savings Interest	12.5		467.5
6	10-Jan		Betting Winnings	43		510.5
7	12-Jan	1007	Tailors		30	480.5
8	14-Jan		Cash from Aunt B	80		560.5
9	30-Jan		January Profits	75		635.5
10						635.5
11						635.5
12	4-Feb		Cave Rental		30	605.5
13	6-Feb		Guild Subscription		15	590.5
14	7-Feb		Savings Interest	12.5		603
15						603
16						603

2 You will see that in the worksheet, dashed lines demarcate the area you have selected. Click on the Print button on the Standard toolbar. Only the print area that you have set will be printed.

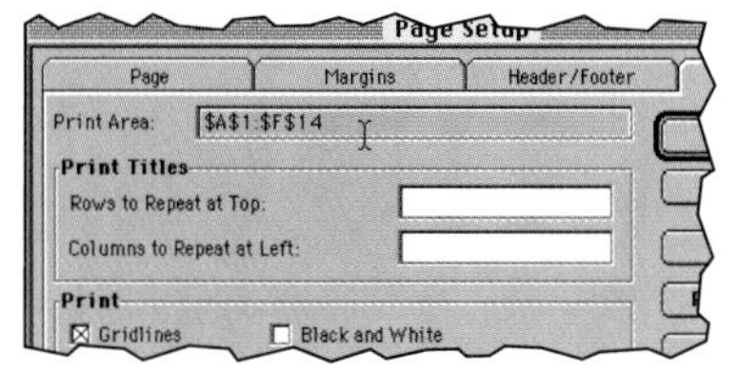

3 Return to the *Page Setup* dialog box. Highlight the contents of the *Print Area* box, delete them, and then click on *OK*. You have redefined the whole worksheet as the print area.

Break Free?
To remove a manual page break, select a cell immediately to the right of or below the break you want to remove. Choose *Remove Page Break* from the *Insert* menu. If this command does not appear, it means you have chosen a cell that is not directly to the right of or below the manual page break. To remove all page breaks, select the entire worksheet and choose *Remove Page Break.*

Pagination

When you are printing a large worksheet, or even part of a large worksheet, you may need to print onto several pages. Excel will set page breaks for you automatically, but you can override these and insert your own page breaks manually. Since a large worksheet may extend over many pages horizontally as well as vertically, you may need to insert vertical as well as horizontal page breaks.

To set a page break, select the row directly below the gridline where you want the break to occur (for a horizontal break) or the column directly to the right of the gridline (for a vertical break), and then choose *Page Break* from the *Insert* menu. To create both a horizontal and a vertical break select the cell directly below and to the right of where you want the page breaks to occur.

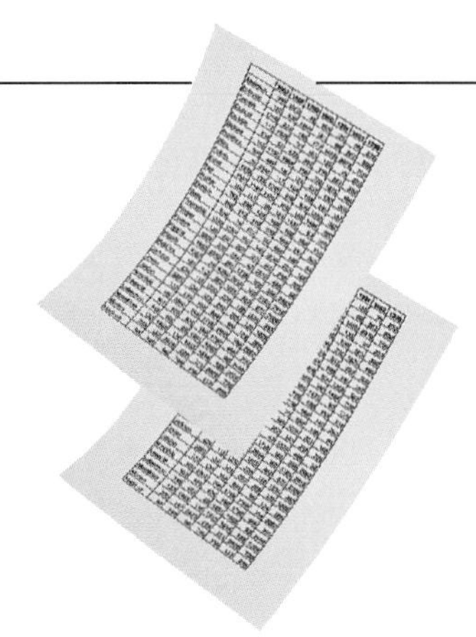

PRINT TITLES

When printing a worksheet over several pages, any row or column labels at the top or left of the worksheet will be printed only once. If you want the labels to appear on every page, you can arrange this by defining the labels as *Print Titles* in the *Page Setup* dialog box.

To practice using manual page breaks and print titles, print the range A1:F20 of the **Checking** worksheet in three monthly sections onto separate pages. You'll use the text labels in row 1 of the worksheet as print titles.

Be Exclusive!
Take care to exclude print titles when you define your print area. If you forget to do this, the print titles will print twice on the first page.

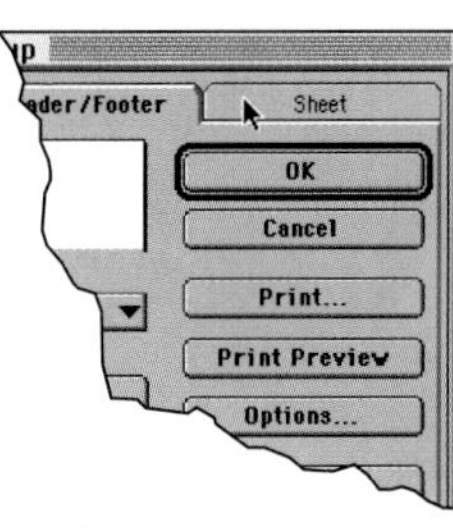

1 Choose *Page Setup* from the *File* menu, and in the *Page Setup* dialog box, click on the *Sheet* tab.

2 Under *Print Titles*, click in the *Rows to Repeat at Top* box. Move the mouse pointer onto the worksheet and click on the row 1 header to select row 1. You will see *$1:$1* appear in the *Rows to Repeat at Top* box. You have defined the column labels in row 1 as the print titles.

3 Now define the print area, excluding any print titles you have defined (in this case row 1). Click in the *Print Area* box, click on cell A2 in your worksheet, and drag the mouse pointer until you see *$A$2:$F$20* in the box. Release the mouse button and click on *OK*. You will see that the range A2:F20 is demarcated as the print area.

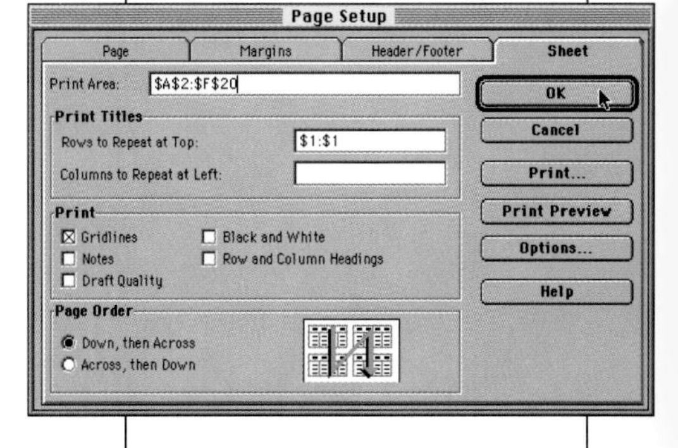

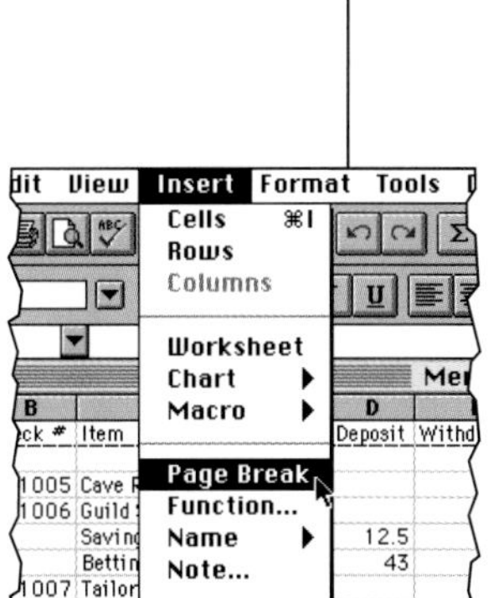

4 Set your manual page breaks. Select row 10 and choose *Page Break* from the *Insert* menu to set a manual break between rows 9 and 10. Select row 15 and repeat the procedure to set a manual page break between rows 14 and 15.

Now click on the Print button on the Standard toolbar. A separate sheet will print for each month, with titles at the top of each page.

In the Middle?
Excel allows you to print your worksheets in the center of the page. To do this, choose *Page Setup* from the *File* menu and select the *Margins* flipcard. Under *Center on Page*, check the *Vertically* and/or *Horizontally* boxes, and then click on *OK*. Your choice will take effect the next time you print.

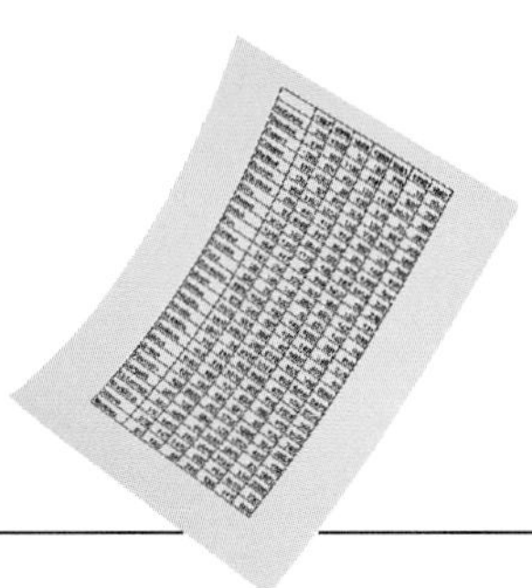

Headers and Footers

Headers and footers are printed at the top (header) and bottom (footer) of each page. You can set them up via the *Header/Footer* flipcard in the *Page Setup* dialog box. A header is not the same as a print title. Although both are printed on each page, a print title is a part of the worksheet, whereas a header is a separately defined piece of text.

Headers and footers can be aligned at the left, center, or right of each page. In addition to text, you can specify values, such as dates and page numbers, by means of header and footer codes. The most common codes, such as *&[Date]* for date, can be inserted using buttons in the *Header* and *Footer* dialog boxes.

You may have noticed headers and footers on the worksheets you have already printed — Excel supplies a default header (the worksheet name) and a default footer (the page number) automatically. Now let's print the **Checking** worksheet again. This time, the header will contain a new title, and the footer will contain a page number and date. Choose *Page Setup* from the *File* menu and click on the *Header/Footer* tab.

Change of Style?

Both the *Header* and *Footer* dialog boxes have a Font button that can be used to access the *Font* dialog box. After selecting text or codes within one of the *Section* boxes, you can use the *Font* dialog box to change the font attributes, such as typeface or type size, of your selection.

1 In the *Header/Footer* flipcard, click on the *Custom Header* button.

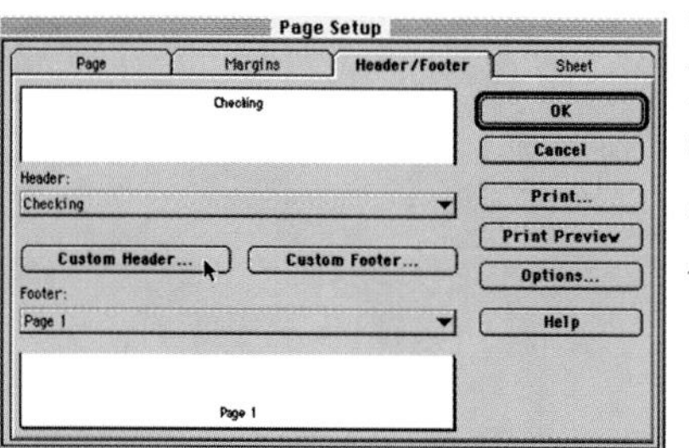

2 In the *Header* dialog box, double-click in the *Center Section* box, clear the existing contents of this box, type in **Merlin Checking Account**, and then click on *OK*.

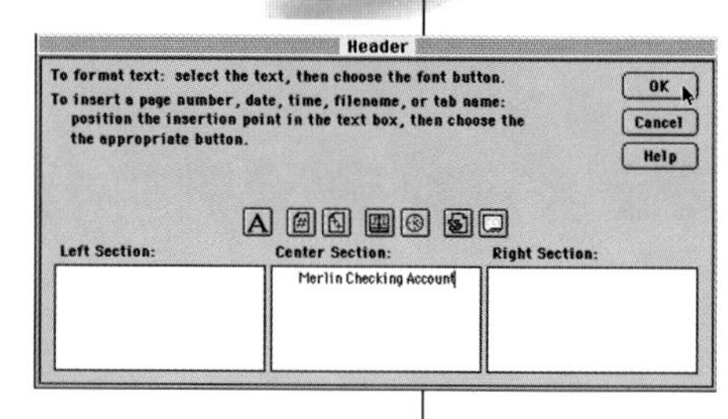

3 Click on the *Custom Footer* button and in the *Footer* dialog box clear the contents of the *Center Section* box. Click in the *Left Section* box, click on the page number button (the second button from the left), type a space, and finally click on the date button (the fourth button from the right). The expression *&[Page] &[Date]* appears in the *Left Section* box. Click on *OK*.

4 The *Header/Footer* flipcard will show you how the headers and footers will appear on your printed page. Click on the *Print* button, and in the *Print* dialog box click on *Print*. The worksheet will be printed out as in the previous example, but this time it will display your specified headers and footers. You can now close your **Merlin** workbook.

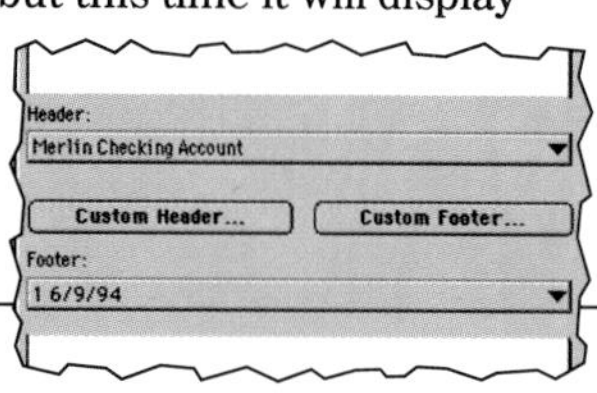

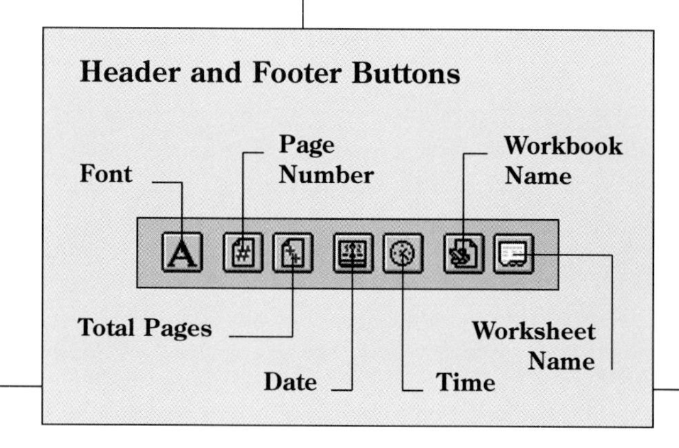

Troubleshooting Printing Problems

When tracking down a printing problem, be prepared to generate and test hypotheses. Questions such as "What is different since I last printed successfully?" or "Might someone have altered the settings since I last printed?" can often furnish clues to help you pin down the problem. This flow chart may help you resolve some common printing problems.

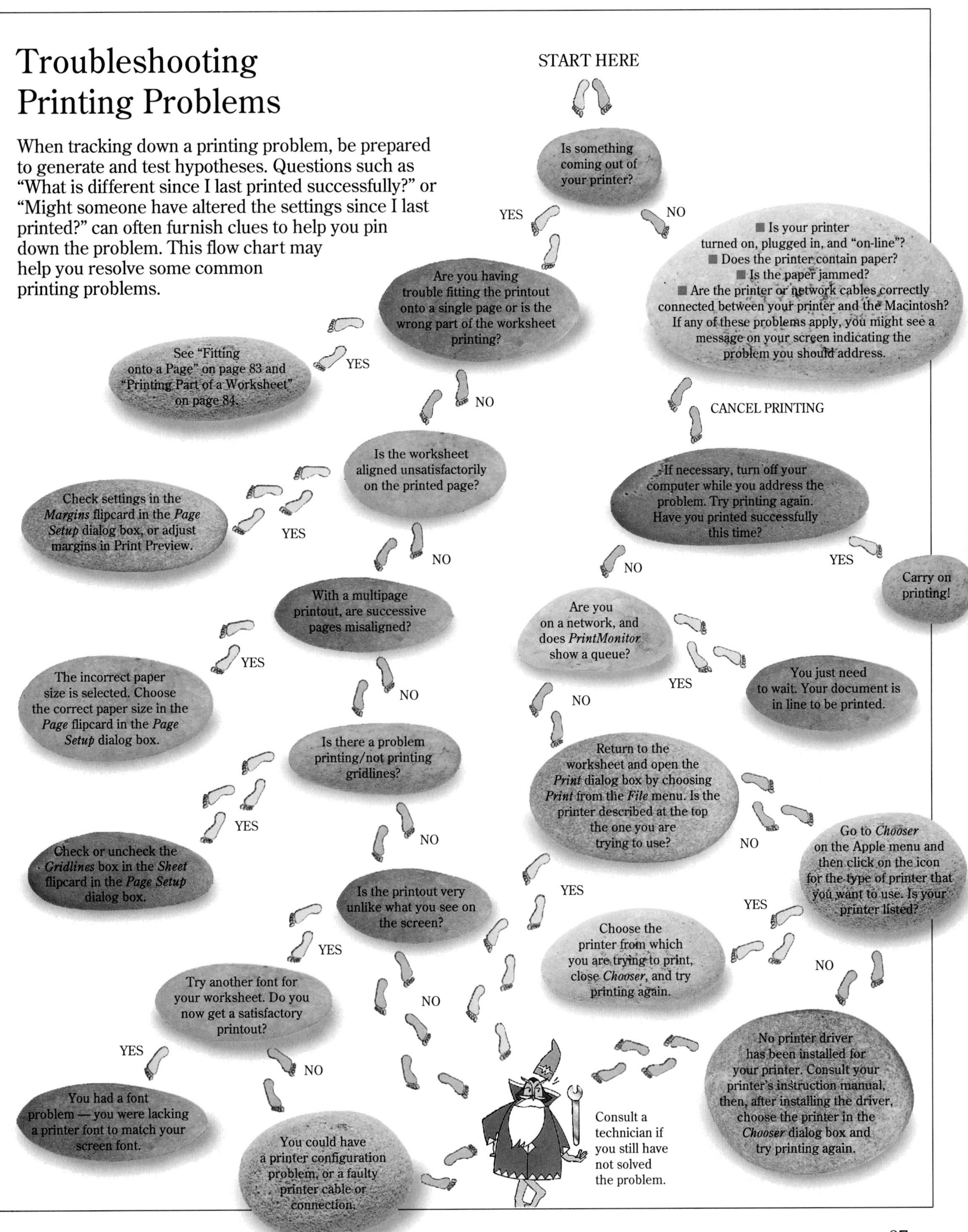

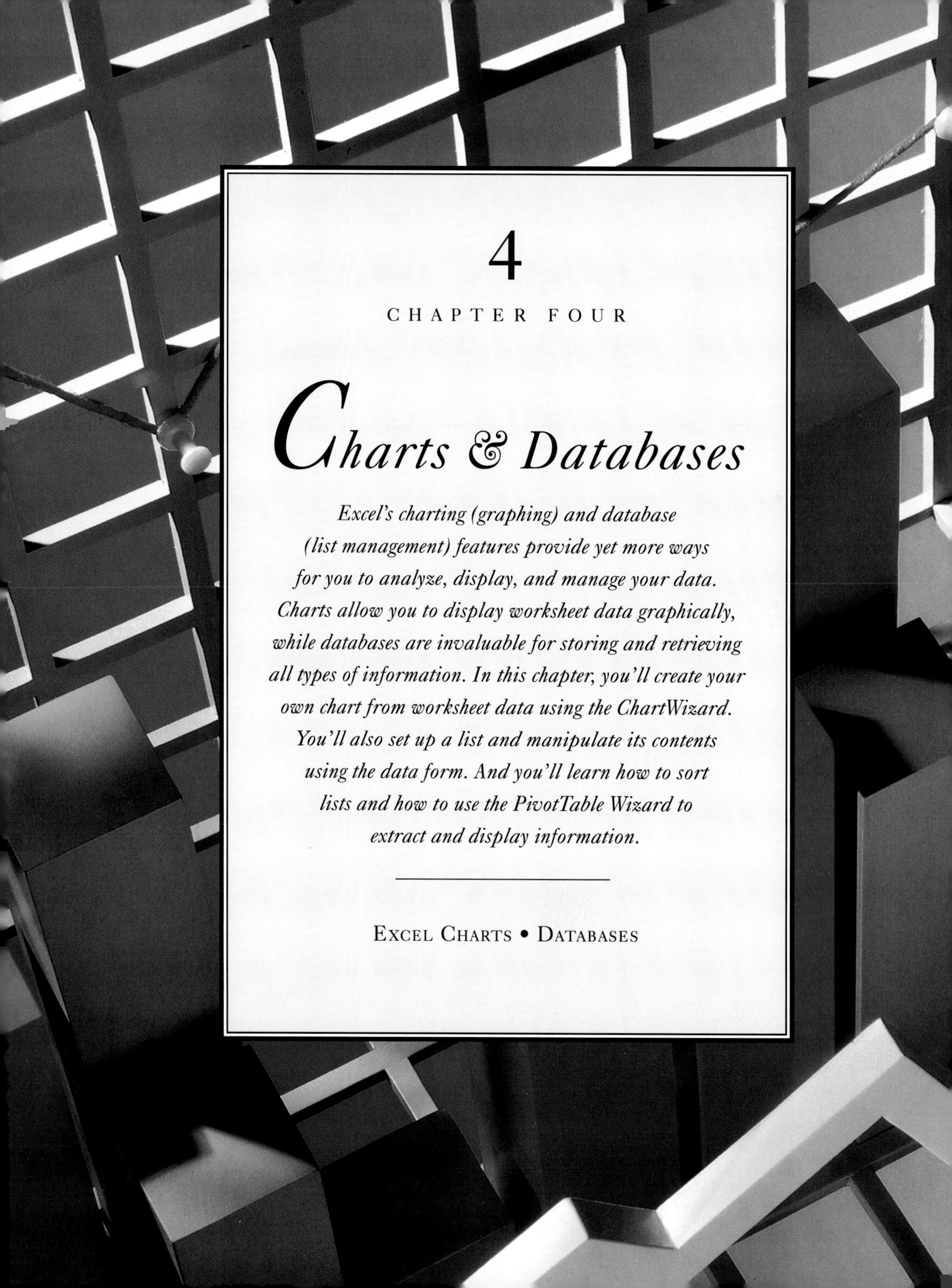

4

CHAPTER FOUR

Charts & Databases

Excel's charting (graphing) and database (list management) features provide yet more ways for you to analyze, display, and manage your data. Charts allow you to display worksheet data graphically, while databases are invaluable for storing and retrieving all types of information. In this chapter, you'll create your own chart from worksheet data using the ChartWizard. You'll also set up a list and manipulate its contents using the data form. And you'll learn how to sort lists and how to use the PivotTable Wizard to extract and display information.

EXCEL CHARTS • DATABASES

EXCEL CHARTS *90*

Discover the different types of charts that Excel can produce, and learn how to create a chart using the ChartWizard. Using the Chart and Formatting toolbars and commands on the Format menu, you'll learn how to modify the chart. You'll also create a graph from pictures.

DATABASES *98*

Use Excel's database features to create your own list. Find out how to add and find records using a data form, how to filter data, and how to change the order in which your data is displayed. You'll also discover how to extract and display worksheet data using the PivotTable Wizard.

Excel Charts

ANY TABLE OF DATA in a worksheet can be depicted graphically in the form of a *chart*. Excel allows you to create many different types of chart, from the simplest bar graphs to complex three-dimensional surfaces. Charts can exist as objects in a worksheet — normally the worksheet containing the source data — in which case they are referred to as *embedded charts*. Alternatively, they can stand alone in their own workbook *chart sheets*. Once you have created a chart, Excel provides the tools to make changes to any of its components.

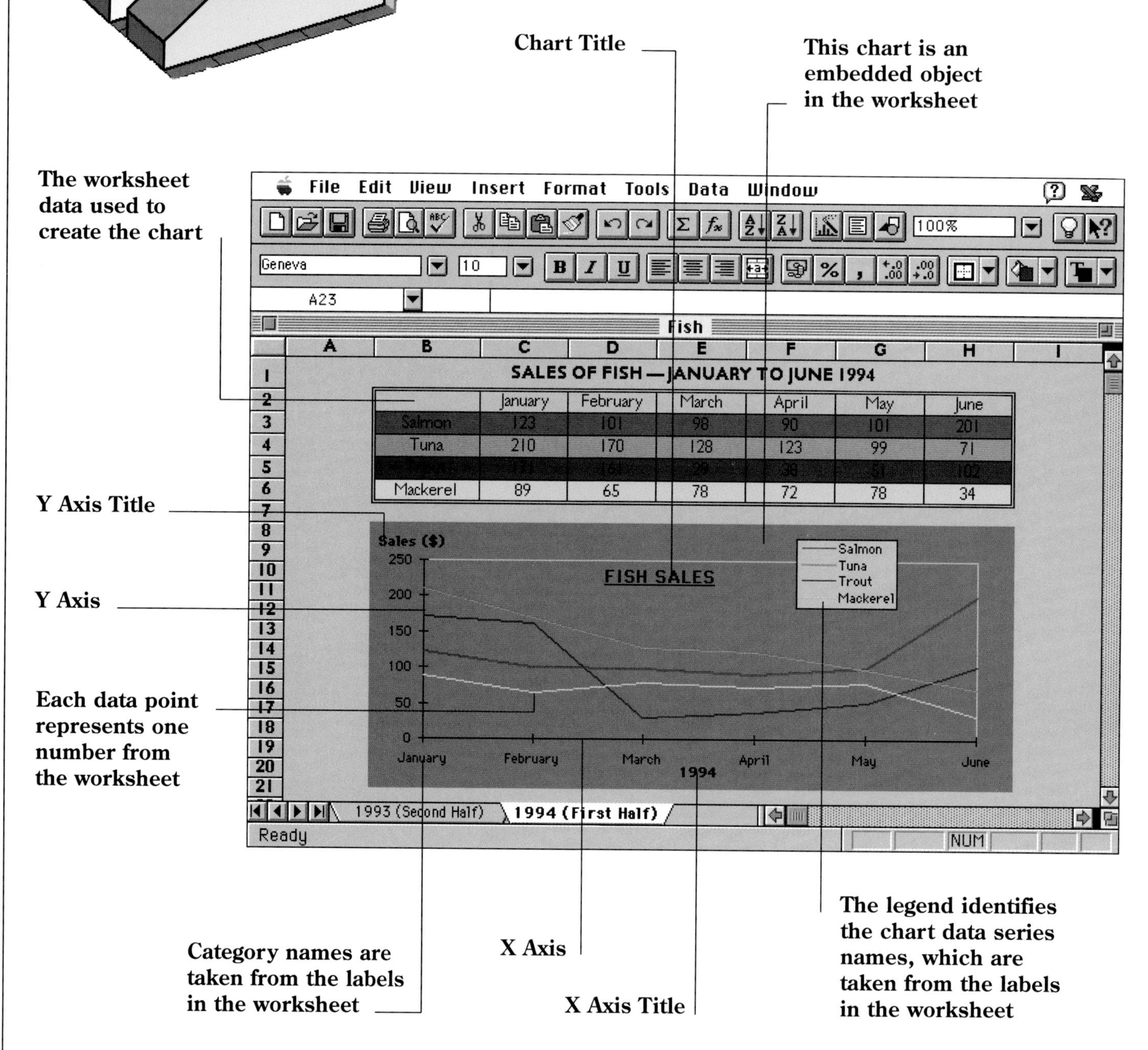

Which Chart?

Charts are usually linked to their source data. If you change that data, the chart automatically reflects those changes. There are many basic chart types to choose from, each with a number of subtypes. Once you have created a chart, you can change it to any other chart type, or customize it with text or pictures. Some of the more commonly used charts are shown here, but you can create many other kinds.

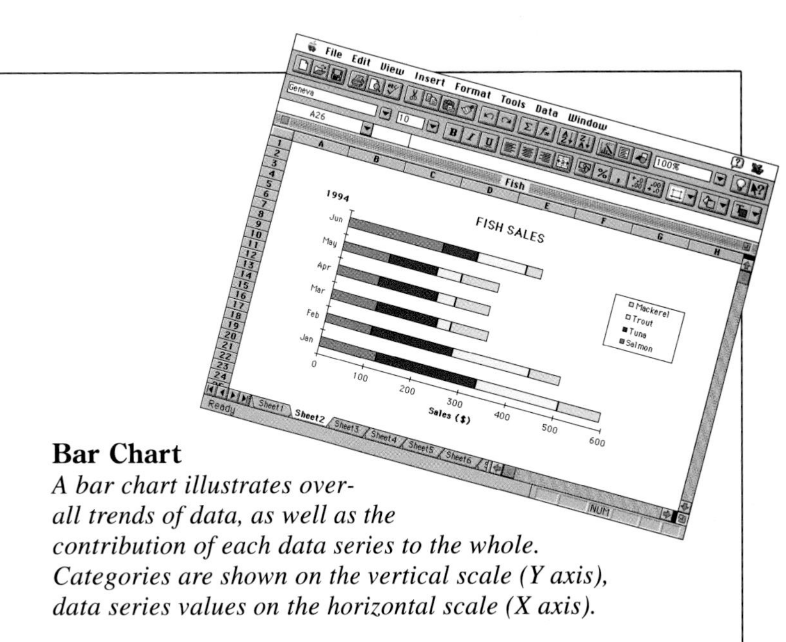

Bar Chart

A bar chart illustrates overall trends of data, as well as the contribution of each data series to the whole. Categories are shown on the vertical scale (Y axis), data series values on the horizontal scale (X axis).

Area Chart

An area chart illustrates changes in each data series from category to category (in this case, from month to month), the relationship of each data series to the whole, and the overall trend of data.

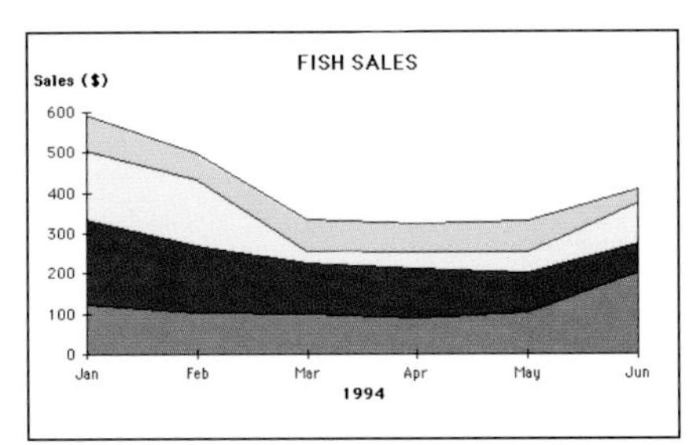

Column Chart

A column chart works on the same principle as a bar chart, except that the categories are organized horizontally and data values are organized vertically. A column chart is useful for comparing data series values within each category.

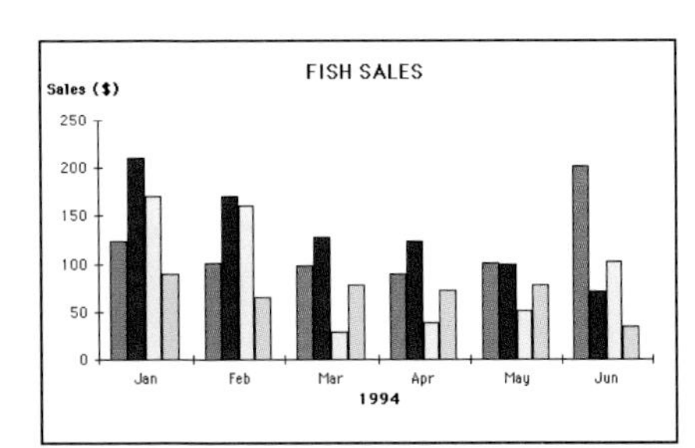

Line Chart

Often used for financial statistics, a line chart is extremely useful for showing changes in data over a period of time.

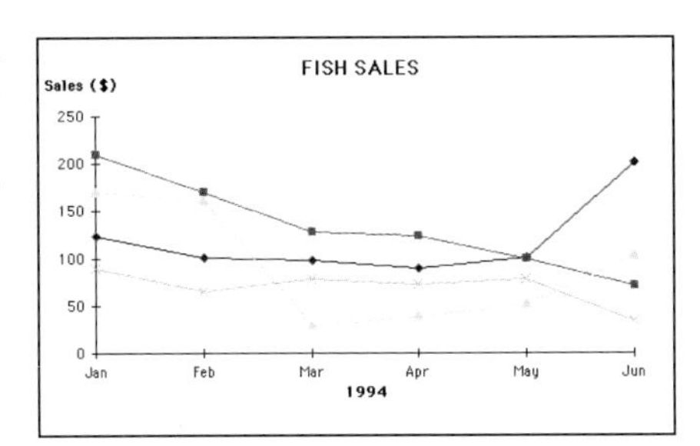

Pie Chart

A pie chart contains only one data series. It shows clearly how each data point (in this example, sales of salmon in each month) contributes to the total.

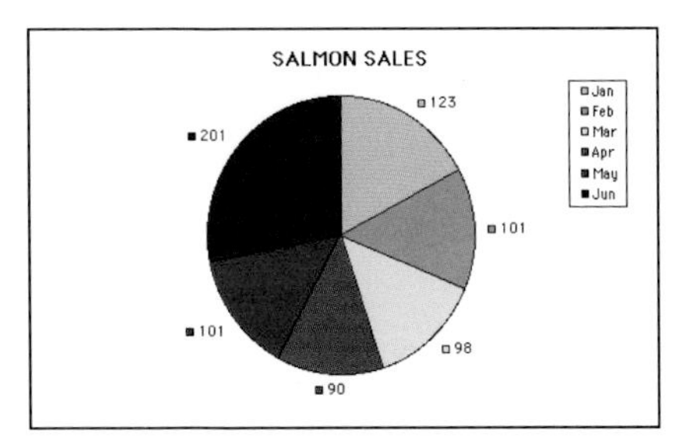

Some Definitions

■ *Data Series* A collection of related values plotted on a chart. In these examples, there are four data series — for the sales of salmon, tuna, trout, and mackerel.

■ *Categories* Individual measurement points or criteria for the data. In these examples there are six categories — the months from January to July.

■ *X and Y Axes* The X axis lies along the bottom of the chart and is usually used for categories. The Y axis goes up one side and is used for data series values. The labels are reversed on bar charts.

Combination Chart

A combination chart shows different data series measured on different scales to show how they correspond. Here, salmon and tuna are displayed in columns against the left-hand scale, and trout and mackerel are displayed as smoothed lines against the right-hand scale.

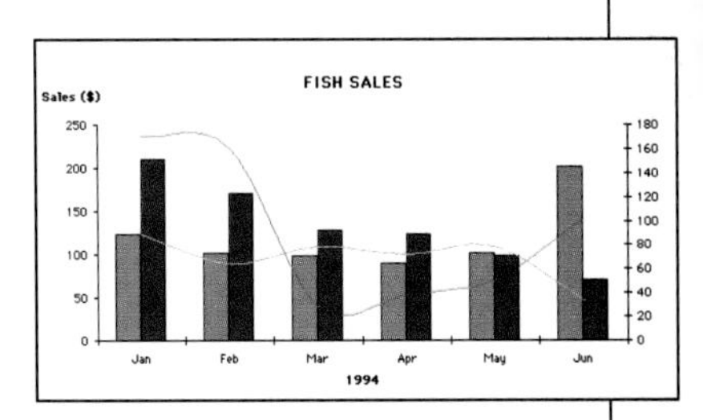

Creating a Chart

Excel creates a chart from data in a worksheet. You select the data to be included and then use Excel's charting tools to produce the type of chart you want. A chart can either be set up to occupy its own workbook sheet — a chart sheet — or embedded in a worksheet.

USING CHARTWIZARD

Charts are created using Excel's ChartWizard feature. Using a series of five dialog boxes, the ChartWizard guides you step-by-step through the process of setting up a chart. All you need to begin is a table of data in a worksheet. Using the charting features of Excel, you can quickly convert these figures into graph format.

Start by opening up a new workbook and entering the sales history data for the WizFood company, shown at left. Rename the worksheet **Sales History** and save the workbook as **WizFood**. Before creating your chart, select the range of data you wish to chart — in this case, cells A2 to G5.

WizFood

	A	B	C	D	E	F	G
1	WizFood Product Sales History						
2		1988	1989	1990	1991	1992	1993
3	Lollipops	108	115	142	86	76	64
4	Choc bars	196	203	234	258	302	349
5	Soft drinks	88	79	93	107	80	100
6							
7							
8							
9							

Worksheet Data
An Excel chart is based on ordinary worksheet data.

The Right Chart?
Sometimes it makes more sense to display a chart within the context of its worksheet data. In such cases, you should use an embedded chart. If you want to display a chart in isolation — perhaps for overhead projection as part of a presentation — then you should create a chart sheet.

1 With the cells selected, choose *Chart* from the *Insert* menu and *As New Sheet* from the submenu.

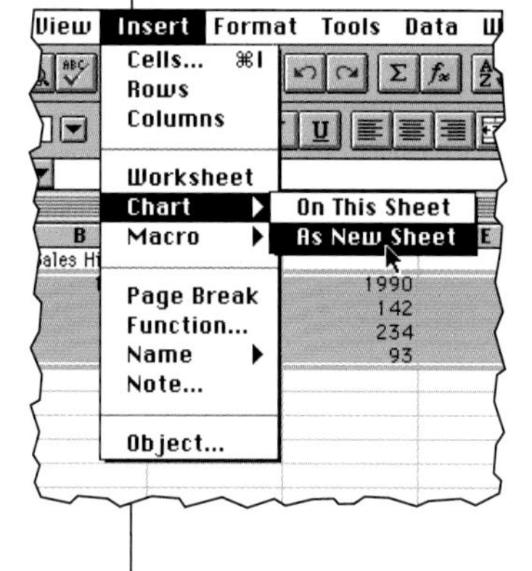

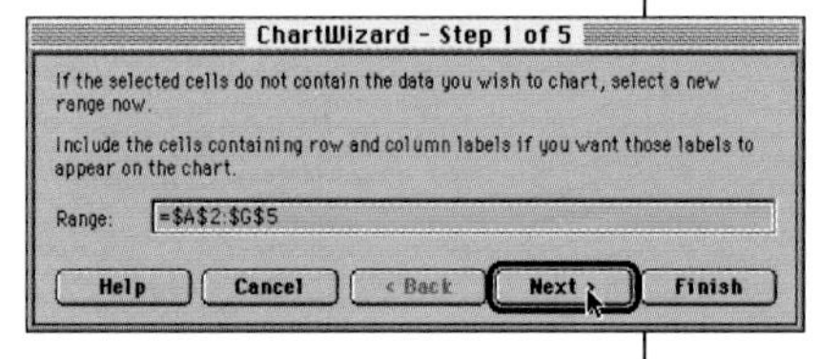

2 The first *ChartWizard* dialog box appears, displaying your cell range selection (A2 to G5). Click on *Next*.

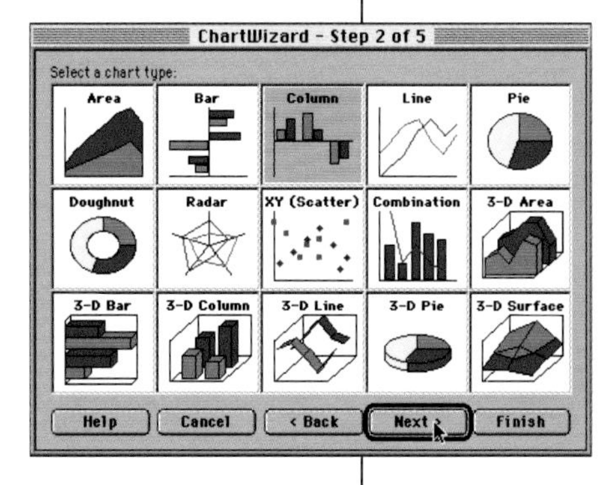

3 The second *ChartWizard* dialog box is displayed. Excel provides 15 basic types of charts for you to choose from. For this example, click on *Column,* and then click on *Next.*

4 The third *ChartWizard* dialog box appears. This shows you that there are ten different subtypes of column charts available. For this example, click on box 3, and then click on *Next.*

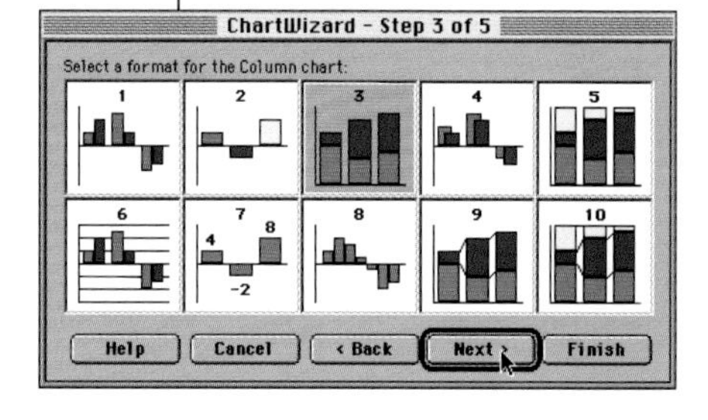

5 The fourth *ChartWizard* dialog box shows how your chart will be displayed and allows you to alter various elements. If you click on the *Columns* option under *Data Series in,* you'll see that instead of a breakdown of sales item-by-item for each year, the chart displays a year-by-year breakdown of each item. Years are now the data series and confectionery items are the categories. Click on the *Rows* option under *Data Series in* to reselect confectionery types as the data series.

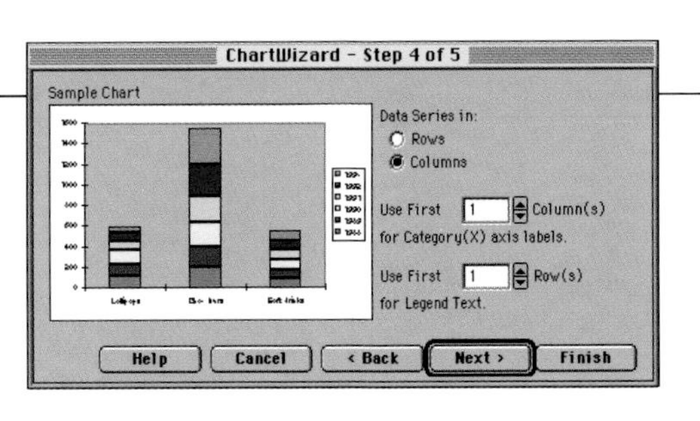

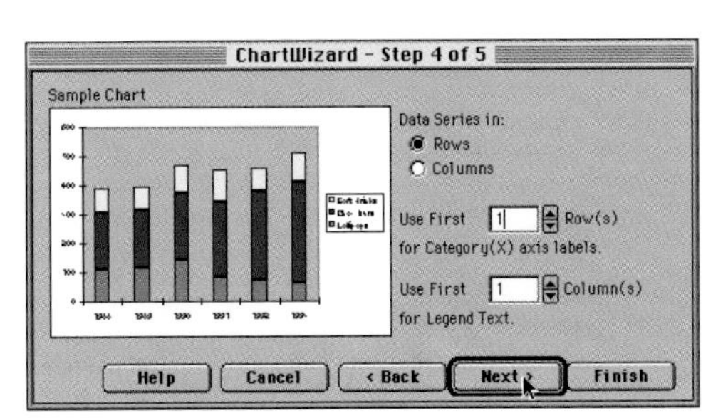

6 If the top left cell in your data selection is blank, or if the first row and column contain text, Excel assumes that the first row contains the category names and the first column contains the chart data series names. If the labels in your worksheet occupy more than one adjacent row or column, specify the number they take up into the *Use First... Rows* and *Use First... Columns* text boxes. In this example, the default value (**1**) is correct in each case. Click on the *Next* button.

Which Button?
The *ChartWizard* dialog boxes include a series of buttons that allow you to navigate through all the stages necessary to produce a chart. The *Next* and *Back* buttons take you forward and backward one step in the process. The *Finish* button uses the ChartWizard's default selections to display the chart.

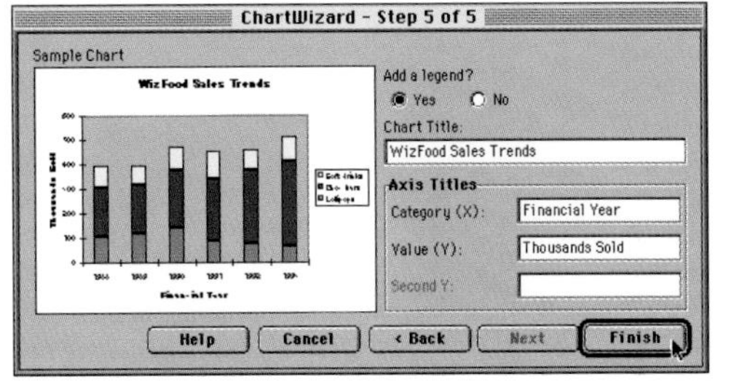

7 The final dialog box lets you add legends and titles. Choose the *Yes* button for the *Add a Legend* option. Type **WizFood Sales Trends** into the *Chart Title* box. Type **Financial Year** into the *Category [X]* box, and **Thousands Sold** into the *Value [Y]* box. Click on the *Finish* button.

8 Your chart sheet is now displayed with the default name *Chart1*. Choose *Sized with Window* from the *View* menu. Double-click on the *Chart1* tab and rename the chart sheet **WizFood Chart**. Save the **WizFood** workbook using the Save button on the Standard toolbar.

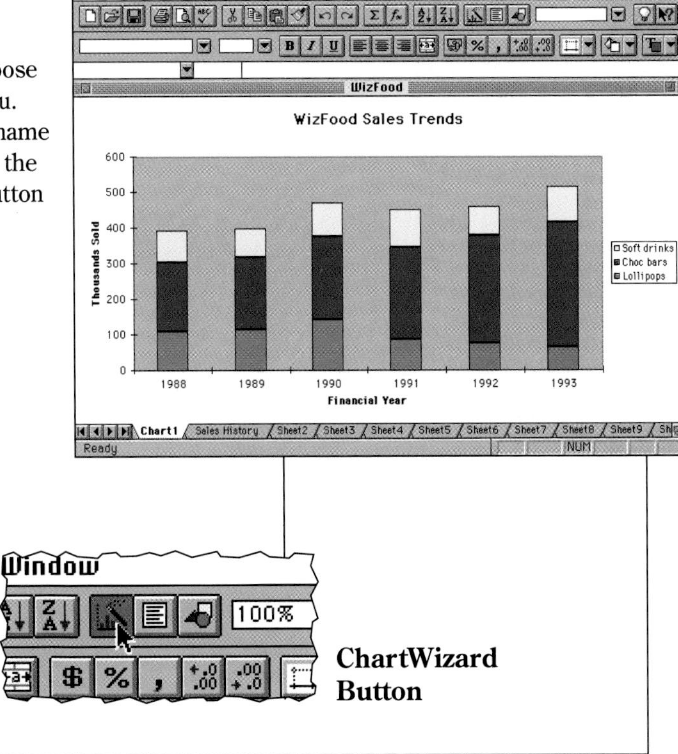

ChartWizard Button

CREATING AN EMBEDDED CHART

A chart can also be embedded in the same worksheet as its data. To create an embedded chart, select a cell range and click on the ChartWizard button on the Standard toolbar. The mouse pointer becomes a crosshair. Drag it to define the area in which you want your chart to be displayed. When you release the mouse button, the ChartWizard is invoked — you then work through the stages in the same way you did above. Choosing *Chart* from the *Insert* menu and *On This Sheet* from the submenu has the same effect as clicking on the ChartWizard button.

Choose Your Chart!
Chart types can also be changed using the Chart toolbar. If the toolbar is not already displayed, choose *Toolbars* from the *View* menu, check the box next to *Chart* under *Toolbars*, and then click on *OK*. To choose a chart type, click on the down-arrow button on the toolbar and then click on your choice from the selection that appears.

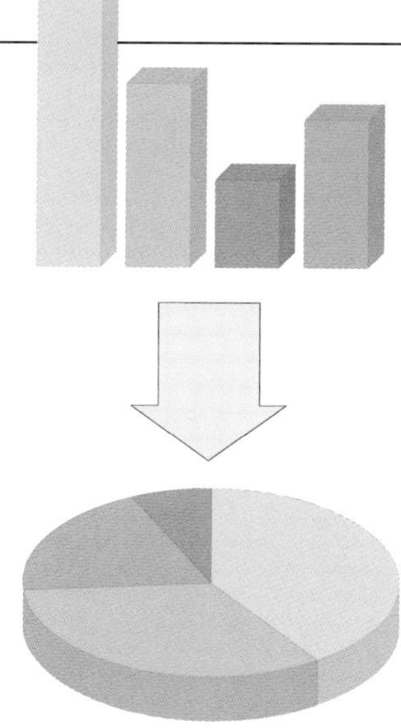

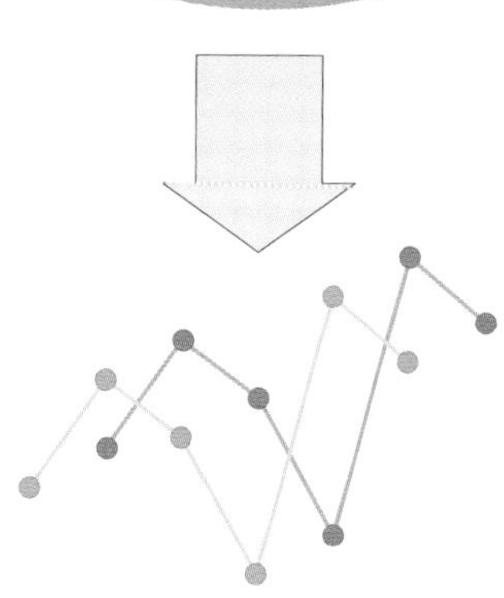

Modifying Your Chart

Although Excel can produce standard charts quickly and easily, the features don't stop there; there are plenty of tools you can use to develop and customize the standard charts to your taste. To make changes to a chart, it must be activated. A chart sheet is activated by clicking on its sheet tab. To activate an embedded chart, double-click anywhere inside it — you'll see that the border changes to a thick outline. When you activate a chart, some of the drop-down menus change to provide commands specific to charts.

CHANGING THE CHART TYPE

There are a number of ways to change the appearance of your chart. To switch to a completely different type of chart, you can use the *Chart Type* command in the *Format* menu. The *Chart Type* dialog box allows you to change the basic chart type and choose other options. Try changing from a column to an area chart. Start by activating the **WizFood Chart** sheet in the **WizFood** workbook.

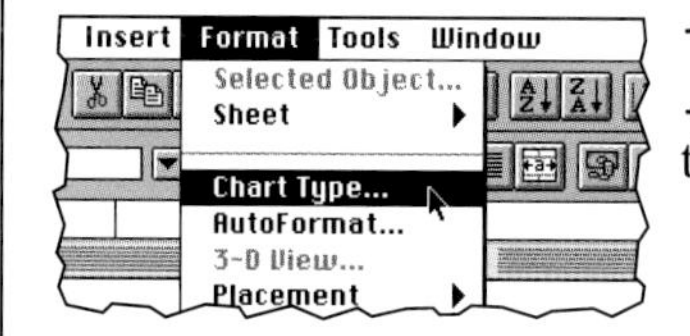

1 Choose the *Chart Type* command from the *Format* menu.

2 The *Chart Type* dialog box is displayed. Click on the *Area* box and then click on the *OK* button. You will see that your column chart has now become an area chart.

CHART SUBTYPES

Excel can produce many subtypes from the basic chart formats. One of the simplest ways of changing a subtype is by using the *AutoFormat* command.

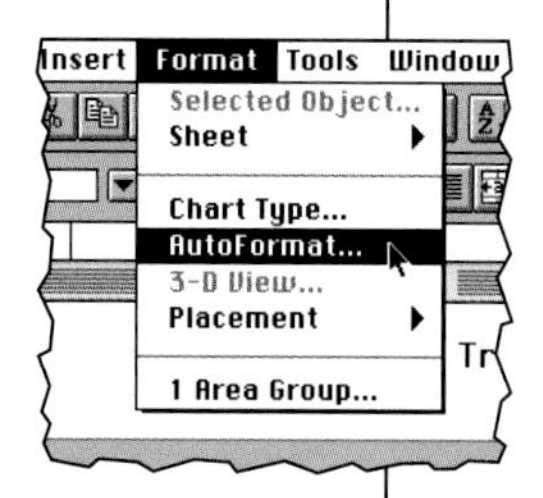

1 Choose the *AutoFormat* command from the *Format* menu. The *AutoFormat* dialog box is displayed.

2 Choose *3-D Column* under *Galleries* (you may have to scroll down to see it). The chart subtypes are displayed under *Formats*. Double-click on box *1*.

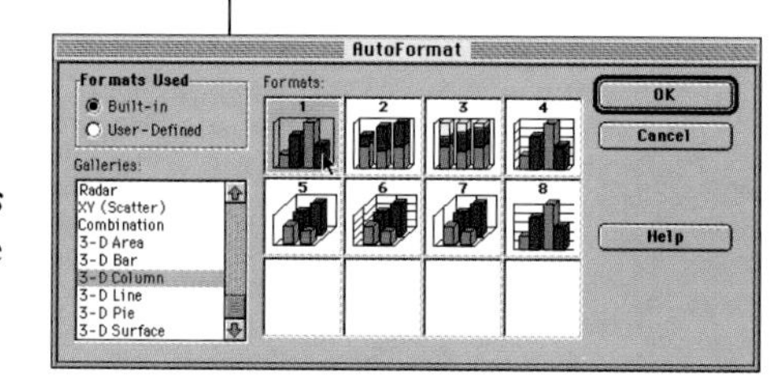

Better Backgrounds?
You can change the background color on which the data series are plotted. With the chart activated, click on the background area. When you choose the *Format* menu, you will notice that the top entry has now changed to *Selected Plot Area* or, for a 3-D chart, *Selected Walls.* Use these commands to show the *Format Plot Area* or *Format Walls* dialog box. Choose a new color or pattern and click on *OK.*

SELECTING AND CHANGING CHART ITEMS

Any of the items that make up a chart can be altered. Before you can alter an item, you must select the item by clicking on it. The name of the item currently selected is always displayed in the name box on the formula bar. You can see this as you select items to change the size of their text — starting with the chart title.

1 Click on the chart title. The chart title's text box is displayed

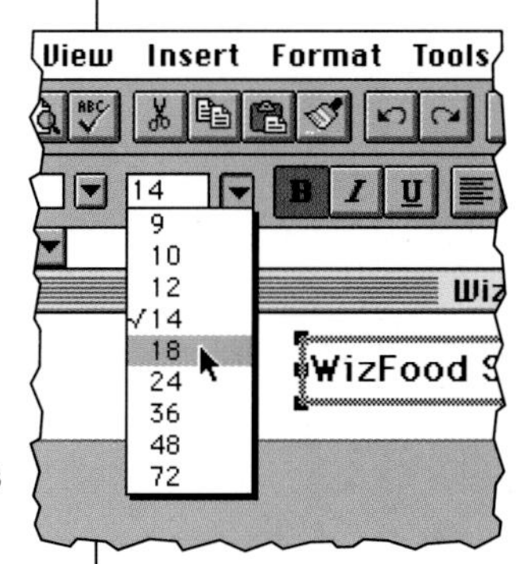

2 Click on the type size down arrow on the Formatting toolbar. From the pop-up list, choose a size of *18* pt. The title of the chart is now displayed in a larger type size.

You can use the Formatting toolbar to change the type size or font of any item that contains text or numbers. Use the same procedure to increase the type size of the legend to 12 pt.

More Text?
You can add text to a chart by using the Text Box button on the Standard toolbar. You can find out more about text boxes on page 80. Also, remember that you can check the spelling of any of the text on your chart by choosing *Spelling* from the *Tools* menu.

CHANGING THE COLORS ON YOUR CHART

You can change any of the colors that appear on your chart. For example, because the WizFood company's lollipop wrappers are red, you might want the lollipop column in your chart also to be red.

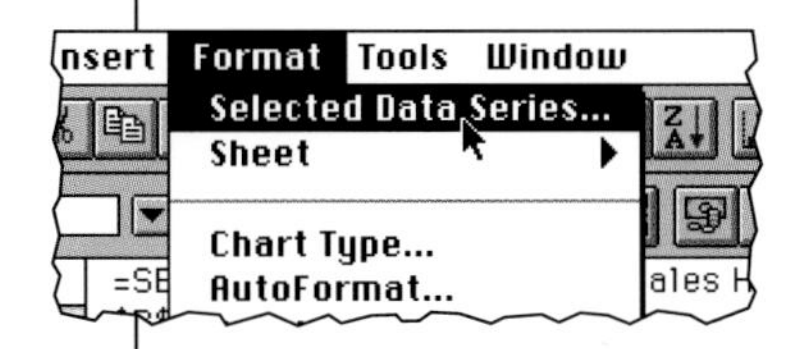

1 Click on any of the columns that represent lollipops, and choose *Selected Data Series* from the *Format* menu.

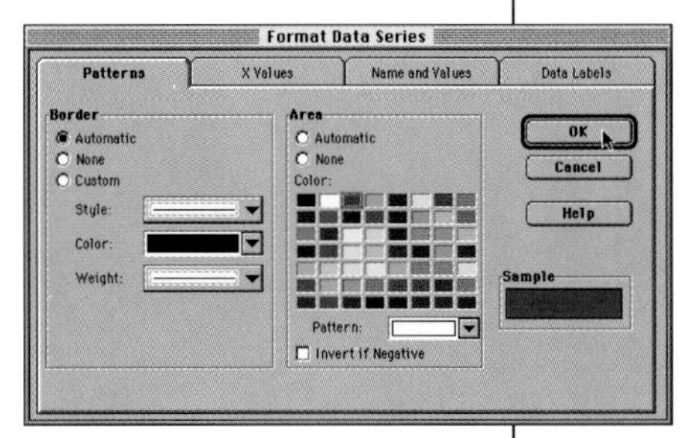

2 The *Format Data Series* dialog box is displayed. Click on the *Patterns* tab. In the *Patterns* flipcard, choose the color red in the *Area* box. Click on *OK.* All of the lollipop columns are now displayed in red.

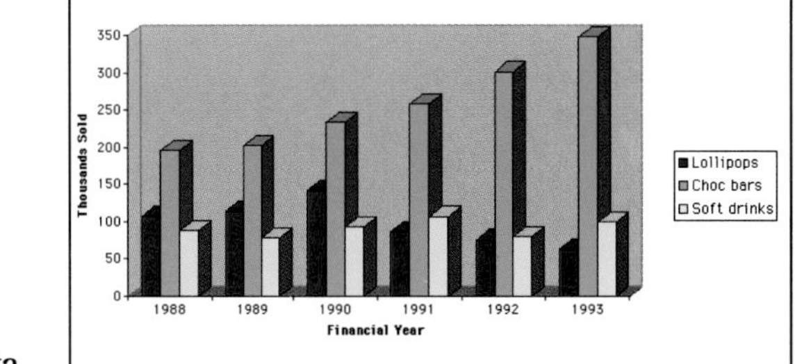

Repeat this procedure for the other two data series. Make the column representing choc bars green, and the column representing soft drinks bright yellow. The chart area should now appear as shown at right.

Graphs with Pictures

In Excel, you can copy pictures created in other graphics applications, or objects drawn with Excel tools, and use them to replace the data markers in a chart. For example, your WizFood column chart might be improved if the columns were replaced with pictures of lollipops, chocolate bars, and soft drinks.

Stretch Graph
Excel can display pictures in charts stretched to fit their data markers.

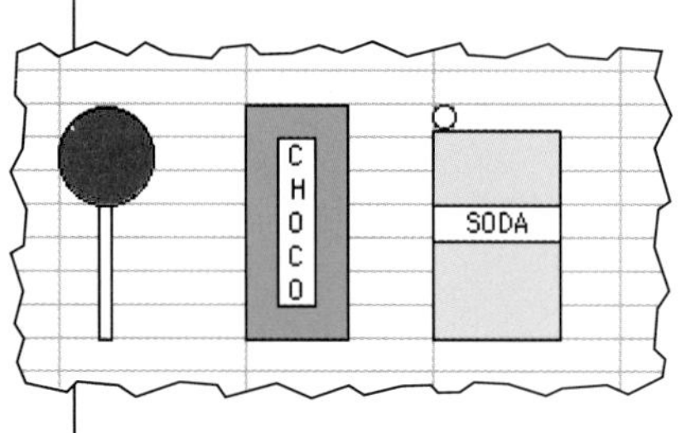

PUTTING PICTURES IN YOUR CHART

First you need some pictures to copy into your chart. Click on the *Sheet2* tab to display an empty worksheet. Refer back to "The Drawing Toolbar" on page 78. Draw pictures of a lollipop, a chocolate bar, and a soft drink. Group the elements that make up each individual picture by selecting each element with the Shift key depressed and then clicking on the Group button on the Drawing toolbar. Finally, close the Drawing toolbar and rename the worksheet **Graphics**.

1 To copy the pictures into your chart, it is helpful to display both sheets. Choose *New Window* from the *Window* menu, and then choose *Arrange* from the *Window* menu and double-click on *Tiled*. Click on the **WizFood Chart** sheet tab in **WizFood:2**.

2 Change the chart type, this time with the Chart toolbar (if it is not already open, choose *Toolbars* from the *View* menu, check the box alongside *Chart*, and click on *OK*). Click on the down arrow and choose a simple column chart.

Moving Pictures
In addition to using pictures produced by Excel's own drawing tools, you can use any type of graphic image from any source — Clipart from Word for Windows, for example — as long as it can be brought into Excel using the *Copy* and *Paste* commands.

3 Return to the **Graphics** worksheet by clicking on the **WizFood:1** window. Click on the lollipop to select it, and then choose *Copy* from the *Edit* menu. Return to **WizFood Chart**.

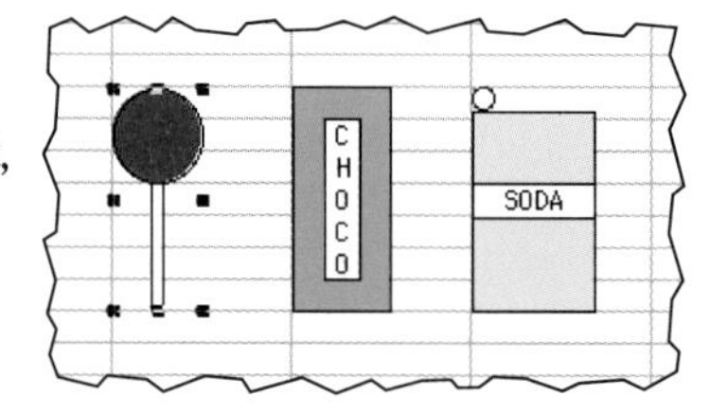

4 Click on any of the six columns that represent lollipop sales. Choose *Paste* from the *Edit* menu. The first column for each year's data is replaced by a picture of a stretched lollipop.

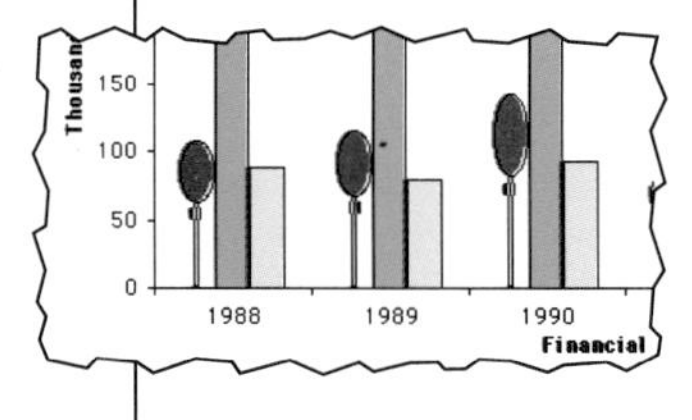

Repeat this procedure, replacing the choc bar and soft drink columns with their pictures. Notice that the legend also uses the pictures. Close the window displaying the **Graphics** worksheet, and click on the zoom box to "maximize" the window with the **WizFood Chart** chart sheet.

Picture Chart
Each data series is now represented by its own picture.

STACKING AND STRETCHING

Excel can display pictures within charts in three different ways: stretched to fit the data marker (which is what you've just done), stacked copies of the picture, or stacked copies scaled to match a value that you specify. Let's stack copies of the pictures so that each picture represents 50,000 units.

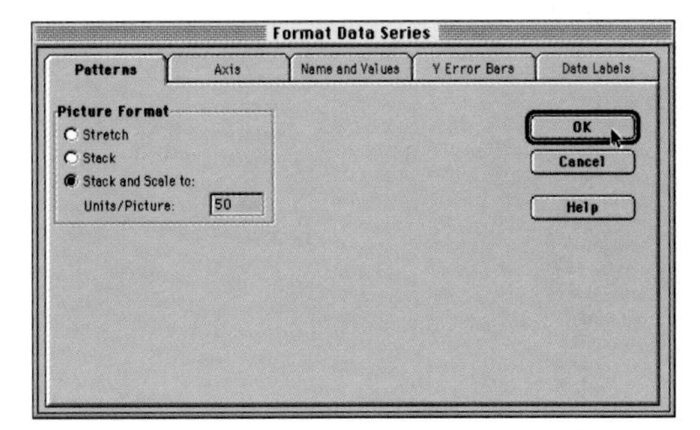

1 Double-click on one of the chocolate bars to display the *Format Data Series* dialog box. In the *Patterns* flipcard, select *Stack and Scale to* from the *Picture Format* options. A *Units/Picture* value is specified — in this instance **50** is appropriate because it coincides with the values on the Y axis.

2 Click on *OK*. The chocolate bars are displayed stacked and scaled. Repeat this with the other pictures.

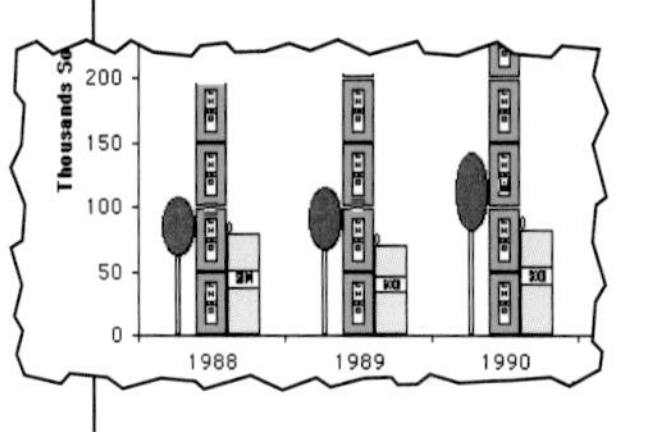

CLEARING A PICTURE

If you no longer want a picture to represent a data marker, you can easily revert the data marker to its original format. You simply click on the picture that you want to clear from the chart, and then choose *Clear* from the *Edit* menu and *Formats* from the submenu. Note that this will also clear any other formats you have applied, such as colors.

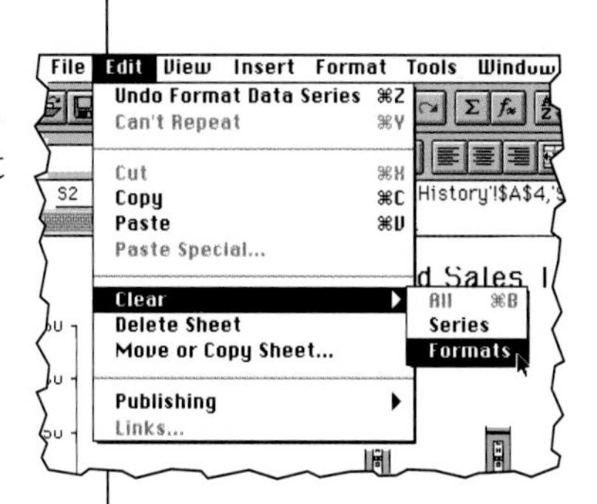

Printing Your Chart

You can print a worksheet containing an embedded chart in the same way as any other worksheet — by clicking on the Print button or by choosing *Print* from the *File* menu. Printing standard worksheets is discussed in more depth on pages 82 to 87.

PRINTING A CHART SHEET

For printing a chart sheet, the principle is similar except that the flipcard options in the *Page Setup* dialog box are specifically oriented toward charts. Your chart will be printed as specified in the *Page Setup* dialog box. So, before you start printing, choose *Page Setup* from the *File* menu and make sure that the settings in all four flipcards fit your requirements. For example, you can alter the page orientation and scale the chart to fit the page.

Page Setup Dialog Box

The Page *flipcard can be used to specify orientation and scaling of your chart when it is printed.*

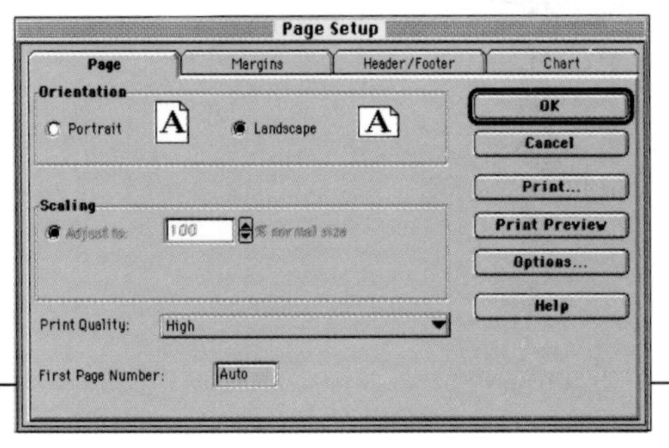

Gray or Black?

If you create a sheet in color, but don't have a color printer, Excel automatically translates the colors into shades of gray. If you want to print only in black and white, choose *Page Setup* from the *File* menu. Select the *Chart* tab, and check the *Print in Black and White* box.

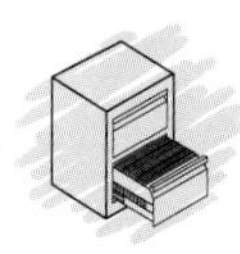

Databases

Some Definitions

- *Record* A collection of related cells making up a single item (row) in the list.
- *Field* A specific piece of information held in each record — the contents of a single cell.
- *Field Name* The heading at the top of each column. A column contains the same type of data for every record.
- *Criteria* The basis on which the sorting and extracting of data is performed. The criteria are defined by you, the user.
- *Filtering* The display of a limited selection of records in a list based on the user's own criteria.
- *Extracting* The selection of specific records from a list based on the user's own criteria, and their display in a different part of a worksheet.

DATABASES ARE TOOLS FOR ORGANIZING, managing, and retrieving data. Typical examples of databases are telephone directories and price lists. Each database is a collection of records that contain the same categories of data, known as *fields*. For example, each record in a telephone directory contains a name, address, and telephone number. With any type of database, it is important to be able to add, change, and extract data easily.

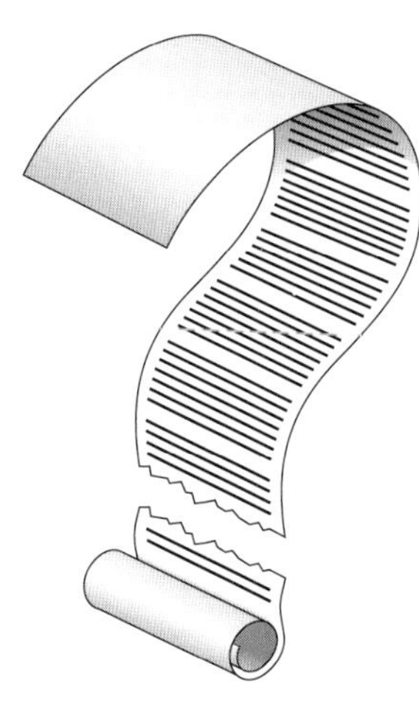

What Is a List?

A list is a simple database. Excel allows you to create your own lists within worksheets. You can enter your data, use tools to extract information, perform calculations, and print the data in any format. The list appears as a range of cells consisting of one or more columns and at least two rows. Each row contains a record, and each cell in a row contains a field.

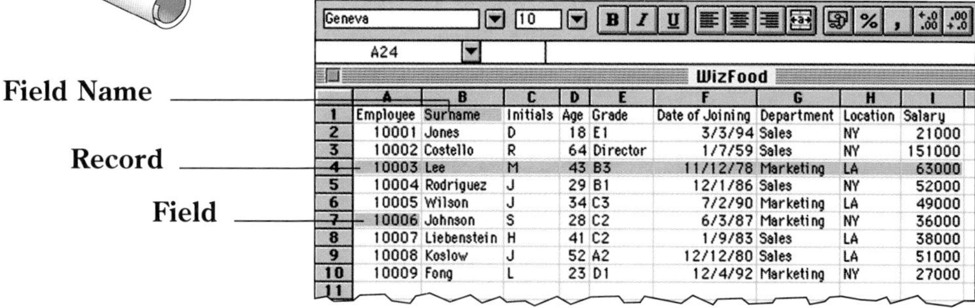

	A	B	C	D	E	F	G	H	I
1	Employee	Surname	Initials	Age	Grade	Date of Joining	Department	Location	Salary
2	10001	Jones	D	18	E1	3/3/94	Sales	NY	21000
3	10002	Costello	R	64	Director	1/7/59	Sales	NY	151000
4	10003	Lee	M	43	B3	11/12/78	Marketing	LA	63000
5	10004	Rodriguez	J	29	B1	12/1/86	Sales	NY	52000
6	10005	Wilson	J	34	C3	7/2/90	Marketing	LA	49000
7	10006	Johnson	S	28	C2	6/3/87	Marketing	NY	36000
8	10007	Liebenstein	H	41	C2	1/9/83	Sales	LA	38000
9	10008	Koslow	J	52	A2	12/12/80	Sales	LA	51000
10	10009	Fong	L	23	D1	12/4/92	Marketing	NY	27000
11									

Creating a List

Try creating your own list containing employee information for the WizFood Corporation. For this list, each row will have entries for information such as employee number, surname, location, and salary. Begin by opening **WizFood**. Click on a new sheet tab *(Sheet3)* and rename it **Personnel List**.

1 Type the field names as column headings in row 1, as shown below. These names define the kind of information that you will enter for every employee. Type the first record in row 2 beneath the appropriate headings.

WizFood

	A	B	C	D	E	F	G	H	I	J
1	Employee	Surname	Initials	Age	Grade	Date of Joining	Department	Location	Salary	
2	10001	Jones	D	18	E1	3/3/94	Sales	NY	21000	
3										
4										

2 To set the column widths, select columns A through I, and choose *Column* from the *Format* menu. From the submenu, choose *AutoFit Selection.*

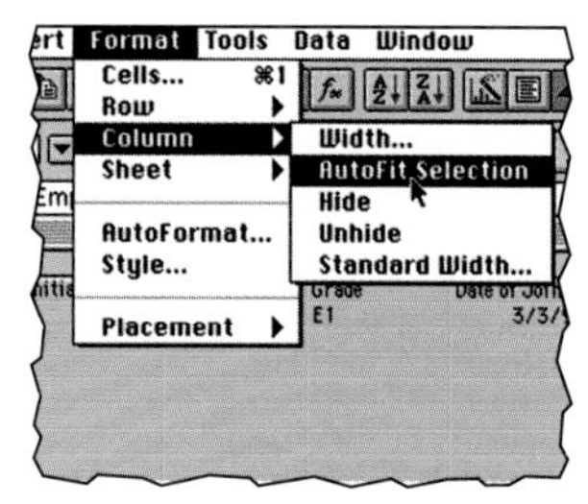

The Data Form

You can add data to your list simply by typing new records in each new row, and you can maintain the data by editing the individual cells. However, Excel also provides a powerful tool — the data form — to help you maintain the information in your list. The data form is a dialog box, created automatically for your list, that makes it easy to enter and maintain data or search for records based on specified criteria.

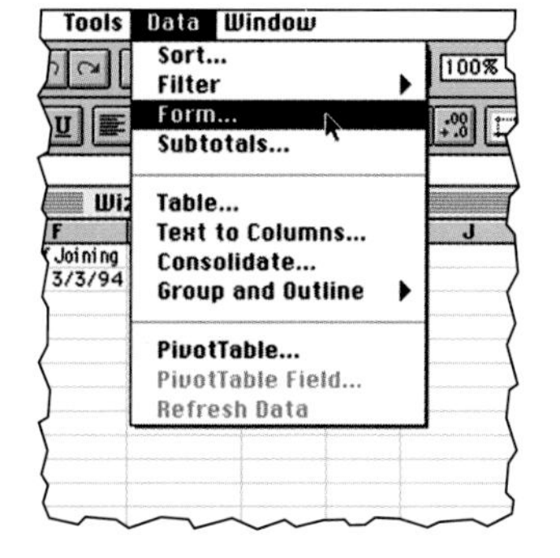

1 To use the data form, select any cell within the list (I2, for example), and then choose *Form* from the *Data* menu.

2 Excel displays the data form and the first record in your list. Note that the data form takes the worksheet name (**Personnel List**) as its heading, and the field names are taken from the column headings in your list.

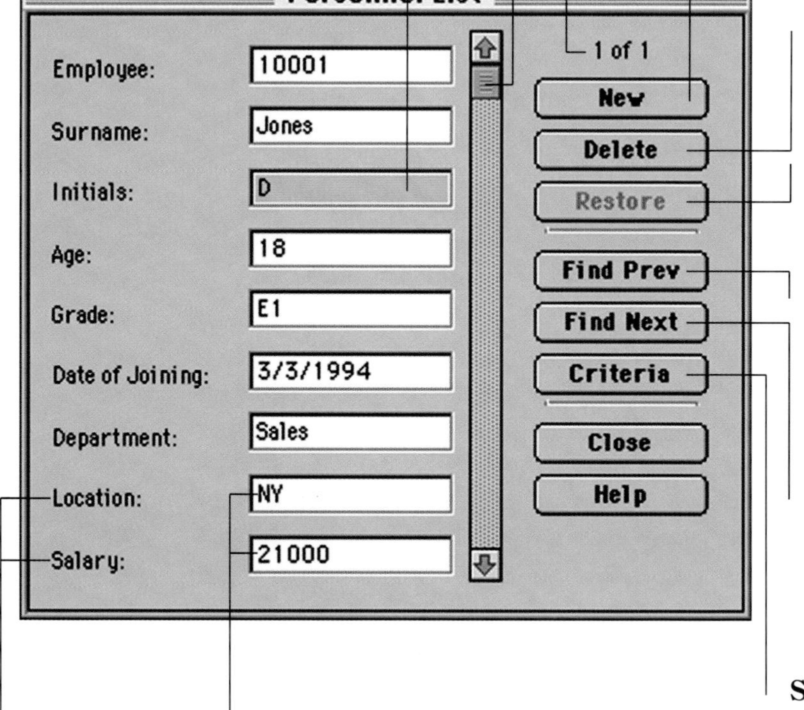

Active data field

Data form title derived from the worksheet name

Drag the scroll box to scroll through records

Record indicator shows the record number and total number of records in the list

Creates a new record

Removes the displayed record from the list

Restores edited fields in the displayed record

Displays the previous record (the Up direction key also does this)

Displays the next record (the Down direction key also does this)

Selects records according to your own criteria

Field names (column headings)

Data fields (pressing Tab moves to the next field and pressing Shift Tab moves to the previous field)

How Many Fields?
A list can be as large as a worksheet (16,384 rows and 256 columns). However, the data form can display only up to 32 fields. If your list contains more than 32 fields, you must enter data or make changes to the remaining fields directly in the worksheet.

Ideas for Databases
There are numerous practical uses for databases, both at work and in the home. A database might be used to keep the addresses and birthdays of your friends and family, or perhaps to store details of your music and video collections. At work, databases can be used to keep lists of business clients or keep track of bill payments.

ADDING RECORDS

Now that you've seen how the data form works, you can use it to add some more employee records to your list. If the *Data Form* dialog box is not active, choose *Form* from the *Data* menu.

1 In the data form, click on the *New* button. You will see that the Record Indicator changes to *New Record.*

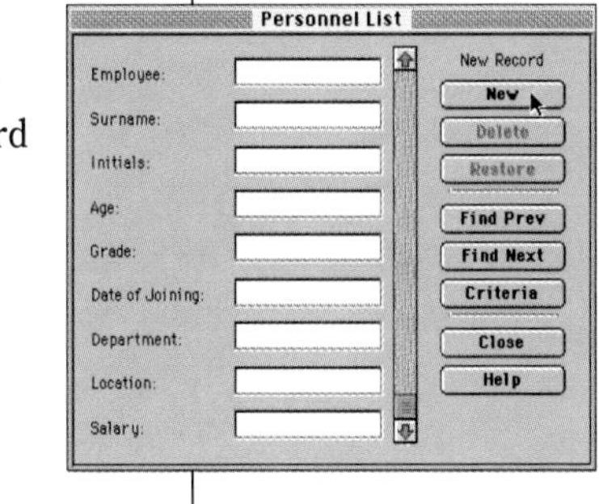

Wizfood

	A	B	C	D	E	F	G	H	I
1	Employee	Surname	Initials	Age	Grade	Date of Joining	Department	Location	Salary
2	10001	Jones	D	18	E1	3/3/94	Sales	NY	21000
3	10002	Costello	R	64	Director	1/7/59	Sales	NY	151000
4	10003	Lee	M	43	B3	11/12/78	Marketing	LA	63000
5	10004	Rodriguez	J	29	B1	12/1/86	Sales	NY	52000
6	10005	Wilson	J	34	C3	7/2/90	Marketing	LA	49000
7	10006	Johnson	S	28	C2	6/3/87	Marketing	NY	36000
8	10007	Liebenstein	H	41	C2	1/9/83	Sales	LA	38000
9	10008	Koslow	J	52	A2	12/12/80	Sales	LA	51000
10	10009	Fong	L	23	D1	12/4/92	Marketing	NY	27000
11									
12									

2 Type the data for the second record shown at left (row 3). To move from field to field, use the mouse or press the Tab key. When you have entered all the data for the record, press the Down direction key or click on the *New* button to begin the next record.

Room for Growth!
As you add new records to a list using the data form, the cell range of the list increases downward. Therefore, you should avoid adding records to a list with other cell entries beneath it. If there is no room to add a new record, an error message is displayed.

Repeat the procedure for rows (records) 4 through 10. When you have finished, click on the *Close* button to view the completed list on the worksheet. Adjust the column widths where necessary.

What Is an Operator?
Standard mathematical operators can be used when selecting from a range. They are:
= *Equals*
> *Greater than*
< *Less than*
>= *Greater than or equal to*
<= *Less than or equal to*
<> *Does not equal*

FINDING A RECORD

Finding specific data is easy; Excel can retrieve data according to criteria that you specify. You can search for specific values or use the standard operators (=, >, <, >=, <=, <>) to search for a range of values. To see how this works, let's find all New York-based employees with a salary of at least $50,000.

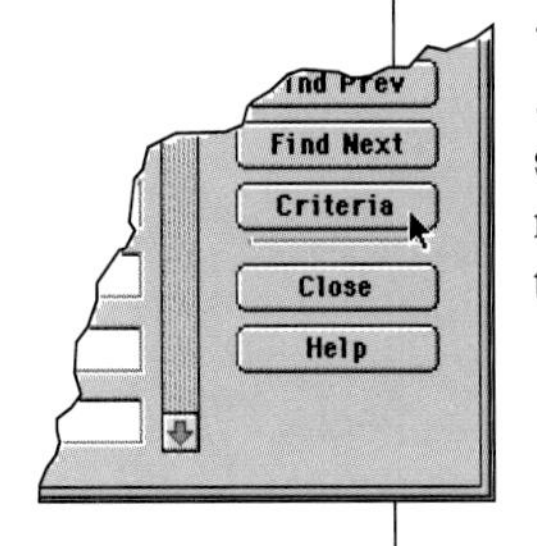

1 Open the data form and use the scroll bar to display record 1. Click on the *Criteria* button.

2 Enter your selection criteria: in the *Location* box, type **NY**; and in the *Salary* box, type **>=50000**. Click on the *Find Next* button. The first record to match your criteria — employee record number 10002 — is displayed.

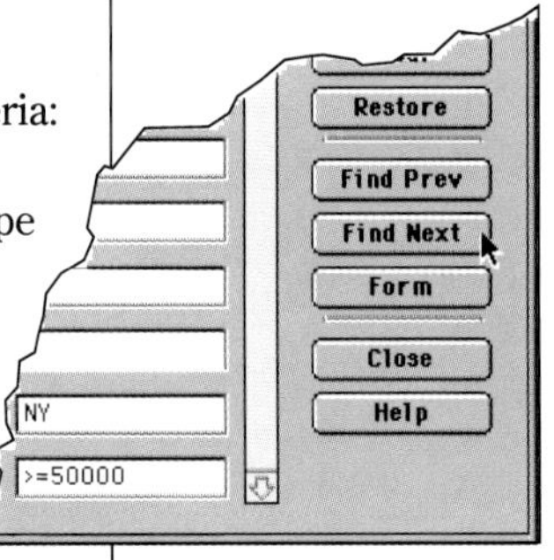

Click on *Find Next* again; a second matching record (employee record number 10004) is displayed. You can use the *Find Next* and *Find Prev* buttons to move forward and backward through the matching records. When you have finished, click on the *Close* button.

Wildcard Characters

When specifying your selection criteria, you can use a question mark (?) to match any single character in a specific position within a field. Use an asterisk (*) to match any number of characters. Here are some examples that apply to your list:

Field	Criteria	Records Found
Surname	JO*	All employees whose surnames begin with **JO**
Surname	JO?????	All seven-letter employee names beginning with **JO**

DELETING A RECORD

You can delete a record displayed in the data form simply by clicking on the *Delete* button. A confirmation dialog box is displayed to prevent you from deleting a record by mistake.

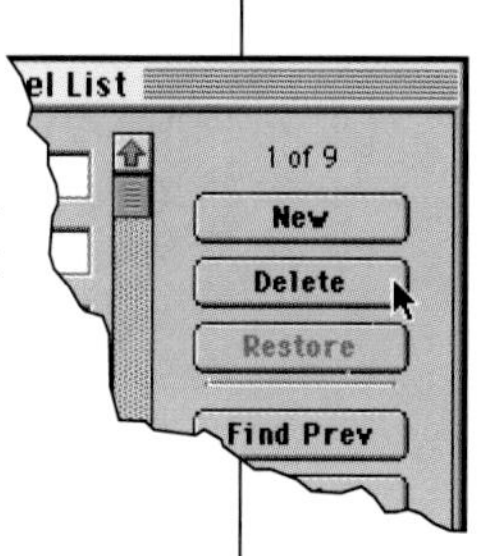

Filtering Records

You can select specified records from a list using the *Filter* command. You can either "hide" the records you don't need, or copy the records you want to another cell range on a worksheet. These extracted records can then be treated like any other worksheet data.

USING THE AUTOFILTER

To see how this works, use AutoFilter to extract from your list all New York employees earning more than $35,000. Start by selecting any cell in your list.

1 Choose *Filter* from the *Data* menu, and from the submenu select *AutoFilter.* A downward-pointing arrow appears in each of the column headings.

2 Click on the down arrow next to *Location* in cell H1. From the pop-up list choose *NY*. All the records *not* containing New York employees are filtered out.

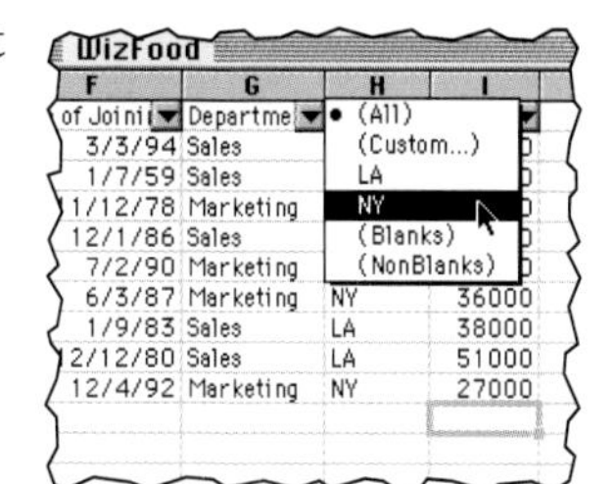

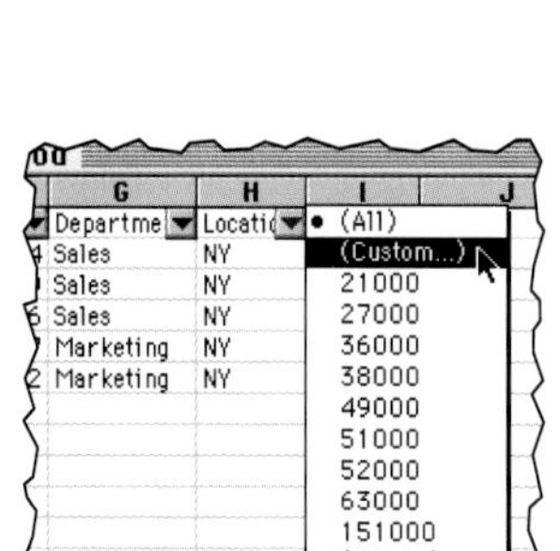

3 Now click on the down arrow next to *Salary* in cell I1 and choose *[Custom]* from the pop-up list. The *Custom AutoFilter* dialog box appears.

4 Click on the down arrow under *Salary* and choose the greater than (>) operator. In the box to its right, type **35000**. Click on *OK*.

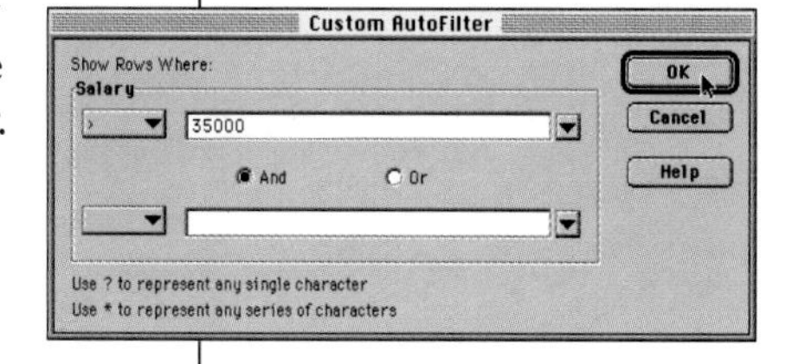

5 You have now filtered out all records except for New York employees earning over $35,000.

Delete or Filter?
When you remove records using the data form or the *Delete* command in the *Edit* menu, you *cannot* retrieve them later unless you've saved a previous version of the workbook. By using the *Filter* command in the *Data* menu, you hide records from view, but they remain in your database. They can easily be retrieved at any time.

RETRIEVING YOUR RECORDS

Rows 2, 4, 6, and 8 to 10 are no longer visible. To retrieve them, choose *Filter* from the *Data* menu, and in the submenu click on the *Show All* option. The hidden rows are then displayed.

To exit from the AutoFilter and remove the arrows from your column headings, choose *Filter* from the *Data* menu again. In the submenu, you will see that the *AutoFilter* option has a check by it, indicating that it is active. Click on *AutoFilter* again to switch it off. Your list reverts to its original form.

Show All

To display your list in full, you choose the Show All *command.*

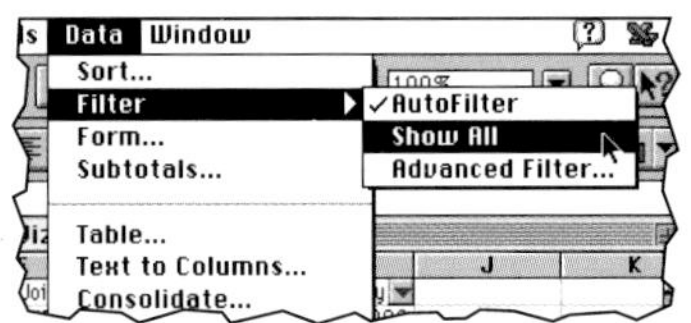

Hide and Seek!

Remember that when you use *AutoFilter*, your filtered records have not been deleted from the list. Excel has simply "hidden" them according to your instructions. To remind you that there are hidden records, the row numbers of the filtered range are displayed in a different color in the worksheet.

Advanced Filtering

Excel also lets you filter a list using more complex criteria. For example, you might want to use multiple comparison criteria to extract simultaneously all Los Angeles employees who earn more than $50,000 and all New York employees who earn less than $30,000. To do this, you specify your criteria in a worksheet range — Excel uses these criteria to extract your list.

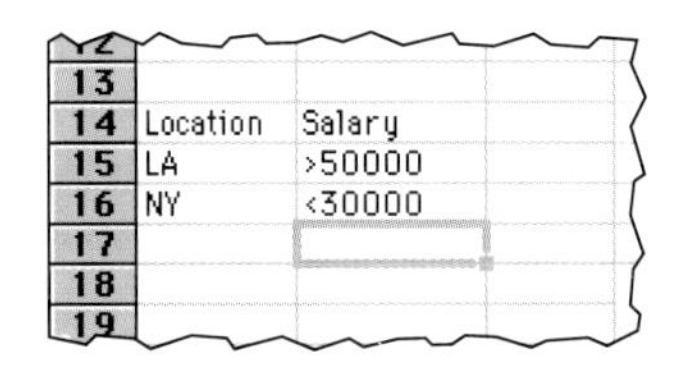

13		
14	Location	Salary
15	LA	>50000
16	NY	<30000
17		
18		
19		

1 Enter the criteria shown above into the cell range A14 to B16. You can enter criteria anywhere in a worksheet, but the column headings must be identical to those in the list.

2 Select any cell in your list, choose *Filter* from the *Data* menu, and then choose *Advanced Filter* from the submenu. The *Advanced Filter* dialog box appears.

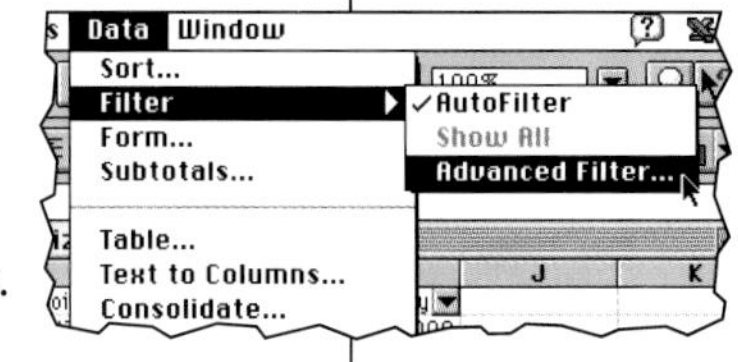

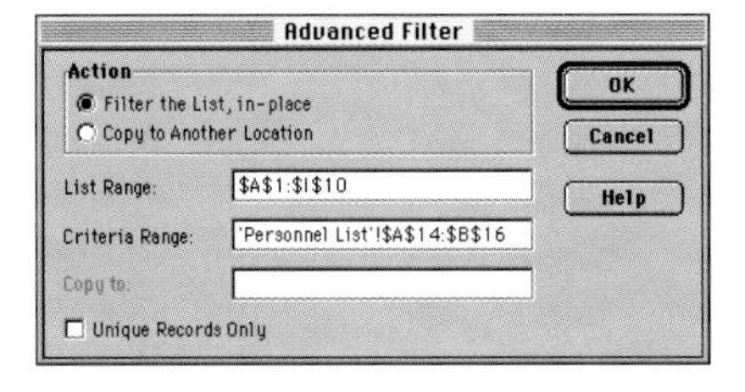

3 In the *List Range* box, you should see *$A$1:$I$10*. This defines the range of your list. Now click in the *Criteria Range* box and select the criteria range (cells A14 to B16).

4 Click on the *Copy to Another Location* button, and then click in the *Copy to* box. Click on cell A20 in your worksheet to define the top left hand corner of the range in which your extracted data will appear. Click on *OK*.

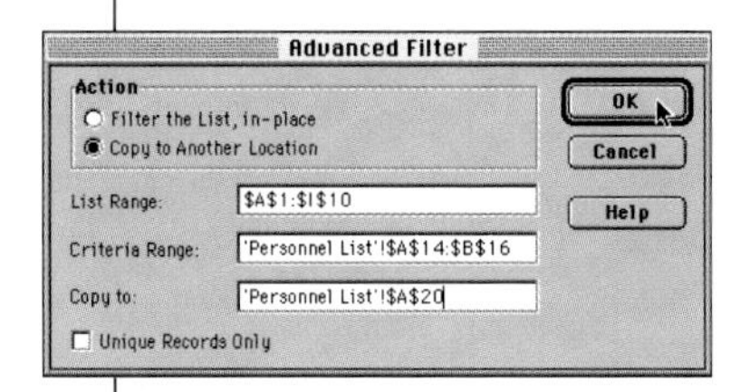

The extracted records are displayed. After examining them to check that the extraction criteria have been satisfied, clear the whole range A14:I24 by selecting this range and choosing *Clear* from the *Edit* menu and *Contents* from the submenu.

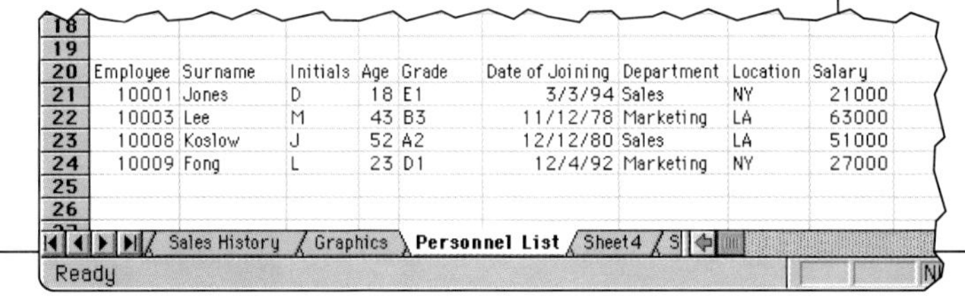

18									
19									
20	Employee	Surname	Initials	Age	Grade	Date of Joining	Department	Location	Salary
21	10001	Jones	D	18	E1	3/3/94	Sales	NY	21000
22	10003	Lee	M	43	B3	11/12/78	Marketing	LA	63000
23	10008	Koslow	J	52	A2	12/12/80	Sales	LA	51000
24	10009	Fong	L	23	D1	12/4/92	Marketing	NY	27000
25									
26									

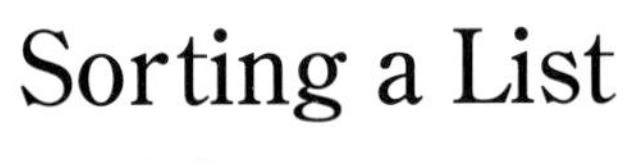

Sorting a List

Excel allows you to reorganize your data alphabetically, numerically, or by date using the *Sort* command on the *Data* menu. First you select the range to be sorted and then you select the sort keys — your criteria for reorganizing your data. A sort key identifies which field name (column) you want to sort by and the sort sequence within that field name. Excel allows you to choose more than one sort key. To see how this works, sort the employees by department and then within each department by their date of joining.

First or Last?
Excel lets you sort your data in either ascending or descending sequence. When you choose *Ascending,* alphabetical data is sorted from A to Z, numbers are sorted with the lowest first, and dates are sorted with the earliest date first. When you choose *Descending,* these rules are reversed.

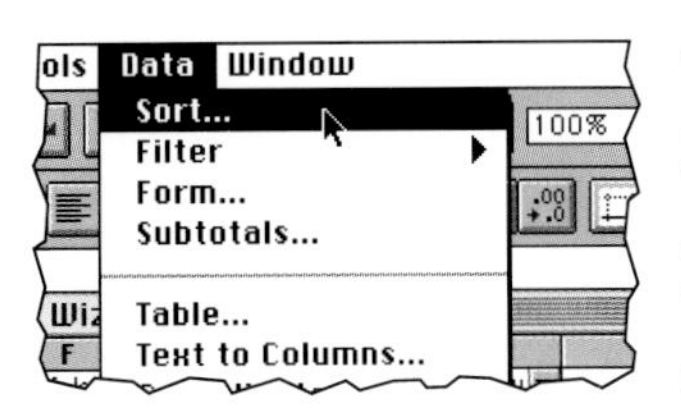

1 Select any cell in your database and choose *Sort* from the *Data* menu. You will see all the records highlighted — this is the data that will be sorted. The field names will remain in the first row and will not be included in the sort.

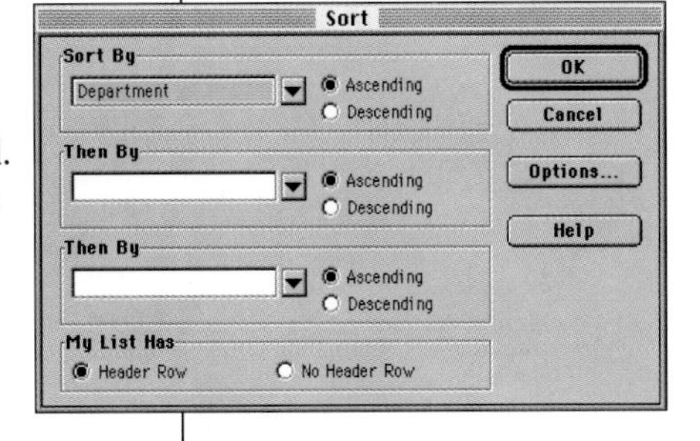

2 The *Sort* dialog box is displayed. Define a sort key by clicking on the down arrow under *Sort By* and selecting *Department*. Choose the *Ascending* option.

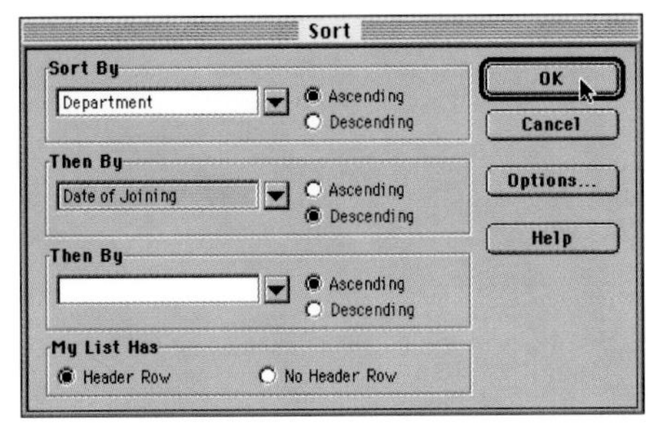

3 To specify the second sort key, click on the down arrow under *Then By*, and then select *Date of Joining*. Click on the *Descending* option, and then click on *OK*.

4 Your data has now been sorted in ascending alphabetical order by department (the first sort key that you specified). Within each department, the employees are sorted according to who joined most recently (the second sort key).

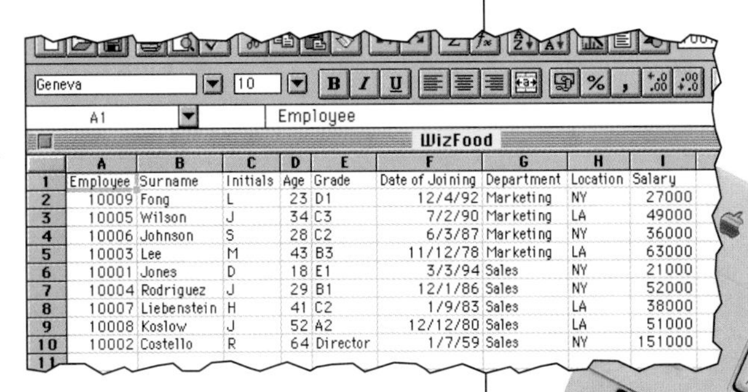

	A	B	C	D	E	F	G	H	I
1	Employee	Surname	Initials	Age	Grade	Date of Joining	Department	Location	Salary
2	10009	Fong	L	23	D1	12/4/92	Marketing	NY	27000
3	10005	Wilson	J	34	C3	7/2/90	Marketing	LA	49000
4	10006	Johnson	S	28	C2	6/3/87	Marketing	NY	36000
5	10003	Lee	M	43	B3	11/12/78	Marketing	LA	63000
6	10001	Jones	D	18	E1	3/3/94	Sales	NY	21000
7	10004	Rodriguez	J	29	B1	12/1/86	Sales	NY	52000
8	10007	Liebenstein	H	41	C2	1/9/83	Sales	LA	38000
9	10008	Koslow	J	52	A2	12/12/80	Sales	LA	51000
10	10002	Costello	R	64	Director	1/7/59	Sales	NY	151000

Undo Sort
Remember that the Undo *command is on the* Edit *menu.*

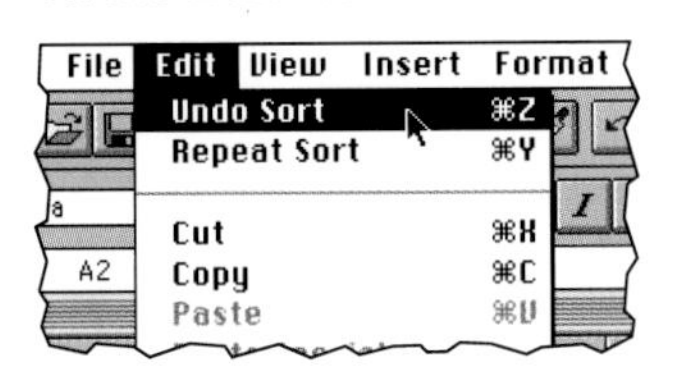

If you don't like the way your data has been sorted, you should immediately use the *Undo Sort* command or use the keyboard shortcut Command-Z. In this instance, you can leave the data sorted as above.

Adding Subtotals to Your List

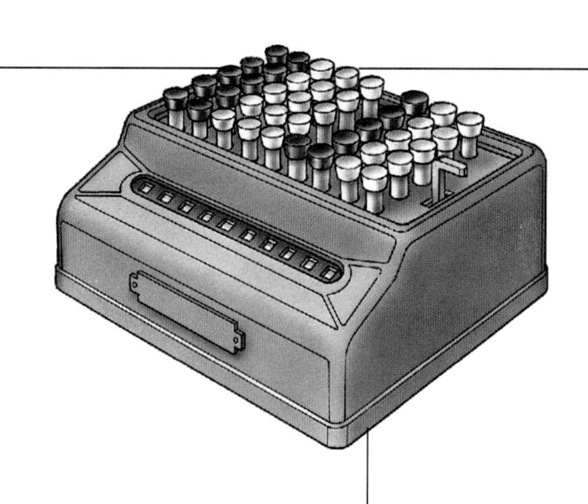

Excel can automatically provide subtotals within any list that contains numeric data. Before you can include subtotals, your list must be sorted into the groups that you want to subtotal. Because you have already sorted the list by department, you can create subtotals for the salaries in each department. Click on any cell in the list.

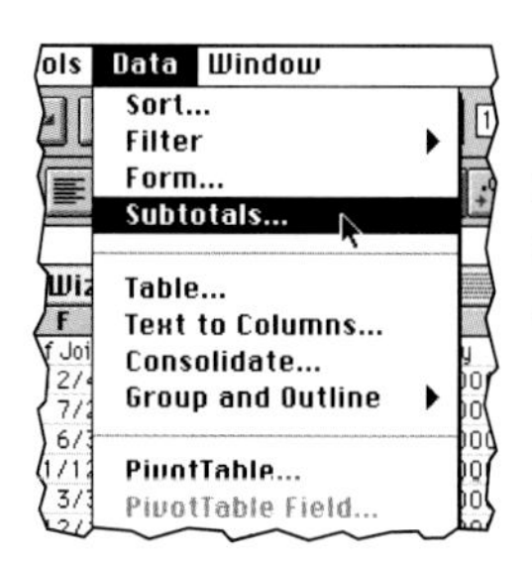

1 Choose *Subtotals* from the *Data* menu. The *Subtotal* dialog box is displayed.

2 Click on the down arrow under *At Each Change in* and choose *Department*. Click on the down arrow under *Use Function* and choose *Sum*. Under *Add Subtotal to*, make sure the box to the left of *Salary* is checked. Click on *OK*.

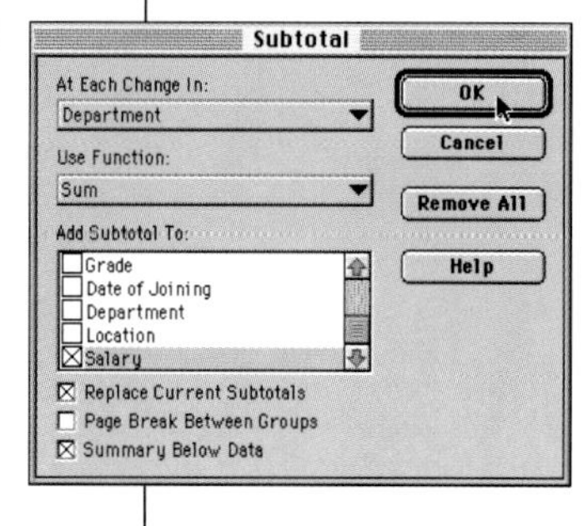

	A	B	C	D	E	F	G	H	I
1	Employee	Surname	Initials	Age	Grade	Date of Joining	Department	Location	Salary
2	10009	Fong	L	23	D1	12/4/92	Marketing	NY	27000
3	10005	Wilson	J	34	C3	7/2/90	Marketing	LA	49000
4	10006	Johnson	S	28	C2	6/3/87	Marketing	NY	36000
5	10003	Lee	M	43	B3	11/12/78	Marketing	LA	63000
6							**Marketing Total**		175000
7	10001	Jones	D	18	E1	3/3/94	Sales	NY	21000
8	10004	Rodriguez	J	29	B1	12/1/86	Sales	NY	52000
9	10007	Liebenstein	H	41	C2	1/9/83	Sales	LA	38000
10	10008	Koslow	J	52	A2	12/12/80	Sales	LA	51000
11	10002	Costello	R	64	Director	1/7/59	Sales	NY	151000
12							**Sales Total**		313000
13							**Grand Total**		488000
14									
15									

Outlining Symbols

3 The brackets and minus buttons that appear at the left of the window are outlining symbols. You'll find out more about these on page 108.

4 To remove the subtotals, choose *Subtotals* from the *Data* menu and click on *Remove All* in the *Subtotal* dialog box.

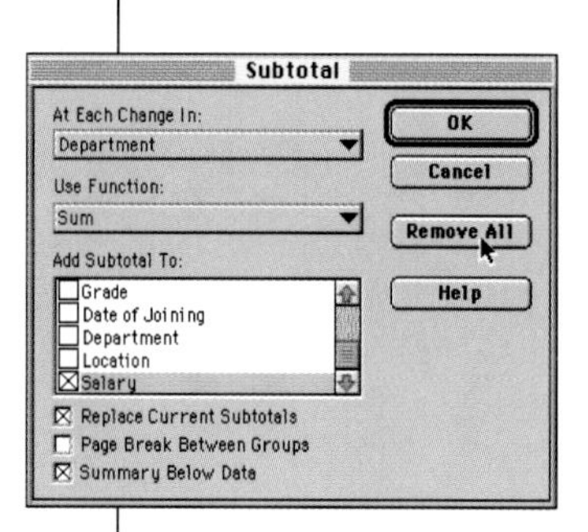

The PivotTable Wizard

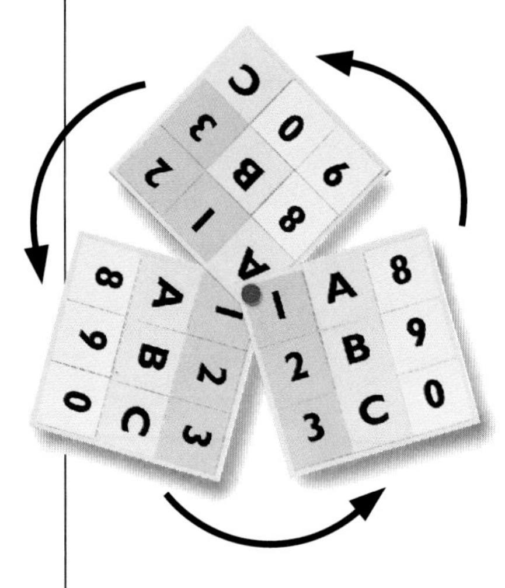

Excel's PivotTable Wizard allows you to extract and summarize information from a list and format it in a table. The PivotTable Wizard is useful for organizing data into newly specified categories and for performing a variety of calculations on that data.

USING THE PIVOTTABLE WIZARD

The PivotTable Wizard is easy to use: you simply work through four dialog boxes following instructions in the boxes. In this example, you'll use the PivotTable Wizard to create a table that shows the annual salary costs for each department and location within your employee list. Start by selecting any cell within the list.

Filtered Out!
Always make sure that you do your filtering before adding subtotals. If you filter a subtotaled list, you will find that Excel does not display subtotals for the newly filtered list.

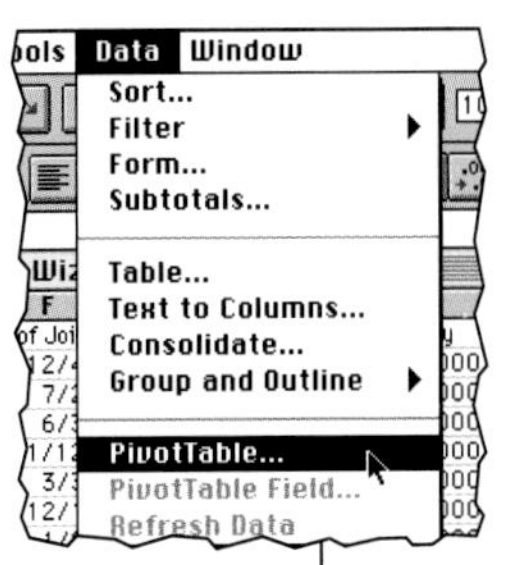

1 To initiate the PivotTable Wizard, choose the *PivotTable* command from the *Data* menu.

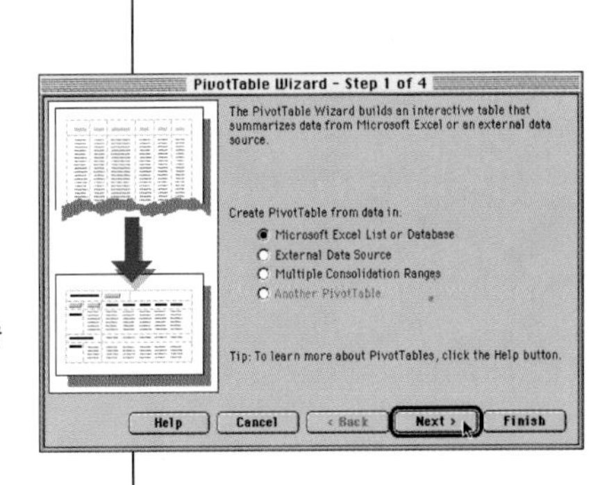

2 The first dialog box appears, in which you select the source of data. Click on the *Microsoft Excel List or Database* option and then on *Next*.

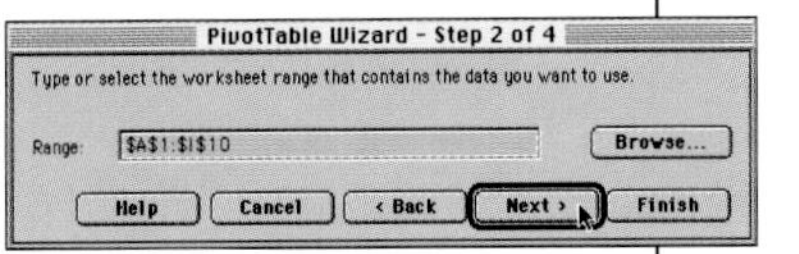

3 The second dialog box confirms your selection range — cells A1 to I10. Click on *Next*.

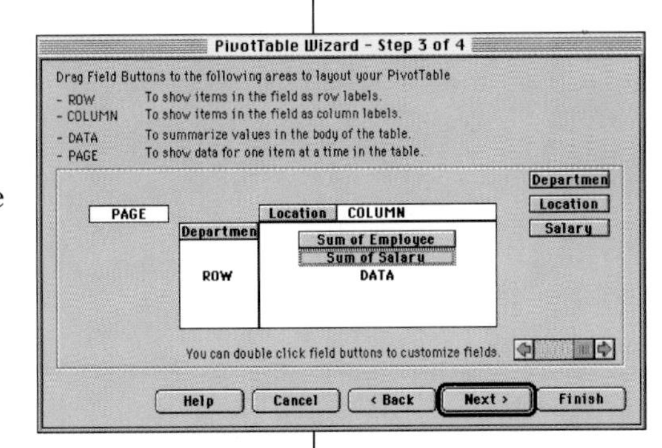

4 In the third dialog box, you specify the contents of the table that you want to create. From the list of fields on the right side of the dialog box, drag *Department* into the box marked *ROW*. Drag *Location* into the *COLUMN* box — then *Employee* and *Salary* into the *DATA* box.

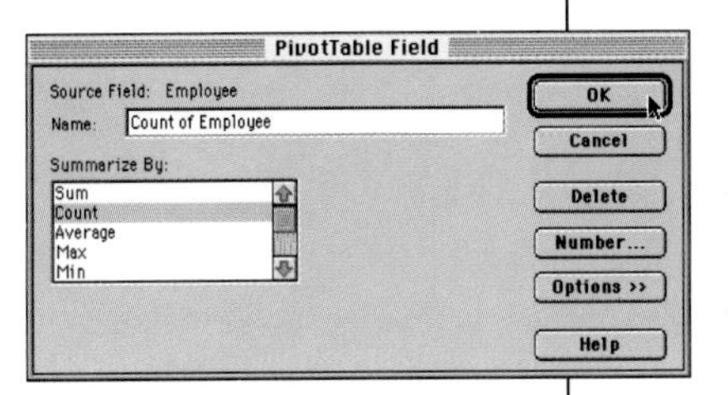

5 You'll notice that the two data fields have been prefixed by "Sum of." This specifies that the data in these fields will be summed in your table. Because you want to count the number of employees, double-click on the *Sum of Employee* box. In the *PivotTable Field* dialog box, select *Count* from the *Summarize By* list. Click on *OK*, then on *Next*.

Table Turning?

By clicking on the PivotTable Field button (second from left in the Query and Pivot toolbar) and using the *PivotTable Field* dialog box, you can modify your table without having to start from scratch. For example, you can choose a different summarizing function, such as *Average* instead of *Sum*, for the salary data.

6 In the final dialog box, you choose where the table will be displayed. Click on cell A14 in the worksheet — this will be used as the top left hand cell of your table. To display the PivotTable, click on *Finish*.

The PivotTable should appear as shown below. You can make changes to a PivotTable by using the Query and Pivot toolbar. If it is not already on screen, you can display the toolbar via the *Toolbars* command on the *View* menu. For information on any toolbar button, click on the button using the Help pointer (see page 16). Now save and close the **WizFood** workbook.

	A	B	C	D	E
13					
14			Location		
15	Department	Data	LA	NY	Grand Total
16	Marketing	Count of Employee	2	2	4
17		Sum of Salary	112000	63000	175000
18	Sales	Count of Employee	2	3	5
19		Sum of Salary	89000	224000	313000
20	Total Count of Employee		4	5	9
21	Total Sum of Salary		201000	287000	488000
22					
23					

Query and Pivot Toolbar

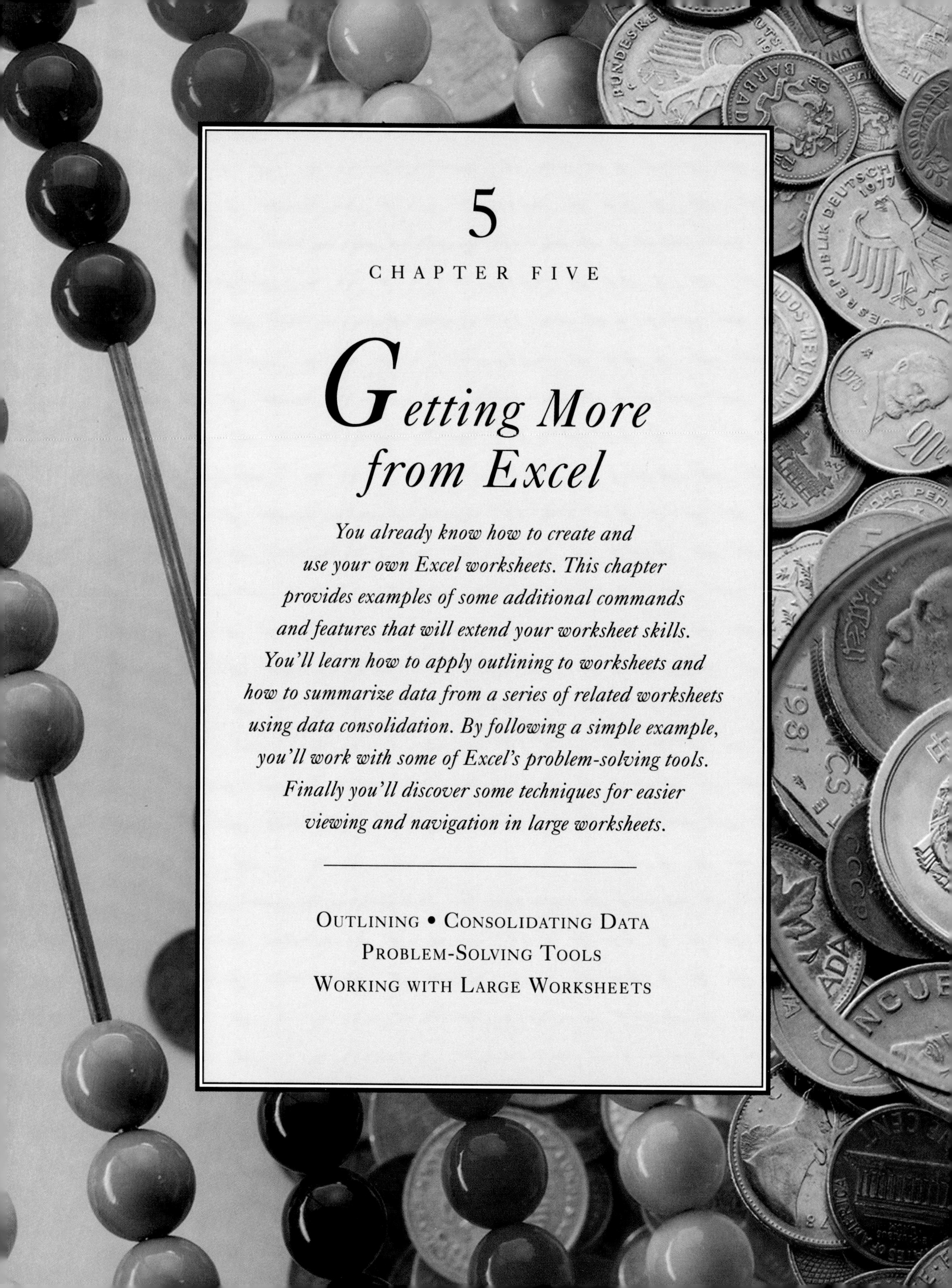

5

CHAPTER FIVE

Getting More from Excel

You already know how to create and use your own Excel worksheets. This chapter provides examples of some additional commands and features that will extend your worksheet skills. You'll learn how to apply outlining to worksheets and how to summarize data from a series of related worksheets using data consolidation. By following a simple example, you'll work with some of Excel's problem-solving tools. Finally you'll discover some techniques for easier viewing and navigation in large worksheets.

OUTLINING • CONSOLIDATING DATA
PROBLEM-SOLVING TOOLS
WORKING WITH LARGE WORKSHEETS

OUTLINING *108*

Worksheets that contain many levels of information can become difficult to read and interpret. Using the outlining feature, you can create a hierarchical structure in your worksheet and then view selected information at different levels.

CONSOLIDATING DATA *110*

Using the *Consolidate* command and any of a range of mathematical functions, you can summarize or combine data from a number of related worksheets into a summary worksheet. You'll also create summaries by "spearing" a series of worksheets in the same workbook.

PROBLEM-SOLVING TOOLS *112*

Learn how to use some of Excel's problem-solving tools. Create your own what-if model based on a simple business example. Then use the *Goal Seek* command and the Solver to find solutions to more complex problems.

WORKING WITH LARGE WORKSHEETS *116*

You already know how to navigate through a worksheet, but for large worksheets Excel offers some time-saving shortcuts. You'll also look at some commands on the *View* and *Window* menus that you'll find useful for viewing large worksheets.

Outlining

> **Keep Within Range!**
> If you choose the *Auto Outline* command when a range is selected, outlining is applied to that range only. If you want to apply automatic outlining to the whole worksheet, select one cell only.

OUTLINING IS A WAY OF STRUCTURING a worksheet into a hierarchy of information. Once a worksheet has been outlined, different levels in the hierarchy can be displayed or hidden with the click of a button. Excel outlines can contain up to eight hierarchical levels.

Automatic Outlining

You can direct Excel to apply automatic outlining to any sheet that contains summary formulas — for example, a list with a series of subtotals or averages. You have already come across an outline in the data sheet on page 104. The *Subtotals* command automatically created an outline structure, which was signified by vertical lines at the left of the worksheet. The *Group and Outline* command is the main outlining command — as you are about to see. Open the **WizFood** workbook, activate *Sheet4,* rename the sheet **Sales Summary**, and then follow the steps starting at right.

Applying an Outline

1 Enter the labels and data shown here. Select rows 7, 11, and 13 and apply bold formatting. Then select the range A3:D13, choose *Column* from the *Format* menu and *AutoFit Selection* from the submenu.

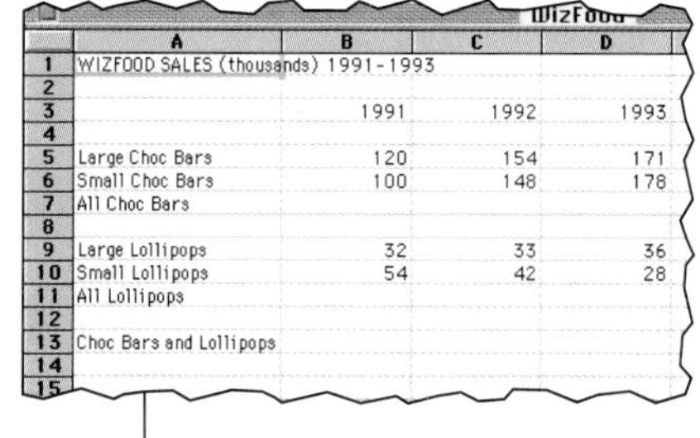

2 Now use formulas to complete the worksheet. In cell B7, enter **=B5+B6**, and then use the fill handle to copy this formula into C7 and D7. In cell B11, enter **=B9+B10**, and copy this formula to C11 and D11. Finally in cell B13 enter the formula **=B7+B11** and copy this formula into the range C13:D13.

3 Select cell A1. Choose *Group and Outline* from the *Data* menu, and then choose *Auto Outline* from the submenu.

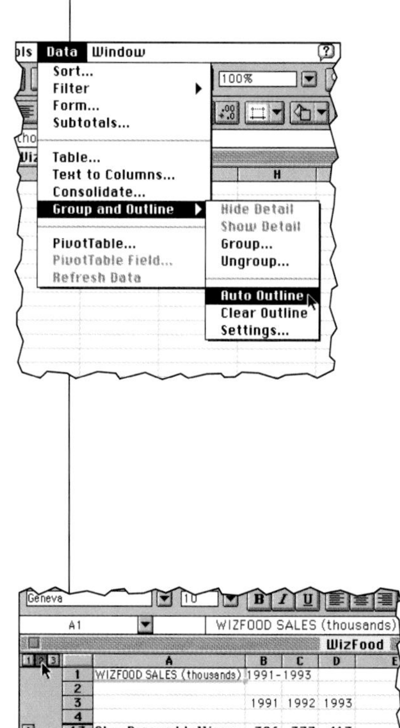

4 Outlining has now automatically been applied to the worksheet. Look at the top left of the worksheet. The three small numbered buttons to the left of the Select All button indicate that Excel has automatically set up three levels of outline in the worksheet. Currently you are at level 3 (fully expanded outline). Click on button 1 to see level 1 (fully collapsed outline).

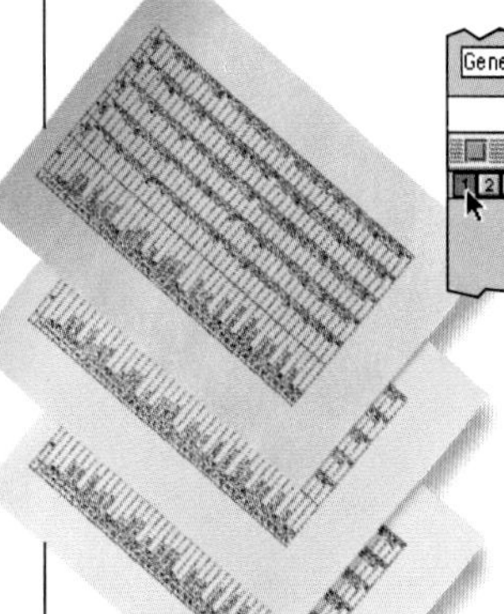

5 Level 1 (fully collapsed outline) is now displayed, so only the grand total line shows. Click on button 2 to see level 2 (partially collapsed outline). Now the subtotals and grand total show.

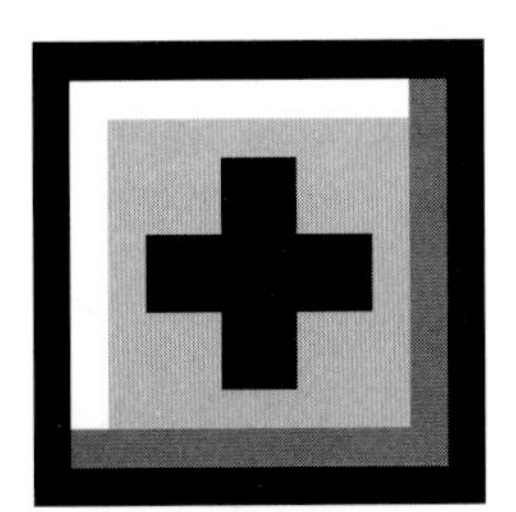

Plus Button
Clicking on a plus button displays detail rows or columns.

A Bit of Style?
Excel can automatically apply different styles to each level of outline. Before you invoke automatic outlining, choose *Group and Outline* from the *Data* menu and *Settings* from the submenu. In the *Outline* dialog box, check the *Automatic Styles* box, and then click on *OK*.

6 In the area below the numbered buttons, you will now see two buttons marked with a plus sign. A plus button appears alongside a summary row and indicates that there are some detail rows hidden above or below it. Click on one of the plus buttons, and the hidden rows are displayed as that part of the outline expands.

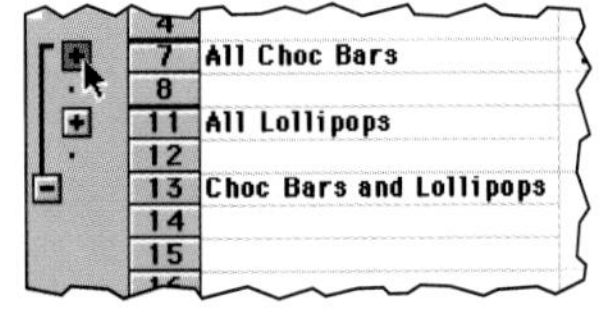

7 The plus button is replaced by a vertical bracket with a minus button at the bottom. The vertical bracket indicates the rows that were previously hidden. Click on the minus button, and these rows will be hidden again. Then experiment with clicking on the various plus and minus buttons to expand or collapse parts of the outline.

Manual Outlining

You can also apply outlining to a worksheet manually. For example, to define three adjacent rows as detail rows and the row immediately below them as a summary row, select the three rows to be defined as details, and then choose the *Group and Outline* command from the *Data* menu and *Group* from the submenu. An outline bar appears against the detail rows and a minus button against the summary row. The detail rows can be hidden or displayed as before.

Clear Outline?
To remove all outlining from a worksheet, choose *Group and Outline* from the *Data* menu and *Clear Outline* from the submenu. To remove any part of an outline, select the detail rows (or columns), choose *Group and Outline* from the *Data* menu and *Ungroup* from the submenu.

Minus Button
Clicking on a minus button hides detail rows or columns.

Horizontal Outlining

Excel supports horizontal outlines too. In your **Sales Summary** worksheet, use the SUM function to enter the totals from 1991, 1992, and 1993 into column E (as shown at right), and then choose the *Auto Outline* command. Excel generates a horizontal outline (as shown here) in addition to the vertical outline. The horizontal outline has two levels. Level 2 (shown) displays the worksheet fully expanded horizontally. Level 1 would show only the summary information in column E. You'll find that the horizontal and vertical outlines can be expanded or collapsed independently of each other.

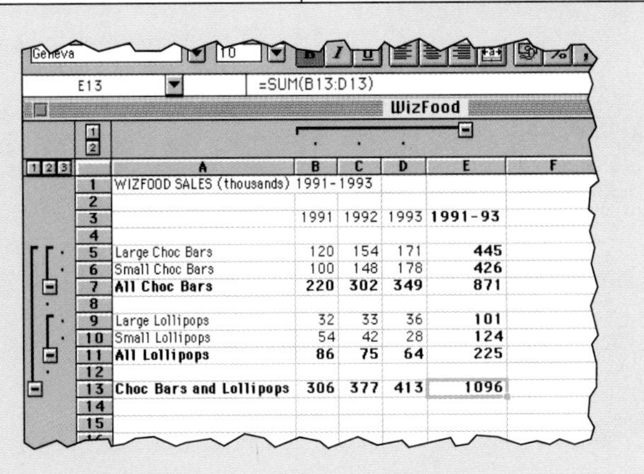

Consolidating Data

YOU MAY SOMETIMES WANT to bring together data from a number of different sources in different worksheets or workbooks, and to combine or summarize the data into a single set of figures on a single worksheet. Excel makes it easy for you to perform this process, which is known as consolidation, in a variety of ways.

"Spearing" Your Worksheets

A simple way of consolidating data is to "spear" a series of cells at the same address in different worksheets. This can give your work in Excel a third dimcnsion. For the technique to be effective, the cells must have a similar meaning in each worksheet. For a simple example, create a workbook detailing weekly sales by three salesmen. Begin by opening a new workbook and saving it as **Salesmen**.

A Four-Sheet Spear

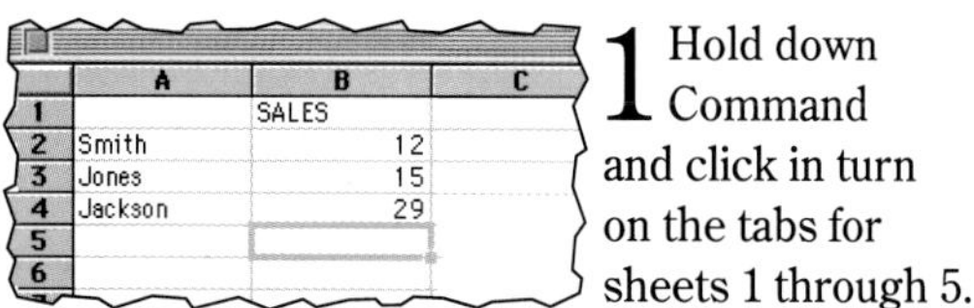

	A	B	C
1		SALES	
2	Smith	12	
3	Jones	15	
4	Jackson	29	
5			
6			

1 Hold down Command and click in turn on the tabs for sheets 1 through 5. Enter the labels in column A and cell B1 shown above. Now ungroup the sheets — hold down Control, click on a sheet tab with the mouse, and choose *Ungroup Sheets* from the shortcut menu. Activate *Sheet1* and enter the sales figures, also shown above.

2 Enter the sales data shown below into *Sheet2*, *Sheet3*, and *Sheet4*. Then click on the *Sheet5* tab.

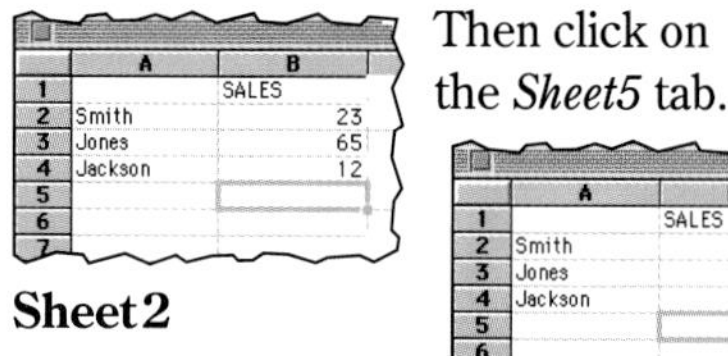

	A	B
1		SALES
2	Smith	23
3	Jones	65
4	Jackson	12
5		
6		
7		

Sheet2

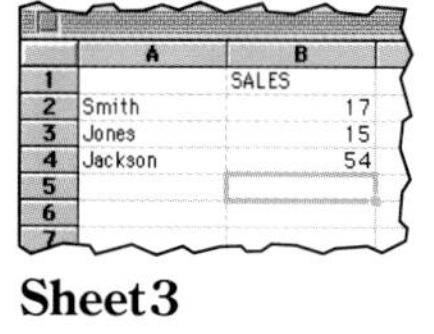

	A	B
1		SALES
2	Smith	17
3	Jones	15
4	Jackson	54
5		
6		
7		

Sheet3

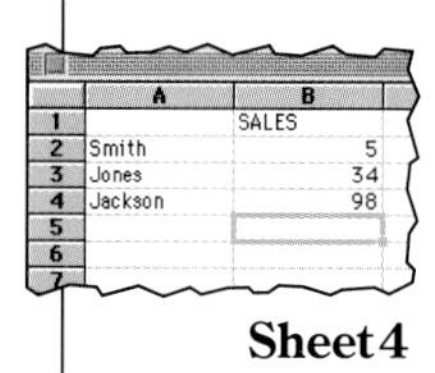

	A	B
1		SALES
2	Smith	5
3	Jones	34
4	Jackson	98
5		
6		
7		

Sheet4

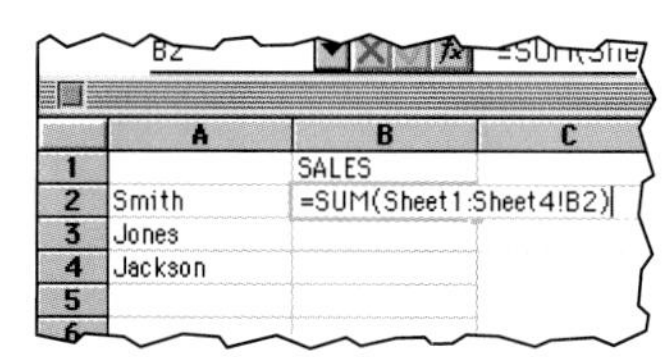

	A	B	C
1		SALES	
2	Smith	=SUM(Sheet1:Sheet4!B2)	
3	Jones		
4	Jackson		
5			

3 In *Sheet5*, click on cell B2 and enter the formula **=SUM(Sheet1:Sheet4!B2)**. This instructs Excel to "spear" cell B2 for the first 4 worksheets and, in this case, to add the values from the four cells and put the result in cell B2 of *Sheet5*. Click on the Enter button.

4 Add the other two sales summaries by clicking on B2 and dragging the fill handle down to B4.

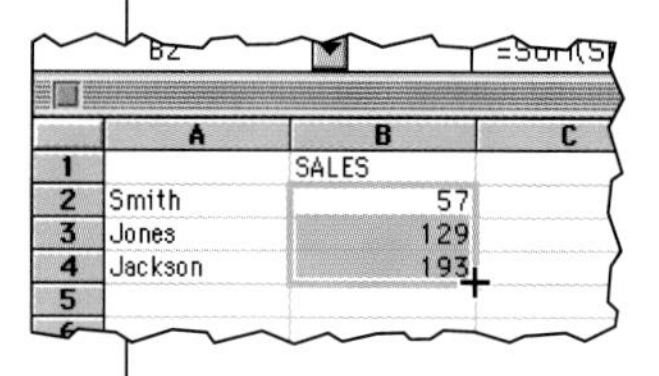

	A	B	C
1		SALES	
2	Smith	57	
3	Jones	129	
4	Jackson	193	
5			

The Consolidate Command

A more flexible way to consolidate data is to use the *Consolidate* command in the *Data* menu. This command can combine information from up to 255 source areas into a single summary worksheet.

Spear and Link!
When you spear a series of worksheets to create summary data, you use the external reference indicator(!), as shown in the formula **=SUM (Sheet1: Sheet4!B2).** This creates a link to the source data. If you change the data in any of the source worksheets, the data shown in the summary sheet will be updated as well.

A Quick Consolidation

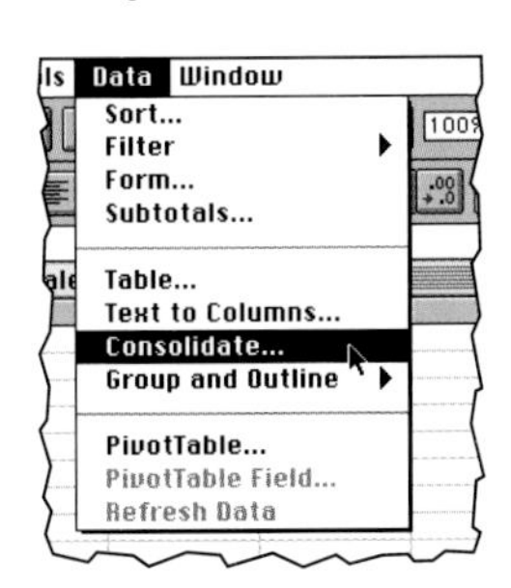

1 Activate *Sheet6* and choose *Consolidate* from the *Data* menu. The *Consolidate* dialog box is displayed.

2 Make sure that *Sum* appears in the *Function* box. Click in the *Reference* box, and then activate *Sheet1* and select cells A1 to B4. *Sheet1!$A$1:$B$4* will appear in the *Reference* box. Click on the *Add* button; this reference is then added to the *All References* box.

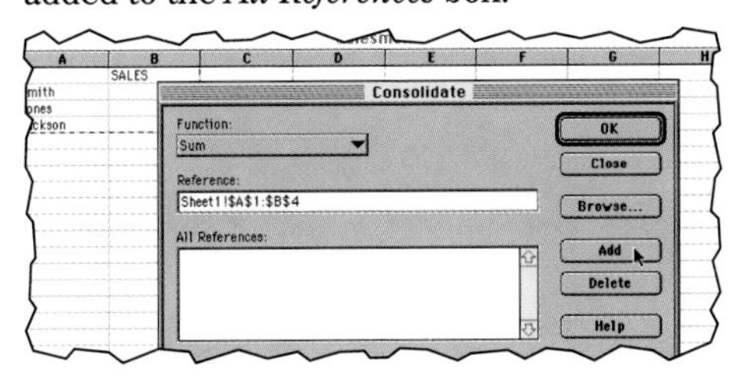

More than Addition?
When consolidating, you can perform any of a number of different operations — not just summation — on the source data. You can choose a function from the *Function* pop-up menu within the *Consolidate* dialog box. You'll find a list of functions that include *Product* (multiplies values together), *Average*, and *Max*, in addition to *Sum*.

3 Now activate *Sheet2*, select cells A1 to B4, and then click on the *Add* button. Repeat this procedure for the same cell range in *Sheet3* and *Sheet4*. Click on both boxes under *Use Labels In* (*Top Row* and *Left Column*). The dialog box should look identical to the one shown at right. Click on *OK*.

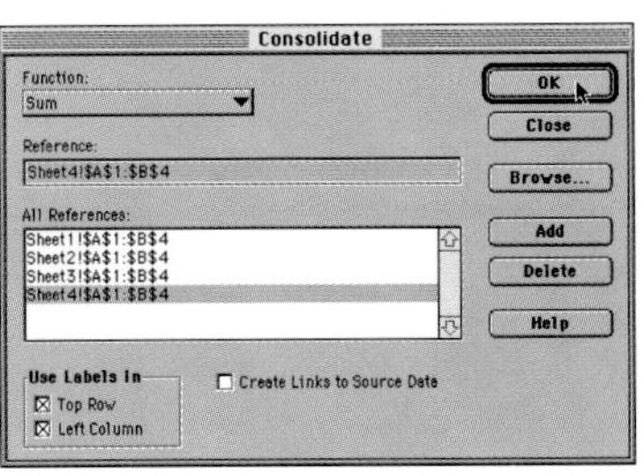

4 You can see that the totals are the same as those you calculated previously in *Sheet5*. However, unlike the data in *Sheet5*, the totals are not linked to the data in the other worksheets.

	A	B	C
1		SALES	
2	Smith	57	
3	Jones	129	
4	Jackson	193	
5			
6			
7			

LINKING TO THE SOURCE DATA

The above method is fine for one-time calculations, but for consolidations in which the source data might change, you should link your consolidated sheet to the source sheets.

1 Click on cell A1 in *Sheet6*, and choose *Consolidate* from the *Data* menu again. Check the *Create Links to Source Data* box. Click on *OK*.

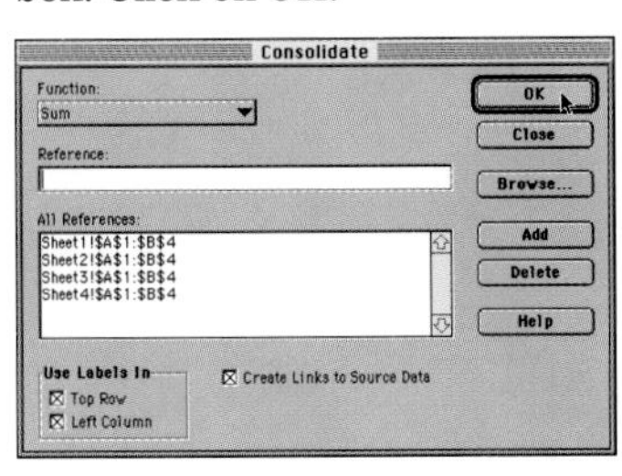

2 This time, Excel has also added an automatic outline to your worksheet.

	A	B	C
1		SALES	
2	Smith	57	

	A	B	C
1			SALES
2		Salesmen	12
3		Salesmen	23
4		Salesmen	17
5		Salesmen	5
6	Smith		57
7		Salesmen	15
8		Salesmen	65
9		Salesmen	15
10		Salesmen	34
11	Jones		129
12		Salesmen	29
13		Salesmen	12
14		Salesmen	54
15		Salesmen	98
16	Jackson		193
17			

3 If you click on cell C6, you will see that it contains the formula *=SUM(C2:C5)*. Click on the outline button number 2 to expand the outline to display the hidden rows.

If you click on cell C2, you'll see that it contains the worksheet and cell reference *=Sheet1!$B$2*. Save and close the **Salesmen** workbook.

Other Workbooks?
Excel doesn't restrict you to taking source data from within the same workbook — you can take it from several different workbooks. Before you choose the *Consolidate* command, make sure that you have all the necessary workbooks open and displayed within multiple windows.

Problem-Solving Tools

EXCEL OFFERS SEVERAL powerful tools for studying problems of a numerical nature — particularly problems in which one or more input values (such as the price of a product) are linked by formulas to specific end results (such as profits from selling the product). By following the simple case study in this section, you can find out how to use some of these tools, in particular the *Goal Seek* command and the Solver.

What Is A2^2?
The ^ character can be used in formulas to calculate exponentials. For example, the expression A2^2 denotes the square of the value in A2, A2^3 denotes the cube of the value in A2, and so on.

WizWands' Profit Problem

The WizWands company makes magic wands, which it currently sells for 65 gold pieces each. Recently, WizWands' profits have been going downhill, and in an attempt to reverse the trend, the company's president has been doing some market research. Wand sales, it seems, are very price-sensitive. In fact, the relationship between sales and price can be accurately modeled by the formula: Monthly sales = 500,000/ $(\text{Price})^2$, where the price is in gold pieces. WizWands also knows the exact cost of manufacturing a wand — 21 gold pieces.

Excel can help WizWands make better decisions and improve its profits outlook. Start by opening a new workbook. Save it as **WizWands**.

Setting Up the Model

1 Enter the column headings shown at right. Using the *Style* command on the *Format* menu, apply the Comma style to columns A, C, and D, the Comma (0) style to column B, and the Percentage style to column E. Select columns A through E, choose *Column* from the *Format* menu, and then choose *AutoFit Selection* from the submenu.

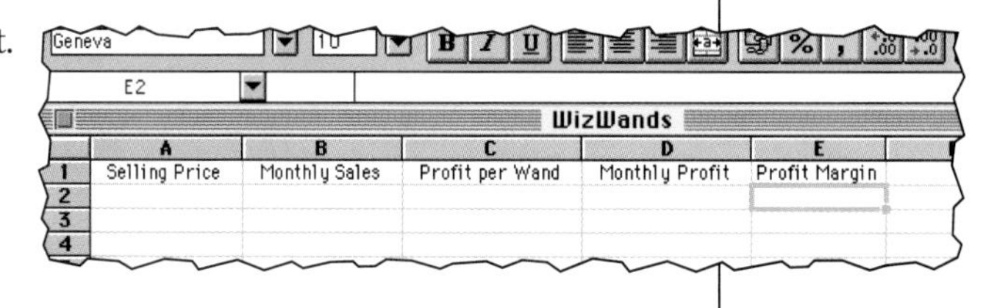

2 In cell A2, enter the current selling price (**65**). In B2, enter the monthly sales formula. Type **=500000/(A2^2)** and press Tab. The anticipated monthly sales figure (118) is displayed.

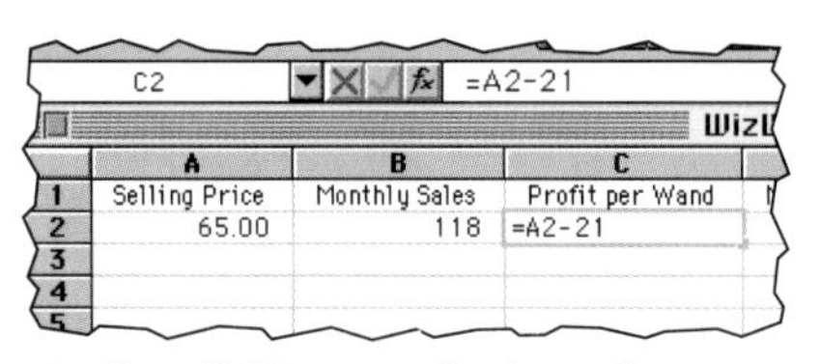

3 In cell C2, enter the formula for the profit per wand. This is the selling price (the value in A2) minus the manufacturing cost (21 gold pieces). Type **=A2-21** and press Tab.

4 Enter the final two formulas. In cell D2, type **=B2*C2**. This is the monthly profit (sales multiplied by profit per wand). In cell E2, type **=C2/A2**. This gives the profit margin (profit per wand as a percentage of selling price).

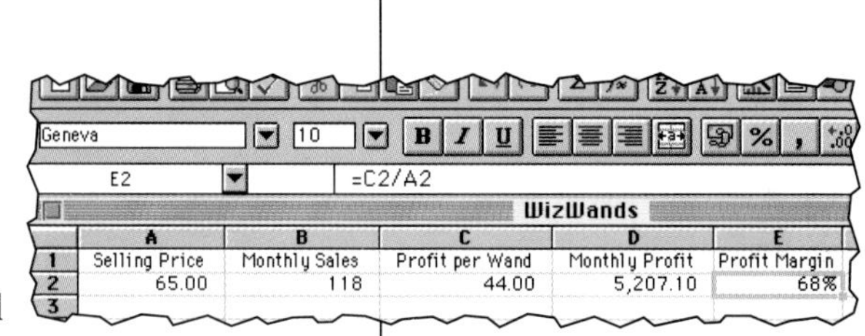

What-If Analysis

By pricing its wands at 65 gold pieces, WizWands is selling only about 118 wands per month and making profits of about 5,200 gold pieces per month. Because all the formulas are linked to the selling price, you can easily find out how changes in the selling price affect sales and profits. Select cell A2, type in a selling price of **50** gold pieces, and click on the Enter button. You can see immediately that the reduction in selling price almost doubles sales to 200 per month and increases monthly profit to 5,800 gold pieces. Try entering some other values such as **75**, **30**, and **20** in cell A2 to see what happens.

WizWands

	A	B	C	D	E
1	Selling Price	Monthly Sales	Profit per Wand	Monthly Profit	Profit Margin
2	50.00	200	29.00	5,800.00	58%

Change Input Only!
Remember that you can perform what-if calculations only by changing your input values. If you try changing the value in a calculated cell by simply typing in the new amount, you will delete the formula.

THE GOAL SEEK COMMAND
A company that supplies WizWands with parts for its wands says it will go out of business unless WizWands can sell at least 250 wands every month. How can WizWands find out what price it should charge to sell 250 wands each month? Trial and error would be one approach — to enter various prices until monthly sales hit 250. But that could be time-consuming. Excel offers a better solution — the *Goal Seek* command.

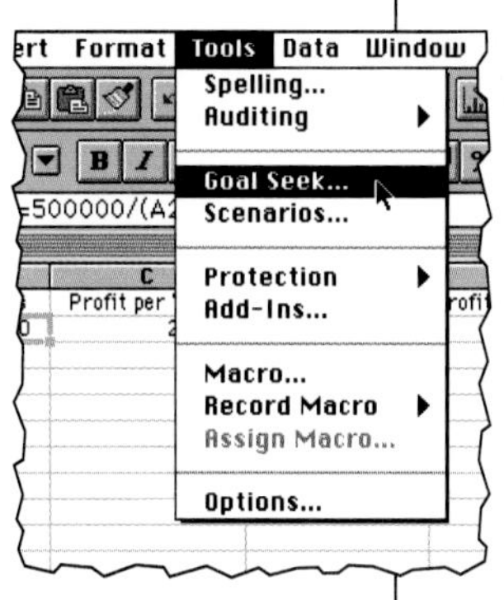

1 Select cell B2 and choose *Goal Seek* from the *Tools* menu. The *Goal Seek* dialog box appears.

2 In the *Set cell* box, you will see an absolute reference to the current active cell (**$B$2**). Click in the *To value* box, and type **250**. This sets your goal — a value in cell B2 (monthly sales) of 250 wands.

Goal Seek
Set cell: $B$2
To value: 250
By changing cell:
OK
Cancel
Help

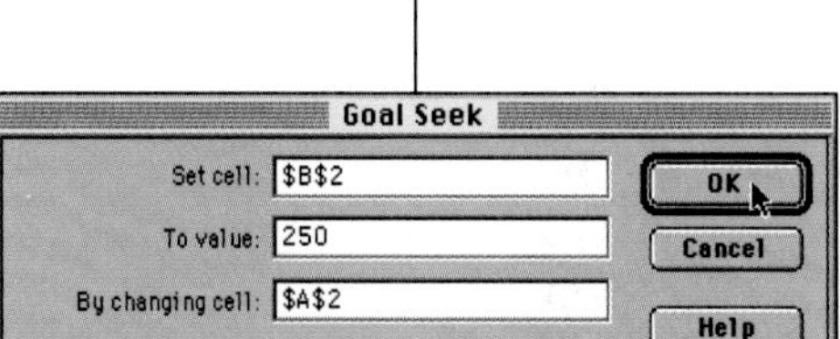

3 Click in the *By changing cell* box, and then click on cell A2. This tells Excel to calculate the selling price (in A2) that will achieve the goal of monthly sales of 250 wands (in cell B2). Click on *OK*.

4 The *Goal Seek Status* dialog box appears, telling you that it has found a solution. Click on *OK*. You can see in the worksheet that to achieve monthly sales of 250 wands, WizWands must reduce its selling price to below 45 gold pieces.

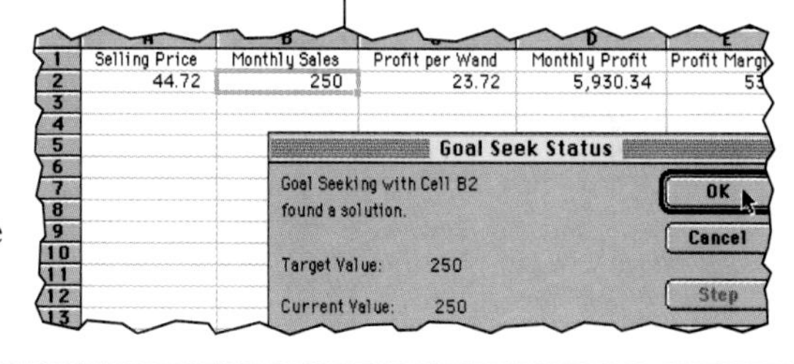

Maximizing Profitability

WizWands wants to find out what selling price to set to achieve the highest level of monthly profits. One of the simplest ways to do this is by creating a table of profit values over a range of selling prices.

Creating a Profit Table

WizWands

A	B	C	D	E
Selling Price	Monthly Sales	Profit per Wand	Monthly Profit	Profit Margin
30.00	556	9.00	5,000.00	30%
35.00				
40.00				
45.00				
50.00				
55.00				
60.00				
65.00				
70.00				

1 Enter a value of **30** in cell A2 and **35** in A3. Select the two cells, and then drag the fill handle down to cell A10. This is the range of your selling price. To copy the formulas over the entire table, highlight cells B2 through E2 and drag the fill handle at the bottom right of cell E2 down to the base of E10.

2 Your table now tells you what will happen to monthly profits if WizWands adopts a variety of different selling prices. You can see from the monthly profit column that the highest profit level (over 5,930 gold pieces per month) is achieved by selling wands for about 40 gold pieces each.

WizWands

A	B	C	D	E
Selling Price	Monthly Sales	Profit per Wand	Monthly Profit	Profit Margin
30.00	556	9.00	5,000.00	30%
35.00	408	14.00	5,714.29	40%
40.00	313	19.00	5,937.50	48%
45.00	247	24.00	5,925.93	53%
50.00	200	29.00	5,800.00	58%
55.00	165	34.00	5,619.83	62%
60.00	139	39.00	5,416.67	65%
65.00	118	44.00	5,207.10	68%
70.00	102	49.00	5,000.00	70%

PROFITABILITY CHARTS
Another way to view profitability is by turning your table into a chart. Select the range A1:A10, hold down Command, select the range D1:D10, and then choose *Chart* from the *Insert* menu and *As New Sheet* from the submenu. Follow the procedure explained on pages 92 to 93, but this time choose a line chart. In the formatted chart shown at left, you can see that the maximum monthly profit (at the peak of the blue line) occurs at a price of between 40 and 45 gold pieces.

Solving Complex Problems

Finding the optimal solution to even a simple numerical problem may take considerable time by trial and error. Methods such as tabulating or charting data, as described above, and then studying the results, may give answers that are only approximate. To find exact solutions to complex problems, Excel provides an add-in program called the Solver.

What's an Add-In?
Some functions that work with Excel are not automatically available — they are either installed when you first load Excel onto your PC, or they can be called up and loaded when they are required. You can see a complete list of the available add-ins by choosing *Add-Ins* from the *Tools* menu.

USING THE SOLVER

WizWands wants to know exactly what selling price to set for its wands in order to maximize profits. However, there are two constraints. The company cannot manufacture more than 275 wands per month. It also wants its profit margin to be at least 50%. You can use the Solver to find a solution. Begin by selecting cells A3 to E10 and clearing their contents by choosing *Clear* from the *Edit* menu and *Contents* from the submenu. Set the value in cell A2 to 40 gold pieces.

1 Select cell D2 and then choose *Solver* from the *Tools* menu. If you can't find the *Solver* command on the menu, choose the *Add-Ins* command from the *Tools* menu. From the list that appears, double-click on *Solver*.

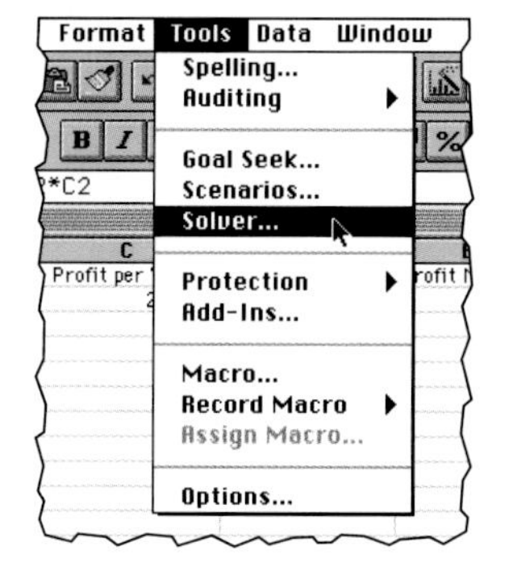

2 The *Solver Parameters* dialog box appears. In the *Set Target Cell* box, you will see the current active cell (D2). Make sure *Max* is selected to the right of *Equal to.*

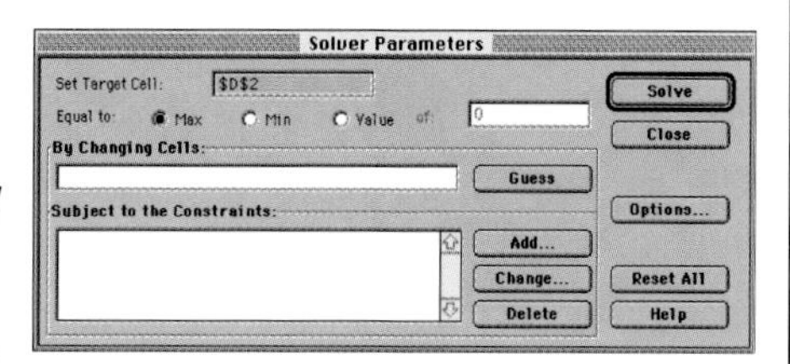

Get in Close!
Because of the method the Solver uses to find solutions, its starting point, embodied in the initial input value(s), is critical. If you start too far away from the solution, Solver may not be able to find the solution, or may stop on a peak other than the highest one. If you can, always try to find an approximate solution and use this for your input value(s) (in our example, the value in A2) before running the Solver.

3 Click in the *By Changing Cells* box and then on cell A2. So far you have told the Solver to find the selling price (A2) that achieves the maximum (Max) monthly profit (D2). Click in the *Subject to the Constraints* box. Now click on the *Add* button. The *Add Constraint* dialog box appears.

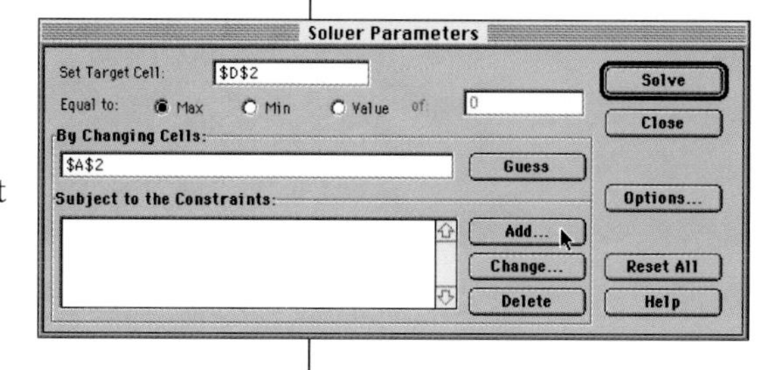

4 Click in the *Cell Reference* box. Click on cell B2. Click on the down arrow, and from the pop-up list choose "Less than or equal to" (<=). Click in the *Constraint* box, and enter a value of **275.** Click on the *Add* button.

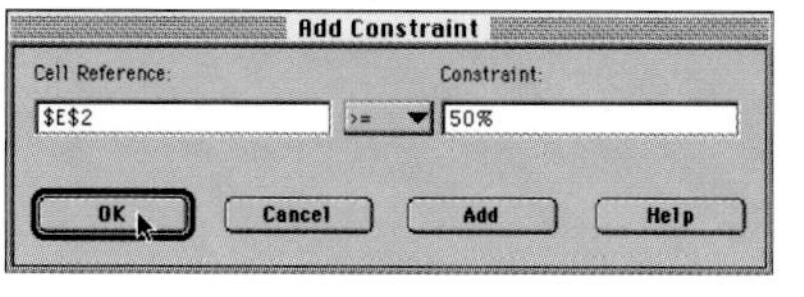

5 The *Add Constraint* dialog box appears again. Follow the same procedure to add the second constraint shown **($E$2 >= 50%).** Click on *OK.*

6 Click on *Solve* in the *Solver Parameters* dialog box. The Solver will now look for a solution.

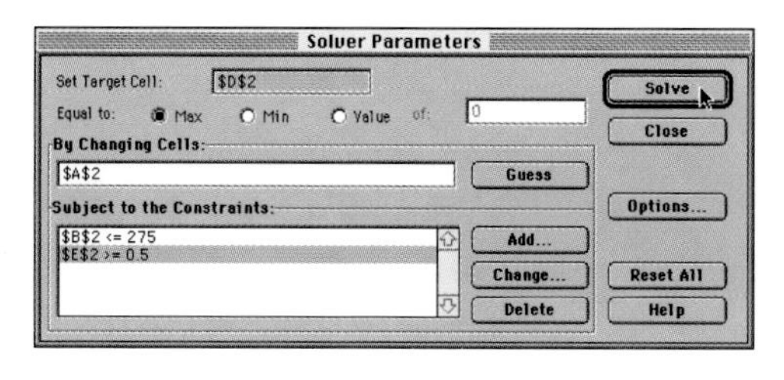

7 The *Solver Results* dialog box appears, telling you that the Solver has found a satisfactory answer. Look at the worksheet to see the values displayed. You will see that WizWands should set a selling price of 42.64 gold pieces to achieve maximum profits within the constraints that have been set. Click on *OK*, and then save and close **WizWands**.

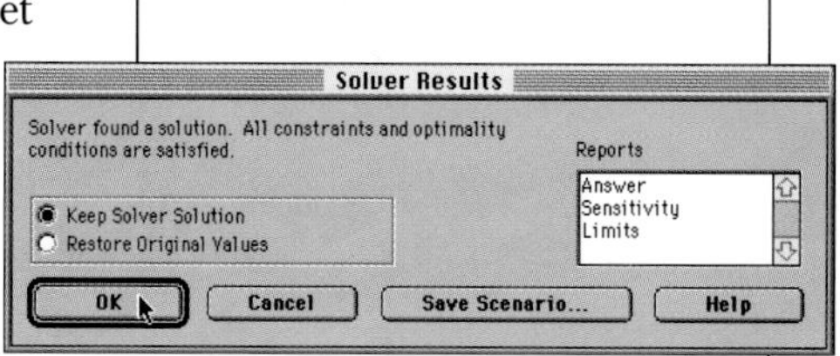

Working with Large Worksheets

Extended Selecting
If you hold down the Shift key when using any method of worksheet navigation (such as the direction keys, the *Go To* command, or double-clicking on the active cell border), you will find that the active cell does not move but serves as an anchor while the cell selection expands or contracts. This can be useful for selecting large ranges.

THE WORKSHEETS YOU HAVE CREATED so far have fit — or nearly fit — into a single full-screen window. But many of the worksheets you are likely to create will be much bigger, so it is useful to know some techniques for navigating large worksheets or for viewing different parts of a worksheet at the same time.

Navigational Shortcuts

Large worksheets usually consist of blocks of related information separated by blank rows and columns. Excel provides ways of moving to the edge of one block, then over a series of blank cells to the next block. To see how this works, open the **Year1** workbook and activate the **Annual Income** worksheet. Select the range A2:M9 and, using the *Copy* and *Paste* commands, copy it to the range A16:M23.

Border-Clicking

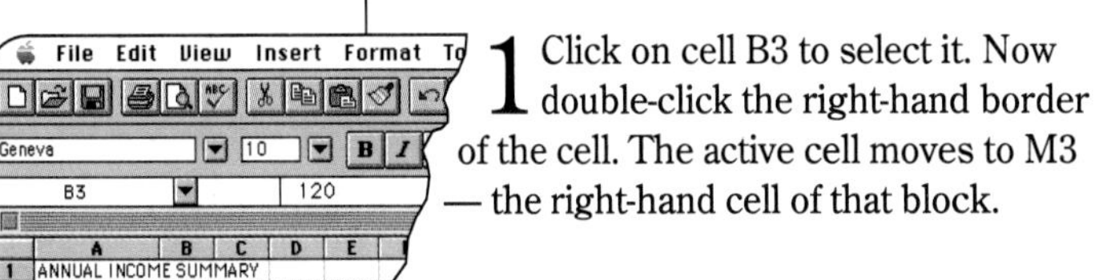

1 Click on cell B3 to select it. Now double-click the right-hand border of the cell. The active cell moves to M3 — the right-hand cell of that block.

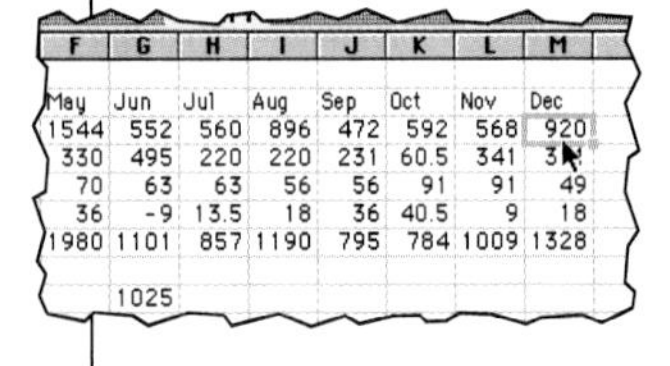

2 Double-click the bottom border of cell M3. The active cell moves to the bottom edge of the block — cell M7.

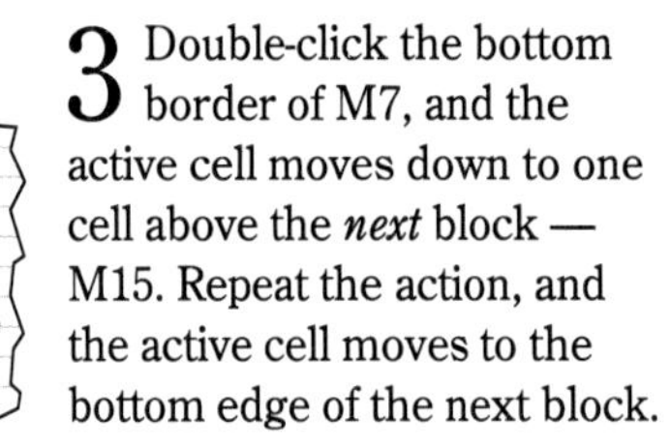

3 Double-click the bottom border of M7, and the active cell moves down to one cell above the *next* block — M15. Repeat the action, and the active cell moves to the bottom edge of the next block.

You can also navigate in this way using the keyboard. Holding down Control and pressing a direction key will take you to the edge of a block or over blank cells to the next block. Try using this method to move back to cell B2. Remember also that you can go to cell A1 in any worksheet simply by pressing Control and Home.

Round Tour?
Holding down Control, Shift, and 8 selects the block of cells containing the active cell. Holding down Control and then pressing the period key takes the active cell on a tour around the four corners of a selected range.

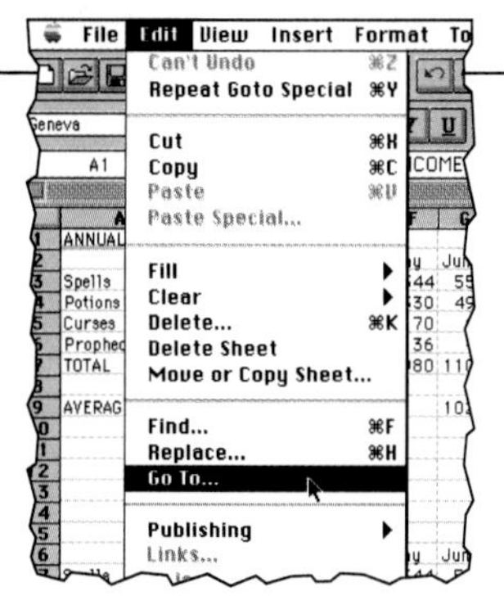

1 Click on cell A1. Choose *Go To* from the *Edit* menu, or press the F5 key.

THE GO TO COMMAND

You can move to any cell address or any named cell or range in the worksheet by using the *Go To* command in the *Edit* menu. This is especially useful for moving to cells or ranges that are not visible in the current window. To see how this works, click the zoom box (at the far right of the workbook title bar) to reduce the size of the workbook window. Drag the size box (at the bottom right of the window) until only columns A to G of the worksheet are visible.

Seeking Out a Name?
The quickest way of going to a named cell or range in the worksheet is to click on the down arrow next to the name box in the formula bar and choose the name from the pop-up list (see page 60).

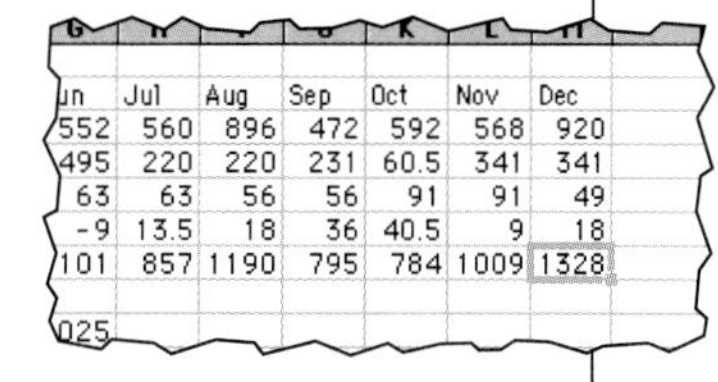

2 The *Go To* dialog box appears, containing a list of all the cell and range names defined on the worksheet. In the *Reference* box, enter the address of the cell you want to go to — M7. Click on *OK*.

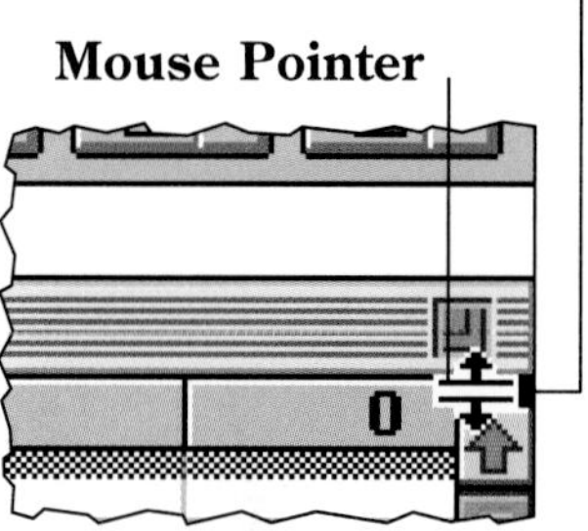

3 The worksheet automatically scrolls in your window and your selection — cell M7 — is displayed.

Window Panes

By using the *Split* command in the *Window* menu, you can split your workbook window into two or four panes, each of which can be scrolled. This allows you to view different parts of a worksheet at the same time. To create two panes, select a cell in the top row or left-most column of the visible part of the worksheet and then choose the *Split* command. To create four panes, select a cell in the middle of the visible worksheet and then choose the *Split* command.

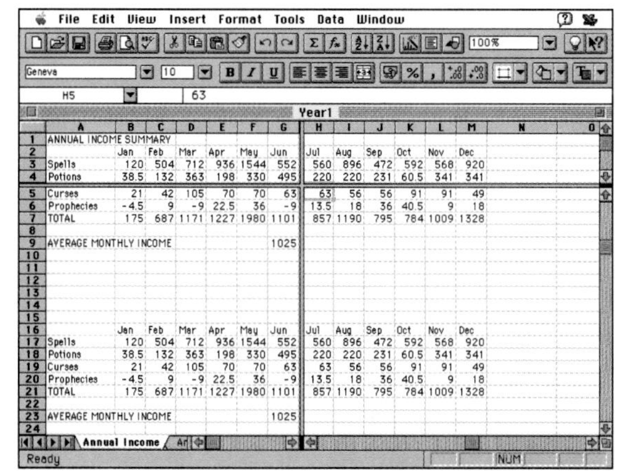

Splitting the Window

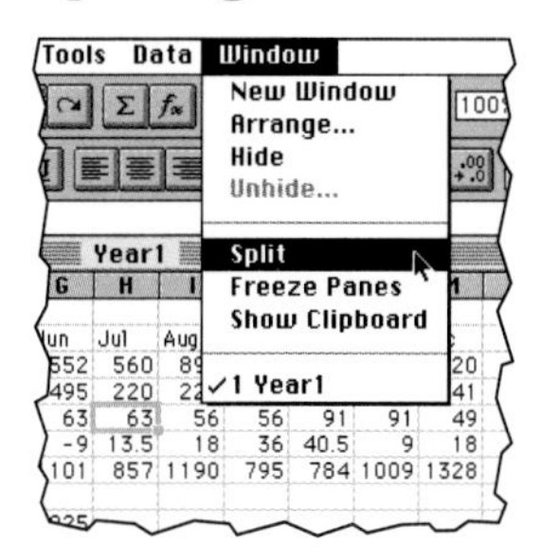

1 Maximize the workbook window again. Click on cell H5, and then choose *Split* from the *Window* menu.

2 Split bars appear above and to the left of cell H5, dividing the window into four panes. If you click on the different horizontal and vertical scroll bars, you'll see that you have access to the entire worksheet in each pane. Double-click on the vertical split bar to remove it. The window is now split into only two panes. Remove the remaining split bar by double-clicking on it or by choosing *Remove Split* from the *Window* menu.

Horizontal Split Box

Mouse Pointer

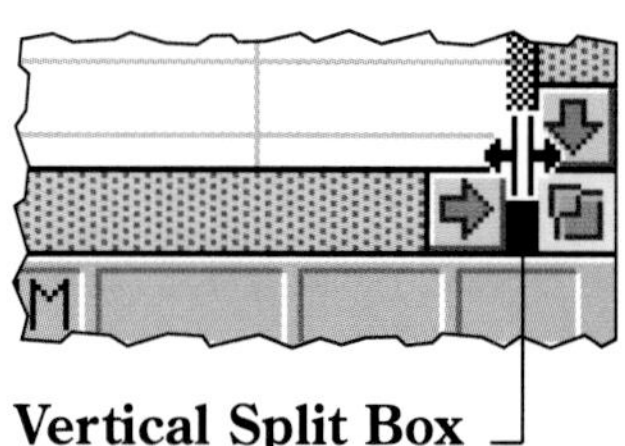

Vertical Split Box

Split Boxes
You can also create panes by dragging a split box. The split boxes are black bars that you'll see above the vertical scroll bar and to the right of the horizontal scroll bar. When you place the mouse pointer over a split box, it takes on a special shape. Just drag the box and a split bar will appear — release the mouse when the window is split as you wish.

Zooming

Excel's zoom feature allows you to move out to see more of a large worksheet or move in for a close-up view. For quick zooming, use the zoom control and pop-up list on the Standard toolbar, which provides five magnification factors — from 25 to 200 percent. You can also specify any magnification factor you want between 10 and 400 percent by typing the factor into the zoom control box.

Zoom to Fit?
To make a particular area of your worksheet fit as neatly as possible into your window, first select the area and then choose *Selection* from the zoom pop-up list.

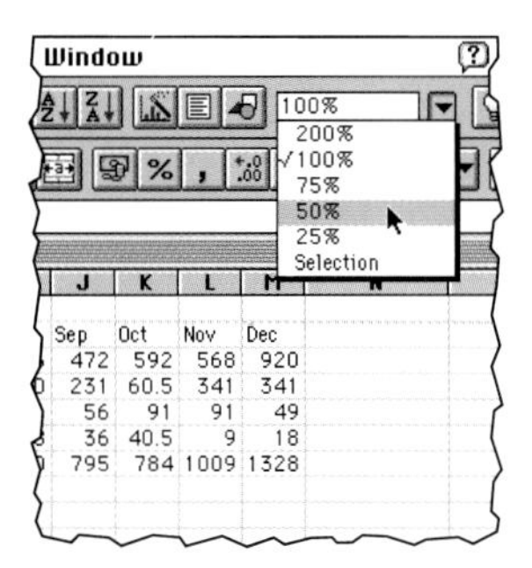

Zooming Out

1 Select cell A1 in the **Annual Income** worksheet and then click on the Zoom Control down-arrow button on the Standard toolbar and choose *50%* from the pop-up list.

2 Both the height and width of everything displayed in the worksheet are reduced to 50%. As a result, the visible part of the worksheet is now four times larger in area. Now try zooming in to 200% before returning to the normal (100%) view.

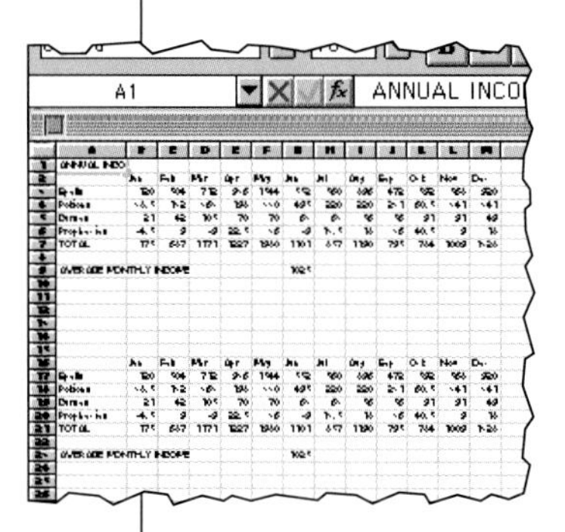

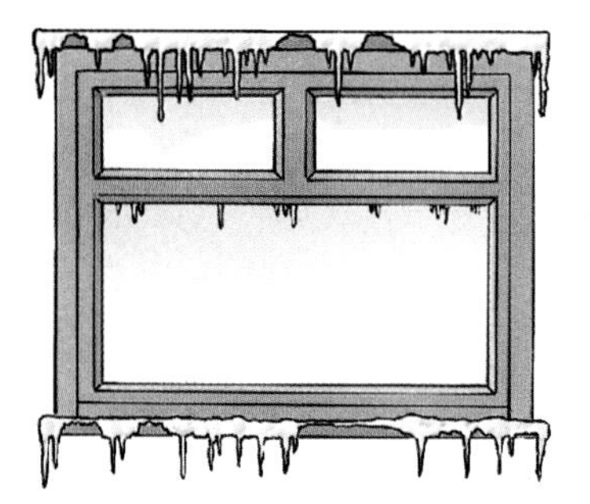

Freezing Panes

The *Freeze Panes* command in the *Window* menu can be used to "freeze" a range of cells at the top or left-hand side of the worksheet. This is a convenient way of turning your row and/or column labels into worksheet titles that stay visible wherever you scroll. If you choose *Freeze Panes* after you have split a window, Excel will freeze the panes at the top and/or left of the window. If you choose the command without having previously split the window, it creates frozen panes above and to the left of the active cell.

Want to See More?
If you want to see the maximum amount possible of a worksheet without zooming, choose *Full Screen* from the *View* menu. This command hides the title bar, formula bar, status bar, and docked toolbars. Choose *Full Screen* again from the *View* menu to return to Normal view.

Freezing Cells

1 Click on cell B3. Choose the *Freeze Panes* command on the *Window* menu.

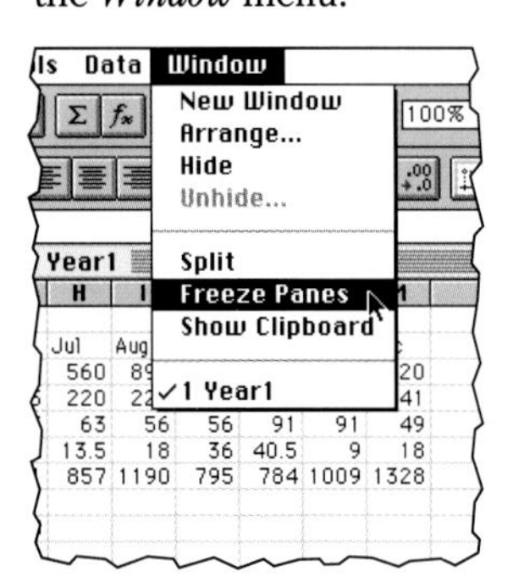

2 Column A and rows 1 and 2 are now frozen. Click on the right-hand arrow in the horizontal scroll bar. Notice that column A always remains visible. Click on the down arrow of the vertical scroll bar — rows 1 and 2 always remain visible. Now choose *Unfreeze Panes* from the *Window* menu.

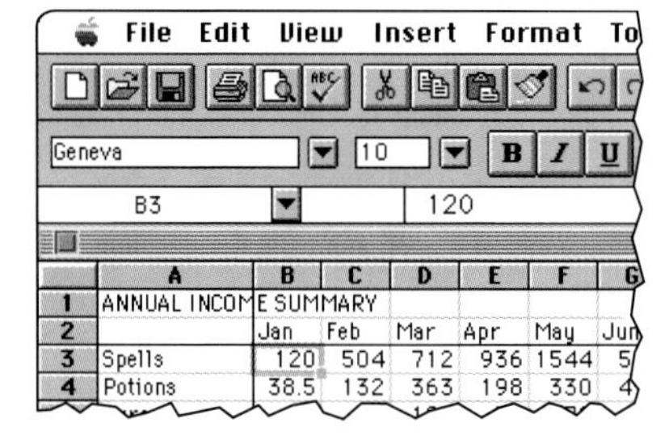

Reference Section

This section provides some additional information to assist you with Excel. The first few pages include advice on organizing your workbook files and the sheets within workbooks. Next you'll find a list of mouse pointer shapes and useful keyboard shortcuts, plus an explanation of how to protect your workbooks with passwords. A panel on error values explains what to do when messages such as #VALUE! appear in your worksheet. The pages on troubleshooting provide some guidance on tracking down the source of errors and demonstrate how you can use Excel's auditing tools. Finally, you'll find an index to the whole volume.

Managing Sheets and Workbooks
Keyboard Shortcuts • Mouse Pointer Shapes
Workbook Security • Error Values
Troubleshooting Worksheet Problems • Index

Managing Sheets and Workbooks

As the folio of work you create and save in Excel grows, you may need to think about how you organize the sheets in your workbooks and the workbook files within the hierarchy of folders on your hard disk.

Organizing Your Sheets

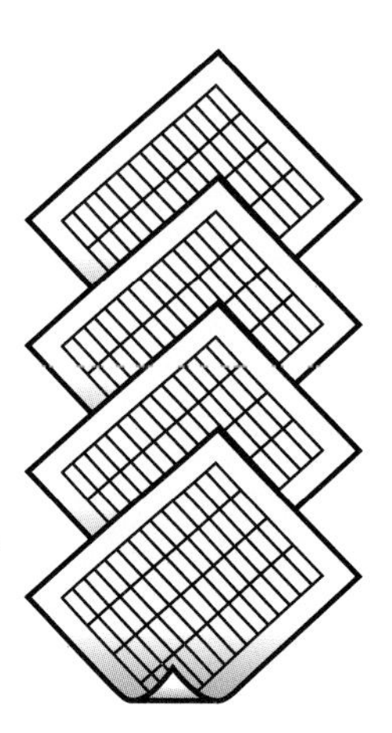

The first level of organization for your work in Excel is the workbook. You should use workbooks to group together related sheets. For example, you might create one workbook for your business accounts, one for your domestic finances, and so on; or you could create separate workbooks for particular years. Each workbook can contain up to 256 sheets — however, you'll probably find that a workbook containing more than about 20 sheets is a little unwieldy.

MOVING SHEETS

From time to time you may decide to reorganize your sheets within a workbook or redistribute some of the sheets to new workbooks. The easiest method of moving sheets within a workbook is to drag their sheet tabs with the mouse (see page 33). To move sheets to new or different workbooks, you must first open both the source and destination workbooks and then do the following:

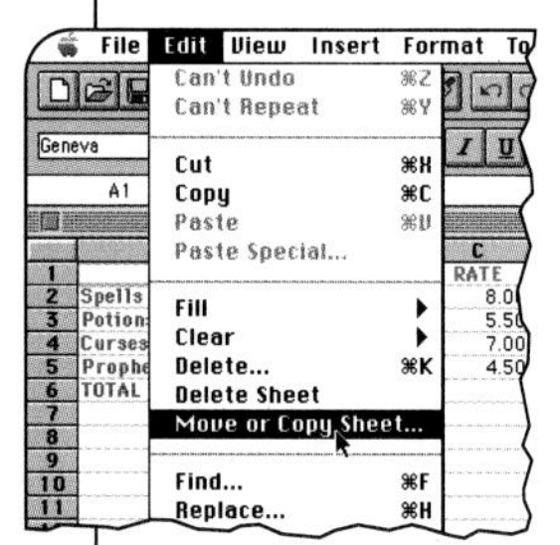

1 Select the sheet(s) you want to move in the source workbook and then choose *Move or Copy Sheet* from the *Edit* menu. The *Move or Copy* dialog box appears.

2 Choose the destination workbook from the *To Book* box. Then choose the new location for the sheet(s) within that workbook from the *Before Sheet* box. Finally, click on *OK*.

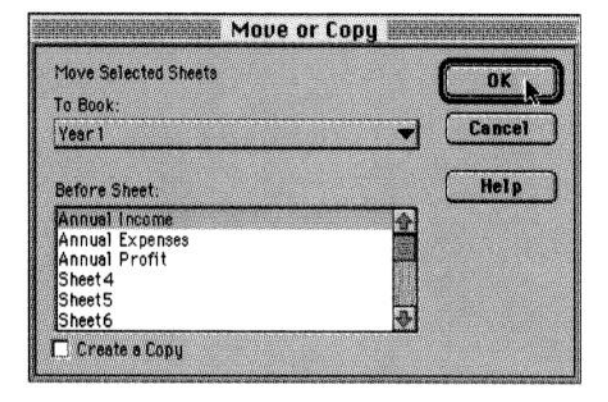

Instead of moving a sheet, you can copy it by checking the *Create a Copy* box in the *Move or Copy* dialog box. A copy of the sheet is then kept within its original location in the source workbook.

File and Folder Organization

The Excel program and its related files should always have their own folder, though you might want to store this within an **Applications** or **Programs** folder. Generally it is most convenient for your Excel workbooks to be stored separately. You might like to group workbooks within the **Excel Workbooks** folder that you created earlier.

Folders stored on the Macintosh's internal hard disk.

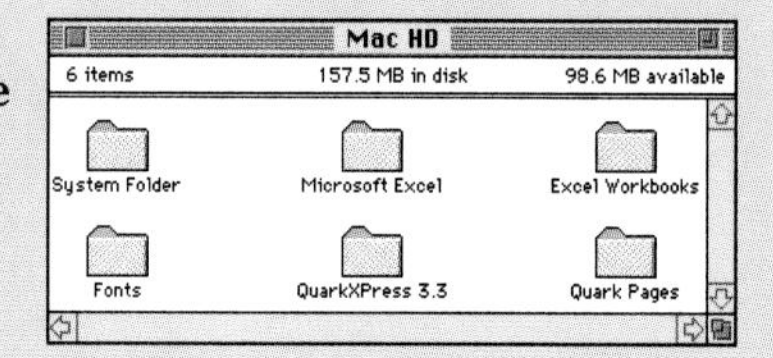

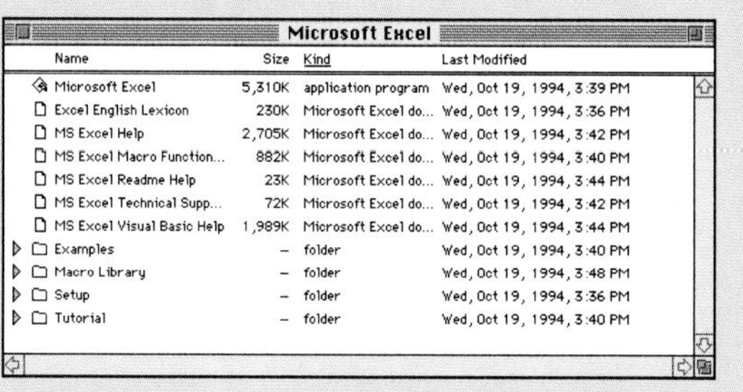

Inside the Microsoft Excel **folder (list views).**

Folders and workbook files within the Excel Workbooks **folder.**

Organizing Workbooks

When performing the example exercises in this book, you created several workbook files that you saved to the **Excel Workbooks** folder on your hard disk. As your files increase in number, you'll find it useful to create new folders to save files in. This facilitates locating particular files and backing up specific data.

CREATING A NEW FOLDER

You can create a new folder by using the Finder. For example, to create a new **Accounts** folder, go to the Finder by clicking on the desktop or using the Application menu. Then use *Hide Others* from the Application menu to give yourself a clear view of your folders and follow the steps on the next page.

1 If it isn't already open, double-click on the hard disk icon to reveal its contents. Choose *New Folder* from the *File* menu.

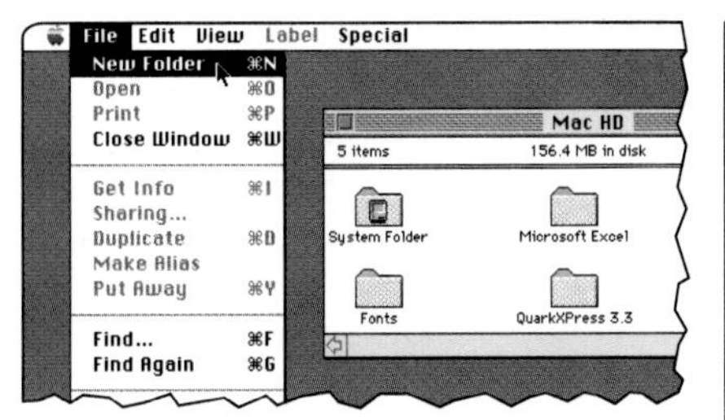

2 With the folder name still selected, type **Accounts**.

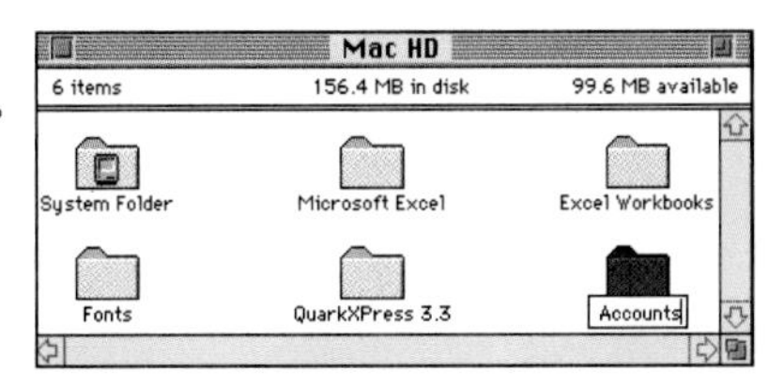

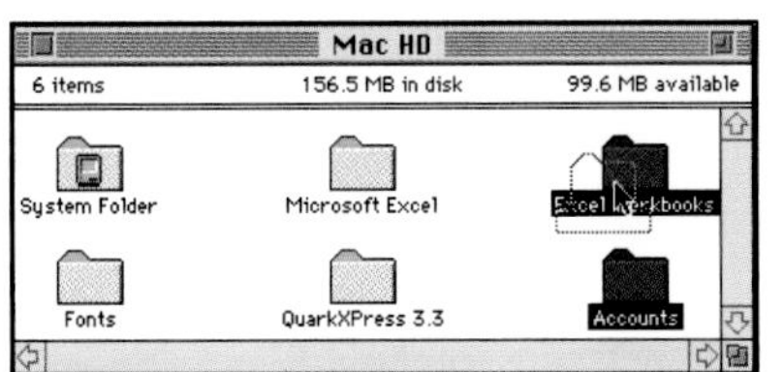

3 If you want to keep your **Accounts** folder within your **Excel Workbooks** folder, move it by dragging and dropping it.

SAVING A WORKBOOK TO A NEW FOLDER

Excel allows you to save a new or existing workbook to any folder on a disk. (When you save an existing workbook, a copy of the workbook will be kept within the original folder.)

Follow the steps below to save a new workbook to the new **Accounts** folder that you have just created on your Macintosh's hard disk.

1 Open a new workbook and then choose *Save As* from the *File* menu to open the dialog box shown at right. The pop-up menu at the top of the dialog box indicates the current folder or disk; if necessary you should use this and the list box to find the **Accounts** folder.

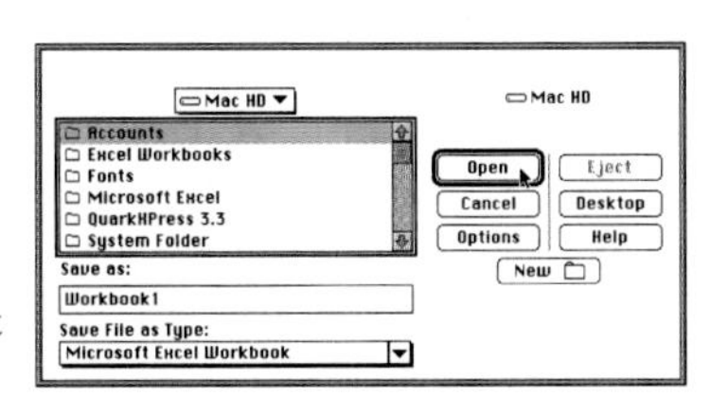

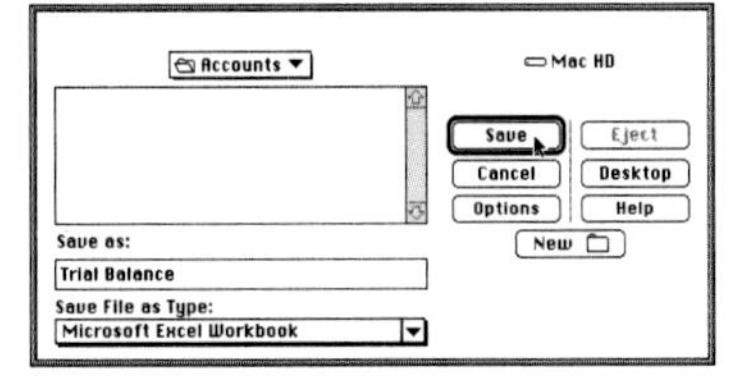

2 Double-click in the *Save as* box and type a name for your workbook (**Trial Balance**, for example). Click on *Save*. The workbook is now saved under that name within the **Accounts** folder. Close the workbook.

LOCATING FILES

Choosing *Open* from the *File* menu brings up a dialog box that you can use to locate and display a saved file from any folder on the hard disk (see page 28). To open a file, use the pop-up menu and list box to find the file that you want to open, then double-click on it.

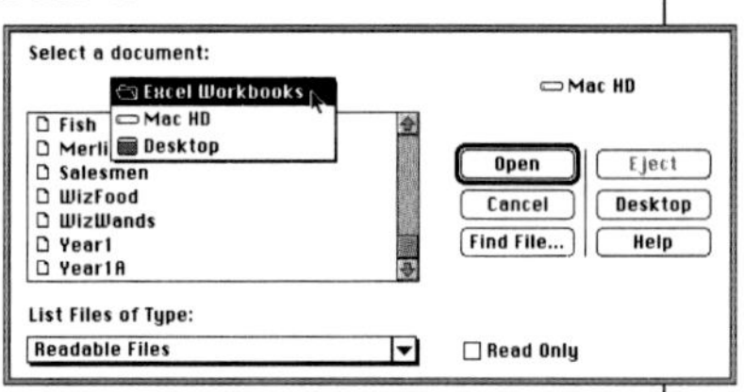

USING FIND FILE

Excel's Find File feature allows you to search for, preview, and open workbook files. It also allows you to print files, copy files, and delete any files you no longer need. To use the feature, choose *Find File* from the *File* menu.

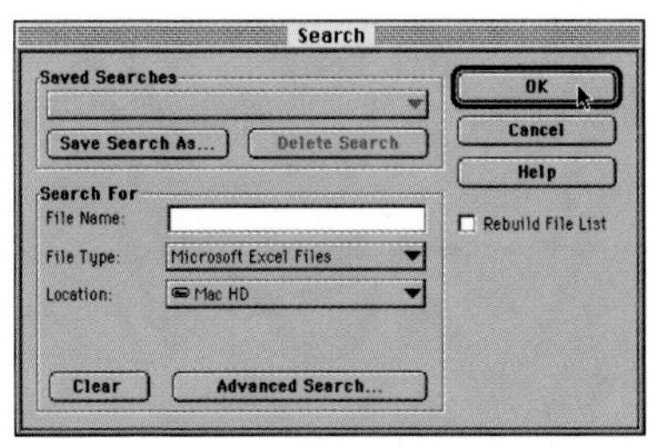

1 The first time you use Find File, the *Search* dialog box appears (subsequent calls go straight to step 2, remembering the details from last time). By setting the *File Type* box to *Microsoft Excel Files* (using the pop-up menu) you can use Find File to list all of the Excel workbooks and macro files on a particular disk or within a particular folder. (Use *Location* to define your search area and *File Name* if you know exactly which file you're after.) Click on OK.

2 In the *Find File* dialog box, under *Listed Files*, you should see a list of Excel workbook and macro files. Click on any workbook file to see its contents in the *Preview of* box. If you wish, you can open the file by clicking on the *Open* button.

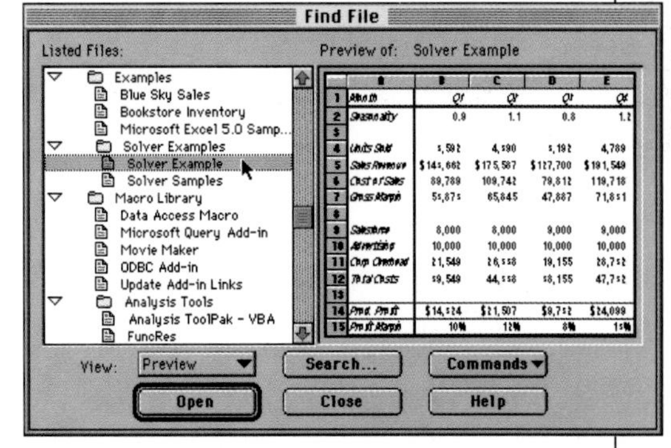

3 Click on the *Commands* button and you will see a list of commands that includes *Print*, *Delete*, and *Copy*. You'll find the *Delete* command very useful for weeding out and discarding any old workbook files you no longer need.

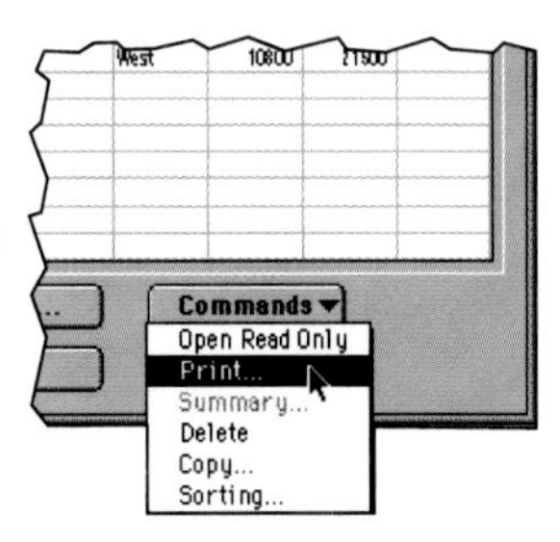

Keyboard Shortcuts

YOU CAN PERFORM most actions in Excel very rapidly with the mouse by choosing commands from the drop-down menus or by clicking on toolbar buttons. But sometimes you'll find it more convenient to use the keyboard. Below are some commonly used keyboard shortcuts that have not already been pointed out in this book. You can obtain a full listing of keyboard commands by choosing *Contents* from the Help menu and then choosing *Reference Information* in the *Help Contents* window. Click on *Keyboard Guide* in the next window and then choose from the many categories of keyboard actions that are listed.

Command	Keyboard Keys
Open new workbook	Command-N
Save workbook	Command-S
Repeat last action	Command-Y
Select column containing active cell	Command-Spacebar
Select row containing active cell	Shift-Spacebar
Open new worksheet	Shift-F11
Move to next sheet in workbook	Control-Page Down
Move to previous sheet in workbook	Control-Page Up
Access *Go To* dialog box	F5
Clear contents of selected cells	Command-B
Access *Format Cells* dialog box	Command-1
Access *Print* dialog box	Command-P
Access *Cell Note* dialog box	Command-Shift-N
Activate Function Wizard	Shift-F3
Activate cell shortcut menu	Shift-F10
Make selected text bold	Command-Shift-B
Make selected text italic	Command-Shift-I
Close workbook	Command-W

Mouse Pointer Shapes

THE MOUSE POINTER takes on different shapes in Excel, depending on its location on the screen and on your actions. The table below shows the mouse pointer shapes and describes the action you take with each.

Mouse Shape		Mouse Action
✚	Normal Pointer in Worksheet	Selects a cell, row, or column when you click or selects a range when you drag.
	Arrow Pointer	Selects a toolbar or other button, sheet tab, chart, or graphic object when you click; or moves cell contents or graphic objects when you drag.
	Arrow Pointer with Plus Sign	Appears when you drag cell contents with Option key depressed; use to copy cell contents in a worksheet.
	I-Beam Pointer	Places insertion point when you click where you want to edit the contents of the formula bar, a cell, or a text box.
+	Fill Handle Pointer	Drag the fill handle of the active cell or a selected range to copy the cell or range contents or to create a series.
	Column Width and Row Height Adjusters	Drag the borders between row and column headers to adjust row heights and column widths.
	Object Resize Pointers	Drag object borders or corners to resize objects vertically, horizontally, or diagonally.
	Split Bar Position Adjusters	Drag vertical or horizontal split boxes or bars to divide window into panes or to adjust sizes of panes.
	Help Pointer	Appears when you click on Help toolbar button; click on any command or screen area for help information.
	Hand Pointer	In Help screens, use to click on underlined terms to obtain more information.
	Zoom Pointer	In Print Preview, magnifies a portion of the page when you click on that portion.
+	Cross-Hair	Appears when you select a drawing tool; drag to draw an object or select a range or group of objects.
	Cross-Hair and Chart Pointer	Appears when you click on the Chart Wizard button; drag in worksheet to delineate chart area.

Workbook Security

IN CHAPTER THREE, you learned how to protect open worksheets or workbooks to prevent unauthorized changes to "locked" cells or to hide formulas in selected "hidden" cells (see pages 76 to 77). You can also assign a protection password to a whole workbook to prevent unauthorized people from opening the workbook or saving changes to it; or you can set up a recommendation that a workbook is used as a read-only file. To activate these options, open the workbook you want to protect, choose *Save As* from the *File* menu, and then click on the *Options* button in the dialog box that appears. This opens the *Save Options* dialog box. Now choose from the options explained below.

Protection Password
To prevent people from opening the workbook unless they know a password, type a password into the Protection Password *box. Click on* OK, *confirm the password, and then click on* Save *in the next dialog box and close the workbook. The next time you open the workbook, you will need to supply the password.*

Write Reservation Password
To assign write-reservation protection to the workbook, type a password into the Write Reservation Password *box. Click on* OK, *confirm the password, and then click on* Save *in the next dialog box. Anyone who opens the workbook in the future won't be able to save changes to it unless they know the password.*

Save Options
Always Create Backup
File Sharing
Protection Password:
Write Reservation Password:
Read-Only Recommended
OK
Cancel
Help

Read-Only Recommended
To set up a recommendation that a workbook is used as a read-only file, check the Read-Only Recommended *box. Press Return, click on* Save *in the next dialog box, and close the workbook. Anyone who opens the workbook in the future will be advised to use it as a read-only file (if the recommendation is accepted, no changes to the workbook can be saved) — however, the user has the option of overriding the recommendation if desired.*

Error Values

EXCEL CALCULATES WORKSHEETS according to a set of rules. When it finds one of these rules has been violated, it normally displays an error value in the cell it is calculating (although for some types of violation it displays an error message in the status bar.) Error values always begin with the # symbol. The meanings of error values, and of circular reference error messages, are explained below. See page 124 for tips on tracing the cause of an error.

########
When a number is too long to fit into a cell, Excel displays a series of # symbols. You can remedy this error by widening the column to accommodate the number.

#DIV/0!
#DIV/0! indicates that a formula is trying to divide by zero. This is an illegal arithmetic operation. It occurs when the divisor in a division formula equates to zero — often caused by a reference to a blank cell.

#NAME?
#NAME? appears when a formula refers to a name that Excel doesn't recognize. It can be caused by misspelling a range name or by using a name that you have not defined in the current workbook.

#NULL!
#NULL! appears if you specify the intersection of two areas that do not intersect, often through using an incorrect range reference.

#NUM!
#NUM! indicates a problem with a numeric value, such as a number that is too large or too small to be represented by Excel, or a formula that cannot be calculated, such as the square root of a negative number.

#N/A!
#N/A! stands for "No value is available." It can occur when you omit one or more of the required arguments for a function. You can enter this error value directly into worksheet cells that will eventually contain data that is not yet available. Formulas referring to those cells will return #N/A! instead of calculating a value.

#REF!
#REF! occurs when you refer to an invalid cell address or a deleted cell. It most often occurs when you delete or paste over a cell referred to in a formula.

#VALUE!
#VALUE! appears when the wrong type of argument has been used for a function. For example, it can occur if you try to add the contents of cells that contain text, not numbers.

Circular:A1
If you try to enter a formula into a cell and the formula refers directly or indirectly back to the value in that cell, an error message "Cannot resolve circular references" appears. Until the problem is resolved, the word *Circular* appears in the status bar, followed by the address of one of the cells involved in the circular reference.

Troubleshooting Worksheet Problems

WORKSHEET PROBLEMS RESULT from a variety of sources. Sometimes, Excel does not accept a formula you enter into a cell because of a simple typing error (for example, if you type **=A1+*A2**). If the cause is not obvious, try breaking the formula down into smaller parts. Other problems include error values (see page 123) and "logic errors." With the latter, the worksheet may appear to function correctly but produces incorrect results — this might result from flawed logic when writing a formula or from careless moving of cells and formulas.

Tracing Errors

To trace the source of errors, you'll find it useful to know about Excel's troubleshooting features. These include various auditing commands, the *Go To Special* command, and the *Info* window.

AUDITING COMMANDS AND THE AUDITING TOOLBAR

A cell displaying an error value causes any cells referencing it — its *dependent cells* — in turn to display the error value. Conversely, when a cell formula containing cell references gives rise to an error value, the problem may lie in the formula itself or in one of the cells referred to — its *precedent* cells. If a worksheet contains complex chains of formulas and a crop of error values suddenly appears, tracing the source of the problem can be time-consuming. Excel's auditing commands, reached by choosing *Auditing* from the *Tools* menu, can simplify the process greatly. The commands are also available via the Auditing toolbar, shown below.

Trace Dependents

Remove All Arrows

Attach Note

Trace Precedents

Auditing

Show Info Window

Remove Precedent Arrows

Trace Error

Remove Dependent Arrows

Excel's Auditing Tools

■ *Trace Error* The most useful of the auditing commands is *Trace Error*. To use this command, the active cell must contain an error value. Choose *Auditing* from the *Tools* menu and *Trace Error* from the submenu or click on the Trace Error button on the Auditing toolbar. Excel shows the path from the first precedent cell containing an error, to the active cell, with a red or dotted arrow (or series of arrows). It also makes that first precedent cell the active cell, and shows the path to it from its own precedents, using blue or solid arrows.

■ *Trace Precedents* and *Trace Dependents* You can also ask for the precedents of any cell containing a formula, or the dependents of any cell, to be displayed by choosing the *Trace Precedents* or *Trace Dependents* commands from the *Auditing* submenu or clicking on the relevant buttons on the Auditing toolbar. Excel will always draw arrows from precedent cell to dependent cell. The arrows are blue unless they lead out of a cell containing an error value; these are displayed in red.

■ *Remove Arrows* You can remove all of the arrows from the worksheet by choosing *Remove All Arrows* from the *Auditing* submenu or clicking on the Remove All Arrows button on the Auditing toolbar.

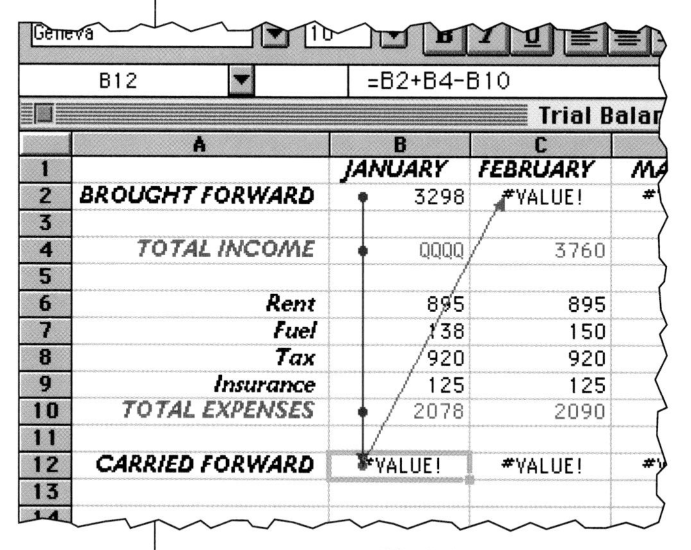

Find the Error

In the error-affected worksheet pictured here, cell C2 (showing the #VALUE! error) was the active cell when the Trace Error *command was invoked. The red arrow from B12 to C2 shows that the first occurrence of an error value in C2's chain of precedents is in B12. B12 is also now the active cell. The blue arrow indicates that cells B2, B4, and B10 are all precedents of cell B12 (this can also be seen from the formula bar, which shows =B2+B4-B10). The ultimate source of the error is cell B4, which contains a text value when it should contain a number.*

GO TO SPECIAL

You have already used the *Go To* command to move around a worksheet (page 117). The *Go To Special* command and dialog box allow you to highlight all cells in the worksheet that meet certain criteria, such as cells that contain formulas or all cells that contain constant data. To use the *Go To Special* command, choose *Go To* from the *Edit* menu, and then click on the *Special* button in the *Go To* dialog box. You can then set your criteria in the *Go To Special* dialog box that appears.

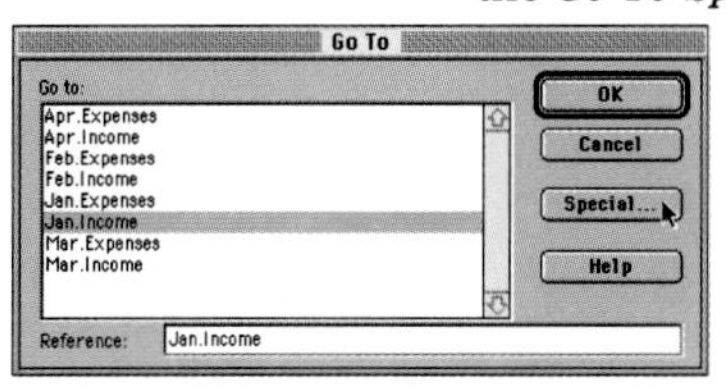

An example of how you could use *Go To Special* to troubleshoot a worksheet would be to highlight all cells that contain formulas. You could then look at each of the highlighted cells in turn to check the formulas for accuracy.

Some of the terminology used in the *Go To Special* dialog box might require explanation. *Logicals* are two special values (TRUE and FALSE) that can be returned by certain formulas based on comparisons. The *current region* of a worksheet is the rectangular block of cells, surrounded by blank columns and rows, that contains the active cell. An *array* is a rectangular block of cells that contain a single formula.

THE INFO WINDOW

The *Info* window displays detailed information about the active cell. It is especially useful for helping you to isolate formatting, data entry, formula, and logic errors in your worksheet. You can access the window by choosing *Options* from the *Tools* menu and checking *Info Window* in the *View* flipcard, or by displaying the Auditing toolbar and then clicking on the Show Info Window button. When the *Info* window is active, a new menu is displayed. You can select the information about the active cell that you want displayed by choosing attributes from the *Info* menu. To get the maximum benefit, open the *Info* window, and then choose *Arrange* from the *Window* menu. You will then have both the *Info* window and your workbook window open at the same time.

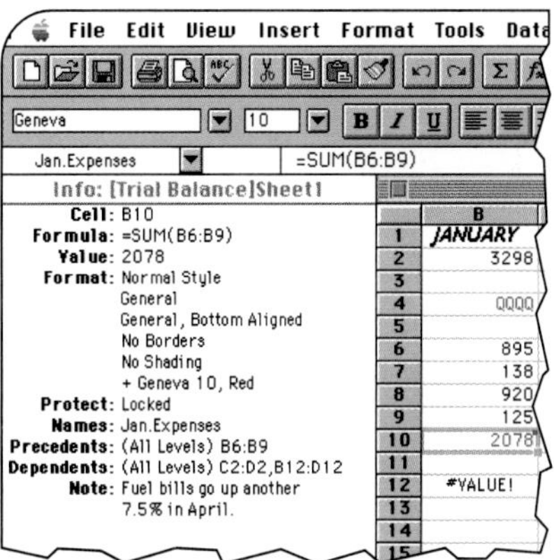

What's in that Cell?

The Info *window shown above lists all the attributes of the active cell in the worksheet — cell B10.*

Go To Special Options

The various options available in the *Go To Special* dialog box are shown here. After setting your criteria, click on *OK* and inspect the cells selected by the command.

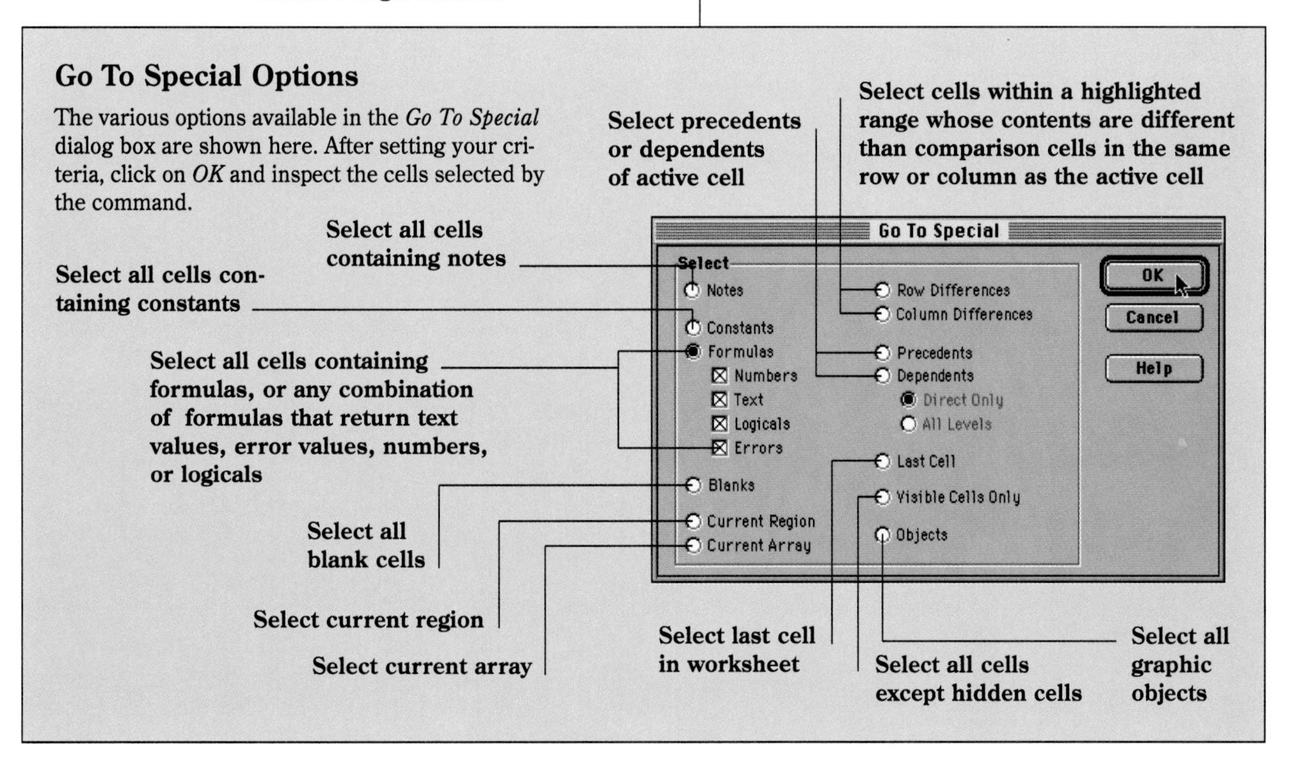

INDEX

r

s

t

u-v

w-z

Equipment suppliers:
The type blocks on pages 66-67 were supplied by James Robinson. The footwear on page 86 was supplied by Hobbs, UK, and Shelleys Shoes, UK. The game pieces and drawing boards on pages 32, 46, 52, and 56 were supplied by Hamleys, UK.

Register Today!

Return this
The Way Microsoft® Excel for the Macintosh® Works
registration card for:

- ✔ a Microsoft Press catalog
- ✔ exclusive offers on specially priced books

Fill in information below and mail postage free.

1-55615-671-5A The Way Microsoft Excel for the Macintosh Works

NAME

COMPANY

ADDRESS

CITY STATE ZIP

Your feedback is important to us.

To help us make future editions even more useful, include your daytime telephone number and we might call to find out how you use *The Way Microsoft Excel for the Macintosh Works*. If we call you, we'll send you a **FREE GIFT** for your time!

( )

DAYTIME TELEPHONE NUMBER

More from the WYSIWYG Series

Microsoft Press and Dorling Kindersley

The Way Word for the Macintosh® Works

Version 6

Peter Gloster

$19.95 ($24.95 Canada)   ISBN 1-55615-672-3

Microsoft Press.

Microsoft Press® books are available wherever quality books are sold and through CompuServe's Electronic Mall—GO MSP.
Call 1-800-MSPRESS for direct ordering information or for placing credit card orders.*
Please refer to BBK when placing your order. Prices subject to change.

*In Canada, contact Macmillan Canada, Attn: Microsoft Press Dept., 164 Commander Blvd., Agincourt, Ontario, Canada M1S 3C7, or call 1-800-667-1115. Outside the U.S. and Canada, write to International Coordinator, Microsoft Press, One Microsoft Way, Redmond, WA 98052-6399 or fax +(206) 936-7329.

NO POSTAGE
NECESSARY
IF MAILED
IN THE
UNITED STATES

BUSINESS REPLY MAIL

FIRST-CLASS MAIL   PERMIT NO. 53   BOTHELL, WA

POSTAGE WILL BE PAID BY ADDRESSEE

MICROSOFT PRESS REGISTRATION
THE WAY MICROSOFT EXCEL FOR THE
MACINTOSH WORKS
PO BOX 3019
BOTHELL WA 98041-9946